Developing Leadership

*Learning from the Experiences
of Women Governors*

Susan R. Madsen

University Press of America,® Inc.
Lanham · Boulder · New York · Toronto · Plymouth, UK

Copyright © 2009 by
University Press of America,® Inc.
4501 Forbes Boulevard
Suite 200
Lanham, Maryland 20706
UPA Acquisitions Department (301) 459-3366

Estover Road
Plymouth PL6 7PY
United Kingdom

All rights reserved
Printed in the United States of America
British Library Cataloging in Publication Information Available

Library of Congress Control Number: 2008932679

ISBN-13: 978-0-7618-4308-5 (paperback : alk. paper)
ISBN-10: 0-7618-4308-6 (paperback : alk. paper)
eISBN-13: 978-0-7618-4309-2
eISBN-10: 0-7618-4309-4

∞™ The paper used in this publication meets the minimum
requirements of American National Standard for Information
Sciences—Permanence of Paper for Printed Library Materials,
ANSI Z39.48—1984

I dedicate this book to my four children: Michael, Brian, Staci, and Scott.
I have learned more from raising them than anything else in my life.
Although it has been a little rough at times,
they have brought me immeasurable joy.
I hope they always remember they are loved.

Contents

Preface   vii
Acknowledgments   ix
Introduction   xi

Part 1: Their Stories

1. Governor Barbara Roberts   3
2. Governor Christine Gregoire   27
3. Governor Christine Todd Whitman   49
4. Governor Jane Dee Hull   75
5. Governor Jane Swift   95
6. Governor Jeanne Shaheen   121
7. Governor Madeleine May Kunin   143
8. Governor Martha Layne Collins   167
9. Governor Nancy Putnam Hollister   189
10. Governor Olene Walker   213

Part II: Themes and Overall Findings

11. Family Influences, Childhoods, and Youth   239
12. College Years and Life Roles   261
13. Career Paths and Political Years   285

References   307
Index   309
About the Author   319

Preface

Upon the completion of this manuscript, I am sitting in my home office this spring morning looking out my front window at the majestic Utah Mountains covered with snow. It has been a long, cold winter in Utah this year for me (I don't like to ski), and it has been a wonderful, long, cold winter for my husband and kids (they love to ski and snowboard). I guess long, cold winters are in the eye of the beholder. Yet, today the sun is shining, birds are chirping, my grass is already getting green, and the flowers will be blooming any day—maybe any minute. It seems to me that there is more hope in the air this morning.

I believe that hope is such a foundational element of developing leadership. A leader must bring hope to his or her followers. I started this project three years ago because I had hope that it could make a difference in some way to emerging leaders (young and old). I wanted to understand the lives of already successful women leaders, so that I could share a blueprint (of sorts) to help others develop the skills they need to make the type of difference these women have already made. This book does just that. It highlights the developmental journeys of ten successful female political leaders. These amazing women had hope that they could make a difference, and they have.

As a professional educator, I am wired to look at students through this developmental lens. I consider what they can learn, how they can grow, and who they can become. I find great joy when I have influenced the positive development of others. Yet, I need to do better, and I need to do more. I challenge myself and all readers to look at everyone you meet (including yourselves) with this type of developmental lens. It is critical that we have more ethical, competent leaders in all sectors of society. We need to be part of the solution.

Writing this book and my last, *On Becoming a Woman Leader: Learning from the Experiences of University Presidents,* has changed my life. I'm a better person because of the developmental journey I have experienced while conducting this research and writing these books. I hope you will also find great value in these pages as you read and reflect on the implications these words and stories may have in your own life. I urge you to let this book provide insight into your life and the lives of others with whom you may influence. Life is short and specific leadership positions are fleeting, but the time you spend developing others will positively influence their lives for many years to come.

Acknowledgments

I am grateful for the support and encouragement of many colleagues including Scott Hammond, Janice Gygi, Jim Fenton, Shauna Peterson, Reba Keele, Doug Miller, Bonner Ritchie, Brad Cook, and Troy Nielson. Their insights and perspectives have been invaluable and their confidence in my ability and potential has been humbling.

I am appreciative of the ten governors who allowed me to interview them and were willing to read and review book chapters.

Thanks to my brother Tim who has played racquetball with me for years and who has always listened to my ramblings about this study. I have valued the listening ears of my neighborhood friends Suzanne Plowman, Denise Gorrell, and Deon Ruff. I am also grateful to my children for their patience, and I am most appreciative to my husband who has always believed I could do anything I wanted to do. Although he quit reviewing manuscripts years ago, he has always believed in the value of my work and dreams. I am also truly grateful for the prayers and encouragement of my parents (Boyd and Helen Willden) and my in-laws (Bob and Peggy Madsen).

Finally, I am very grateful to those who provided travel funding and support for this research: The NEA (National Education Association) Foundation; C. Charles Jackson Foundation; Woodbury Family Endowment; Utah Valley University Presidential Scholarship fund; NASPA (Student Affairs Administrators in Higher Education) Region V and WISA (Women in Student Affairs) Research Fund; Utah Valley University School of Business; and an anonymous donor who believed in the importance of this project.

Introduction

*What lies behind us and what lies before us are tiny matters
compared to what lies within us.*

~ Ralph Waldo Emerson

For many years, I have dedicated a major portion of my time to the study of leadership development. I have been fascinated with exploring and understanding how people, particularly women, became leaders. Warren Bennis taught in his book, *On Becoming a Leader,* that "the process of becoming a leader is much the same as the process of becoming an integrated human being" (Bennis 1989, 4). Therefore, studying the lives of extraordinary human beings is often also the study of remarkable leaders. Understanding the processes and experiences of *becoming* is never an easy task, but it can be rewarding as helpful patterns and themes begin to emerge. It is clear that this *becoming* process is closely connected to self-discovery. Bennis also argued, "Becoming a leader is synonymous with becoming yourself. It's precisely that simple, and it's also that difficult" (9).

This book is about the lifetime development of leadership in ten strong, competent, and fascinating women governors in the United States. It shares their leadership development journeys through experiences, stories, and insights. It shows how they were able to develop the knowledge and competencies throughout their lives to become the leaders they became. It describes commonalities and differences among these women and provides themes that can be useful in addressing development issues for future women leaders.

Why read this book? Although there are multitudes of leadership books available on bookshelves today, not much has been published about how women developed throughout their lives to become prominent leaders. There are even fewer books that focus on women and leadership development issues within any domain, but particularly in appointed and elected political positions. Until now, no one has studied such a large number of influential women who have served as leaders in the same governmental position—such as a governor—in enough depth to provide commonalities and differences among their childhoods, adolescence, and adulthoods. If we are truly interested in figuring out how to develop strong, competent women leaders for the future, then we must look at those who have succeeded in the past and those who are succeeding now. We need to understand how they learned to lead throughout their lives.

THE STUDY

To understand these issues, experiences, and themes, I designed a research study that would use a rigorous qualitative research methodology called "phenomenology." This method would help me explore all of the governors' "lived experiences" so as to gain a deeper understanding of their lives, experiences, and perceptions. I wanted to probe beyond their outward behaviors and accomplishments to investigate the underlying meanings and influences of their experiences. It became clear during the early conceptualization of this project that it was essential for me to *hear* the women's own voices as they described their journeys and reflected upon their own beliefs and interpretations. I needed them to open up and share stories, emotions, and passions. My hope was that the resulting data could provide insights into the development of the leadership competencies that are essential for effective leadership today, and it did.

Between the summers of 2005 and 2006, I traveled to the homes and offices of ten women governors. At the time of the interviews, there were only twenty living women governors, many of whom were not currently in office. I felt privileged to have spent two to four hours with ten of these twenty women for in-depth interviews. I asked them a detailed set of open-ended, probing questions to explore their past experiences and perceptions. All of the interviews were transcribed in full, which resulted in nearly 600 pages of text. The transcripts were then reviewed by the governors for accuracy and completeness. Other steps included a preliminary analysis, combined categorization, in-depth analysis, and finally theme generation. I maintained a continuous relationship with the governors so that they could review the manuscripts for accuracy. Throughout the process some governors shared additional insights, which added more richness to the data. It was important to me that my writings were authentic representations of the governors' true perceptions and experiences.

THE GOVERNORS

Although the governors' information is included in their individual chapters, I have summarized some basic collective demographic information about these women:

- At the time of the interviews, nine were past governors and one was currently in office.
- Seven were elected outright as governors, and three were inaugurated after the resignation of a governor (while serving as lieutenant governor).
- Six were lieutenant governors.
- All ten are Caucasian.
- The majority were the first female governors of their states.

Introduction

- Seven were legislators at one point and all chaired or served on key committees.
- The age range of these governors fell between forty-two and seventy-four at the time of the interviews with most being in their late 50s to late 60s.
- Nine were born in the United States, and one immigrated when she was young.
- Eight have bachelor's degrees, three masters' degrees, and two completed doctoral programs.
- The states they governed are spread throughout the United States. These included Arizona, Kentucky, Massachusetts, New Hampshire, New Jersey, Ohio, Oregon, Utah, Vermont, and Washington.

AUDIENCES

I have shared the results of this research with many audiences—old and young, women and men—within government, education, and business realms. The interest of so many individuals with such varied backgrounds, positions, and current responsibilities reflects the broad application of this material. These groups have included:

- College students
- Community members
- Corporate leaders and employees
- General public
- Government leaders and employees
- High school and college/university counselors
- Human resource leaders and staff (business, government, nonprofit, and education)
- International leaders
- Junior high and high school students
- K–12 leaders and educators
- Nonprofit leaders and employees (national and international)
- Parents and family members (aunts, uncles, siblings, grandparents)
- Post-secondary leaders and educators

Each group acknowledged these leadership attributes across organizational and industry boundaries and each has also contributed important insights.

In today's constantly changing environment, we must have competent and effective leaders. Developing such leaders is no small task; yet, developing yourself and others for leadership responsibilities is a rewarding experience. It can and does happen successfully. In today's society, I believe we cannot be comfortable with preparing only a selected few for leadership. Preparing for effective leadership is a critical endeavor for all who are up to the challenge. Everyone can learn to lead somewhere at something. We must have individuals who have the capabilities to lead in every facet of life (e.g., home, church, schools, non-profits, government, business, and community). The bottom line is this: we should encourage all girls and women to develop effective leadership skills. This book will provide helpful nuggets of information about all life phases that may provide new ideas and potential strategies for future leadership development efforts.

THE BOOK

This book is one of a kind. It not only shares insightful and intriguing information (based on a scholarly research study), it is about the lifetime development of leadership knowledge, skills, and competencies in women governors. It shares the commonalities and perspectives of ten women on their own personal journeys in developing leadership throughout childhood, youth, young adulthood, and adulthood. These ten women reflect a journey shared, in part, by all leaders.

The book not only highlights each governor in her own chapter, but it includes chapters that summarize general findings on life phases across all of the interviews. Remember that both similarities and differences are important and interesting information. Often what is *not* found can be as enlightening as what *is* found. Hence, Part I includes ten chapters, one on each of the women governors. Importantly, I am not trying to provide a full biography of their lives, but rather a leadership development journey though stories, themes, and experiences that are most closely linked to this developmental process. Part II includes the final three chapters of the book (11, 12, and 13), which reveal the primary themes that surfaced throughout all ten interviews.

This book is dedicated to teaching you what I've learned from this research, and it is also dedicated to providing thought-provoking experiences, so you can reflect on issues—both brought to light and those not directly articulated—so you can draw connections in your own lives and teach yourselves. I believe that this can be the most powerful type of learning there is. Enjoy, reflect, and learn!

Part I

Their Stories

Chapter One

Governor Barbara Roberts

As a governor, I had to confront and sometimes go against powerful people and powerful organizations. I learned I had this strength and ability because of my experiences in making public education available to my autistic son and other disabled youth.

~ Governor Barbara Roberts

I interviewed Governor Barbara Roberts at her condominium in Portland, Oregon on November 30, 2005. She was inaugurated as Oregon's first woman governor on January 14, 1991, and she completed her service in 1995. She was recognized as a strong advocate for environmental management, human and civil rights, and creative workforce development. Although she has many notable accomplishments, the purpose of my interview was to discuss how she developed the knowledge, skills, and abilities to become the leader she became. I will not attempt to share her entire life story, but rather share her thoughts and experiences that are most important and applicable in understanding her lifetime of leadership development.

FAMILY BACKGROUND

Barbara Roberts was born in Corvallis, Oregon on December 21, 1936, and grew up in the small town of Sheridan. Being a fourth generation Oregonian, she takes great pride in her heritage and spoke of her ancestors coming west on the Oregon Trail. Throughout the years this has given her a "sense of identification" with her state.

Governor Roberts grew up in a blue-collar family with a sister Pat who was two years younger. Barbara summed up her parent's relationship by saying they were "absolutely meant for each other." She spoke of their kindness and lovingness toward each other. There were periods when her parents did very well financial, and there were periods where they had to live thriftily. She explained,

We always had clothes and a roof over our heads. We never were without that, even if it wasn't very fancy. My dad and mom always made wherever we were a

> *real home. I always had this sense of stability and this sense of being loved and adored.*

She believes this stability was important in developing self-esteem, confidence, basic leadership skills, and sense of commitment to family.

Barbara's family lived in Los Angeles during World War II. They moved from California to Washington and then to Oregon all in one year. She said that in fourth grade she "actually went to school in three states without missing a beat." She found this to be an "enlightening experience" which taught her to adapt, adjust, and deal with change. These skills have proven to be very helpful throughout her life and career. Because she liked people and was a good student, she felt that adjustment was relatively easy for her. She explained,

> *I had lots of friends who had gone to school their whole lives in the same town, same school, and with the same friends. They went from first grade through high school and never moved. They never knew what it was like to make new friends, start over, and to be the new kid in school. I think it was actually good for me to move around a little during my childhood. The ability to adapt and adjust was very important later in my life as I served in formal leadership positions.*

Parents

Barbara's father, Bob Hughey, was a machinist for most of his life. He graduated from high school, which in those days didn't happen for about fifty percent of the youth as many worked on the farms or in the woods, joined the military, or got married. Few ever went to college. Her father was a preacher's son and came from "solid stock." He had six sisters and two brothers. During his youth, his parents divorced and his father moved to another state. Barbara explained that after that her father "was pretty much raised in a female house." She explained how this positively influenced his relationship with his own daughters.

> *He thought females were real people, and that was a wonderful thing. He never felt shortchanged that he didn't have sons. It was a time when men felt they had to have "their" boys, but he never felt that way. I grew up feeling loved and secure.*

As an adult, Barbara's father was involved in the community with the Masonic Lodge, volunteer fire department, and with other issues and projects. She explained that although he became master of his lodge, "he would not have run for mayor or another formal position."

Barbara's mother, Carmen, was a full-time homemaker for most of Barbara's upbringing. Carmen began working outside the home for a local newspaper when Barbara was a freshman in high school. Carmen's father was a farmer in Montana, so she was raised to have a very strong work ethic and believed that her own children should learn to work hard as well. From the time Barbara was very young, she was expected to work hard and be responsible and dependable.

Carmen was also very thrifty and could make a little bit of money go a long way. She also had domestic skills, such as being a very good cook and making beautiful clothes for her daughters when they were young. Barbara explained, "We always had lots of cute little things to wear because my mother sewed a lot. We were always very well dressed because of her ability to do that." Barbara spoke about her mother being a strong, kind, and very competitive individual:

> If you played cards with my mother, you knew she was playing to win. She did not play for sport. No, she played to win. In Montana, where she grew up, she and her sister played on a girl's basketball team, and they won the state championship. Girls in Montana played full court basketball. After that we went through the years when people thought females couldn't run up and down the full court because their ovaries would fall out or some such thing!

Carmen's involvement in the community included being a Girl Scout leader, Red Cross Blood Bank volunteer, and Eastern Star Lodge member. After she started working for the local paper, her primary community involvement revolved around the political and local issues she covered as a journalist.

Extended Family
During Barbara's upbringing, her extended family was very united, and she always had a sense of belonging. When she was younger, she remembers spending time with her mother's family and having aunts, uncles, and cousins around. She remembers going to ball games together on Sundays and then picnicking together after the games with many relatives. This extended family also got together often for meals and card playing. She felt that her relationships with her extended family enriched her life. Later she was able to spend time with her father's family. They were much more conservative and religious, especially her paternal grandmother, and she remembers, "We had to be real careful and extra good when we went there because we couldn't misbehave." She learned early that her families behaved differently and were not the same.

CHILDHOOD AND YOUTH

Personality and Activities
Barbara was a happy and energetic child and "probably a little flamboyant." She stated jokingly, "I think in another time period I might have been called hyperactive, but we didn't have a word for that then." She was always busy doing a variety of things. She loved being around people. She described herself as being achievement-oriented and having a desire to accomplish all kind of things. She was a confident child stating, "I don't think you could come out of my household and not be confident because of the stability, love, affection, and encouragement."

Barbara remembers leaving a one-room country school house and moving to Sheridan where there was a bigger school and more opportunity, and she became involved in all kinds of activities during this time. She belonged to Girl Scouts where her mother was the troop leader. Her dad was the coach of her summer softball team. She liked being in sports (particularly softball and volleyball) because all her friends were playing, but she also loved being a cheerleader and in school plays.

Barbara described herself as competitive and explained, "Although I was definitely competitive, it was probably not so much in athletics as it was in other places." If there was a talent show or contest, she would always do her best to win and typically did. She remembered the following frustrating experience:

When I was in the eighth grade I remember studying Oregon history. We put on a big play that we had worked on all year. We built canoes, and we were Lewis, Clark, and Sacagawea. I felt very strongly that the boys had all the good parts. There was only one good part for a female—Sacagawea! I remember that I wanted to see if we couldn't expand the parts a little bit. The girls were just making costumes and doing other side jobs. I remember being disturbed by the lack of good visual roles for girls. I didn't even get a shot at Sacagawea because we actually had Native Americans in our class, so the Sacagawea role went right away. I remember so well wanting to have more involvement in that play. I don't think the teachers listened to those concerns at all.

She also told of the natural competition of fitting in during her childhood:

A few summers ago four women from my high school stayed with me a couple of days in Portland. We were talking about when I moved to Sheridan in the fifth grade. When I moved there, the teacher announced that there was going to be a new student coming into the class that day. She didn't tell them anything about the student, and my friends told me how disappointed they were when I turned out to be a cute little blonde girl. They were hoping for a really cute guy. They did not want the competition of another girl. I was unique because I came from someplace else, and my dad didn't work in the forest products industry, nor did he work in agriculture. He ran the local machine shop. He did something that most the fathers didn't do. It was a competitive environment even when I was young and trying to fit in.

When Barbara was in seventh and eighth grade she and all her girlfriends had boyfriends. In a small town that wasn't uncommon, particularly during that period of time when girls married at eighteen with many young women not even graduating from high school. She told the following story to demonstrate her competitive nature in a social setting:

I was dating in those grades, although that is probably a strong word for what we did. We held hands, went to the movies together, and the boy would give you a ring to put on a chain or something. There were boys and girls that you identified as sort of "going steady," and it was pretty competitive. You bet I had a boyfriend. I was smart and pretty popular, and I'd moved into town from someplace else, which was a unique characteristic. I'd lived in other states like California and Washington, while most of the kids lived in Sheridan their whole lives and had never known anything else. We were all very competitive back then for girlfriends and boyfriends, and it seemed I had some advantages and definitely used them.

During adolescence, young women didn't have a lot of choices for activities that they could excel or "stand out" in. Females were never student body presidents or athletic stars, so competitive speaking was a good avenue for her to take. Barbara found out in high school that she was good at public speaking and that she could have fun doing it. This gave her a "real sense of accomplishment." She had given up competitive sports and said, "There were always people so much better than I so it didn't make sense for me to put a lot of energy into it when I became older." By the time she entered high school, she had other activities to occupy her time. She was in the service club, Honor Society, and on the newspaper and yearbook staffs. She was the editor of the high school newspaper for two years. This paper was actually published in the weekly town newspaper, so she had experience preparing all the copy for a professional paper and learned how to do all the related duties and tasks. She became comfortable with having that responsibility, being professional, and interacting with adults. She went into the newspaper every week with copy and worked with the editor.

She was also involved in a number of other activities. She was a cheerleader and believed some of the other women governors likely had that experience. She explained,

When we interviewed all of the women who were in the Oregon legislature in the 1980s, a huge percentage of them had been cheerleaders. It was one of the places females could excel during their adolescent years. It's one of the places a female could be a leader. In the 1950s when I went to high school, there were not many places (particularly in a small town school) for girls to excel. Cheerleading was someplace to stand out. We had to get up in front of the crowd and be organized and responsible. It was good for us.

She also sang in the school chorus and was involved in all the school plays. She remembers that she got the lead in many school plays and admitted she was a little bit of a "show-off," although she didn't consider herself one at the time. She wasn't afraid to be in front of audiences, which made a significant difference in her choice of activities. Many of these activities continued to be competitive in nature, which helped her learn to be comfortable with and effective in the competitiveness of a political environment later in life. She also believes that participation in a wide range of activities provides important leadership development opportunities. Small schools make that participation easier. She believes that she learned something from everything she did during those years.

Parental Influence

Barbara's parents remained very influential throughout her childhood and youth, in part because of their lovingness and supportiveness. She said, "They really cared about what we were doing in school and the other activities we were involved in. They liked to attend my games and other events." Her parents, but her dad in particular, encouraged their girls to try new things. For example, her sister wanted to learn to paint, but there were no art classes in their high school so her father took her sister and bought paints and then found an adult painting group for her to join. Barbara said that she didn't feel there was ever any attempt by either of her parents to put them "in any kind of box." Her mother and father encouraged self-discovery and wanted their daughters to be involved with whatever they chose.

It is important to note that Barbara's parents had certain expectations about their daughters' behavior. As other parents, they wanted their girls to be good. In a small town everyone knew what everyone else was doing. As she explained, "They didn't want us to be kids who were smoking, drinking, and getting pregnant." She said, "We pretty much towed the line in terms of what we did, not because there was sternness about it but because we never wanted to disappoint our parents." She told the following story to illustrate this point and what she learned when she did not follow the rules:

> When I was a freshman in high school there was a senior boy (the captain of the football team) who wanted to go out with me. My dad told me I couldn't go out with him because he was too old. But, it was very tempting. In fact, it was so tempting that I went out with him anyway. I learned very quickly that my dad had been absolutely right. My dad had an interesting rule for my sister and me. The rule was that if we went someplace with a boy in a car, and the boy got too amorous (nice way to put it) and was crossing a line we weren't comfortable with, then we could get out of the car and walk to the nearest phone and call him. He would come and get us with no questions asked. We only had to do that once for the boy to understand that my dad knew, and then every boy in town knew. They weren't necessarily scared of my dad; they actually all loved him, and they didn't want him to know that they'd misbehaved. Of course if we called our dad he wouldn't let us go out with the boy again. So my father was absolutely right about that senior boy, and I had made a bad mistake. He was too old for me and too mature. I learned a lot from that experience. I learned that you could say no. It was an important lesson for me to learn, that I had control of that kind of situation. My dad taught us that by simply giving us the ability to leave a situation without making us feel bad or guilty.

Barbara was also raised to believe that being vocal and opinionated was a good quality even for a girl. Her parents also allowed her to express her own opinion, which provided her an opportunity to find her own "voice." She explained,

> My father had six sisters and two brothers, and my dad was definitely the black sheep, at least religiously. He didn't stay active in church. He was kind of the

> "wild hare" when he was a young guy. He was used to not having to "tow the line," meaning he believed people had a right to their own religious and political thinking. My parents were both very interesting people, and they were very serious voters. They always cared about voting, they talked about voting, and they talked about elections. They were both very strong Democrats. We talked about all of these issues at the dinner table and in the evenings. I remember these discussions well, and I could always express my own views. I can remember when Truman was running for President, and for the first time in our lives we had a political sign in our front yard out in the country. People didn't do lawn signs at that time.

Barbara spoke about her parent's political interest and discussions growing up. She remembers in-depth conversations about FDR and Harry Truman. She explained that their discussions were primarily at the presidential level until her mother went to work at the newspaper office when Barbara was about fourteen. She said,

> Things changed because my mother was now so aware of things going on in the community. At the newspaper office, the candidates would come by, even U.S. senators and congressmen, because they wanted endorsements and wanted the paper to say nice things about them. My mother met all these important people because she worked for the paper. She'd come home really excited and talk about what they had said. I can remember thinking that it was a really big deal that my mother knew these important people. My mother (a Democrat) and the newspaper editor (a Republican) were both pretty political, and they would talk about all of the issues. We would get that conversation over dinner.

These conversations became important to her during her adolescent years. Barbara and her sister grew up thinking that everyone had to vote in every election.

Barbara was raised to 1) believe she had strengths, options, and opportunities; 2) understand certain broad behaviors were socially acceptable; 3) listen to other's views; 4) share her own opinions and be heard; and 5) observe people, events, and situations for content, dynamics, and meaning.

Influential Individuals
Barbara spoke of two women teachers who were particularly influential because they were encouraging and involved. The first was a teacher and coach.

> When I was in the seventh grade, I had a teacher/volleyball coach named Bernice Cody. She had her own children, two sons, but she sort of adopted six of us girls that were in her class. We actually went out in the summer and stayed in their barn. It is probably inappropriate by today's standards, but she liked having us around. She was very influential during those years. She treated us different from other kids at school, so it made us feel special. She also talked about when she went to college. She was a college-educated woman, so we did have an example. Interestingly, she never asked us if we wanted to go to college. In fact, only one of the six girls went to college. She talked to us a lot and

also listened. She had lived in other places and would talk about her experiences, which was exciting to the girls since most had never lived anywhere else.

The second was a high school English/speech teacher and volleyball coach named Fern Eberheart. She was divorced with two children. A divorced woman teacher in those years was pretty unusual. Barbara explained,

She played a very special role in my life. I loved public speaking, and she was my speech coach and helped me get really involved in competitive high school speech. I began going to speech competitions and competed in extemporaneous and other kinds of speaking. I also played volleyball during my freshman year for her. She really encouraged me to study, yet she didn't talk much about college. However, she taught me to find joy in learning. She told me that one should never quit learning in life. She showed me I could find excitement in learning and developing my mind. She encouraged me to read. She did this by telling me about a book in the school library that I might like. I would check it out from the library and read it. I think she was very purposeful in what she suggested I read. She wanted me to broaden my thinking. She would talk with me much differently than other adults talked to me. She always talked to me like I was an adult.

These two adults were important in Barbara's development. They fueled her desire to learn, encouraged her to expand and develop her skills, listened to her, and believed in her mind, abilities, and ideas.

Barbara shared a memorable experience that demonstrates some essential elements important in leadership development. It also provides an example of another adult who listened to her ideas. When she was in high school four or five boys got suspended or expelled for ten days because they skipped school for the opening day of fishing season. They were boys who lived in the country, and fishing was very important to them. She remembers telling Fern, her high school English/speech teacher, that expelling them didn't make any sense as a punishment. Fern asked Barbara if she wanted to talk to the principal about it. After she agreed, Fern took her into the principal's office to speak to him. Barbara told him of her concerns and made the statement that the punishment didn't make any sense at all. She said,

Mr. Smith, these boys are in trouble for skipping a day of school, and now you have them out for ten days. As you know they're probably fishing now for ten days straight, and there's nothing sensible about that. I said, "You've given them exactly what they want." I suggested that the suspension stop and that he bring them back to school and make them do long study halls to make up for what they missed. He told me that suspension was the only real form of punishment they had for skipping school.

She remembered saying, "But there are other forms. It doesn't have to be this way." Again, she was listened to by these adults who seemed to value her opinion during her teenage years. After this incident she ended up working in the principal's office her junior and senior years, which gave her the opportunity to get to know all the teachers kind of as colleagues.

These individuals helped Barbara learn to 1) care about the development of others, 2) find joy in learning and in developing her mind, 3) read and think broadly, 4) share her views and ideas with others, and 5) know that her contributions would be respected.

Employment

Barbara started picking crops in the summer after sixth grade. This was something a lot of kids in her small town did. She got on a bus at 5:30 a.m. and went to the fields to pick strawberries and string beans. It was somewhat of a competitive environment. She decided that since she was up so early and getting dirty doing the job anyway, she better do it well. The better you performed the more money you made. She was very clear about her status as a top picker and picked crops from the sixth grade through the summer before her junior year in high school.

Barbara went to work before her senior year of high school in the office of the company where her father worked managing a machine shop. His boss hired her to do secretarial work all summer. She explained,

> *It was one of my first experiences working in the setting where I was the only female, and that was a learning experience for me. There were blue-collar men, me, and my dad who was the foreman. I wasn't necessarily uncomfortable with these men; it was just a new experience. Interestingly, since that time I have spent most of my workplace experiences in settings with predominantly men.*

She found out that summer that it was a lot nicer to work in an office than it was in the fields, and she could also make more money. She remembers enjoying that work experience and also going out to lunch with her father. She also said that although she was always an organized person, this job gave her the opportunity to practice that and other important skills like phone etiquette, interpersonal communication, taking messages, being accurate, and answering questions. As mentioned previously, Barbara also learned some of these skills from working in the principal's office during school and being the editor of her high school paper. She felt her youth employment experiences were very helpful developmental experiences. She stated, "I'm sure confidence breeds confidence. If you're feeling fairly confident about yourself, then people allow you to do things you wouldn't be able to do otherwise."

In addition to the skills already mentioned, early employment experience taught Barbara that 1) hard work could lead to success, 2) healthy competition motivated some workers, 3) she preferred working with her mind more than hard physical labor, and 4) successful experiences increased confidence.

College Plans

As a youth, Barbara watched many of her peers drop out of high school, and she knew she was not going to do this. However, she didn't grow up with the expectation that she would attend college. She wasn't encouraged by her parents and extended family to do so. Although she was the salutatorian of her high school graduating class, a student body officer, and a speech winner, she didn't feel she received encouragement by anyone to attend college, including high school counselors/advisors.

At that period of time, particularly in a small Oregon town, most girls graduated from high school, got married, and then had families. Those were the expectations for most young women, including Barbara. In fact, most married women didn't even work outside their homes. Young women didn't have female role models who did anything different from the norm of the times. She mentioned that there was one woman who owned the beauty parlor in her town when she was growing up and "that was about it." She said, "In terms of female role models, there were no women doctors, no women lawyers, no women principals, no women elected officials, and no women school board members. That was how it was in the 1950s." Barbara didn't consider any other options until later in her life. She would have never believed, during those years, that a woman could become the governor of Oregon.

PERSONAL AND FAMILY LIFE

Early Married Life
Barbara married at eighteen, five months before her high school graduation. She was committed, however, to graduating. Her husband was two years older and had joined the military hoping to get a college education on the GI bill. She explained,

> *My fiancé had joined the Air Force and was in Texas and Mississippi. He was coming home on Christmas leave, and we decided we wanted to get married on that Christmas leave during my senior year. He was going to turn right around and go back to Mississippi. Then he was supposed to get assigned to Europe, and we both wanted to go. The idea of going to Europe was so exciting for me. It was like going to the moon. We figured that if we got married, the military would then pay to move me over there too.*

However, shortly before her high school graduation her fiancé was sent to Texas instead of Europe and ended up spending the rest of his enlistment (3 ½ years) in the Air Force in Texas. So, the morning after her graduation from high school Barbara moved to southern Texas. She had difficulty leaving her family because they were very close. This was a huge change and adjustment for her. Her first son was born in Texas and her second was born shortly after returning to Oregon. She spoke of the stress of the timing of the birth of her second child. The young couple wanted to make sure they had moved from Texas before he was born, because they were afraid if that baby was born there they would be too poor to move home to Oregon. However, on the other hand they needed the military insurance to cover the delivery. Barbara went home early to be with her parents and waited for her husband to be discharged. She had her second child four days before his discharge.

Her husband returned, and they started a new life. He hadn't gone to college yet, but now he had the GI bill. He knew when he got ready to go to college it would be there. However, his immediate worry was to support a wife and two children. They lived with her parents for a few months and then moved to Portland where he began working at a local television studio.

Although these military years were difficult, Barbara learned and developed important competencies during that time, including patience, being comfortable with new circumstances, financial frugality, and awareness of others' situations and circumstances.

Motherhood

Barbara spoke of patience being something that parenthood helped her learn. Motherhood also helped her become more organized and improved her time management skills. She explained,

> *I had two children, and it was important to get them both down for a nap at the same time. I had to figure out the types of things best to do when they were awake and save particular tasks for naptime. For example, I could do laundry and cook when they were up running around. I had to prioritize.*

Barbara told the story of her oldest son who was autistic and a difficult child. Mike didn't sleep a lot so she didn't get the advantage of long nap times with him, which was an added challenge. She stated,

> *Nobody knew what was happening with him. We knew something was amiss, but he was my first child and I had no preparation for this challenging behavior. So, boy did I learn patience! I think in some ways it softened me so that I had more patience with other people. I could see other people's points of view more because of those experiences. I was not so quick to judge either. Maybe it was my recognition that something wasn't okay with my son. It's amazing how nonjudgmental one becomes.*

Barbara also spoke of how she learned the lesson of "picking your battles wisely" very early in her motherhood experiences. She remembers that when her son was six years old, the school officials sent him home from the first grade and said he could never come back to school. This would have been devastating for any mother! There was no special education required by any state in the nation or by the federal government at that time. She said,

> *Here I was with a difficult six-year-old, and he couldn't go to school. Parents just expect children to go to school. That's what children do. He ended up at the Health Science University, and they put him through diagnostic work and decided that he had a severe emotional disturbance. They didn't use the term autism back then. They recommended that we permanently institutionalize him.*

> *They said that he would never be able to function, and that he would never be able to go to school. They said that he would never be able to work, and that he would never be able to live alone. Basically, he would never be able to be independent in any way. This child was hopeless as far as they were concerned, and they suggested we permanently institutionalize him. That was a huge blow, a huge blow. It was not only a blow for him and for me, but it was also a blow to my marriage. Lots of fathers have trouble accepting children with severe disabilities.*

Barbara spoke of the challenges with her son and her marriage and how she learned about herself during these years. She began developing a personal strength that would continue to grow through the years. Importantly, as Warren Bennis (1989, 9) stated, "Becoming a leader is synonymous with becoming yourself." This is definitely the case for Barbara Roberts.

Barbara decided that she would temporarily institutionalize her son to get the only available help for him. She took him to a facility that dealt with emotionally disturbed children. Her son was only six at the time, so it was very difficult for her. For a while she could see him once a week and then visits increased. During these years, the mental health counselor told her that something in his "environment" had caused his condition. The expert writer on autism at that time said that autistic children were caused by "refrigerator mothers" who were cold, uncaring, unfeeling. She said,

> *But I would not let the counselor blame me for this, and I argued with him about this for three years. I knew he was wrong. I knew my child and knew something had been different with this child from the beginning. It did hurt that I was blamed, but I kept saying, "No, it's not true. You're wrong." He just kept saying, "Barbara, you're in denial. You've got to accept this. If you can accept that you were at fault then we'll be able to help him more." Interestingly, years later the counselor sent me a long letter of apology for what he'd done. I accepted his apology. This was another profound learning experience related to what it means to stand up for what you know is right.*

This institution made sure she never met any other parents whose children were patients there. There was no support system, and parents felt very alone. Parents had to develop a sort of survival strength to get through that experience. This experience gave her the opportunity to continue developing internal strength and resolve. She used this learned skill to her advantage when she was governor. As Barbara stated,

> *As a governor, I had to confront and sometimes go against powerful people and powerful organizations. I learned I had this strength and ability because of my experiences in making public education available to my autistic son and other disabled youth.*

Barbara was able to move forward productively and did not allow her circumstances to become a roadblock. She rose to the challenge when many others had given up. She learned to dig deep to understand herself during these years. She learned that she could survive in the face of being challenged to the very core of her existence.

When Barbara's son went into the institution, she began working outside the home as a secretary/bookkeeper in the construction field to help pay for his care. She still had another child at home, a job, a husband, a house, and other responsibilities. So, she had to deal with the huge emotional cost of her oldest child being away, the needs of her other child at home, and a deteriorating marriage. She believes that personal struggles like this helped shape her character and insights.

These motherhood experiences taught Barbara very powerful lessons that were critical for her leadership success later in her life. She learned or strengthened her knowledge and skills in surviving, patience, organization, time management, prioritization, personal strength, and digging deep inside. She learned to listen to others' views, delay judgment, pick battles wisely, trust her instincts, and challenge authority figures appropriately. She began to 1) understand the importance of learning from challenges, 2) learn more about herself, and 3) comprehend the connection between responsibility and relationships.

Creating Support
When her son came out of the institution, he still couldn't go to public school because there were still no special education programs. She enrolled him in a special program that was funded by the National Institute of Mental Health. It was an experimental program to see if children with autism could be educated in a public school setting. The children had their own schoolroom, but they ate lunch and played on the playground with the other kids. This program came with a requirement that there be a parents' group that met with a psychologist every two weeks. The group talked about how they and their children were doing and how the kids were doing educationally. It was the first time that she had other parents to talk with.

In the middle of her divorce, the federally funded program her son was attending was coming to an end, so once again her child was not going to be able to go to school. There was not another existing, appropriate program available. The parents' group from this program decided that they could and should do something about it. They saw a need and initiated a solution. Barbara told the following story:

> *We went to Frank Roberts, who was our state representative for the area, and told him that we wanted a bill in the legislature that would put funding for special education into state law. It was kind of a "dreamer" bill, and we knew it. However, he agreed to sponsor a bill for us. He introduced the bill with a funding requirement as well as the specifics about opting into the program. Every district that opted in had to have parent support and advisory groups as part of their program, and the state had to have an advisory group for what was labeled in the bill "emotionally disturbed" children. Frank introduced the bill, and I became the volunteer lobbyist for the group in 1971.*

> *No one else in the group was willing to do it because they were all scared to death. By then I had been involved with a small amount (very small) of politics. My first husband had run for the legislature and lost. I was also doing a little bit of Democratic Party volunteer work. I agreed to take one day a week off work. The group promised to pay my expenses and gasoline to drive back and forth to Salem one day a week. I was receiving no child support by then, so it was financially difficult. Taking a day off a week meant that I was taking a 1/5th cut in pay to lobby this bill. However, through this experience Frank taught me the legislative process. He was my political mentor. In five months, I lobbied the bill through the legislature, and it became Oregon law. There wasn't a lot of funding in the bill then, but I found out that I could literally change people's lives through the legislative process. This was a huge lesson for me, and I found new confidence. I also found out I was good at the political process and liked it very much. I was hooked by the end of that session.*

She believes, and says that others agree, that it was the first required special education bill in the United States. The federal law passed about six years later. During these years her passion to move forward in life came from the determination that stemmed from fighting for her son's rights. She concluded, "There's not much question that my son's disability gave me the ability to do many meaningful things in my life." Through these and related experiences she developed an interest in government, a feeling of empowerment, and confidence, skills, networks, determination, and purpose. During these years she developed and strengthened the ability to be proactive by seeking out solutions and individuals who could help her make the difference that needed to be made. These skills proved very beneficial as she rose through the ranks to become governor.

Second Marriage
During her time as a citizen lobbyist, she not only learned the legislative process, but she and Representative Frank Roberts (who was also single) became really good friends. They eventually developed a relationship that resulted in her second marriage three years later. It was a "massive change" in her life. Frank was both a college professor and a state representative at the time, and he later became a state senator. Barbara said, "We were just totally simpatico. I mean, it was just amazing. We both loved the political realm, we both loved the public speaking realm, and we loved each other." By this time, her two sons were adults and her oldest son was doing better and living in his own apartment.

Frank's approach was central in empowering her during that process. His influence became the steadiness she needed to move forward, and it gave her the confidence and support to move through the career path that she ultimately chose to take.

Work-life Strategy
Barbara's work-life strategy through the years has focused on conscientiously balancing personal and professional responsibilities. As a young single woman she was able to separate her work time from her family time fairly well. Al-

though she worked for the survival of her family, she felt fortunate to have had positions (office manager and accountant) during these early years that didn't require her to bring home any work. When she walked out of the office she was done with work for the day. By the time she was doing a lot of other types of jobs and activities, her kids were older. In fact, by the time she was in the legislature, both of her children were adults. She did serve on the school board while her boys were young, but she explained that she attended a monthly meeting, and most of her other responsibilities could be done in the evening after her children were in bed.

CAREER

The opportunity Barbara had to serve in various positions, paid and non-paid, throughout her career provided important development through experience. Barbara spoke about what she learned from each of her positions including school and college boards, advocacy work, county commission, legislative, and secretary of state.

School and College Boards
Barbara was elected to her position on the school board in part because of her work with the special education bill, and during some of the same time she also served on a community college board. She explained what she learned from these experiences saying the school board was an "in-your-face government kind of situation." This is when people "who care about the issues and choices meet you face-to-face and demand results." It didn't matter whether it was about school bus routes, chocolate milk, athletics, or arithmetic. The issues were about their kids, and Barbara dealt with passionate individuals who felt strongly about their own issue. Barbara said,

> *I learned to make those decisions looking them in the eye. That's true of the community college boards and later positions as well. These earlier experiences helped me because when I became a legislator and had to make decisions, I'd had similar pressure before. I wasn't afraid to make a tough decision.*

Advocacy Work
Barbara already had experiences because of her son's disability that gave her strength and confidence in advocacy positions. She actually lobbied her first bill, her son's right for an education, with major associations in opposition including the Oregon Education Association, Oregon School Board Association, Confederation of School Board Administrators, and other formal education groups. She had practice in advocating against strong groups from the start. She believes that she continued developing toughness and perspective from these experiences. She feels that each of the offices she held or committees she served on were helpful in her development. For example, she was a strong contributor on the

House Revenue Committee because she knew school finance from the perspective of a school board member.

County Commission
Frank was very supportive of Barbara's ambitions and success, and he was a fan and advocate for her. When a county commissioner vacancy became available for appointment she decided to become involved. She told this story:

> We were watching the news every night to see who had been added to the list of potential candidates. I was whining one night at Frank and said, "That can't be the list!" I complained about it off and on all evening. He finally said, "If you don't like the list, put your name on it." I said, "I don't think so." I couldn't imagine that I would have an actual paid political job, and I was also recovering from some surgery. We went to bed that night, and he went to sleep. I couldn't sleep. By morning, I was ready to do it. I remember him opening his eyes and saying, "Well look who looks like a commissioner this morning."

She submitted her name with an endorsement from the powerful Oregon Women's Political Caucus who supported her enthusiastically. She was also able to get the endorsement of some labor unions as well as her own party. She got the county commission appointment and served for nine months in this very public position. This provided her with new visibility as well as new experiences and perspectives that enriched her leadership foundation. Her increased ability to use effective support systems, network, and remain aware of opportunities and political dynamics became critical. It's important to note that she was still serving on the local school board and community college board, both unpaid positions.

Legislative Positions
Following her term as a county commissioner she went back to work as Frank's chief of staff in the legislature, which she had done for a number of years previously. She continued to learn and develop leadership skills from these experiences and also learned more about politics. She said,

> He and I really had a partnership in that office because we really both understood the issues and were very involved. I sometimes testified for him in front of committees. When that 1979 session was over, I decided that I really wanted to run for the legislature. Frank was my senator and I couldn't run against him. My state representative (George Starr) and his wife were and are very, very close friends. George knew how much I wanted to run, so he stepped down and let me run. Truthfully I think he really wasn't quite ready.

Barbara ran for the legislature in 1980 and won. She had been so visible with all of her past positions that no one ran against her. She had good credentials, many of them for unpaid volunteer positions. For example, the fact that she'd been on a school board and understood about school finance, teachers' contracts, and other educational issues was incredibly helpful. She was immediately appointed to the Revenue Committee of the House. Although she was a freshman, because of her experience people did not treat her as such. Her colleagues chose her to represent the freshman's Democratic class, so she was able to sit in on leadership meetings right from the beginning of her service.

When she was running for a second term, she helped the majority leader with recruiting new Democratic candidates, and then helping those recruits with their campaigns, working with a variety of candidates from all over the state. The majority leader decided he was going to run for Speaker, leaving an opening. Barbara decided to run for majority leader. No second term Oregon legislator had ever successfully been elected to that role. Because she had been helping others with their campaigns for years, knowing a lot about politics and developing other important competencies made her a strong contender for the spot. Soon she was reelected as state representative and also started her second term in the House as the majority leader. This was quite an accomplishment and a surprise to many since no woman had ever been House majority leader in Oregon. She felt that majority leader was important in her development of leadership, particularly in the political domain. The knowledge and abilities gained through these years built a crucial foundation she later applied when she became governor.

Secretary of State

She was still serving on the Revenue Committee and chairing the Rules Committee, which were both important assignments. By the end of that 1983 session, the Speaker of the House decided he was going to run for state treasurer. Barbara knew if she stayed in the House she could be majority leader again or even Speaker. However, there was an opening for secretary of state, and she wanted to do that. She loved the kind of work that office entailed and knew she'd be good at it. It was a huge risk because she would lose her seat in the House to run. However, by the time that race ended, she had won the statewide race handily. She was the first Democrat to hold that position in Oregon in 110 years. She felt she won in part because of her selling skills, confidence, and assertiveness, which had been developed through her life through a variety of experiences. These three, according to Barbara, are important in running for a political office. She also believed that her ability to get good endorsements was important. She continued to develop many leadership competencies like working with people, networking, persuasion, and public speaking through this process and position.

When she became secretary of state, she also became the manager of a large government agency, which was a new experience for her. She suddenly had to manage an agency with around 300 people, and she was faced with the responsibility for agencies or divisions, such as Elections, Archives, Auditing, and others. She explained,

> *I began managing individuals and providing oversight for all of those people and departments. I did develop new skills by doing this. I went into an agency where the head of every one of those departments had been hired by someone*

else. I had to determine if I wanted to leave the person in the position or whether there might be someone better to run that operation. I had that choice. I had to look at the work that each of those divisions did and decide if they were doing the best work possible. In some cases, I decided they were not. We ended up doing better work with stronger results using the same people.

She learned about evaluating and managing people and processes. These new experiences as secretary of state helped her develop the competencies and skills needed to become a successful governor. More specifically, she had a broader "portfolio" of experiences and abilities, and she used this experience to demonstrate her skills and outreach when she ran for governor. During these years, she gave approximately two hundred speeches a year. When she ran for governor, there was hardly an audience in the state that she hadn't already spoken to and people all across the state already knew her.

Barriers
Barbara started her political career in the 1970s and believes many gender barriers have changed over those years. She believes that it's "a little easier for women today because there have been so many women office holders in many states now." She knows she lost votes from people who believed that a divorced woman must not have the competence to be a legislative member or leader. She explained that many voters can't understand situations and experiences beyond their own. She also felt the assumption from many that a male had more leadership qualities than a female. She always felt that she had to prove herself because she was a woman; yet even with these limitations, Barbara believed that once she was able to work and show her competence and commitment, she was able to harness the respect needed from leaders, colleagues, and the public to progress in her career.

FORMAL EDUCATION AND TRAINING

Barbara spoke about a number of developmental opportunities that came through both formal and informal education and training that were helpful in her career. Although Barbara never earned a college degree, she was able to take advantage of college courses throughout her professional life. When her first husband was going to college full time, she also went part time for about three years at the university extension center. When she was secretary of state, she went back to college part time majoring in speech communication, which was challenging to fit into her schedule at that stage of her career. She wrote extensive class papers until 1:00 or 2:00 in the morning to meet her educational requirements.

During the time she was secretary of state, Barbara also spent three weeks at the Kennedy School of Government at Harvard University in their leadership program. I asked her if it was helpful in her development, and this was her response:

> Oh, my god! It changed my life, absolutely changed my life. I was secretary of state, so I'd already been a school board member, a county commissioner, and a legislator. When I went to the program, I was holding a statewide office. I had won this fellowship in a competitive program with the Women Executives in State Government Organization. They offered three of these fellowships every year. I competed and won one year, and so I went back to the Kennedy School for three weeks. It was a very intense program. We worked seven days a week from morning until night; they pushed us all of the time.
>
> There were about sixty state and local government leaders from all over the country in the leadership program. After about a week in the program, there were about five of us who sort of emerged as the leaders among leaders. It took me awhile to recognize that it had happened, because I didn't expect it. I was a statewide office holder, and many of them were county office holders, county and city agency heads, or legislators. I guess I had a little bit of status because of this. The five of us took on informal leadership roles in that class. In fact, one day we challenged a professor about something as a group. By the time I had finished those three weeks, I was transformed. I recognized for the first time I was truly a leader. It was life changing.

This was a pivotal experience for her and a springboard for what would come next. She was involved in this program during the summer of 1989, and soon afterward the current governor of Oregon dropped out of his reelection campaign. She announced her candidacy for governor the next day and believed she would not have had the courage and confidence to do so without the Harvard leadership program.

Barbara also participated in a lot of leadership programs and seminars within women's political conferences and women's organizations. She felt they were all very helpful for a number of reasons. Networking and open discussions with women's groups were refreshing. She said that part of it was that these events brought in women who held high public office and who really understood what leadership meant. They spoke of concepts like balancing work and family in the political environment. They talked about decision making, ethics in public and private lives, and lessons learned. She participated in a lot of these programs, including weekend retreats with the Oregon Women's Political Caucus. She enjoyed these women-only retreats because they were so unusual and unique for her. The retreat participants studied a lot of issues with a particular focus on running for office and learning about "issues that the women's movement cared about like child care and reproductive choice."

Barbara enjoyed learning from others in these leadership programs. When she first became governor, she went on a three day New Governors' Conference. She attended similar training when she was secretary of state/lieutenant governor for both of these positions. She explained,

> These conferences were really good growing experiences for me. Listening to

> the high quality speakers who were involved in similar work was helpful. I really think that during every step of my career, even as a school board member, I went to related conferences and gained from every one of those experiences. There was just always so much to learn, and I took advantage of every experience.

INFLUENTIAL INDIVIDUALS

Barbara also learned leadership knowledge and competencies through interactions with influential individuals. Listening and learning from colleagues, including her own spouse, was particularly beneficial in her personal development. She explained,

> *I learned so much from them about policy, the ethics of serving, how to deal with the lobby, how to be part of a decision making process, and about learning how to listen and not just talk. Those experienced legislators were really invaluable to me.*

Barbara believes that her second husband, Frank Roberts, was the most important influential individual and helpful support system she had. He was a mentor, a cheerleader, and believed in her leadership potential. As she rose up the political ladder, his support made her comfortable in taking on new challenges, as he was always encouraging her to not be afraid. Because he was a political leader and a skilled public speaker himself, she felt she had the most ideal and skilled mentor possible. She stated, "He loved to teach, and I was a very ready student. It was a great combination."

Barbara also spoke of a few others who were influential. Of course she was one of the first, or at least one of a few, women on boards and in leadership positions. Although the women in common leadership positions didn't always start by getting along, she became close friends with many. She believes that the "cadre of energized women" helped each other in their development of leadership abilities. She felt that the camaraderie between many women in the legislature was very helpful; however, when she became a governor the dynamics changed. She provided this explanation:

> *In a way that was the thing I missed when I became governor. You don't have another governor in the state. You don't have someone who is holding an equivalent position in your state whom you can be a colleague with. You can go to the National Governor's Association or the Democratic Governor's Association, and then you have colleagues. But, you don't really have that in the state you are serving. It is sometimes lonely. I did pick up the phone sometimes and call a governor that I trusted in another state. There is just nobody else who is going through what you are going through at that time in your own state. Only a former governor or a current governor can really feel that.*

As others have said for years, it is often lonely at the top, and Barbara seemed to agree.

Barbara said that many individuals actually influenced her through the years because of her own ability to observe by watching and learning from a variety of people. She explained, "If you're involved in the legislative process, you have a broad opportunity to learn." She was applying the best practices she was observing; she watched how people acted and reacted to various situations and pressures and learned to implement good ideas and practices into her own leadership style.

MOTIVATIONS

Barbara's motivations for leadership were originally initiated by her son's disability and his rights to an education. She said, "I don't know that I particularly sought the early leadership roles; I think they just came." She said that she was always good at articulating her opinions and enjoyed being part of a discussion. She felt that because of these characteristics "it didn't take long for me to rise to a role of leadership in other people's eyes." However, she also addressed the issue of the few opportunities she and other girls had to lead during her youth. She said,

> *I think probably part of my desire to lead, serve, and make a difference was because I didn't have the scope of opportunity and ability to do that in a small high school in the 1950s. Maybe I was left with an unfulfilled desire to try that. It was terrific once I found I could lead in an adult setting.*

Particularly as an adult, titles never meant as much to her as the chance to positively change things in the community and society. She said, "I loved serving, and I always felt privileged to be in an elective office at any level. Suddenly people had chosen me to help make their community or school or county better. That's a thrill and a privilege!" She felt that it was a gift that she had the "wonderful opportunity to make a difference, to make positive changes, to serve the community, and to be creative in terms of looking for solutions." This brought her great satisfaction. She also enjoyed having influence. She always had strong achievement needs, even as a child, which was also a motivation for seeking and accepting leadership roles.

LEADERSHIP STYLES AND PHILOSOPHIES

Barbara Roberts feels that the people who worked for her would agree that she had a collaborative style of leadership and also made the public part of the decision making of government by listening to them. She believed it was important to reach out to the public when looking at issues in order to see different perspectives. Her staff would say that she was a good listener and a good questioner. For example, after reading or listening to a report, she liked to sit down and ask the questions that allowed her administration to move either toward decision making or toward a point of needing more information before a decision was made. She felt that that sort of analytical skill, knowing how to question, is a very useful part of leadership. She was comfortable asking others for information and assistance.

Barbara spoke of being a risk taker and how important that is in political work. She believes that a great leader should be willing to take risks. She said,

I'm a risk taker but not a kamikaze, and there's a lot of difference between the two. I will stand up for something even if I'm standing alone. But I will not do something totally stupid just to prove that I've got a little courage. You've got to know that compromise is not a dirty word. I've really taken leadership on some very controversial issues. When I was sworn in as secretary of state in the state capitol rotunda, the Portland Gay Men's Chorus sang at my swearing in. It blew people's minds. They were the best chorus in the state, and that was part of the reason I chose them. The other reason I chose them was that I thought if you stood for something that was hard to stand for your first day in statewide office, you'd never be afraid to stand again. People told me, "Oh, my god, Barbara, you'll never be elected statewide again." Every newspaper in the state reported it. The next time I ran for reelection for secretary of state, I won every county in the state.

She believed in taking calculated risks as long as there was a clear purpose and it was sending a message that would be helpful in the future.

Her leadership philosophy is based on the belief that no leader can truly be successful without taking care of one's family, staff, public, and the people who helped them get where they are. She explained, "I think it's absolutely essential for good leaders to take care of those who support them." She also said that a good leader should have other important qualities:

To be a great leader you should also have passion. You must be ready to act and contribute. I think you have to be willing to get in and do that tough stuff. I need to really understand how it works to be successful. You should also be willing to take the heat because sometimes you have to make tough decisions.

Barbara felt that it was particularly important for a leader to be concerned with the development of others. She spoke of working with a lot of women and minorities to give them opportunities to expand their ability to work effectively within the government setting. For example, she spoke of the woman who was her chief of staff for three of the four years she was governor. This woman started out as a secretary in Frank's legislative office and then was promoted at the time Barbara ran his legislative office. This individual came and ran Barbara's general election for secretary of state, worked in an administrative role in the secretary of state's office, ran her campaign for governor, and then became her chief of staff. She explained,

It was like watching a child that you'd raised. I felt this great joy when she expanded her skills. She was very intelligent and strategic. Once she learned how to apply those two characteristics, she was really quite extraordinary.

Barbara enjoyed being part of the development and growth of others, and she supported those who demonstrated that they were bright and talented.

Barbara also believes that a strong leader must be able to hire effectively and fire effectively. Ensuring that she had the most competent and dependable employees was always a critical issue. She spoke of the importance of being perfectly comfortable hiring people who are smarter than she is. She explained,

I never felt threatened to surround myself with really bright people. I also don't like to be surrounded by "yes" people. These are people who just tell you how wonderful you are and how right you are. If this is the case, then they never really question any decisions or actions. That's a very poor way to lead, a very poor way to manage and govern.

She spoke of the opportunities that her staff had to be involved in the decision-making process in her office. However, once the decision was made, she expected some loyalty to that decision. If someone disagreed with that decision, they didn't talk about it to the press or at public forums. According to Barbara, if this does not happen, then strong leaders must be willing to fire. She also believes that strong leaders must be transparent, clear about their expectations, and candid about their position on issues.

ADVICE

Barbara has given advice throughout the years to many young women who had desires to pursue political and government leadership opportunities. She believes that political science courses in college can be helpful. However, as Barbara exclaimed, "political science is the only science that doesn't require a lab. It is very philosophical in its teachings and not an applied subject at many academic institutions." Before taking political science, however, she recommends other types of coursework (e.g., accounting, public speaking, and debate). She spoke of the importance of learning to be comfortable in front of audiences and articulate ideas effectively. She also recommends women take courses in nonprofit management or operations if they are available. Barbara said,

I tell young women all the time to learn and understand finance and get a sense of who they are, philosophically. I tell them that they can't let somebody else decide their philosophical views. One of the ways young women can do this is to watch a political campaign up close. You learn a lot about your own philosophy and your own ethics, and you can examine other people's philosophy in that kind of a setting. You've got to be able to walk away from a campaign, too. I really, really believe that sometimes people get involved in campaigns and then feel uncomfortable about the ethics of the campaign. You must be willing to walk away. There's a great deal of learning in that.

She suggests that young women work on small campaigns, like city council, school board races, and community legislative races where they can actually get to know the candidates and see the detailed campaign workings. She explained that working on a presidential campaign or even U.S. Senate races doesn't provide an opportunity to see and be involved in the decision making process. The smaller races also help volunteers learn about ethics as well. The presidential races are a lot more exciting than a local city council race, but Barbara believes that young people won't get the same kind of learning from those experiences, particularly if the larger ones make up all of their learning experiences.

One of the things Barbara has taught young women is that, when they are working on a campaign, they need to cite their credentials before they cite their opinions. This is particularly true when they are the one running for office. She explained,

> *When I was running for governor or secretary of state, I would say, "As a person who's served for four years on the Revenue Committee of the House and who has a background in a private business in the accounting arena, one of things I feel about the taxation system is . . ." Men are assumed to know those things and have that knowledge base. People hear women better if they give their experience base before they give their opinion. It was something I learned along the way. It has just seemed logical to me that if people doubt my skills and ability to understand issues, then it is important to give them my credentials. Then they would listen. It really made a difference for me. I even did this when I talked about Oregon. I would sometimes say, "My family came to this state on the Oregon Trail, and one of the things I feel about Oregon is . . ." It gave people a sense of my long commitment to the state. It gave me a place in history. It was very hard for many people to understand that a woman could know anything about economic development, forestry, manufacturing, agriculture, or very male kind of businesses, so I had to help them see that I could and did understand.*

FINAL THOUGHTS

It was clear that Barbara has loved and thrived on learning throughout her life. Each of her experiences has helped her develop leadership competencies that served her well in her governorship and beyond. She has always yearned to make a difference, and she has. Following her passion for helping others through the governmental processes has brought her fulfillment in life. She stands as an example for many women who have similar desires to do work that really matters. Barbara has left a legacy through her example, and she continues to show her passion and commitment to the people of the state of Oregon.

Chapter Two

Governor Christine Gregoire

Two of the most profound influences in my life were my mother and John F. Kennedy. My mother provided the steady drumbeat that education was my ticket to success and that we should always reach out to help others at every occasion. JFK's speeches helped me realize that I could channel all my energy into making a real difference in the world.

~ Governor Christine Gregoire

On July 22, 2005, I interviewed Governor Christine Gregoire at her office in the Washington State Capitol where she currently serves as the governor. Chris was inaugurated as the state's 22nd governor on January 12, 2004. She is known for her tireless work ethic, courage, and independence to fight for the people of Washington. She continues to be recognized as a strong advocate for low-income children, education, expanded health care, social services, and transportation. Before being elected as governor, she served three terms as attorney general, being the first woman to serve in that position. During this time she led the comprehensive reform of the state's juvenile justice system and worked to pass a tough new ethics law for the state. She has become well known for her leadership in the state's lawsuit against the tobacco industry, which claimed the largest financial settlement in history. Although Governor Gregoire has had many other notable accomplishments, my interview focused on how she developed the leadership knowledge and competencies to become the successful leader she has become. This chapter will share Governor Gregoire's thoughts, stories, and experiences, helping us understand her lifelong leadership development journey.

FAMILY BACKGROUND

Christine (Chris) Gregoire was born on March 24, 1947, in Auburn, Washington. Auburn was a small town, larger now, but "it was not much back then." Chris was an only child born to parents who divorced while she was young. She never really knew her father as he left early in her life, and her mother ultimately had to get a restraining order against him. From that time forward, she hasn't had any contact with him, nor does she remember him or his influence. Therefore, her upbringing included many years as a child of a single parent.

Chris lived on a small farm out in the country where she raised calves to sell, rode horses for recreation, and raised chickens for their own personal consumption. She was given a lot of responsibility as a child/youth and was definitely expected to work. She said, "I always laugh at people who say that because I was an only child I was probably coddled. I was an only child; therefore all the chores came to me!"

Although her mother was a single breadwinner, she was able to earn enough to provide and care for Chris adequately. As Chris looks back on her upbringing, she said that they must have been poor, but she never knew it. Although her home was turbulent at times because of a stepfather's presence and influence, Chris felt that she had a fairly steady and stable upbringing. Home life with her mother was good.

Mother

Chris' mother, Sybil O. Jacob, was employed as a short order cook and never finished high school or attended college. Chris described her mother as follows:

> *My mother was the salt of the earth! I don't know of anybody that could have worked harder than my mother did. She would sometimes work two or three extra hours with no pay just to make sure that wherever she was working was the best. She was absolutely dedicated.*

As an only child, Chris always felt that she was very important to her mother. Chris knew without a doubt that she came first in her mother's life. In fact, Chris explained that the greatest influence her mother had in her life was the "steady drum beat of—education is your ticket to success."

Chris felt that her mother's consistent encouragement came in part because Sybil Jacob had not attended college herself. Chris told the following story:

> *During the war, my mother had to quit school to help her family. She worked in the town's sawmill and helped at home. These were very difficult times. Time went on, and she just never went back to school. She always had that desire to get a college education, but the opportunity for her (in her mind) was never there. Interestingly, one of her sisters who got a high school diploma went back to college in her forties. My mother was unbelievably envious of her sister, I think in part because mother just didn't have the confidence in herself to do it. My mother had dropped out of high school, so she didn't feel she could go on and get a college degree.*

Chris spoke of how unfortunate that was because "my mother was one of the brighter people I've ever met." She believed her mother didn't really need, in some ways, much formal education because she was naturally very bright. According to Chris, "Because my mother did not have the opportunity to go to college herself, her constant refrain for me was 'education, education, education'!"

Although she would be the first female in her family to attend college, it became a foundational expectation for Chris. She stated,

Because of our close relationship, I would never have done anything throughout my mother's life to disappoint her. Not going to college would have been a huge disappointment. I always knew I would attend college and that education would give me some options in my life.

Chris attributes her desire to do "something that would help others" to her mother. She explained, "My mother was always of the mind that we should help others. She believed that if people receive a little help, they would pull themselves out of the situation they were in." Chris said, "My mother always wanted us to reach out to others on every occasion we could to help others." Her mother was a "big believer" that

Those who found the wrong path in life should never be given up on whether they were incarcerated or otherwise. I think it was just a real inward reflection on her. She believed that if people just had some opportunities, they could turn their lives around.

Stepfather
Chris had a stepfather, a car salesman, during part of her childhood and much of her adolescent years. Although Chris describes him as a "good person with a good heart," she explained that he was an alcoholic, which ultimately caused him to die prematurely. He "never could face up to his problem and as a result, as in the case of any alcoholic, he couldn't get the necessary help." She remembers the sadness of that experience and also noted that when he was drunk, there was some physical abuse to her mother. Chris spoke about what she learned from these experiences:

I've come to admire and respect unbelievably those who face up to that type of problem and get help, because I've seen what happens when you can't see the consequences of it. In fact, it really made me very concerned about marriage for myself. I didn't want to end up in a situation where I found that my spouse had a drinking problem and raise a family in that environment. As a result, my husband and I were together for five years before we got married. I wanted to be certain that I would have no surprises like finding out I had a husband with a drinking problem. Years later, I asked my mother time and time again if she knew he was an alcoholic while they were dating, and she did not. So, I learned to respect those who face up to the problem, and I learned to be very careful about my choice of a spouse.

Chris explained that she wouldn't bring most friends home during those years because of the embarrassment. Interestingly, today she looks back with fondness on her stepfather as a human being but with disdain for his illness. Through the years, possibly even starting with these experiences, Chris learned to see the good in people and situations even though there may be grave problems and shortcomings. This kind of optimism and hope is important in successful leadership.

Extended Family
Chris' maternal grandfather died when she was very young, and she only vaguely remembers her grandmother. She never knew her father's parents, so her grandparents weren't directly influential in her life. As Chris became a teenager, the more influential family members were her aunt and uncle—the sister and brother-in-law of her mother. These relatives lived in a small town, Enacel, not far from her home. They had one son (an only child) a few years older than she, who was the first family member to go to college. This aunt and uncle were influential in Chris' life (particularly in matters of faith), and she was able to spend a good amount of time with them during her upbringing.

Chris also had another aunt who lived in a very remote area in eastern Washington. This aunt's husband worked on the railroad there, and she took in foster children. Chris told the following story:

> *My aunt adopted two children. One of these children turned out to be developmentally disabled. He's the exact same age as I am, and he wouldn't really do anything for anybody else but me. For whatever reason, he would respond to me. So, I spent several summers while I was growing up (fifth, sixth, seventh, and eighth grades) teaching him how to play baseball and swim as well as how to do math, read, and so forth. It wasn't a sibling-type relationship, because I was teaching him. He wasn't accepted by the kids in that community because he was developmentally disabled, but if they wouldn't accept him then I wasn't about to be a part of them. So, he became accepted. It was a real growing experience for me.*

Chris spoke of how much she enjoyed these experiences. She had learned from her mother that if you give people a little help and respect, they could and would progress. She said she just treated this cousin like any other person, and out of that he learned to do many things. Chris found joy and satisfaction in seeing him learn, grow, and develop. This was not a job; it was simply a life-defining experience. Interestingly, he is still alive to this day, although he was only supposed to live until thirty. Chris is his legal guardian and described him as a "wonderful gentleman."

CHILDHOOD AND YOUTH

Personality and Attributes
Chris described herself as very shy in grade school. She believes this shyness stemmed from being an only child and not having daycare or other modes of interacting with children. When she started school and had all kinds of children around her, it was a new experience. Although she remained quite shy throughout elementary school, it is clear that she had confidence in areas that provided a

foundation for future confidence building and leadership. She believes that this confidence was possibly based in academic performance as she said that she "always got straight As."

When she started junior high, she blossomed and "picked up all of these really good friends." She explained,

> I can't account for what happened next. I just came out of my shell in junior high. I had a better time and enjoyed it. I got involved in activities and actually started and became the editor of a newspaper that hadn't previously existed. These experiences just kind of launched me into doing a lot of things. In high school, all of the students voted annually for the friendliest freshman, sophomore, junior, and senior. I think I got that award three out of the four years. There was a remarkable difference between my grade school and secondary school behaviors.

Chris believes that the reinforcement she received in junior high and high school that people liked her actually helped her become more outgoing. She stated, "The more reinforcement I received, the more outgoing I became." She had a wonderful time in school.

Chris mentioned a number of other personality traits or characteristics she had during her upbringing. She was a very conscientious and responsible child and was dependable "without question." She was driven to do well and was competitive in many ways. During her childhood she was achievement and accomplishment focused, which emerged more sharply during her adolescent years. She was respectful of those around her, particularly adults, and she was generally obedient. I asked Chris if she was a reflective child, and although she said she was not, she did speak of observing her surroundings by watching and listening, which are traits of initial reflective abilities. Children and adolescents who observe people and situations and then try to understand why certain things happen often develop reflective behavior.

School and Activities

Chris loved school in general but also thrived there because, being an only child living on a ranch in the country, school became her social realm. Chris enjoyed learning all kinds of subjects and, although she read often during her earlier grades, she became particularly enthralled with reading during her sixth grade year. Because she lived out in the country and her mother worked full time, she had many chores and responsibilities at home, which accounted for most of her non-school time.

Chris' junior high school had a Girls Club, which "in that day was kind of a big deal." This club was made up of all kinds of groups, and she was not interested in affiliating with a single group. She seemed to develop her social confidence during these years due in part because girls in all of those groups liked her. She enjoyed having lots of friends particularly because when she left school in the afternoons she could not hang out with friends due to living so far out in the country. She knew the other girls would continue doing activities with friends outside of school, because they all lived in the same neighborhood. She ended up running for president of Girls Club in seventh grade. She explained, "At the beginning I don't think anyone would have said I was going to win at all, but I did." She won in part because of a great speech she gave. People were "wowed." She said, "I surprised myself as I can't tell you where my speaking ability came from." She thinks some of it may have been natural, but because of this and other experiences, she continued to develop her public speaking and communication skills throughout her teenage years.

Chris became more involved in various activities in high school. She loved athletics and played sports, but spoke of the lack of organized sports for females during those years. She believed that sports taught her how to 1) react to wins and losses, 2) fail and move forward, 3) be tough and thick-skinned when appropriate, and 4) enjoy and learn from challenges and difficulties. She was also involved in service clubs and many other activities, as she stated, "You name it; I did it."

Chris was in leadership positions throughout junior high and high school. I asked her how she got into these leadership positions and why people wanted her to lead. She answered,

> *It was just kind of assumed by everybody. I remember going to an awards ceremony during our freshman year, and everybody said, "I want to sit with you because you're going to get all the awards." I remember thinking "What? What's up with this?" This helped my confidence and social skills in that middle school setting. It was my time to bloom.*

Chris felt that people wanted her to be the leader because "we got stuff done." She spoke of the kind of activities and tasks they were able to complete, many of which had never been done before. During high school, she also went to Girls State where she had the opportunity to give speeches, listen to others' arguments, and encourage and support her peers. She ended up graduating from high school being awarded the "Most Likely to Succeed."

Before she was fourteen or fifteen years old, Chris knew that she had the capability to accomplish things and to get people to participate. At that time, socializing was her primary motivation, as she believed that people should have fun while also getting things done. These groups of youth did indeed get things done. Through these efforts Chris was already developing and practicing the skill of motivating people to follow a cause. For example, she organized and led a competitive activity between the Girls Club and the Boys Club related to decorating cars. They had scores of cars and prepared for a parade by having everybody come out and make part of the float. She said, "To me it was fun to bring people together and have a good time and also get something done." After she reached high school, Chris began to be influenced heavily by John F. Kennedy and tapped into a growing desire to make a real difference in people's lives and to the community through service.

After Chris had this paradigm shift, she became more involved in leading food drives and other service-related activities. She started focusing on the types of activities that could help "things be better." Chris has been interested and involved in positive change since her early teenage years. As a youth, she seemed to have the ability to look for the gaps—places where things needed to be improved. Her greatest strength today as a governor is problem solving. She spoke of opportunities during her youth that helped her to begin developing and strengthening this skill.

> *If you ask people who know me well what my greatest strength is, they would tell you it is problem solving. I can bring people in, identify tough problems, confront them head on (not shying away), be direct and open without being offensive and confrontational, then help groups come to a solution. I started the beginnings of these types of facilitation and problem-solving processes during many of the activities and responsibilities I had during my adolescence. Opportunities for problem solving escalated dramatically during my college years. My skills in this area are strong now because of the years of experience that started in my youth.*

Chris clearly began developing and strengthening this and many other leadership skills at a young age because of the many opportunities she had in school.

Youth Employment

Chris continued to have farm duties during her teenage years and during the summers worked down the road picking berries at the Metzler's Blueberry Farm. She ended up being shed boss for a couple of years, so she had additional responsibilities during the season and beyond as she helped with the pruning and other tasks, including having pickers reporting to her. She said, "There is no question that I was able to practice and develop leadership skills through this job." She was reporting to the owner so she learned accountability, organization, responsibility, and work ethic.

On weekends, Chris would answer the phone at her stepfather's work. She said that she was bored to tears because the phone calls were few and far between. She didn't believe she acquired much applicable development out of that experience, other than maybe learning how to be nice on the phone. However, she admitted that this experience helped her understand that she only wanted jobs that would keep her busy and motivated.

Influential Individuals

During her childhood and youth, Chris was influenced by a number of individuals other than those already discussed (mother, stepfather, aunts, uncles, and cousin). She shared some insights about influential individuals who were role models, coaches, or mentors, such as schoolteachers and a national political figure.

Chris had a sixth-grade teacher who was particularly influential. He actually came to her swearing-in ceremony as governor, and he continues to write on occasion. Further, the town of Auburn was a blue-collar community; Chris and her mother didn't travel a great deal, noting that "traveling" meant going fishing in Montana for a couple of weeks in the summertime. This sixth-grade teacher, whom she described as "a true gentleman," came along and "just kind of took me under his wing." He told Chris, "You can travel; you just have to travel through books." This teacher instilled in Chris a love for and a great appreciation of reading that she has retained throughout her life. He spent one-on-one time with Chris telling her "that he thought I was bright and that I had a great future ahead." Ray gave Chris a little guidance so that she could begin excelling academically. In fact, after she began excelling, the school administration unsuccessfully tried to get her to skip a grade. Chris provides an interesting explanation:

> *My sixth-grade teacher thought I was bright. But I actually think some of that was not really so true. As a sixth grader, I was sitting in a class where it was fourth, fifth, and sixth graders. No wonder I was bright! Yet because people thought I was bright, I listened more at school, and I think I tried harder.*

Chris spoke briefly of other influential teachers during her youth. She remembers an incredibly bright math teacher who had no arms. He became Chris' symbol of how one doesn't need to let handicaps get in the way of success. She said, "He did not! I could see his strength." She also had a physical education teacher who was as "tough as any drill sergeant on God's green earth." This teacher was an example of a very strong woman, and Chris liked her and the class. She also felt that other teachers and administrators had subtle influences on her by the things they said or by their passion in what they did and how they did it. She noted, however, that even with these influences during high school, no teacher actually talked to her specifically about college.

As I briefly mentioned in a previous section of this chapter, Chris was profoundly influenced by John F. Kennedy. This came to light in her response to a question about her desire to make a difference during her youth. She answered, "Intellectually, my understanding of this occurred with John F. Kennedy. I really understood then that I could channel all my energy into making a real difference in the world." JFK died when Chris was in high school, and she was absolutely crushed. She spoke of how he inspired so many people of that era. She learned that "public service is a noble calling," and that it was right for her. From listening to his words, she understood that we are all so blessed to live in this country and that it is necessary for us to give back so as to continue to make this country strong. She was moved by his speeches and keeps a book of his speeches in her office. She explained that her deep interest in public service and making a difference "really matured when Kennedy was inaugurated." During her high school and college years, she remembers often thinking, "I'm going to dedicate my life to helping others"; she continues to live by that motto. To this day, she has a picture and a bust of JFK in her office for inspiration.

College Plans

Chris always knew she would not only attend but also graduate from college with an undergraduate degree. She wasn't going to let her mother down. Although she knew she would have some options in life, during some of her upbringing she had the influence of her stepfather who told her that the only kind of job that females could get was a teaching job. Chris felt that he kept pushing her down that pathway, which she ended up taking. Although she was interested in children, she was not necessarily interested in teaching. Her deep desire was to become a juvenile probation and parole officer. She was very interested in dealing with at-risk, troubled youth. She always thought she could help turn them around.

During high school and the very beginning of college, Chris went through a time when she actually believed she might want to become a pharmacist. As this statement seemed uncharacteristic, I probed for a deeper explanation, and she told the following story:

> *I would spend my Saturdays as a youth going to work with my mother. I would sit in the back of the restaurant for the entire shift and read. I didn't want to stay home; I wanted to be close to her. I suppose it was boring, but I didn't let it be boring. I watched people constantly. If you've ever sat and watched people in restaurants and thought of things, it's great. Eventually I also started going down to the local corner pharmacy, and I became very close to the pharmacist. I volunteered to help him clean up and did so. What I didn't understand is that I liked him, not his job. Interestingly, because of his positive influence, I went off to college thinking I wanted to be a pharmacist. I dispelled of that very quickly, thank goodness. I started taking some of the classes, but realized it may not be the right major for me. When I started having concerns, I went over to the fifth-year program to watch what they were doing. Finally, I realized that "Oh my God, I'm going to be counting pills." There is no way that I would be well suited for that field.*

She was reminded by this experience that she needed to choose an educational path that would help her work with others to make a difference for the community and society at large.

During high school, she had the life expectation that she would graduate from college and then get a job and work. She had spent years seeing her mother provide the financial support for the family, so she planned on working and supporting herself.

UNDERGRADUATE COLLEGE YEARS

Chris attended the University of Washington and graduated in four years. She ended up majoring in speech and English with a secondary-education teaching certificate. During her first few years of college, she took a required sociology class and found that field fascinating. She started progressing down the sociology path while, at the same time, maintaining speech and English classes for her degree. She said, "It was kind of an eclectic group of classes," but she loved her educational experience.

A part of Chris' college experience felt somewhat chaotic or turbulent. There were so many dramatic events that occurred during these years. For example, John F. Kennedy, Martin Luther King, and Bobby Kennedy were all assassinated during her high school and college years. The United States was also at war and there were all kinds of emotions around those issues. In fact, Chris described her freshman year as a disaster. It was the fall of 1965, which was a very tumultuous time, when one young college student next door tried to kill herself by not taking her insulin. She had written a goodbye letter, so they knew it was a serious attempt. Chris and her roommate tore down the dorm room door and got help for her before it was too late. It wasn't until after the fact that Chris and her roommate began to realize the grave seriousness of such an event.

Activities and Involvement
Keeping in mind the tumultuous times, as president of the sorority Chris dealt with one hundred diverse women as they were dealing with day-to-day problems. Chris became somewhat of a mother figure in a way. She said she learned a great deal about listening during this time. She stated, "I spent most of my time in my room listening to others." She believes this experience provided her many leadership insights and experiences by helping her learn to listen, care, counsel/advise, problem solve, and motivate others.

Through her sorority leadership experiences, she also had opportunities to lead change. When Chris joined her sorority, she discovered that it had a discriminatory policy in place. She was shocked at the policy and knew that it wasn't just. She remembers very distinctly saying to herself, "I can either walk away, or I can stay and try to change things." In those days, people who walked away stood out on the front steps to scream, yell, rant, rave, and picket. She knew this was not her style. She chose to stay in the sorority, particularly when she became involved in its leadership and worked to change the system. In fact, she ended up attending a national convention and standing on the floor of that convention to tell people that this discriminatory policy wasn't right. She remembers people telling her that she was "gutsy to do that." These and other efforts resulted in the policy being changed. She believes that if she had walked away the policy would have continued. Through these experiences she began learning what it means to become involved in controversial issues and how to use appropriate methods and strategies to lead change. She came inside the group, and then convinced them that this was not the way things should be done. She continues to use this change strategy today.

In addition to becoming involved in sorority activities and leadership, she also spoke of other campus activities. She became the head of the Program Panel for the university. She shared the following experience:

> *At one point, I became an officer in the Program Panel that brought all the speakers to the campus. Because of this involvement, I somehow organized and led a very interesting demonstration against the war but **for** our military personnel. I knew I didn't want to blame them, but I wanted us to distinguish the difference between being against the Vietnam War and doing what we were doing to the soldiers when they returned home. The demonstration did not work well at all. I thought I had recruited all of these people, but I found out many people would not actually come out to make the case. I learned that you can't motivate everyone, even if they intellectually agree with you. I learned that people worried about being misunderstood.*

Chris was also the campaign manager for a classmate's student body presidential campaign, which provided her with a taste of political involvement on a larger scale. She was also very active in a number of extracurricular activities during these years. She believes that practicing leadership in these forums was definitely helpful in the development of leadership skills.

Influential Individuals

Although she felt that a number of people positively influenced her during her undergraduate college years, Chris focused her comments to me on describing the family that would change her life in many ways. During her junior year of college, Chris met a young woman named Annette Faber-Slaybaugh who became her dear friend for life. Outside her immediate family, Annette was the most influential person in Chris' adult life. In fact, today Chris is a godparent to her two sons, and Annette is a godparent to Chris' two daughters. Annette's two brothers became like her own siblings, and Annette's father became the father figure she never had. Chris shared the following story:

> *Annette's dad and I used to have arguments for hours. They were so much fun. We solved the world's problems. My friend loved the arguments too, but she'd finally get tired and leave. He and I would continue these discussions into the late evenings.*
>
> *He and his wife had a great marriage. I finally had an example of a solid, functioning, thriving marriage. This family was an amazing influence in my life. Ultimately, when I decided to go to law school, I was in no position to pay for it and of course neither was my mother. Since I had worked for the state for a while, I took out my retirement for part of it, however, Annette's family helped me financially, and I was able to attend a private university.*

Although Annette's father has now passed on, Chris still remains in close contact with Annette's mother. This family provided additional stability and support in her life. She loved to spend time with them, because they listened to her and challenged her ideas. They respected her for who she was. She recognized that these lessons worked well in the development of others, which is a critical leadership competency.

CAREER AND LAW SCHOOL

When she was a freshman in college, there was a huge outcry and concern in the United States that there were not enough teachers. As a certified teacher, Chris expected to graduate and get a teaching position fairly quickly. However, by the time she graduated with her teaching certificate, there were too many education graduates and no one was hiring. She knew she would not find a teaching position, so she tried to figure out a job choice where she could still help children. She inquired about working with juveniles at risk in juvenile probation or a related area. Since Chris had no experience, this avenue was also challenging.

Clerk Typist II
Chris decided she'd need to start by working with adults. So, in 1969, she got a job as a Clerk Typist II for Adult Probation and Parole in the central area of Seattle. She was a young Caucasian adult from Auburn, Washington who grew up on a farm, and was working in the poorest, most averse area of Seattle. Thinking back on her initial work experiences in this new job, Chris said "Talk about an education, man, oh man, oh man!" She got an education quickly! She explained, "I think I learned more as a clerk typist than I learned from any book I ever read."

After she worked as a clerk typist for a time, she took the agency's formal test and passed it with a very high score. She was then directed to go to Olympia to interview with the head of the agency. It is important to point out that no one else had to interview with the head of the agency, and it was a big deal. She did the interview, and he approved her. During this process, she didn't understand why she had to do these extra interviews but quickly figured it out. When she went back to the regional administrator in Seattle, she got the news. Their region had already hired a "token" [woman], and they didn't need to hire any more. She explained,

> *He told me this very clearly. However, not all of the people who worked there felt this way. I worked with men who knew of my competence, but the administrators had issues. I had a very high score on the test, and the interviews with the higher-level leaders had apparently gone very well. However, this regional administrator said they didn't need any more women. I knew it was wrong, but I felt helpless. That's the lesson I learned. I didn't know at that age that I wasn't helpless. I'm angry with myself—that I didn't do more. It wasn't right, and I should have done something about it. I think this experience was my motivation to ultimately go to law school. I knew that those kinds of experiences shouldn't happen to anybody.*

In 1970, Chris left this agency after working there for approximately eighteen months.

Case Worker
Shortly after she left, in 1970, she moved to Everett, Washington and became an

"Entry Services Case Worker" in the Social and Health Services agency. She ended up working in this field for four years. Although she felt she was having an impact on specific individual clients, she again began thinking about her continued desire to make a difference on a larger scale. That strong desire to "change the world" and make a broader impact reemerged. She stated,

> For me, it wasn't satisfying to make a difference for this one person. I wanted to make a difference for a much broader spectrum of society. I pondered about what I needed to do next to put myself in this position. I was convinced that the law was the way to make the difference. The law was the way I could make fundamental changes. So, I think it was both influences. First, it was the influence of what had happened to me—discrimination—and my understanding that it shouldn't happen to others. And second, my frustration about this caseload and thinking "I'm never going to change the world here one day at a time. I need something bigger." I somehow understood that the law was the vehicle to do so. I have never regretted that because I've determined that my thinking was absolutely right. I've never regretted a moment of saying that was where I should go.

Law School

In 1974, Chris started law school at Gonzaga University in Spokane, Washington. Although she didn't work during her first year of school, between her first and second years she went back to Seattle and did some criminal investigative work, which she found quite interesting. She got married the end of that summer and went back to school and started working in the attorney general's office throughout the rest of her law school experience.

Chris said that law is a great discipline for developing leadership knowledge and skills. It teaches one to "get into the head of the other person." She learned in law school that she didn't "hold the answers to all problems." She stated,

> I believe that none of us are as good as the collective whole. We need to get into each others' heads to figure out what each person has to offer at the table. Law school teaches you to anticipate the defense. You need to figure out what they're going to do, and you can't do that if you're not willing to get inside. My personality coupled with that legal training has taken me a long way towards succeeding in various settings. I've been able to bring about change because I'm so respectful of another person's opinion. I continually seek out their opinions and try to understand what they want to achieve. I will tell you more often than not, I don't care how big the issue is, people can agree on the goal. What has brought them to an impassable state is that people and groups get so immersed in not agreeing **how** to do something that they forget they agree on the goal. I help them remember, and it helps everyone move forward in crafting a new way to achieve the goal.

Chris spoke of the pure joy she finds in doing this very thing. She said, "I love it! I really do!" She loves bringing chaos to order through good end results. She continues to thrive on the complexity of these types of issues and problems. Law school helped in her development of these abilities. She loved some of the specific courses she took and enjoyed the mental discipline of the overall schooling. Although her problem-solving skills were already somewhat developed, Chris explained that completing law school and becoming a lawyer dramatically strengthened those abilities. She mentioned many times that these skills are critical for successful leadership in public and political domains.

Attorney General's Officer
Chris' early work in the attorney general's office helped her learn and develop a number of important competencies. She explained,

> *Law school is interesting. Law school is this nice intellectual approach to law. It's not particularly application-oriented or practical. So, working in a public law office gave me a much greater appreciation for really how to practice law and what the practice of law was really about. At the same time, I was able to get the intellectual piece. Another very powerful experience was what we used to call Rule 9—not allowed in private practice. When you work in the attorney general's office, you can literally take cases to court as long as you've got that supervising attorney in attendance. I ended up getting much more experience than any of my classmates who were working part time or summertime in private firms. Once I actually graduated from law school, I already had some actual practical experience.*

This experience increased her confidence in her own ability to apply what she had learned in school.

Career Employment
After Chris graduated from law school, she became an assistant attorney general. And, after a few years she became the head of the Social Health Services section of the attorney general's office in Spokane. In 1980, she was then promoted to the head of the Spokane office, and in 1982, Chris was promoted to a deputy attorney general. In 1988, Chris served as the director of the Department of Ecology, and then in 1992, she ran for and was elected as attorney general. Chris explained that each of these positions provided her with new responsibilities, challenges, and opportunities to learn and develop the knowledge and skills she now uses as governor. Experience itself was clearly Chris' strongest strategy for developing leadership. Each experience provided an opportunity to develop new networks of individuals and groups who in turn provided insight and support. Chris spoke specifically about using many of the competencies she had developed and strengthen though the years—like problem solving and negotiation—in this position as she led the efforts surrounding the Tobacco Settlement. Her years of leadership development experiences, even dating back to her youth, were helpful in her success in her later career duties.

Career Path
Chris said that she never actually sat down and figured out a career path for her

life, stating she had no "official career path." She did know that she wanted to work with kids. She was given that opportunity in the attorney general's office by working with child advocacy cases. From there, she believes that other people saw leadership and management skills in her and gave her opportunities. She said, "To all of those people who saw that in me, I say thanks." For example, one chief deputy of the attorney general's office was insistent that she become the head of the Spokane office. She turned him down, but he came back and convinced her by telling her that she was a natural born leader and that it was what she needed to do with her life. Another example was a new state attorney general who came to her and told her that she was the kind of leader he needed, and he wanted her to take a promotion. She also got to know the current governor at that time and, despite an ongoing national search, he called and asked her if she would come and talk to him privately about the Department of Ecology directorship. She turned him down, and he called back two weeks later and finally persuaded her to take the position. Finally, a few years later, this governor, and others, encouraged her to run for attorney general. She said,

> *It's been people along the way who told me I had leadership and management skills. They told me they wanted me to move into certain positions. This has allowed me to move through my career the way I have. That's why I keep trying to tell everybody in my administration, look for the people inside who have talent. Nurture it; bring it up; give them opportunities, and let them stretch. It's there.*

Barriers

When it comes to gender issues, Chris believes there are always little subtleties. She said, "I don't want to suggest that I can't see it or feel it, but I have never let it stand in the way." For example, when she first became a member of the National Association of Attorney Generals, the membership would play basketball for their social time. Chris played basketball and would be out on the court, but of course the men wouldn't throw her the ball. She assisted in changing that organization, at least in the years she was there. They began offering other kinds of events that didn't favor one gender. She explained,

> *I think we were good with our male colleagues at saying, "You know I wouldn't say this is sexist, but we're just saying times have changed." We explained that if we really want to work together, be collegial, and establish a comradeship, then we're going to have to think about things differently. They were great. What I have found is that when you bring something to the forefront and put it out on the table, it can be discussed and seen for what it is by all.*

This seems like a much more effective approach than others who take a victim mentality in these types of situations.

When I asked Chris if she felt that things would have been different or easier if she had been a man, she said simply, "No." Other than her initial confrontation with hiring discrimination, she believes that she has received all of the opportunities she has needed to become successful. She believes she can, particularly in her role as governor, truly make the difference she has sought throughout her life.

PERSONAL AND FAMILY LIFE

Chris met her husband, Mike, when he returned from Vietnam and immediately began working at the Social and Health Services agency where she was working. He also had a teaching certificate and could not find a teaching position. During their courtship, Chris started law school at Gonzaga University. As mentioned previously, they dated for five years before marrying. Chris and Mike got married between her first and second years in law school in 1975.

Children and Support

Their first daughter, Courtney, was born in Spokane in 1979. Chris had finished law school in 1977 and was working as an assistant attorney general doing predominately child abuse cases at the time. Her stepfather had died during her first year of law school and, being the only child, Chris was in what she termed a "tug of war" for the next few years. Her mother was now living alone and adjusting to all of those related changes. When their daughter was born, she and Mike debated about how to best care for her daughter, as Chris went right back to work full time. At this point she was trying to get up enough courage to ask her mother to care for her daughter believing it was what her mother needed in her own life at that point. Before Chris asked, however, her mother actually suggested that she would be willing to provide care for her granddaughter. Sybil sold her home and moved to Spokane, living with Chris and Mike long enough to find her own home. Chris explained,

> When I look back on that period, I recognized at the time, but even more so now, how fortunate I was to be able to raise both of my daughters with the help of my mom. I was able to work while never having doubts in my mind that my girls were cared for and loved while I was out of the home.

Chris then spoke of the offer she received to serve as a deputy attorney general, which was technically one of the highest-ranking roles in the state. She would be the first woman to fill this position in the Washington State Attorney General's Office. Despite the rare professional opportunity, it was a family decision, and it had to be unanimous, as the family would need to relocate to the west side of the state. They voted to have Chris accept the position, and the family would move. Her mother moved with them and then eventually moved into her own place. Chris' second daughter, Michelle, was born in Olympia in 1984. Chris' mother continued to provide childcare. According to Chris, this connection "was probably one of the most bonding experiences for me, let alone my daughters. It allowed me to work as hard and as long as I did without a lot of pressure related to childcare responsibilities." Her mother also felt needed and discovered continued purpose during her later years. She described the whole situation as a tremendous experience saying,

> *I've lost my mom now, but her life was so fulfilled by our two daughters and her providing care for them. The fact that she could live with us during some of those years was perfect, but she was real independent and so ultimately had her own place. We totally respected that and helped her do that. This whole situation was a gift for all of us.*

Motherhood

Chris spoke of the many types of competencies she developed from motherhood. She never did babysitting as she was growing up and didn't have younger siblings, so having a child of her own was a very new and different experience. She remembers very distinctly coming home from the hospital with her first child. She put the baby on the bed and looked at her husband and said, "There is no button to push, now what?" She then spoke of how natural being a mom became.

Chris has found that motherhood helped her develop more patience than she would have otherwise. It also allowed her the forum to express her nurturing side. Motherhood helped her strengthen her skills in helping others find ways to work out and deal with differences. It assisted her in improving her ability to manage schedules and keep things organized so things were in order. Chris explained,

> *I would literally make all of the meals for the week each Sunday afternoon. I would have them designated so that if perchance something should happen where I wasn't able to come home, those meals were already made for the entire week.*

Chris also spoke of the lessons learned from raising teenage daughters. She said,

> *Not that they are the most foreboding in the world, but they were challenging as most teenage daughters are. They were blossoming and exercising their independence. At that, point you just hope and pray that what you've tried to instill in them along the way guides them in making good choices.*

She also learned that sometimes a mother just has to stand back and watch. Of course sometimes it's easier to do that when one thinks their children are making the right kinds of decisions. Chris explained that it was hard, as a mom, to adjust to the fact that she needed to step back and let them spread their wings. She feels that she and Mike have been very lucky. They've let their daughters spread their wings, and their daughters have made good choices. She said, "They are great kids and are going to be wonderful citizens. They're going to be great spouses and parents. We just are very fortunate."

Husband

Mike Gregoire spent his early career in the military and the next thirty years of his professional career working as a health care investigator for the State of Washington. Mike and Chris have been married now for over thirty-two years. She stated, "So see, my mother taught me to be careful and I was; it worked!" I asked Chris about her husband and his support through the years. She quickly replied:

> *I couldn't do what I've done without this kind of spouse. He is quite unique because he didn't care how powerful I was or how much money I made. None of that was important. From the beginning, he was a parent. We both planned on being deeply involved in our children's lives, and he has always been there.*

Chris said that she has always traditionally done more of the cleaning and the cooking, but when it came to parenting, Mike definitely pulled his fair share. Mike always did whatever he needed to do around the house as well. When Chris was in the middle of the tobacco negotiation settlement, she was gone a lot. This actually gave Mike and her younger daughter a chance to establish a relationship they didn't have before. Out of that time together grew a much more positive relationship between father and daughter. She said that both of their daughters have unique relationships with their dad.

Chris spoke of her husband's wonderful qualities as a great father and spouse. Chris said he is very different than she is. "He is patient, laid back, and finds humor in everything." One of her daughters has actually picked up these traits and is much more like Mike, while the other daughter is more like Chris. Mike was clearly the most important "support system" Chris had in her life. He has encouraged, supported, and listened throughout the years.

Work-life Strategy

Chris has always believed that she shouldn't take work home with her. She said that her daughters feel now that this was helpful for them growing up. They knew their mother would give them attention and read to them when she arrived home. Chris felt that it didn't matter how good or bad her day had been, she tried very hard not to bring work and its emotions home in the evenings. Even today as governor she tries as much as possible not take work home, but her current schedule demands make it more difficult. Her daughters are now raised and her husband is much more involved in her work than he has ever been; today work and family have blended together.

Chris considered her husband, mother, and daughters in all of her career decisions. She always wanted their girls to have as normal an upbringing as they could. When Chris was attorney general, she worked hard to make sure her children were not in the media. She kept them from being exposed during campaigns until they wanted to be involved, and even then she stressed that it was their choice and made sure her daughters knew the consequences of being involved.

OTHER DEVELOPMENTAL INFLUENCES

Influential Individuals
A number of people continued to be particularly influential throughout Chris' adult life. Chris feels this constant influence helped her continue to strengthen her leadership through the years. Their encouragement and support provided the confidence Chris needed to work hard and perform well in her career. These individuals, both personal and professional, provided her encouragement to take new positions and opportunities that would help her learn and grow. From Chris' mother and husband to her college friend and her friend's family, she continued to be very supported and encouraged throughout the years. Chris explained,

> *My good friend from college and her father have served as significant supporters. They are like family to me. I still talk to this friend several times a week. Our relationship was made up of both mentorship and friendship. Annette and her father provided a certain grounding for me through the years.*

Chris was also positively influenced by a property professor, Richard Amonte, her first year of law school. He was the dean of another law school and had taken a sabbatical to come to Gonzaga University to teach first-year property law. He and Chris became friends, with his influence being quite helpful to her in learning and understanding a "different kind of appreciation for the law than the actual law school experience."

Other individuals who became influential in Chris' development were former governors of Washington, such as Booth Gardner. She met him after moving from Spokane. He started calling her office when he had a big legal mess. He told the attorney general at that time, "I need the best and brightest mind that you've got over there. I want Chris Gregoire." He and Chris struck up a friendship and, to this day, she'll occasionally call him for advice.

Chris also spoke about being very fortunate that she had encouraging supervisors, who provided vital support in her competency development throughout her early and mid-career. She believes that says a lot for Washington State. She has been fortunate enough to have supervisors who have reached down into the organization and decided to give a chance to high performing individuals.

Chris was positively influenced through the years by a variety of others. Different people influenced her thinking and helped to answer questions and clarify ideas. She believes that she was influenced as she interacted with them, watched them, and listened to them. Chris was able to sort through the large amounts of conscious and unconscious information she processed to find ways to continue to improve her leadership knowledge and skills in practical ways.

Training and Development
Chris took advantage of a variety of leadership training and development programs. She said that the best, without exception, was the Kennedy School. At

the time she attended this program, she was the director of the Department of Ecology. She found it "absolutely helpful." She explained,

> *Of course in law school I learned the Socratic Method; at the Kennedy School I had to take it and apply it in public policy. This allowed all of us in the program to use the exact same thing. I had used both the Socratic legal skills of getting in and trying to understand the other side, but the Kennedy School program was much more helpful in helping me see how to adapt it to the public policy arena.*

This developmental experience was the most practical of any she has participated in.

She spoke of the helpfulness of a women-only annual dinner group she helped form, which began meeting at the National Association of Attorneys General each year. This professional organization was unique because, "as an attorney general, there is really no one in one's state to relate to." She said that the dinner "was very fun, but it was also very enlightening because all of these women had gone through various stages of political work and campaigns." For example, today one is secretary of the interior, and she still comes to these dinners. During these get-togethers the women talked their way through many issues, including balancing work and personal life. It gave the women insight into the various stages and what to expect next. It became a support mechanism for each of them. Chris felt this was helpful for her because it gave her other colleagues to interact with who could understand her situations and provide ideas/advice for future challenges.

LEADERSHIP STYLE AND PHILOSOPHY

Chris said that her staff and others would first describe her leadership style as energetic. They say that her energy level is "like trying to take a sip out of a fire hydrant." Second, they would say that she is competitive with everything. If someone brings up something, it often turns into a competition. If an individual or group gives her a challenge, her first thought is "You want to bet?" She explained that although she is very competitive, it is in a good-natured manner. She doesn't get angry but loves just doing it for fun. The bottom line is that she enjoys laughing and having a good time with friendly competition. Third, she is collaborative. She likes bringing people together to make decisions and enjoys listening and responding. She told the following story:

> *We have a group of outreach employees here who are all very young. They come up with the darndest ideas about what I can or can't do. The expectation was that I would send out a list of rules. Instead, they were surprised because I brought them all into my office and said, "Let's talk about this issue. You may know something I don't know." I told them that we needed to talk about why they were scheduling me to do certain things, so that I could understand what*

they were thinking. They were surprised. They opened up, and I saw real value in what they had to say.

Fourth, she said that the staff would also say that she was a good team player, decisive, and outgoing. She gets inspired and acquires more energy from the people around her. Finally, she spoke of what her staff had told a recent hire for the governor's office:

Recently, we hired somebody to represent our office in southwest Washington. This individual told me that he checked me out with the staff that is closest to me at the capitol. They told him they would probably not be able to work for another politician because, as far as they were concerned, it wasn't about working for the governor or a politician; it was about working for me. They told him they are inspired by my work ethic, values, and vision. They told him they liked working for me as opposed to just someone in the position of governor or someone leading a particularly issue. They told him that they find it inspiring and fun to work for me.

When I asked Chris about her general philosophy about leadership, she spoke about the importance of the leader making the ultimate decision. However, she spoke again of her belief that many people should work together to come up with answers and solutions. She provided an example of this philosophy:

If you had a meeting with me today where you were going to discuss a problem, I would throw a decision out on the table. People have to get used to me because they assume I've made up my mind. Now, what I'm actually doing is trying to move the meeting along. So, I'll throw something out on the table (that I may or may not agree with), then everybody starts in on it. Out of that generates the next idea. So, then we get down to figuring out where we need to go from here and what we need to do. It is hard sometimes for some people to get used to my style. Before coming in to such a meeting, I've already been briefed on the problem and had a chance to ask questions. This process seems to work well for us.

ADVICE

Chris provided a few pieces of advice in her interview. She strongly advises youth that they should not short change themselves by getting through high school on some kind of fast track. She spoke of always talking to her daughters about how much fun and growth she had during her own high school years. She said, "I learned so much that no book can ever teach you about sports, leadership, working with people, and all of that. Seat time and books are really not what education is all about." She explained that when teenagers bypass high school, they are missing all of the valuable learning that occurs beyond the books and lectures, which maybe the most powerful learning that occurs during those years.

Chris also advised, as previously noted, that managers and leaders should look to promote people already inside their organizations. Many people already have the talent to lead and just need the opportunity and training. She said, "Nurture it, give them opportunities, and then let them stretch. It's there."

Chris also believes that throughout their lives women should practice working well with others in a variety of settings (work, home, and community) and in different roles. Learning from being a follower can often be as helpful in learning leadership as is serving in a specific leadership role. Chris said, "Times have changed. We really need to work together, be collegial, and establish a comradeship."

FINAL THOUGHTS

When I interviewed Governor Gregoire in 2005, she shared a then recent experience:

> *Just last Sunday, I threw out the first pitch at the Mariners game. I'm sure most people at the game thought, "Well here comes this fifty-eight-year-old girl who ain't going to be able to do this." I practiced before I did it, and I warmed up before the game. In fact, I was more nervous about that task than I think I would have been giving a half hour speech to them that day. It ended up working out perfectly, and it went just fine. The pitch got across the plate perfectly, and I was relieved!*

Chris continues to throw strikes in many ways as she continues (at the time of this writing) in her role as governor of Washington. She is able to do so because of a lifetime of experiences and opportunities that have allowed her to develop and strengthen her leadership abilities. Although many would argue that she has already made that difference, Chris continues to yearn and work toward making the continued difference she has always been driven to make. After spending only a few hours with Governor Gregoire, it is quite clear that her deep desires for facilitating good for others will continue for many years to come.

Chapter Three

Governor Christine Todd Whitman

What has made my career in politics possible was my good fortune in having a strong partner with whom to share the demands of political life, my husband, John. While politics provided a good fit for me as I was able to balance the demands of young children with part-time political office holding, having the support of my spouse was key . . . none of it would have worked without him . . . he was also my chief cheerleader and supporter, urging me on even when I was ready to call it quits.

~ Governor Christine T. Whitman

I interviewed Governor Christine Todd Whitman at her farm in Oldwick, New Jersey on January 13, 2006. She was elected governor in 1993, becoming the first woman to hold that office in the state of New Jersey. She served for seven years (nearly two terms) between January 1994 and December 2000. She resigned in January 2001 when she was named the administrator of the Environmental Protection Agency (EPA) by President George W. Bush. As governor she worked to permanently preserve one million acres of open space and farmland and fought for tougher anti-crime measures, including Megan's Law and "Three Strikes and You're In." She worked on efforts related to education reform, the environment, women's health and rights, and programs to enhance workers' education, skills, and earnings. Although Governor Whitman has been very successful on many fronts, my interview with her focused on how she developed the leadership knowledge and competencies to become the successful leader she became. With her permission, I supplemented the data I gathered from my interview with information from the book *Talking Leadership: Conversations with Powerful Women* (Hartman, 1999) and her own book titled *It's My Party Too: The Battle for the Heart of the GOP and the Future of America* (Whitman, 2005).

FAMILY BACKGROUND

Christie Todd was born on September 26, 1946, in New York City and was raised in the small farming community of Oldwick in Hunterdon County, New

Jersey. She was the youngest child (by eight years) of four children. Her older siblings are about eight, ten, and twelve years older than she is. Her sister is the eldest and then she has two brothers. She said, "By the time I came along, I think my parents were pretty inert to the kids, and I was so much the last one." She was treated "somewhat like an only child" during much of her upbringing; yet, her parents had "all the experience with the older kids to know how to raise a child." She said,

> *I was in a rather unique situation being the youngest by eight years. They'd worn out their discipline on the older ones! Mother raised me more on her own, and she used to say that while Dad was the disciplinarian with the others, she was able to keep him at bay with me!*

Christie was raised in a fairly affluent home and was well cared for physically, financially, and emotionally. She described her home as a place where she was able to "strengthen her own religious faith throughout the years." Although Christie had a close family who "loved each other deeply," she didn't come from a "hug and kiss" home environment. Interestingly, the way they showed affection was to be "kind of rude, but jokingly so." They just had a totally different way of expressing themselves than many other families.

Christie was raised within a strong family structure, and her parents were the dominant influence in her life. Because she was much younger than her siblings were, her parents treated her like an adult in many ways from the very beginning. For example, they didn't change their dinner table conversation because she was there. She said,

> *We had dinner together almost every night, except when my parents were out politicking. There was never any "seen but not heard." I think they figured out early on that wasn't going to work anyway. I believe those family dinner conversations steered me toward public service.*

These conversations typically focused on government, politics, and current issues. According to Christie, "Neither parent was the slightest bit shy about sharing his or her views. Their mutual respect for each other definitely didn't get in the way of some very lively supper conversations." Christie's parents had a good partnership. Her father (Webster) respected her mother (Eleanor) and encouraged her; and Eleanor was constantly promoting him. Although they had somewhat different political views, she said that her "parents worked closely as a team so it's hard to separate their influence."

Christie was raised around politics her entire life. In fact, in many ways her family embodied what was once known as the Republican eastern establishment. She explained,

> *My parents, and their parents before them, had been active in the GOP since the early days of the twentieth century, holding leadership positions in the state and national party. My parents actually met at the 1932 Republican National*

Convention in Chicago, where their parents played matchmaker and introduced them to one another.

She remembers being intrigued by all of her parents' political activities. Her father was always working behind the scenes and her mother was constantly going to one political meeting or another. She began going with them to political meetings and events as a child. In fact, her parents even took her along with them when they voted. They were determined to instill in their children the importance of participation. Christie said that she can still hear her father saying, "If you don't participate, you lose your right to complain." That made an impression on her as a child because, as she explained, "the last thing I wanted to do was to lose my right to complain!"

Both of Christie's parents loved nature and open space. Her parents had bought the farm on which she grew up shortly after their marriage in 1933. It continues to be a beautiful place nestled in the rolling hills of western New Jersey, about fifty miles outside New York City. It was a working farm, and she still remembers, "all too well the hot, sweaty, dusty job of bringing in the hay and stacking the bales in the hayloft." Her parents believed that there was a certain democracy about farm life, and when there was work be done, everyone had to pitch in and do it. Among the skills they taught her were "the fine art of mucking out stalls, the proper way to groom a horse, and how to tell when a cow, horse, or pig is about to give birth." She said,

> *Although the farm was not the main source of my parents' income, it defined the rhythm of their day-to-day life. My father was never happier than when he came home from a long day in New York City and could spend a few hours on the seat of his tractor mowing a field.*

Christie developed her deep commitment to environmental protection from the farm and her parent's love of the outdoors.

Although Christie mainly grew up in Oldwick, during her upbringing she and her parents lived in Paris for a year when her father was appointed the economic minister to OECD (Organisation for Economic Co-operation and Development).

Father

Christie's father, Webster Todd, was very educated and became a tough businessman. He was born in 1899, so he was "much older" by the time Christie was born. In fact, he was thirty-two or thirty-three when he married her mother. He went to Princeton, got an engineering degree from Stevens and a law degree from Cambridge. Webster and his father owned and managed a major construction company (Todd and Brown and Todd and Todd). In fact, they built Rockefeller Center, Radio City Music Hall, and Williamsburg. Her father did more than general contracting. She said,

> *He was the one who interviewed all the artists to find Diego Rivera, who painted the mural at Radio City. He hired Rockcie, who did the Rockets. It was general contracting with a big "G." I've heard that my grandfather was brilliant, but not very nice at times. He was the one who came up with the idea of putting all the architects for Rockefeller Center in one place, so that they could plan together and weren't working in a vacuum. That was a first. Rockefeller Center was the first multi-use development in the country.*

When Christie was growing up, her father wasn't a "major factor" in her life. He left early to catch the train to commute into New York and came home in time for dinner and bed. On weekends her parents would play golf or attend political events. However, she did get closer to him as she grew older. By the time Christie was a teenager, her father had retired from his New York business and was more focused on politics. He became the New Jersey Republican state chairman, but he still went into New York every day for years because he had investments and was on boards. He eventually held official appointments from both President Eisenhower and President Nixon.

Christie described her father as a perfectionist. "If you did anything, you did it right. You didn't fail, you didn't lie, and your word was your bond. Anything worth doing was worth doing well." Christie believes this taught her to always try to do her best in whatever she did. Webster was well respected. Although he never was a great speaker, the honesty of his personality always came through. He had friends on both sides of the aisle and all walks of life, a characteristic that Christie developed in part because of his example.

Mother

Christie's mother, Eleanor, was a twenty-one-year-old college student when she married Webster. She didn't continue her education once she was wed. She was interested in English and history, and when Christie was in high school, Eleanor returned to college and graduated one month before Christie's high school graduation. Christie described her mother as follows:

> *My mother was a very determined and very strong woman. Her nickname was "the Hurricane"; she scared some people because of her presence and her security. She was very secure in herself and was a strong presence. She didn't let herself get discouraged easily or be backed off of things easily. She was involved in a full host of political roles and events before women were really involved.*

Eleanor was a full-time, stay-at-home mother and held volunteer positions. She was patient, "soft around the edges," and realistic in her expectations. Eleanor never held a paying position, and she never ran for office. Yet, she became very influential because of numerous community efforts. She was someone who was in the "forefront in areas where women weren't usually taken seriously." For example, she was part of a group that established the Gateway National Park between New York and New Jersey. Christie explained,

> *My mother was very involved locally and politically. She was on the state board of higher education and served in a lot of those kinds of positions. I remember hearing stories about her during World War II. She worked as a volunteer for the Red Cross and would drive an ambulance. The military was up in the hills back here, and she would take up coffee and doughnuts. She also used to drive the water truck to the local school. She was a tough woman.*

Christie's father actually deferred to Eleanor's opinion on many things, and he'd always push her rather than himself when people started talking about running for public office. He even wanted her to replace a U.S. Senator who was resigning. Ironically, her mother was always turning it around and would do the same thing to her father. Eleanor wanted Webster to get the recognition and awards.

Eventually, Eleanor became the chair of the New Jersey Federation of Republican Women and vice chair of the Republican National Committee. Back in the mid-1950s, New Jersey's largest newspaper even listed her as a woman who could one day be New Jersey's first female governor. Eleanor didn't want a political life as a career, but she had an ethic of public service that she instilled in all of her children. Christie learned from her mother that "women can do anything." Christie's mother provided her a nontraditional example of a strong woman who wanted to make a difference.

Extended Family
Both sides of Christie's family lived close and were influential in her life. Christie spoke primarily of two interesting women in her family. Her maternal grandmother was particularly influential in her life. This woman went to finishing school as a youth but never graduated from college. Christie described her as a "southern type of sweet Steel Magnolia." She said that people who saw her and didn't know her "had no idea how tough she really was." Christie said, "My grandmother was one of those carefree spirits who did everything well. She'd shoot, play golf, ride, play bridge, and do politics. She did everything." Everyone loved this woman for being a free spirit. Although she was elderly by the time Christie spent time with her, she remembers her grandmother's personality and positive influence.

Christie also remembers a "crazy aunt" who was a little flighty, but who was wonderful. She said, "My aunt lived fairly close and reminded me of Peter Pan." Christie learned from her about enjoying life, even as an adult. She remembers singing the Peter Pan song a lot when she was young. Christie learned that "you don't need to over analyze everything in life." She said,

> *The ability to, at least every once in awhile, just step back, enjoy life, and not analyze is important. I learned from my aunt that I needed to relax and just take a deep breath sometimes. I still have to remind myself to do this.*

Chapter Three
CHILDHOOD AND YOUTH

Personality
Christie described herself as "opinioned, bossy, a spoiled brat, and a pain in the ass" as a child. She was not particularly reflective and was "pretty competitive." She didn't have a lot of friends, but always had a few very close ones. She believes her lack of friends probably stemmed from the fact that she was sometimes too bossy to other children. She even recalls threatening to beat people up in the schoolyard if they didn't want to do what she wanted them to do. For example, she wanted to organize everybody into West Point, which was a television series she loved, and "the ones that didn't want to play felt my wrath." She enjoyed "bossing others around." She said, "I think I was pretty awful as I child, yet I just couldn't understand why all of my peers wouldn't just do what I wanted them to do!"

Christie said that when her family lived in France—when she was ten or eleven years old—"mother was desperate to get rid of me for the summer because she had all kinds of diplomatic duties." Eleanor sent her to a camp in Switzerland, which she "absolutely hated." The following incident provides additional insight into Christie's personality:

> *We had a counselor I really liked, but she got married and left. They were going to give us a new counselor whom none of us liked. I organized all of the kids and then told them to get one of their favorite items from the cabin. I then had all the kids climb up a tree. I climbed up last and took the bottom branch so nobody could get down. We just stayed up there until I negotiated a new counselor for the cabin. It worked.*

Christie clearly wanted influence, control, and power as a child.

Grade School and Childhood Activities
Christie went to a fairly small grade school in Far Hills, New Jersey. She felt she had a stable and solid education during those years (K-8). However, as mentioned, one of her grade school years was spent overseas. It was particularly difficult, as she explained:

> *When we moved to France my mother first put me in an American school, but I must have become bored quickly. My mother tells me that for "show and tell" one day, I made up a story of my father chasing my mother around the house with a hatchet. The head mistress actually believed it and called home to speak with my mother. My mother figured the head mistress wasn't that smart, so she took me out of that school and put me in a nearby all French school where no one spoke English. I enjoyed it and learned to speak French quickly, but unfortunately it was only half a day and my mother struggled with what to do with me for the rest of the day. My parents then put me in a Catholic school, which didn't work at all, as I didn't hit it off well with the nuns. I threatened to run away several times, so my mother just kept me home for the rest of that year.*

Even with these challenges, Christie enjoyed living overseas. She believes that the international experience was very helpful and beneficial for her long-term development. She learned that there are other places in the world, different languages, and people who think and act differently. She began developing adaptability and the value of continuous learning. She also "picked up an ear for languages," which has been helpful in her career, as she has been involved in international travel and work.

Many of Christie's memorable childhood activities revolve around the family farm. She and her best friend had their own ponies, and they spent a lot of time riding horses. Christie said, "We'd get home from school, get on our ponies, and ride all over. We played all sorts of games, like cowboys and Indians." She found riding enjoyable, relaxing, and entertaining. She also enjoyed farm life in general, as she explained:

Some of my fondest early memories are of chasing after wayward chickens, riding my pony, and fishing in the stream that ran through our property. I remember my father and brothers stretching an old fishing net across the stream and dragging it along the streambed in a futile effort to decrease the population of snapping turtles that were constantly getting the ducks that lived along the banks. I remember swimming in the stream and then putting salt on my legs to remove the leeches after we were done.

She also remembers caring for milk cows, beef cattle, and pigs on their farm.

Christie said that throughout her life she has spent as much time as possible enjoying the outdoors. She has always enjoyed hiking, kayaking, fishing, mountain biking, riding, or just appreciating the beauty of nature. She finds the outdoors refreshing and invigorating. Nearly every summer during her childhood, Christie and her family would travel out west for vacation, more often than not spending a week on a ranch in Idaho, Montana, or Wyoming. She said, "These were active vacations spent riding horses, shooting skeet, fishing some of America's greatest trout streams, and sleeping in a bedroll out under the skies."

Besides outdoor activities, Christie remembers enjoying other activities as well. For example, she has always loved to read and has read a lot through the years. As previously mentioned, she also went with her parents to many political events. In fact, one of her earliest memories was going with her mother to count paper ballots in Oldwick until two o'clock in the morning. She was allowed to stay up late on election night, and she loved it. She remembers, at the age of nine, attending her first national convention. She said,

Though I didn't fully appreciate at the time just how special the experience was, as I look back, I realize what an extraordinary opportunity my parents gave me by taking me along to that and future conventions. Because my mother was a convention official in 1956, she could take me anywhere in the hall. Of course, at that age, the political issues at stake escaped me, but I was entranced by the excitement. On the last night of the convention, when Eisenhower was to make his acceptance speech, Ma positioned me next to the stairs leading to the podium so I could see him up close. After his speech and the frenzy that followed, he left the platform and, spotting my mother, he stopped to thank her for all her hard work. Ma then introduced me to him. It was memorable for me. As much as I enjoyed my first convention, it certainly would have been easier for my parents to have left me home at the farm. But what made an even bigger impression on me was the pageantry: the sheer size of the hall and the crowd, the hundreds of handmade signs and the thousands of trinkets and balloons, the bands and the funny hats people wore. All of that was exciting to a nine-year-old who realized that politics could be very interesting indeed.

High School and Youth Activities
Christie spoke of struggles and experiences with her schooling during her high school years. Both her mother and sister had gone to Foxcroft boarding high school (a quasi-military school) in Middleburg, Virginia and had loved the experience. In 1960, Christie found herself away from home for the first time attending this same school and having a terrible experience. She said,

> *The school was organized along the lines of a military academy, complete with demerits, marching wooden rifle drills, and room inspections. Having been raised essentially as an only child, I was used to having the run of the farm. I felt as if I had been confined to quarters. I went there for one year and absolutely hated it. I would call my mother every day in tears. I was massively homesick, yet I learned many things about myself while away. I learned I was not one to accept rules for their own sake. I discovered that I missed the daily dose of politics I had with my parents at dinner. I learned that many people didn't care about politics, and this was a foreign concept to me. My mother tried to help me feel involved by sending me autographs of various politicians they had met on the campaign trail, but it didn't help much.*

Christie began failing every course (save one) and getting constant demerits. Her mother finally took her out before the end of the school year. Christie ended up attending an all-girls private high school in New York for the rest of her high school years. She learned a unique lesson from this experience. Because her mother wanted to her to attend Foxcroft, Christie had someone to blame for her unhappiness. She learned that it was important to give people their own choices, so they can accept the outcomes.

During Christie's high school years, she was involved in a number of organized activities, events, and clubs. She had a group of friends who were always organizing activities and had fun doing so. Christie remembers creating and running the current events club. In 1968, she convinced the head mistress to allow her to be in charge of a school assembly in order to run a political convention. She said,

> *Half of my classmates didn't have a clue about politics. I had grown up in an intensely political family and couldn't understand why people didn't care or understand. I wanted to organize this event to help the other students understand the process. I organized the event, and it worked pretty well. I designed a*

> build up period for people to do research on candidates, write the platform, and so forth. Then, during one assembly period we had nominations from the floor, nominating speeches, and a vote. I enjoyed leading this event and believe it helped some of the students.

Christie also belonged to the drama society and acted in a few dramatic productions. She recalls even being an understudy for one of the leads in "Blithe Spirit." She also played and "absolutely loved" contact sports, like baseball and field hockey. She said, "I was a very good defender in field hockey because I'd go for the shins instead of the ball. This kept people away from my side of the field, and it worked very well. I liked anything like that." She also spent a lot of time skiing and playing tennis. Interestingly, she refused to learn to golf as a teen because her parents and siblings talked about it so much, and she thought it was boring. Christie believes that, through a variety of high school activities and opportunities, she started building her capacity to network and to motivate others.

Christie also continued to attend political events with her parents. Some of it was "glamorous and a lot of fun," but she also did a lot of the "stuffing, stamping, sealing, and sending." She even loved doing door-to-door contacts for candidates. She said,

> Although I did plenty of grunt work, I was also able to see the excitement and the glamorous parts of it. I loved meeting all the people; I knew I wanted to be involved in government for a long time, even though I didn't know what I would do.

Employment
Although Christie didn't have paid employment during the school year, she was involved in volunteer work. She remembers being a candy striper at the local hospital and having to change bedpans. She learned some important lessons through this volunteerism that were helpful for future leadership. She said,

> I had the responsibility of going to a job and had to be there at certain times on specific days. I took it very seriously. I learned that people really seemed to benefit from seeing a smiling face or hearing a hello. My volunteerism efforts as a youth definitely helped me begin to understand others' experiences, perspectives, and needs.

She also had paid employment during the summers as she got older. She remembers working at a school for handicapped children. She spoke briefly of her experience: "I saw potential in these kids, and I grew to understand the challenges that people faced who had more struggles in their lives than I did. It helped me understand how lucky I really was."

Influential Individuals
In addition to the influential individuals already mentioned (e.g., mother, father,

grandmother, aunt, and political role models), Christie had a female teacher in grade school who was influential in her life. This woman taught Latin, literature, English, grammar, history, music, and drama to children between kindergarten and eighth grades. Christie remembers this woman's attention to detail and was influenced by the breadth of her understanding, interests, and knowledge. She said, "This woman did everything at school and was so competent. She even taught piano and voice lessons after school. She was very good at everything, and I admired that quality." Christie always loved creative writing, and this woman was very encouraging to her about her writing. This teacher had the important ability to figure out people's strengths and then help the students "bring those out."

Christie mentioned a few other individuals as well. She had a few good friends during these years who gave her a sense of companionship and accepted her with her own set of strengths and weaknesses. She appreciated friends who were candid and told her what they thought. In addition, she remembers watching a number of "trailblazing" women who inspired her, two of which were congresswomen in New Jersey who became her role models. She had an appreciation for strong, independent, competent, courageous women who sought to make a difference in their own ways.

College Plans
Attending college was always an expectation for Christie and her siblings. She said, "I was expected to go to college, but if I got married and didn't go, that was no big deal." When she was considering college and looking at careers, her father always said, "Well, you've got to learn how to type." Christie didn't want to learn how to type because if she put it on an application then she would "end up with a typing job." Then he'd tell her she should go to law school as a "fall-back position." She didn't want to do either. Her mother's message was different. Eleanor said, "You can do whatever you want." Interestingly, neither parent pushed or even suggested that she consider a career in politics.

COLLEGE YEARS

After graduating from high school, Christie went directly to the all-female Wheaton College in Massachusetts. She lived in the dorms on campus and "had a wonderful time in college." In 1964, most college campuses were still peaceful. Even as the politics of protest heated up in the coming years, "most college campuses like Wheaton were largely isolated from the unrest." She attended only one protest during her four years in college, and it was about birth control. However, she kept current with the issues of the day and followed what was going on in Vietnam. In fact, during the spring of 1966, she was one of two student members on a campus-wide, student-faculty panel discussion on Vietnam. Yet, by the time she graduated from college, the "intensity of political upheaval was pervading American life."

When Christie started college, she had never been a "terribly great student." She was good in English and creative writing, and "that was about it." She did poorly with rote memorization, so she hated classes that required a lot of that. However, things changed in college and she began to excel. Christie ended up majoring in international government. She explained,

> *I didn't take a single domestic political science course because, in the arrogance of youth, I sort of figured that they wouldn't be able to teach me much. I had grown up in it. I had gone campaigning since I was a child. I thought I knew a lot about it, so I took only international courses that would broaden my horizons, and I loved my education. I thought that maybe I'd like to be an ambassador or become a Foreign Service officer in the State Department, because I knew French and Spanish. I finally decided that I wanted to be involved in something that could make a difference, but I didn't know exactly what.*

Christie believes that she learned a great deal from her coursework in general. In 1968, after four years at Wheaton, Christie graduated with honors and received a B.A. in government.

Influential Individuals
Christie continued to stay close to her family, and they remained influential during her college years. She and some friends would travel to her hometown during spring fling, and they'd spend long weekends with her family.

Christie had a lot of good friends at college, and although she had a difficult time being specific on their particular influence, she said,

> *We were continually influencing each other, often subtly. We could talk openly and bluntly to each other. We provided important feedback to each other about our behaviors and circumstances. Many of us have remained friends. In fact, to this day, we actually get together once a year for a long weekend in Florida.*

Christie had a number of very good professors throughout her college years as well. She had one "particularly great professor" who made an "enormous impact" on her life. He was brilliant and was really good at allowing and encouraging his students to express their opinions. This professor, Daniel Lewin, helped her learn to form her thoughts and then speak out. He had a passion for teaching and a respect for his students. In reflecting about his influence, she remembers that he gave her and others meaningful, individual attention. He never put students down. If students' arguments weren't cohesive or coherent, he had a good way of pointing it out. He pushed students in a positive way. Because he knew she had potential, as a sophomore he put her into his senior seminar to challenge her.

Lewin was an epileptic, and he controlled it pretty well until the year Christie participated in his senior seminar. He started coming to class disoriented more often, and then something happened:

> *One day he went missing. I got in my car with friends, and we drove all over. His wife was also a professor, but she was at Brown and was away this particular day. He had apparently had a seizure at home while she was gone. Because of the endocrines that come along with a seizure, he got very depressed. He ended up in a local river and died. Whether it was suicide or not, who knows. We drove by as they were getting him out of the river. I was nineteen or twenty and was just devastated. We went to see his wife after this happened and were totally blown away. She told us that he never knew how much the students really loved him. We all assumed he knew because we doted on him, worshiped him, followed him, and took his courses. We worked so hard in his classes because we thought he was so great. This really made an impression on me about the importance of letting people know what you think of them.*

This experience was devastating for Christie and her classmates. This was the first time she started understanding how fragile life was and how people don't have all the time in life they might think. She started understanding that people can have much different perspectives on the same events and situations. She and her classmates thought Lewin knew how much he was valued. This experience helped her become more proactive in communicating to others their value.

Christie was also influenced during her college years by some political figures of the day. For example, she adored Ed Brook, who was a senator for Massachusetts at that time. He was the first African American Republican senator, and she was able to meet him personally. During college, she was also able to meet the governor of Rhode Island at the time, John Chafee, who also became a role model.

Influential Opportunities

Christie continued to be involved in both service activities and political volunteerism. She was president of the Republican Club on campus and "put together a pretty active speakers program that year." She was able to practice her influencing skills to convince speakers to come to campus and to get students to attend. She joined the debate society on campus and remembers debating Vietnam. Christie also served as the vice president of her senior class.

Between her junior and senior year of college Christie worked as an intern in Washington for the Republican senator of New Jersey, Cliff Case. She loved it. Among other things, she wrote a speech for him to give on the Senate floor. She said,

> *I remember writing a speech in fairly strong language, and I got it sent back to me about three times for not being strong enough. When I wrote the final draft I said that something was "akin to extortion and blackmail." I never thought a senator would actually say that, but he really liked the speech and gave it. This was a great experience for me.*

This internship program also included visiting embassies, seeing some of the inner workings in politics, and touring various parts of Washington. During this experience Christie lived in a house with other young women, with one of her roommates working for a congressman named Donald Rumsfeld. Christie calls this "serendipity," as it led to a future employment opportunity. This internship was a powerful learning experience for her in many ways.

CAREER

Christie said that her plan was to graduate from college and then start working; however, she had no idea what type of job she wanted to have. She assumed she would marry and have children sometime in the future, but knew she wanted to work for a time after graduation. She had always been taught, "If you want to move up the ladder, you try to do a good job where you are. If you don't, you're not going to get anywhere." She knew she could work hard and believed that results would eventually lead her along the best path to making a difference.

Political Researcher and OEO Special Assistant
Immediately after graduating from college in 1968, Christie spent the summer working for Nelson Rockefeller on his presidential campaign. She lived in New York and earned $100 a week doing research and writing position papers. She was quite proud of that opportunity, but it ended with the summer.

Interestingly, around this time, one of Christie's past roommates from her internship experience in Washington called her to see if she wanted to work for her boss, Donald Rumsfeld, who had just been appointed to head the Office of Economic Opportunity (OEO). She told Christie that he needed a special assistant, so Christie agreed and moved to Washington, D.C. to take the position. During her brief stint at the OEO, her duties were largely limited to administrative support. She was eager to make a "more substantial contribution and was on the lookout for how she might create that opportunity."

Early that spring, a perfect opportunity arose. The new chairman of the Republican National Committee (RNC) was holding a lunch for all the state party chairmen. Her father was then the Republican chairman in New Jersey, so she attended to see him. At this luncheon, her father introduced her to the national chairman, and Christie was able to speak with him about an idea she'd "been kicking around for some time." At twenty-two, she pitched some ideas about how to expand the reach of the Republican Party. She suggested the RNC send someone out into the country to listen to groups of youth, blacks, and seniors talk about what political issues were most important to them and what they thought about the Republican Party. She convinced the chairman that the information would help improve the party's outreach efforts. Within a few weeks, she found herself on the staff of the RNC, in charge of the Listening Program.

Director of the Listening Program
So, at a fairly young age, Christie found herself directing the national Republican Party's Listening Program. She traveled all around the country talking to groups of individuals who were not engaged in politics. She asked them ques-

tions about their political involvement and views. She discovered the issues they cared about. In addition to strengthening her skills in speaking, organizing, leading, planning, and writing, most importantly, Christine learned how to listen. She facilitated sessions with senior citizens, college students, and blacks everywhere she went. At that time, these groups were not organized into political advocacy groups as they are now and weren't as influential. She shared a story of one particular learning experience.

> *I was too stupid to be nervous during some of my experiences. I had a contact person in each state who would set things up for me. I didn't typically travel with anyone, but when I went to the Bronx, one of the blacks who worked at the national committee said, "You're crazy to go up there by yourself." One time the head of the Young Republicans wanted to come with me for one of these trips. We were in East Chicago, late at night with members of the Black Disciples gang who all came in with their stocking caps. They were pretty tough group. It was January in Chicago after dark. This guy was so scared. I didn't typically do these sessions with gangs, but I figured it was important to hear what the gangs were all about. At the time, they were starting to get more attention and were really a substitute for the family.*

Christie did the Listening Program for a little over a year and then submitted her final report acquiring some good exposure from her work. During this year, one of the most helpful things she learned was that she really didn't have all of the answers (as she had assumed during her teens). She learned that there is "far more that unites us as people than divides us," and that by truly hearing people out you can be better prepared to respond, even when meeting with people who are fully prepared to oppose you. These were all lessons that helped her develop the skills she needed for her future leadership roles. She said, "Without question, this year of my life was enormously helpful for me."

Campaign Manager
In 1970, after the Learning Program ended, the RNC sent Christie to Colorado for four months to do a congressional campaign. Although the candidate didn't "stand a chance," the party still needed someone in Colorado to run his campaign. Christie lived out on a ranch in Colorado, worked hard, and had "all sorts of good times." She was able to create a strategy and become the day-to-day manager of a statewide campaign. Even with multiple challenges, Christie "had a ball" and thrived on the learning experience. She developed a more in-depth understanding of the candidacy process that eventually helped her in her own future elections. In addition, the experiences she had, from living with rodents, rattlers, and tin showers, were "probably good" for her as "you learn from all that." Although she was young, she never doubted that others took her seriously, and she continued to develop confidence in her own abilities.

Teacher, Freeholder, and Board of Public Utilities
Christie and her husband (see upcoming "Marriage and Motherhood" section of

this chapter for more details) taught courses in an English as a Second Language program in New York City in the 1970s. In 1982, Christie entered New Jersey electoral politics winning election to the Somerset County Board of Chosen Freeholders, to which she was reelected in 1985. During her five-year tenure as a county freeholder, she served as both deputy director and director, implementing numerous projects including the establishment of a shelter for Somerset County's homeless people. During the time she was a freeholder, she wanted to learn and understand the specific issues they were facing. She had learned so much from being "out in the field" with her Listening Program that she began to use some "hands-on" strategies to understand county issues. She said, for example,

> *When I became a freeholder in Summerset County, they were instituting mandatory recycling and working with the Association of Retarded Citizens. I went with them for a day on the recycling trucks picking up recycling to figure out why it was that they required citizens to do things in a certain way. I wanted to understand what it was like for the people who worked on the trucks.*

She discovered that these types of experiences helped her develop additional leadership knowledge and competencies.

In 1988, Governor Thomas Kean appointed Christie to be the president of the New Jersey Board of Public Utilities, where she emphasized ethical responsibility and won the respect of many constituents, including union leaders. When she started, she knew very little about regulating utilities. However, she thrived on challenges and new learning opportunities; she listened and quickly learned what she needed to know to be successful in this role. This was a wonderful position for her, and she was delighted to have it; however, she couldn't wait to get back to elective office. She missed the connection to the people that elective office has over appointive office.

Running for Senate

In 1990, the current congressman in her district had decided that he wasn't going to seek reelection. She said,

> *Everybody expected me to go for that seat, and I would have won. But I really didn't want to go someplace where I was going to have to run every two years. I figured that if I was going to have to raise a million dollars, I might as well go for the statewide experience. By that time, I knew that I wanted to become governor and thought a statewide election would help me get more recognition across the state.*

The state chairwoman at the time asked Christie if she would consider running for the Senate race in 1990. Since there were only two statewide elections—gubernatorial and U.S. Senate—Christie was interested and ran against popular incumbent Bill Bradley. In a strong showing, she came within two percentage points of Bradley; most importantly, however, the campaign gave her statewide recognition as she hoped. During the campaign, she spent time "going after all the Republican bases," showing up at every one of the counties and making sure people knew she was "alive and well."

The most important statewide recognition events Christie took part in during her campaign were two televised debates with Bradley. At first, he refused to debate, but she "pulled the feminist card and said he was probably scared to debate a woman." Bradley then agreed but stipulated they have one debate on domestic policy and the other on international issues. The debates became a national story. She provided the following background:

> *I think he really thought he was going to hammer me on the international issues because a lot of it was going to be around defense. I looked around to figure out who was the brightest person in this area in the world, and he happened to be living in the state of New Jersey—Richard Nixon. Nixon spent an hour with me just taking me around the world and talking about defense policy and weapons systems and everything. During the debate, Bradley would throw out some acronym for a weapons system, and I knew just what he was talking about. It caught everybody off guard. Nobody knew me and the fact that I was a woman and able to put two sentences together made me look brilliant. When I could actually stand up and go back on some of the weapons policy and what was happening in the world, I really gained some credibility that I never could have gotten any other way.*

This Senate race was the key to her success in being elected as governor in 1994. She spent the interim years doing party building—just going out and campaigning for every candidate—no matter what they were running for including mayor, local council, freeholder, or sheriff.

Governorship and EPA Administrator

In 1993, Christie was able to win the gubernatorial election. Being the first woman in New Jersey to win statewide office was a big achievement, but to defeat an incumbent governor was even better. She became a popular and visible figure as one of a handful of women governors. She was reelected in 1997 and remained a leading moderate Republican. She loved being governor because it is a "wonderful position from which to effect change." She felt she could do more from that position than any other. She got a lot of hands-on contact with people and issues. She enjoyed being involved in the National Governors Association because the other governors were "great fun." At these meetings, party didn't matter because they were all good people facing so many of the same problems.

Christie resigned from her governorship the last year of her second term to become the head of the EPA. She was term limited as governor and was thinking ahead for new opportunities. She felt it was an honor to be appointed to serve nationally in this position. She thought she could make a difference, but unfortunately found out quickly she could not make the kind of difference she wanted to. She learned that she wasn't really in charge and that it was "terribly political." She resigned after 2 ½ years of service, but gained valuable insight from the experience.

Career Path
Christie admits that she never had a formal career plan. She knew she wanted to be in government or politics, but she didn't have any idea the positions or areas she wanted to be involved in. Although she admits she may have said to her peers in college that the best job in the world would be to become the governor of New Jersey, she followed up saying, "I didn't seriously think I'd be governor." She noted, "My career has been all over place, but I've learned from everything and gained valuable experience from each position." Her career focus was choosing work that would help her learn. In recalling her experiences, Christie spoke of her low threshold for boredom:

> *Each new position sent me up a learning curve, and when I stopped going up that curve, positions became much less attractive. I found that I got very bored very quickly because of this. So I always like to have people around me, attend events, or participate in things where I'm learning too. I love exchanging ideas and strategizing.*

She said that politics has been a good place for her because moving from job to job "isn't held against you." In fact, the longest job she's had was being governor for seven years.

Christie acknowledged that there are all kinds of paths or routes to political leadership. Each person can take a different path to arrive in the same place. However, their leadership will be based on their lifetime of experiences up to that point in their lives.

MARRIAGE AND MOTHERHOOD

Spouse
Christie first met her husband, John, at her high school graduation party. He was the date of one of her classmates. After briefly meeting at the party, they "were sort of like ships crossing in the night for many years." They kept running into each other at odd times. For example, when she was in Washington working at the OEO, he had a fellowship from Harvard to do a study in Washington at the Department of Transportation. Yet, he was dating someone else at the time. Christie and John "didn't like each other much during these years." She said,

> *I thought I was going to run the world, and he thought he knew what was wrong with the Transportation Trust Fund and was going to fix it. When we looked at each other we thought, "Yeah right. You're one of those." We were both quite opinionated.*

In 1973, Christie needed a date for the inaugural ball of Richard Nixon's second term. She had just broken up from a serious relationship and wanted to invite someone who could dance well to go with her. She loved to dance, and it happened that John was a wonderful dancer. Since they didn't like each other, she assumed he was a safe choice, so she invited him to the ball. After this, they started dating and "that was that!"

Christie said that John has always been very supportive "for better, worse, or for politics." She explained,

> *What has made my career in politics possible was my good fortune in having a strong partner with whom to share the demands of political life, my husband, John. While politics provided a good fit for me as I was able to balance the demands of young children with part-time political office holding, having the support of my spouse was key. Had John not been there to attend school functions I had to miss or to drive the kids to various events when I couldn't, none of it would have worked. He not only filled the gaps my career created (while still very successful pursuing his own career), but he was also my chief cheerleader and supporter, urging me on even when I was ready to call it quits.*

John never hesitated to do more than his fair share in raising the kids and running the household. Christie said, "John has been integral to our children's lives from the beginning."

Early Marriage and Children
The first four years of their marriage they focused on John's career. During this time, they moved to England where Christie couldn't work because she didn't have a green card. She went "nuts" for the first year trying to keep busy by taking classes in English silver, visiting museums, and doing walking tours of London. She didn't feel productive, and it drove her crazy! She had always worked full time from the time she graduated from college until she went to Europe; then all of a sudden she wasn't working at all. However, after living in Europe for one year she gave birth to their daughter, Kate, which seemed to help.

They returned to the United States after 2 ½ years, and Christie chose to continue focusing most of her time and energy on her family. However, she did start getting re-involved as a member of the board of the Somerset County Community College. A little less than two years after Kate was born, Christie gave birth to their son, Taylor. She loved being a mother and adored her children, even though parenthood was not without its own challenges. Through the years, she said that Kate and Taylor have exhibited great patience with the demands of her career. They believed in Christie and her work, and they gave her their "complete and unconditional love and support, which has been an indispensable ingredient" to her success. She felt it was important that her children and husband always knew that her family came first. She said, "No matter what happens during the course of your career, it's your family that will always be there."

Motherhood

Christie believes that motherhood helped her learn patience and balance, both important qualities for good leadership. Because John was the primary breadwinner, she was fortunate enough to be able to raise her children and work part time for many years. This gave her practice in learning to balance priorities. She learned to accept the fact that there were going to be nights that she'd cry herself to sleep because she thought she wasn't the best mother, and other times she would struggle with feeling she wasn't doing enough for her job. But she learned that she could find a balance that somehow worked. She came to understand that it wasn't going to be perfect and that there would still be frustration. This ability was important when she became governor. She was constantly making choices with her time between important priorities and decisions. She learned to move forward without expecting perfection and peace.

Christie also felt that motherhood helped her develop other skills. She developed a deeper ability to look at things from another's perspective. Motherhood definitely helped her increase her multitasking skills. She also said that being a mother helped reaffirm the fact that life was not black and white, as "children teach you that there is often a lot of gray." Motherhood also influenced the first piece of legislation she signed after becoming governor—a mandatory 24-hour (vaginal delivery) or 72-hour (cesarean delivery) hospital stay for a woman after she gave birth. Motherhood has not only helped her develop important leadership competencies, but has influenced her focus regarding many political issues.

VALUABLE CHALLENGES AND INFLUENCES

Work-Life Challenges

While her children were young, Christie became a freeholder and started working part time. John could be home with the children most of the time that she needed to be gone. However, she still felt the conflict that arises in a mother's heart when there is a need to be in two places at once. She said, "I finally decided I was always going to have those times." She explained,

> *If you are a wife or a mother or in any other way responsible for another person in your life, you will inevitably confront those times when you are torn between responsibilities. Many nights I couldn't sleep agonizing over something I hadn't done for the children or for work. Over time, however, I found the right balance for both my family and my career.*

Although she had to deal with initial judgments from her male colleagues, Christie believes she may have been helpful in giving them the courage to put their families first as well.

> *I'll never forget the first time I told my colleagues (all men) on the county board of freeholders (my first elected position) that I would have to miss a*

> *meeting because my daughter was playing in an important soccer game. There was a fair amount of judgmental throat clearing in the room, but I couldn't help but notice that after I had opened the door, others followed. In the months and years ahead, some of my male colleagues who had children at home would miss an occasional meeting to attend one of their children's special events. I like to think I helped show my colleagues it was possible to put our kids first and still do our jobs well.*

After she started working full time and the children were in school, Christie said that she became very good at "shutting things off." When she came home in the evenings, she didn't bring a lot of work home from the office. She learned to compartmentalize; when she was home, she focused on family, and when she was at work, she focused on work. However, she doesn't believe that it is entirely possible to totally compartmentalize work and family responsibilities because "women do have a different set of life experiences and expectations." Christie learned to keep a lot of "balls in the air" and had to learn to compromise and acknowledge to herself that she "couldn't do it all." Despite the challenges, Christie believes that a career in politics has been a good fit for her. She said, "It has enabled me to balance the demands of my career with the priorities of my family while allowing me to make a difference."

Gender Challenges
Christie found that gender played an important role—for good and bad—in her career. She believes that through the years she has been evaluated differently because she is a woman. The first gender-related experience she remembers was when she was interviewed to be a freeholder. There were two slots open, and she and a man were the two designated candidates. She remembers the screening committee asking her whether she had a college degree. Of course she did, so there was no problem. Yet, she realized something. She said,

> *I didn't really reflect on the fact that they didn't ask my running mate if he had a college degree. It wasn't until I got on the board that I discovered that only one other member had actually graduated from college. The other three male members of the board had not. Yet I don't think I would have gotten the nomination if I hadn't had a college degree. There was definitely a double standard. I still see it today to a degree. I think it comes from the fact that we don't have as many women in prominent political positions as we need to have. Each female represents us in a much more personal way.*

Christie believes that in politics women don't get credit for life experience. Life experience is an incredible preparation for political office and leadership, but it doesn't seem to count for women. She believes that all of the experiences in a woman's life—work and non-work—should be given credit as preparation for politics.

Christie feels that the women's movement opened a lot of doors for her. Even if people didn't believe that women belonged in politics, "it was harder for them to keep women out." In fact, she believes that voters still hold women candidates to a more rigorous standard than they do their male counterparts. She also believes that women voters are tougher on women politicians than they are on most male politicians, which is a primary reason there are still few women in public office. Regarding gender she stated,

> *Since my gender isn't something I can do anything about, I have tried to avoid letting it define who I am as a political figure, but the difference is obvious. How that difference has actually affected my career is harder to pin down.*

Christie does believe that the road has been a little harder because of her gender, but she doesn't want to spend her whole life "thinking and complaining about it." She believes that "you can't get anything done that way."

Experience

In thinking about the types of experiences that were most helpful in developing leadership, Christie noted that she never attended any leadership training programs or courses, although she said she should have done so. She has always learned more through experience—by watching and doing. She said,

> *I watched how others around me were doing things. I probably unconsciously analyzed their methods. I haven't sat down and studied various leadership approaches to determine what I should do. I always do what works for me. I probably should have analyzed more people, but I didn't do it that way. Yet, everybody was an influence. I think I became a sponge so that I could pick up a little from everyone in all my experiences.*

She loved new experiences. For example, she asked a colleague who attended AA meetings if she could attend one of his meetings. She went and said it was a real eye opener for her because it was not at all what she had expected. She had all these prejudices of what a group of alcoholics would look like and be like. She said, "It was totally different, and it was a very good experience. I've always liked to do things like this. This is how I've learned about people and developed leadership."

Many hands-on experiences informed her leadership. For example, before running for governor, she spent a time in Newark traveling with a hospital community van and in the emergency room. She wanted to see what was happening first hand. She explained,

> *When we put the state troopers in Camden, I went out with them for two nights to see what I was really asking these people to do. It was an extraordinarily eye-opening experience to see the city at night. I had spent a lot of time in it during the day, but it was totally different city at night. We went into a block where many people were isolated in one house with bars on every window. I heard the lookouts for the drug guys yell warnings. I saw police go into the houses that had been booby trapped for the police. This experience was very important for me, and it informed a lot of what I did when I had to send the Na-*

tional Guard in to board some of these homes up in order to take down some of the drug dens.

Christie continued to develop these leadership competencies through the years in all of her positions. For example, although she said that taking criticism well doesn't come naturally for most women, experiences helped her develop a thick skin and learn to "deal with it." She said that criticism never goes away in the political environment, so politicians have to learn to handle it gracefully. Even with criticism, "practice brings more calmness and confidence."

Influential Individuals

Different individuals also influenced Christie throughout the years. First, her boss at the Republican National Committee, Roger Morton, was terrific. He gave her extraordinary responsibility and experiences. He mentored her through many situations and choices. He liked her ideas, was very open, and provided Christie with valuable opportunities. Second, the deputy chairman at that time was also very helpful. On one particular occasion she disagreed with an effort he was leading and didn't want to help. He asked her questions to clarify her motivations and reasoning for not wanting to be involved, and then respected her views and found others to cover. He didn't push her to be involved and, most importantly, didn't hold it against her. He taught her that she could be "honest and open" and gave her another example of someone with integrity within the political environment. Although she supported most of the efforts and projects this job required, this man taught her that she could speak her mind and still remain a valuable member of the team. Third, during her time as director of the Listening program, she brought in another person to work with her. Nancy Risque had been working for the national committee in France and was very sharp. She and Christie became best friends quickly and continue their friendship today. She believes that enriching, open, honest friendships can help people learn more about themselves and others—a critical task in effective leadership.

Christie believes that she has learned a great deal from many different people in small ways. She admitted that it was hard for her to identify specific individuals as influential because many of her peers and compatriots have been very important all throughout her professional career. She said, "We talk, we share, and we learn from one another. From these conversations, I get ideas or thoughts." However, she also noted that she has also learned from negative examples. She said, "Observing supervisors and leaders who were not effective helped me figure out what I needed to do to lead well."

LEADERSHIP MOTIVATION, STYLE, AND PHILOSOPHY

Motivation

Christie has had a variety of motivations for leadership through the years. At times, she prefers to lead because she doesn't like to be told what to do. She enjoys having goals, "finishing things," and thrives on achievement and accomplishment. She has had a desire, at least since her college days, to lead the type of changes needed to make a difference for others. This was clearly her motivation at the age of twenty-two when she proposed and directed the Listening Program. She knew she had good ideas and wanted them heard, and leadership provided a way for her to be heard. It has also provided her opportunities to continually learn new things and develop herself.

Style
Christie believes that her staff would say she has a collaborative leadership style and likes to hire really good people and trust them. Once hired, she believes in assisting them in professional development. In fact, she finds great satisfaction in assisting others to become more skilled, knowledgably, and competent. When she sees special ability in individuals, she enjoys giving them opportunities to excel and grow. She likes giving her "really good people" the flexibility to make decisions and come up with solutions on their own. She typically "sets out the broad agenda" and then lets her "staff figure out how to get there." She then would facilitate meetings where the team members discuss the issues and proposed solutions. She said, "It's great fun to watch people develop. Although I've had a couple of cabinet members that I really needed to put the brakes on, I'd far rather have a horse to hold back rather than one I had to kick." She found particular satisfaction from reaching out to women and minorities who had "incredible potential" and needed opportunities to help them attain their potential.

Christie is also certain that her staff would say that her leadership style includes compromising and listening. She believes that life is all about compromising, "whether you're dealing with your kids, negotiating with your life partner, or serving as a member of a school board." She said, "There's nothing wrong with that as long as you're still focused on the right goals and moving toward those goals and not compromising principles." She also figured out in her early professional years that leaders don't have to have all the answers. She said,

> As long as you are willing to look for people who know more than you do and listen to them—you can do all right. You get up the learning curve pretty fast. Probably because I've been exposed to so many people from so many different walks of life over my lifetime, one thing I'm good at is figuring out who's opinions I can trust. I am a pretty good judge of people, and that's helped.

Once she found people she valued and trusted, she listened. She believes in listening to others, respecting their ideas and then incorporating their ideas into solutions.

I asked Christie if she has become reflective throughout her personal and professional life. She quickly said that she has not. Yet, most effective leaders are reflective. Since a number of governors had this initial reaction, I inquired more deeply into her reasoning, and she responded,

> *I really don't spend a lot of time reflecting in the sense that I need to take the time to sit in an orchard and think deep thoughts. I do categorize information, note what's happened, and figure out what can be done better. There are times when I may stop and admit we screwed up and need to analyze what happened. For example, after 9/11 we were the first agency of the federal government to do a "lessons learned." This is something I always did after a crisis when I was governor. That's what you should do. You should always go back and review what happened, how you responded, and how to do better the next time. I don't like to sit and spend a lot of time thinking through things; I just look back at events and issues and figure out where we went right and where we went wrong.*

Her response clearly demonstrates her reflective qualities, but in a different way than she had envisioned reflection to be. She believes in absorbing what other people have done and to "observe and pick up the big trends rather than stopping to dissect each different way of problem solving." She said, "I've never had that much time!" She noted that government leaders don't have much time to reflect on everything in the past.

Philosophy

One of Christie's philosophies of leadership in the political environment is that women have an obligation to support each other by bringing them into politics and mentoring them. She explained,

> *I was fortunate; I had my mother and my older sister as role models for women in politics, but very few women have that same good fortune. That's why we must be deliberate about being mentors to qualified women; we must support them in their efforts, we must celebrate their success, we must help pick them up when they stumble, and we must look for opportunities to help them get ahead. That is what I have tried to do—from appointing many "female firsts" to campaigning and raising money for women candidates from Maine to Hawaii.*

Christie also believes mentoring must be an important part of women leaders' work—not just one-on-one mentoring but in a systematic way. She believes that if women ever hope to reach a "critical mass in politics," they must consider quality and quantity. She doesn't believe it's enough just to hire women. Women leaders must set the tone by creating and enforcing family-friendly policies that make it possible for women and men in politics to work and still have a life.

ADVICE

Christie provided some intriguing advice for girls and women of all ages interested in developing themselves for political leadership. She said, "Go for it!" Regarding educational preparation, she shared a recent conversation she had:

A woman asked me the other day about her daughter who wanted to go into politics and couldn't decide whether to get an advanced degree in law school, business, or political science. I said, "If she's interested in getting a graduate degree, then go get it. Then she'll have something to fall back on." Although graduate degrees will certainly help, they aren't essential to being in politics. I probably would have benefited from an MBA or law degree, but there is no degree in public office holding or in how to become a governor.

Christie recommends doing volunteer work and getting involved in part-time politics early. She said, "The nice thing about politics is that it doesn't have to be a full-time position; you can do it part time."

The most important piece of advice she gives to young people, however, is that they need to find out what their passions are and what they really love and care about. After discovering their passions, they then need to find out what needs to be done. She explained,

I think a good place to start is focusing on issues not positions. Find the causes and figure out where you stand. If other people aren't doing what you think they ought to be doing, then get involved and start to influence. You must have the passion, because it is not about the job.

She noted that politics is not for the faint of heart. It is a "pretty brutal job" and politicians get attacked at all different angles. She explained that it can only be satisfying if there is a "reason bigger than yourself to do it." She stated,

You have really got to find out what it is—and it can be many things—that you care about. It can even be a method of approaching problems that you think is wrong. It can be as broad as you want it to be. But the bottom-line is that you really have to know why you want to get involved to make a difference and to be successful.

FINAL THOUGHTS

Christie and John currently live on the same family farm where she grew up, and they continue to love the farm, outdoors, and staying active. She remains busy and committed to the political efforts she has lead for many years. She runs her own management consulting strategic planning business and heads a political action committee now in thirty-one states. Although she has already made a difference for many throughout her years in official leadership positions, her passion for positive change and improvement continues to drive her continued efforts in improving political dialogue.

Although it can be difficult, Christie believes that politics is a good career for women because a lot of positions are part time and the hours are often flexible. Women can also go "in and out of politics" as their lives change. It can also meet the needs of women who also have yearnings to make a difference in the world around them. It has definitely been a good career for Christie.

Chapter 4

Governor Jane Dee Hull

Teaching on the Navajo Indian reservation was an incredibly profound experience in my life. The students and environment were challenging but very rewarding. My eyes were opened to real diversity. I learned to look at situations and circumstances with more insightfulness and understanding. I learned to listen in a much broader and deeper way. This experience helped me develop some abilities that were particularly useful as a governor.

~ Governor Jane Dee Hull

I interviewed Governor Jane Dee Hull in Phoenix, Arizona on February 1, 2006. She served as the governor of Arizona from September 1997 to January of 2003. As governor of the second-fastest growing state in the nation during those years, her top priorities were education, healthcare, the economy, and preserving the State's natural beauty. Throughout her time as governor, she led the fight for dramatic improvements in each of these areas. Prior to her position as governor, she served in the Arizona House of Representatives, the last four years as Speaker of the House, and then became secretary of state. I spent a few hours with Governor Hull as she shared insights, stories, and experiences related to how she developed the knowledge and competencies in leadership throughout her life to eventually become a successful governor. Her career path is quite remarkable, as she seems to have learned to lead from both unique and rather ordinary opportunities and experiences.

FAMILY BACKGROUND

Jane Dee Bowersock was born in Kansas City, Missouri on August 8, 1935. She grew up as an only child in a newspaper family; her father was an editor for the city's paper. Because of this newspaper influence, politics were often discussed in her home. Jane said that although her parents didn't tell her what political opinions she should have, the family had wonderful political conversations around the dinner table in the evenings. She reminded me that those were the "days before TV and talk radio so there was time and space for these kinds of conversations at home." The newspaper her father worked for was very political, and this helped fuel the engaging dinnertime conversations. She noted that because she and her parents were all Republicans, they didn't necessarily argue about politics but discussed the many issues and happenings of the day.

Jane felt well cared for by her parents during her upbringing in a "very middle-income family." She had a "typical" family situation for that time period, which included a father who worked full time and a stay-at-home mother. Even though they were a middle-income family, Jane said that because of her father's occupation she was "given the opportunity to see a lot of places," particularly within the community and state. Jane's father took the family with him to various events. For example, she had her fourth birthday on a TWA constellation plane. She believes it was possibly the "first one of its kind and probably just circled the city." Although she doesn't remember the experience, she still has photos. Jane's mother was a Lutheran and her father was an agnostic, but Jane wasn't exposed or involved much in religion as a child. Overall, Jane felt she had a steady and stable home environment. Jane said that she lived in the same house from the age of four until she left home. In fact, her mother lived in that same home until she died at the age of ninety-two.

Parents
Justin Bowersock, Jane's father, attended Kansas State University and received his bachelor's degree in journalism. As mentioned, during Jane's childhood and youth, Justin was the aviation editor of a very political, Republican newspaper called the Kansas City Star. Her father worked as a photographer for the Kansas City Star during the Prendergast crime era in Kansas City, and he was shot at while covering the mob uprising at Union Station. Although this happened before Jane was born, her father spoke about it occasionally through the years, as it was "a big event in his life." A second major event in her father's life was his coverage of a 1950s plane crash in the Grand Canyon. Her father traveled from Kansas City to Arizona to cover the story of two planes that had crashed and could not be found. Jane told the following story:

> *Many authorities and volunteers were searching for both planes, and my father shockingly sat on a stool at a local bar while everybody else went out and worked. Because he waited, he was the first reporter authorities spoke to when they brought in the remains of one of the planes. My father received umpteen awards for AP and Kansas City Star newsman because he was right there when the story unfolded. It was always a joke, that he didn't go out and get himself dirty. He just sat and waited for the story to come to him, which is interestingly the way I always feel about politics.*

Other than the community involvement inherent in being a reporter for the paper, Jane's father was not particularly involved in any other community groups or efforts.

Jane's mother, Mildred Swenson Bowersock, attended Kansas State University for four years and graduated before Jane was born. Mildred worked as a registered dietician at a hospital even after she married, which Jane noted was quite unusual for the time period (1928–1934). However, after Jane's birth Mildred became a stay-at-home mother and started her involvement in volunteer work. Jane remembers that for many years her mother was a PTA volunteer as a dietician to help plan school menus. Jane always had a very close relationship with her mother. Jane believes her mother was actually more intellectually grounded than her father was, and she was the "rock in the family." Jane's father was a writer and kind of "here and there," while her mother was "always there."

Extended Family
Jane described three women in her extended family that were influential as role models. First, she knew her paternal grandmother and remembers her "working at a fraternity dorm to help raise the kids." Jane's paternal grandfather died early, so she never knew him. The fact that this grandmother went to work in a university setting let Jane know that this woman had a strong commitment to education. Because of this, all of the children in this family (three boys and a girl) became college educated. Jane has always admired her paternal grandmother for her strength, work ethic, and perseverance.

Second, Jane's maternal grandmother, Hilda Swenson, was Swedish and born on a boat coming to America. Jane's maternal grandfather died when her mother was only six months old, so Jane didn't have the influence of that grandfather either. Hilda had a family farm and six children. She was a strong woman who worked hard and eventually put all six children through college, including her two daughters. Hilda was also a role model for Jane as she spent time listening to her stories through the years. Because of her example and words, Jane knew a college education was very important to her maternal grandmother.

Third, Jane remembers one of her father's aunts who was influential as a role model when Jane was young. This woman took care of Jane's grandmother and never married. She held paid employment and was very independent. Jane remembers her primarily for her independence and sense of humor.

Interestingly, all three of these influential relatives were women who did not have husbands for at least part of their adult lives. They were independent, strong, and selfless women and mothers. They were strongly committed to education and hard work and believed these were the most important elements to gaining self-sufficiency and life success. These elements were also the priorities Jane developed as a youth. She now believes these characteristics became very important and useful as she rose through the ranks to become governor.

CHILDHOOD AND YOUTH

Personality and Activities
Jane went to a K–8 school and then to high school, as they didn't have a junior/middle school in her area. She loved school and enjoyed learning. Her favorite subjects were English and Spanish.

Jane described a number of her personality traits or characteristics. Although she was "not real athletic," she would have liked to be, but she was not competitive in sports. She was, however, a good student and always received "As." Jane felt driven to excel in school; she remembers that her parents wanted her to get good grades but would not "pay her for grades as some of her friends' parents did." She was somewhat competitive with herself and others regarding academic grades and activities but doesn't remember being particularly competitive as a child/youth in other ways, particularly during her K–8 educational experience. Jane described her own personality as follows: "I was shy, and I think I was probably relatively introverted being an only child. I did, however, have close friends in both grade school and high school." She also noted that she was responsible, obedient, and respectful as she was growing up. Overall, Jane believes that she had confidence as a child and was comfortable with herself. In high school, she became much more social and describes herself as follows:

> *If I wasn't going to church with my mother, I was going to whichever teenage group had the best parties at whichever church. I had been everything except Catholic, but my choices were certainly based on social things—who was doing what at which church. Interestingly, later in life I married a Catholic and converted to Catholicism.*

Jane described herself as a reflective individual. She watched people, paid attention to what they did and said, and was generally observant. She liked to look at how things happened and then considered how they should have been done differently for better success. Although she was not involved in politics during her youth, Jane enjoyed the topics and discussions, but not the arguments. She confessed that she has always had "somewhat of a passive aggressive personality."

Jane spoke about the enjoyment she found with her family and friends in her "rather ordinary childhood." Jane remembers being involved in a few activities as a child. She took piano lessons for many years, but she admits that she can't play it today. She became involved in Girls Scouts and enjoyed setting goals, earning badges, and participating in the activities and projects. She spoke of being an avid reader and the enjoyment she found as a child/youth in exploring many topics and stories through books.

During high school, Jane continued to enjoy academic achievement and also began migrating toward activities that helped her and others "accomplish things." For example, she became quickly and heavily involved in journalism, obviously influenced by her father. Her work during these years in publishing school newspapers and yearbooks provided her great satisfaction. In fact, Jane felt this opportunity was the budding of her "hallmark strength as a governor"— pulling people together and moving them toward a common goal. She explained,

> *I was very active with the yearbook and newspaper in my school. In fact, I became the editor of the newspaper at one point. During this time, I also began to understand that I could pull people together and accomplish goals if it didn't*

matter to me who got the credit. I learned early that it is really important that everybody gets the credit.

Although she loved written communication, she never took debate or speech and did not do a lot of public speaking during these years.

In high school, Jane began her interest and "involvement in clubs, leadership, and boys." She took a year of Latin and also belonged to the Latin club, which she said helped her tremendously later in life when she was teaching on an Indian reservation. She also took three years of Spanish and ended up passing the university test before attending college. Jane was a member of the student council and remembers being a secretary at one point, which she noted was one of the few leadership roles available for women at that time. Even with these limitations, she stated, "I don't remember it ever entering my mind—from day one—that women couldn't do whatever women wanted to do." She also mentioned going to football games and dances as most of her friends also did during those years. She summarized her activity interests as follows:

Although there is a thin line between academic and social activities in high school, I felt that I leaned toward the intellectual or academic interests. I wanted to be involved in pursuits that made me feel like I was accomplishing something.

She also enjoyed dating and actually met her future husband (of now more than fifty years) during high school.

Jane worked through high school as a secretary at a company in Kansas City. Although she doesn't remember learning a lot from that experience that helped her in the development of leadership, she did admit that she learned some independence by taking the bus into the city for work and "going to downtown shops to buy lunch." She mentioned that she was glad that she learned to type in high school, as she typed for this job and has used those skills throughout her life, certainly in today's world of computers.

Influential Individuals

In addition to the influence of her parents and relatives, Jane spoke of a few others who were influential during her upbringing. She described her fifth-grade teacher, Miss Grinstead, as "a very good teacher" who somehow inspired her to begin thinking about elementary education as a college major. Jane remembers her as "very tough, yet very good." Early in life, Jane seemed to enjoy healthy challenges and appreciated rigorous teachers who pushed her to develop and learn.

Jane remembers that she had a geometry teacher in high school that was also influential. Although she never liked geometry and barely passed his class, he was also the school newspaper advisor. He and Jane worked quite closely, and she felt that his one-on-one mentoring helped her increase confidence and develop skills that became very important later in her life.

College Plans and Future Expectations

Jane always planned on attending and graduating from college, as both of her parents had done in their early adulthoods. She doesn't remember feeling pressure; college attendance was just expected. She always planned to attend Kansas State University because her parents and their siblings were alumni. She didn't, however, necessarily expect to seek full-time employment when she finished college. She explained,

> *Young women during those years typically got married and started a family after high school and/or during or after college. I doubt that any of the people I ran around with during high school ever thought that they would do anything but get married and have babies. I don't think I ever thought that far ahead, frankly. I've always tried to be flexible and open to what comes next.*

COLLEGE AND EARLY MARRIED LIFE

Jane went straight to college after graduating from high school and moved into the women's dorms until she married. She started as a journalism major, but that didn't last long. She explained,

> *I'm sure I was influenced by my father on that. It didn't take me long to figure that it was not a job that I wanted. It wasn't the stability that I needed. I knew I couldn't be running around at all hours of the day and night and also be a mother of children. Having children grounds you.*

Because she liked teaching, she quickly changed her major to elementary education.

During her first year of college, Jane remembers being heavily involved in her dorm's musical production. She explained,

> *This was my first year, and I was only eighteen. I ended up pulling this presentation together. I couldn't sing or dance, so this was where I fit in. I wasn't necessarily the one who pushed, but I coordinated and organized. My peers recognized quickly that I had a talent for doing this.*

Because she doesn't like disorganization, Jane stepped forward quickly to take the role of coordinator. It seemed like a good role to assume because, as she said, "If they are smart, no one else wants the job anyway!" Yet, Jane always enjoyed and thrived in this management role. The presentation went very well, and she felt great satisfaction from her efforts.

Marriage and Children

During the second semester of her freshman year, Jane and her husband, Terry, were married. Terry was only six months older than Jane was and today she wonders how they ever made it through. Although Terry did have a stepbrother who was serving in WWII when his mother remarried, Terry was also raised as an only child. Jane and Terry moved into their own apartment, and Jane remained in school. Both sets of parents "did well financially" by then, so the couple received financial help throughout college. Jane's parents paid her tuition, and Terry's parents paid for his and also helped with some of the couple's living expenses. They both worked part time as well.

One year after her marriage, at age nineteen, Jane gave birth to their first daughter, Jeanette, and then two years later to another girl, Robin. Terry worked full time during the summers to earn money to support the family. They moved into Terry's parent's guesthouse during some of these summers, and Jane and Terry both worked while the grandmothers cared for the little girls. Interestingly, Terry graduated in June and Jane in August after their second daughter was born. The couple's parents continued to be very supportive. When I asked Jane why she continued her college education when many women in that day dropped out after marriage, Jane replied, "I don't think I ever thought about dropping out. I never thought of not having a college degree."

Terry continued his education by entering medical school as he had always planned to do. Jane commented that some of "those years were very isolating" for her. Jane didn't work Terry's first year of medical school, as she was heavily involved with children, neighbors, and friends. Jane then taught sixth grade for about three years at an elementary school about two miles from the medical center in Kansas City. She found these teaching years were very important experiences in helping her learn and develop leadership and organizational skills. During this time, there were no specialty teachers, and Jane recognized that she had weakness in some areas (music and physical education), so she traded with another teacher. Jane taught art and square dancing, while the other teacher taught music. She concluded, "I love teaching, I really do. It was fun. I did a lot and worked hard, but I loved it." Jane has used her teaching skills throughout her career, so those early developmental experiences as a teacher were important. She explained:

When I was Speaker of the House, I taught. In fact, my full-time job was teaching. It was teaching ethics, rules, politeness, mature behavior, and appropriate dress to legislators. I continued teaching ethics as secretary of state and as governor.

Jane learned how to juggle work and family during these years. While she was teaching school, her mother or mother-in-law would watch her children once a week and then a friend (a medical student's wife) took care of her girls the rest of the week. Jane felt she had excellent help and a wonderful support system during these years. Her husband was gone all the time, so she learned to be very independent. Medical students and their families tend to live close to each other, so she had friends who also had young children. She said, "Everyone was poor and just survived, and we all shared those same experiences." She did struggle with balancing work and family, as she had to bring homework to complete after her children were in bed in the evenings. She went to bed totally exhausted many nights. After medical school, she got pregnant again and had their third child, Jeffrey, during Terry's internship.

Move to the Indian Reservation

In 1962, after her husband finished medical school, Jane (at the age of twenty-six) and her husband moved from Kansas to Arizona. Jane and Terry felt Arizona would have "no boundaries" compared to "the old Kansas City society that has to bless you in everything you do." They were excited about a change and had made up their minds that they wanted to move to Arizona. Terry had decided he wanted to go into public health, so he accepted a position as a physician on a reservation in Arizona for two years. Public health sounded great to them, and it was a way to get to Arizona. Jane smiled as she described their entry on to the reservation:

> *They put us in Chinle, Arizona which is not close to anything! We knew we were getting ourselves into quite an adventure when we saw hogans as we drove down the hill with two kids in the back seat and a baby screaming. My first thought was "What in God's name have we gotten ourselves into?"*

They lived in government housing next to the other five doctors' families, which was actually the nicest housing they'd had up to that point in their marriage. At that time, Chinle had one gas station and one trading post that only carried milk and eggs, so they drove long distances for groceries. They quickly became involved in the Navaho community, and they became part of a very close-knit society. They also made lasting friendships with the other doctors and their families. Jane assured me that they did have "a lot of fun." She said,

> *I always say that the Navaho reservation was a land of "room enough and time enough." It was the first time in our lives that I had time enough to think, talk, play games, or whatever. It was a very good experience for us. It was a totally different life, and we loved it.*

During this time, Jane gave birth to their fourth child, Michael, although she did deliver him at a hospital off the reservation. She remembers, "I went to the doctor when I was five months pregnant, and he told me that I wasn't pregnant. I told him he was wrong, and I delivered Michael the next time I saw him. I knew what I was doing." She took only five days off from work to recover.

Teaching on the Reservation

Jane had children when she arrived at the reservation and had not planned on working while they were young. However, she began substitute teaching because there weren't enough teachers on the reservation. She said, "What an experience! It opened my eyes to real diversity." She substituted the first year and received her Arizona teaching certification by correspondence. The reservation was desperate for substitutes and full-time teachers. She provided an interesting description of her experiences.

> The administrators assigned me to teach chemistry classes because the teacher was out sick for two weeks. Chemistry was not my area, so it was tough teaching. I learned a whole lot. The school was divided into high, medium, and low levels, so they had all of the smart kids together. I must say that I preferred teaching mixed levels together. The lowest level Navahos did not even speak English. I remember that one of my students was a twenty-one-year-old who was trying to pass his GED so he could go into the service. It was one of my goals to help him do this. Overall, it was a challenge to keep things under control, and it toughened me up. Although I knew I was pregnant the second year, the schools didn't have enough teachers and really wanted me to sign a contract. I finally took sixth-, seventh-, and eighth-grade English, but taught classes with all three levels. On the one hand, I was reading books to some students and teaching them third- and fourth-grade English. Yet, I could follow the state curriculum with others.

Jane's experiences on the reservation were quite profound—from her teaching experience, to the differences and diversity in the people she interacted with, to the closeness they had with the Navaho employees. Jane learned to look at situations and circumstances with more insightfulness and understanding than she had previously done. She felt teaching on the reservation was a very important experience in helping her prepare for her future governorship. She learned to listen and understand various constituencies, cultures, and points of view.

Motherhood
Jane believes that motherhood helped her develop many competencies important in leadership. The first word that came to her mind was discipline, particularly self-discipline. Motherhood also provided opportunities that continually pushed and challenged her to get things accomplished—often in uncertain and chaotic circumstances. Jane also attributes motherhood with teaching her the art of multitasking. As an only child, she did not get much multitasking practice during her upbringing. She also spoke of learning the importance of being flexible and able to change one's mind when better information is available. She gave this example: "We always swore that our children would not have drivers' licenses at sixteen years old. Yet, as soon as my firstborn turned sixteen, she was in the car helping me by driving the rest of the kids around. I learned and adjusted." Jane stated that motherhood helped her develop more empathy, which is also important in leadership. Since so much of motherhood is focused on teaching, Jane also believes that mothers have continuous opportunities to strengthen their teaching skills. She explained, "Although sometimes you don't know you are doing it, you are continually teaching, promoting, and pushing your children to improve." She believes that teaching and developing others is central to good leadership. Motherhood also helped Jane strengthen her skills in organization and "pulling people together," as well as providing many opportunities to practice negotiation skills, such as "keeping the peace with two little boys." She jokingly said, "Keeping the peace in politics was *almost* as challenging as keeping the peace among my own children." When her children became teenagers, she

also learned a great deal about conflict management. She stated, "Being a mother of teenagers helps you learn how to pick your battles wisely. I learned that it wasn't good to fight about the little things."

Jane said that she and Terry felt they survived pretty well for both being only children, "We learned as we went along." Unconsciously, this probably gave her continued confidence later in life that she could handle new and undefined situations and responsibilities. She learned to trust that she could learn from her experiences and figure out how to accomplish what needed to be done. Jane stated many times how much she enjoyed raising her children. She feels they have been a powerful gift in her life, teaching her leadership and helping her develop the skills needed to lead as a governor. She simply concluded, "They were fun and wonderful years."

CAREER AND VOLUNTEERISM

Early Politics
After two years on the Navajo reservation, Jane and her family moved to Phoenix. Her four children ranged in age from one to ten at the time of the move. Jane had been interested in politics from her youth, but circumstances had not permitted her to do much volunteer work during her early married life. However, she did a small amount of volunteer work for Barry Goldwater's presidential campaign and continued to keep abreast of the political issues of the day.

After moving to Phoenix, Jane kept too busy with work and kids to be involved in politics for a number of years. She was, however, involved in other volunteer work, such as being a Girl Scout leader and joining the Medical Wives and Florence Crittendon Auxiliaries—"the things doctor's wives were supposed to do." However, in 1968, she joined a Republican Women's Club. She began doing some speaking and eventually became the president of the club. She kept busy during the day with her volunteer work and would be home when her children arrived home from school in the afternoons. She also served in a number of different positions with the Republican Party in Arizona.

Political Activism
Around 1974, Jane had started a pattern of working on campaigns every other year. In the off years, she would "do something in the community like the PTA." She'd be home for a year, and then her friends wouldn't see her for a while. When she was involved in a campaign, she dropped out of the bridge group and other activities and commitments for about six months. She'd then return and pick up her former life with some new community volunteer responsibilities. Her husband was very patient and, according to Jane, "has always been supportive." Her daughters were teenagers by this time, so increased involvement in political work was "not that much of a problem." She stated, "I enjoyed it. I just balanced family, campaign work, and community involvement."

Jane liked organizing behind the scenes, even in PTA, and described herself as "a good solider for things like that." It was clear that Jane did not have specific plans for a career as a politician. She didn't seek that kind of position or want to take charge of anything, but she enjoyed being involved. During this time, Jane became involved in a few political issues surrounding education. As her children grew older and she had more flexibility with her time, she started getting involved with campaigns during the primaries.

By 1974, Jane decided to take on the major responsibility of co-chairing and "kind of managing" a governor's campaign in the state. Although this candidate won the primary handily, he lost the election because it was the year of Watergate. The newly elected governor was eventually the subject of a recall and resigned to become the ambassador to Argentina, and the Secretary of State took over the office. Two years later, Jane chaired a county attorney's race. She learned some good leadership lessons in each of these experiences. She learned more about the issues, politics, and campaigns in general. Because of the various campaigns she had managed, people began to know of her work.

Jane's motivation for leadership throughout her career was to make a difference for individuals and the community. She loved party politics and the people involved. She loved the work but never considered running for office herself during these years. She just planned on being a faithful volunteer, yet she continued to accept some leadership responsibilities.

House of Representatives

In 1978, one of the representatives in their district decided not to run for reelection, so the district came to Jane and asked her to run for the seat. She said, "I'd been involved with campaigns, the community, and the party for years; however, this was the first time I'd even thought of running for myself!" The district leaders wanted her to run against another woman who had spent the previous year watching the legislature from the gallery, a very effective way to learn about the political process. These were the days when the districts were small enough candidates could walk door to door to campaign. Both candidates canvassed the district often. Jane told the following story about the start of her own campaign:

> *I committed to run and got about six or seven couples (good friends) together in our house. I gave my first little political speech. I told them they were going to have to listen and not fall over dead. That was how it started. I had a lot to get done.*

Jane latched onto the issues quickly as she already knew many of them from her previous campaign involvement. She began moving forward quickly and aggressively and won the election. Jane used many of her previously developed skills (e.g., pulling people together). She learned that she could convince others to believe in her vision, and she was able to secure the support of the business community.

During that era, freshman representatives were "seen and not heard." The House had a very strong majority leader, which meant that Jane wasn't able to become a committee chair until her third term. She was from the majority leader's district, so it was very safe for this leader *not* to put her out in front and just try to "manipulate her behind the scenes." Hence, she did a lot of work behind the scenes. However, people knew she was a hard worker. She always served on the same five committees, including Education and Land and Water. She felt that her service on these committees helped her in learning about specific areas of government. She acquired insight into various perspectives and issues, which helped her to become more effective and insightful in her later roles. Jane never left for the Senate, although she had opportunities to do so. She said she liked the "hustle and the bustle of the House."

During these years, she did not have other paid employment. She explained, "I had a husband who supported me, thank goodness. When I became a representative, we were paid $6,000 a year. I had the time to work hard at the job, and it became full-time employment for me."

Majority Whip

Jane became the majority whip for one term (1986–1988). She had the ability to move between the moderate and the conservative factions. She was careful about her choices. For example, she would not serve on the Health Committee, because her husband was a physician, and she didn't believe it would be ethical. Her later years as a representative were very tumultuous, as there were impeachments, resignations, and heated debates on ethical issues. Jane carefully watched what was happening and why people became ineffective. She observed and reflected on her surroundings during the impeachment of a Republican governor in 1987. She learned that "you can't stop the investigation once it starts." She pondered on her reasons for being involved and questioned her motivations and ended up learning a great deal from the events of those days. Although not enjoyable, she did believe that involvement in these challenges and issues was helpful for her development. She learned to forecast future situations and potential needs and tried to predict when she would need help so she would be prepared.

Speaker of the House

In 1988, Jane became Speaker of the House of Representatives. During her two terms as Speaker, she led the House as it became more divisive because of the challenging issues and dynamic circumstances. She enjoyed this leadership role and feels it provided her the additional competencies and knowledge needed to become an effective governor. She served in the House for a total of fifteen years.

Secretary of State and Governor

During her second term as Speaker, several people suggested that she run for secretary of state. She had known for some time that she would enjoy this role, so in 1993, she decided to resign as a representative to run for Arizona secretary of state. She explained, "I didn't want to sit here and watch while I knew I could be more involved in making a difference." Her campaign was successful, and she was elected.

As secretary of state, she was excited about the new opportunity to manage and lead in an office; she was interested in seeing what could be done. In this position, she was able to make the necessary changes to "do a lot with limited funds." The morale of the employees improved during her service. She talked a lot about education and policy during those years, as it is "difficult to talk about filing UCC forms for very long, since it's very boring." However, she did learn a great deal about policy and budget during those years, which were particularly helpful in preparing her to become governor. In September of 1997, Jane became the twentieth governor of Arizona upon the resignation of the sitting governor. In 1998, Jane ran for her second term as governor. She was elected overwhelmingly and served until term limited in 2003.

Career Development and Barriers

Jane didn't plan to have a career in politics. She never had a formal career path focused on running for public office or ultimately becoming the governor. Her choices and career moves happened as she continuously prepared herself to become more effective and influential so she could make the difference she yearned to make. She transitioned into positions that were interesting to her and also provided challenges. She had prepared herself from each paid or unpaid position or assignment. Each helped her learn valuable knowledge and skills needed to be successful in the next professional and personal career step she took. She said, "Each one builds a person. If you are paying attention, everything you do can build and develop you for whatever comes ahead."

When I asked Jane if she felt that being a woman was a barrier in her career progression, she said, "No." I also asked her if she thought her career would have been easier if she had been a man, she also responded with a resounding "No!" Jane believes that the public now votes more on how effective the individual candidate is instead of considering their gender, and she said that the public obviously did not cast their votes on gender when she was elected. In fact, Arizona has had many women in high appointed and elected positions throughout the past few decades.

Jane believes that some women, including herself, became legislators because they were stay-at-home mothers involved in educating their children and had flexible schedules. Jane did not have a full-time job and was able to become more involved in community and political work. She did "not need a second income in her family," which she believes allowed her many political opportunities in her life. She said that it was this flexibility that ultimately allowed her to become the governor. She noted, "I think it's tough for anybody that has a full-time job, unless it is very flexible, to be a legislator. Most people are not looking to stepping up that way." Being a wife of a husband who could support the family made it easier for Jane to be "at the right place at the right time." She was able to prepare herself in unique ways to be ready for such responsibility.

Balancing Professional and Personal Life
When her children were young, Jane integrated her family, political, and volunteerism roles effectively. She was able to move between these roles as time and commitments allowed. Her husband and children were supportive of her endeavors. Although this became challenging at times, she enjoyed being involved in each role and felt driven to continue her involved in each.

As her children left home, Jane then used the compartmentalization strategy to balance her work, family, and life demands. She knew she needed to spend certain amounts of time in her different roles and responsibilities. She also knew that she needed personal time to relax, so she tried to maintain time to be physically active and also rest. She continued, even as governor, to have her family over for dinner once a week and even cooked much of the time. She made real efforts to see her children. She had to continuously prioritize and keep family events on her calendar, so that she could keep doing them. Her political positions could have easily taken over her life in full, but she set boundaries and kept things prioritized.

Her husband worked hard for many years in his occupation. She explained that he retired halfway through her governorship because he had severe back surgery, which prohibited him from delivering any more babies as an OBGYN. She said, "We just traded roles. He was very good at becoming the governor's spouse." She and her husband would meet and decide which events they would attend together, which ones he was willing to do alone, and which she would do. This worked well for them.

DEVELOPMENTAL INFLUENCES

Support Systems
Jane's family has been her biggest support throughout her professional career in politics and government. Her youngest son was thirteen when she ran for the legislature, so her children were older and busy with their own lives. By the time Jane became governor, she had eight grandchildren. Her children and grandchildren have always provided support and encouragement. For over thirty-five years, Jane and Terry have had very good friends that have provided encouragement as well. Even as a governor, Jane made time to see her friends. She said several times,

> *I always intended to leave the office with the same family and the same friendships that I came into office with. This goal grounded me and helped me continue with insight and perspective about the things that really matter. This was a priority.*

This personal and professional support can typically be directly and indirectly linked to assisting individuals in their development of leadership. In Jane's case, having this encouragement and assistance opened doors for her to be able to continue to learn and grow through her experiences and opportunities.

Influential Individuals
A number of individuals influenced Jane throughout her political career. First, she became close friends with most of her freshman class of legislators, as they supported each other and provided her with "some sort of a balance." This group of men and women got along very well professionally and socially. Second, she also became very good friends with two women legislators in the House who provided valuable insight, ideas, and encouragement. Third, as a legislator, her majority leader was also influential. Although she "fought with him all the time," she said, "When push came to shove, he always knew he had my vote." Fourth, Jane spoke briefly of Dodie Londen, the state party chairman in the early 1990s who was one of Jane's very good friends. Because they were both involved in the Republican women's group, Jane was able to watch this friend operate very effectively in her role as chairman. "She did a lot, and she did it very, very well." This individual was both a good friend and a role model. Jane watched and observed her and learned a great deal from her. This friend also gave Jane encouragement, which was particularly meaningful because Jane truly respected her. Finally, the long-time former mayor of Phoenix, Margaret Hance, also served as an important role model for Jane early in her legislative career.

Jane also shared a unique experience she had with President Bush. She attended a Border Governors' meeting with nine Mexican governors and watched and learned from Bush's facilitation skills. The first part of this particular program was scripted and formal. However, after dinner something interesting happened.

> *Governor George W. Bush leaned back and said, "Okay, now let's talk about the real issues. Let's talk about drugs." This discussion was so much better than the rest. We were there for another hour and people let their hair down and were comfortable. I stayed until the men started smoking cigars, and I decided that was enough of that. That is what I have always found with the President. I watched him work crowds and talk to groups. He has some amazing skills that I admire.*

Jane also had lots of people who reminded her of her role and helped her keep things in perspective. Their comments (whether she implemented them or not) were helpful.

Training and Development
When Jane was a freshman/sophomore legislator, there was a fellowship available through the Council of State Governments. They invited one or two people from each state—from judges to legislators to administrators—for an in-depth leadership development experience. Someone had suggested that she participate.

Jane did so and believes that it was a broadening experience, as she interacted with people from different positions and states. She said, "I just listened to their ideas and challenges." It provided her with new insight, and "it was very helpful."

Jane also attended leadership programs specifically for women. These programs were usually scheduled on long weekends. Some of these were helpful, as they provided interaction with women leaders across the country. After one such program, Jane became more involved in teaching leadership and ethics. She believes that it is important to meet and interact with individuals who serve in the same position in other states. Listening to others who are dealing with similar concerns and issues can be helpful. These discussions provide Jane with new ideas and support.

When Jane was in the House, she participated in the Josephson School of Ethics. She was particularly interested because of the legislative scandals in the early 1990s. She took a five-day ethics course and used what she had learned throughout the rest of her political career. As governor, she even hired an individual to create a "Character Counts" program to work with teachers on how to teach ethics to children and youth.

Jane mentioned three additional training and/or developmental opportunities that she utilized. First, during her governorship, Jane attended the "winter meetings of the governors, because they were kind of broad based and for everybody." However, she wasn't able to participate in many of these programs while serving as governor; she feared the press would criticize her trips because they "didn't like travel!" Second, she received informal training by belonging to and meeting with different women's groups through the years. Jane mentioned groups like the Arizona Women's Forum and Charter 100. She said that these groups are "good for all women to be a part of because they include varied groups of people getting together, talking, and learning from each other." Finally, while serving as secretary of state, Jane had a good friend who was a voice coach who worked with her on speaking.

Challenges and Difficulties

Jane learned a great deal from the many challenges she faced in her different roles. For example, she inherited a Speaker's office that was bankrupt because of an impeachment. She also took over the secretary of state office when it was bankrupt. She took over the governor's office when it was "in a mess." She admitted, however, that she does enjoy these kinds of challenges. She said, "I have the ability to bring in the right people, and that's what I did." In fact, she had to make her transition to governor within twenty-four hours. She explained,

> *I could not keep a lot of staff from the past governor. Although I was not a threat to them when I was secretary of state, his staff was absolutely paranoid that I wanted to be governor. In fact, during my term as secretary there was little communication between him and me. It was hard to come into office so suddenly, but we did establish an effective office very quickly.*

Jane mentioned many challenges and difficulties throughout my interview (e.g., finishing her education with two small children, balancing work and family, working in difficult circumstances) most of which have already been addressed. However, one final challenge she spoke about was her difficulties with the press. Interestingly, this topic was mentioned by most of the women leaders I have interviewed. Jane worried about the press for many years, but said she was "very tired of it by the end" of her governorship. She had learned about the press through her previous roles, and knew that she couldn't ever let her guard down, that she had to develop thick skin, and that she couldn't question her own abilities by what was reported.

LEADERSHIP STYLE AND PHILOSOPHY

Leadership Style

I asked Jane what her staff would say if I asked them to describe her leadership style. Jane spoke of four characteristics she felt were central: 1) clear and candid communication, 2) collaboration, 3) flexibility, and 4) assertiveness regarding the development of others.

First, Jane speaks clearly and candidly and has done so throughout her career. For example, as the Speaker she felt strongly that CEOs were totally out of touch with what their lobbyists were doing. She said,

> The CEOs would come in and tell me they wanted something. Then the lobbyists would say, "No, they want their taxes cut" or whatever. I just decided I was not going to mess around a lot or have "a kitchen cabinet of lobbyists." I was candid about why I didn't have lobbyists immediately involved in my campaign.

Jane also explained that sometimes she had specific issues or topics that she had strong feelings about, and she just laid them out clearly and told her staff that was the way things were going to be. She didn't want to waste her time or theirs. She said,

> I was sixty-two when I became governor and had eight grandchildren. Thank goodness I was in good health. It is a twenty-four hour a day job. If you don't stay up all night, you end up worrying half the night. It was better to just be clear and open with my staff and others.

Second, Jane said her staff would talk of her collaborative leadership style. Jane liked to discuss most bills and issues with her staff. For example, her staff would go over proposed bills six times and then sometimes still have concerns. She would always give them opportunities to voice their concerns. She did note, however, that there were some issues where she just needed to say, "This one's not for discussion. I know what I'm going to do." Because she was so collaborative with most issues, they knew they needed to back off when she had made a final decision. They knew and agreed that she would make the final decisions.

Jane also led with an open-door policy, which also alludes to her collaborativeness. Her staff knew she would listen and that any of them could come in and talk. They knew she relied heavily on them and wanted to hear their views and ideas. She wasn't afraid to appoint and listen to those whom she didn't totally agree with philosophically.

Third, Jane also spoke about her own ability to "take a lot of things as they come" and even laugh about them. She believes this is a quality important in a strong leader. She said,

If you can't laugh in some of these situations, you cry. Governors don't cry, except for September 11. You have to present strength, and yet you still have to be a woman. That's a very difficult line to walk. That's again why I think I've always wanted to pull people together behind the scenes.

Finally, Jane has always had a passion for developing others in a variety of ways, and the people who worked for her knew this well. She enjoyed giving individuals different assignments that would help them grow and develop. She is particularly proud of how many people who worked for her developed into competent leaders, in part, from the opportunities they received while working for her (e.g., women she appointed to be chairs in the House, a man who became Jane's education specialist and legislative liaison, and the first Hispanic to ever be superintendent of schools in the state of Arizona). Jane explained, "I kind of look at them all like my children, and I love to see that all of them have done so well." Jane believes that being influential in the development of others means that leaders should give appropriate credit to those who deserve it. She believes that women do this much better than many men do.

Jane believes that she was open to changing the status quo and provided women, many of whom had not had opportunities before, to lead in critical positions or assignments. This was one way Jane tried to strengthen potential women leaders. When she became Speaker of the House, women had been on certain committees (e.g., Education, Human Resources) and men were on the more powerful ones (e.g., Ways and Means, Appropriations). She watched these dynamics very carefully. When Jane became Speaker, she made a very competent woman the Transportation chairman, another woman the chair of the Ways and Means Committee, and a third female the Banking and Insurance Committee chair. She exclaimed, "They handled the responsibility beautifully. You think I didn't shake up the men!"

Leadership Philosophy

Jane spoke of two primary leadership philosophies: 1) hiring and firing effectively and 2) the importance of professional and personal ethics. As a political leader, Jane always believed that it was imperative to hire people who were better and smarter than she was. She learned from watching previous leaders retain ineffective employees, which in turn resulted in ineffective performance from the leaders' offices or administrations. Jane learned that she needed to hire the best people who understood the system and then trust them to do their jobs. She also believed that you need to pay these people appropriately. Also important to her was the need to fire people who are not performing well in their jobs and replace them with high performers. Although she does not feel she was ever good at firing people outright, she demonstrated the ability to "thin the dead weight out" when she became governor. By the end of her governorship, she cared deeply about her staff and said, "We spent the last two months getting everybody situated so they had new positions. I wanted to take care of my own before they got swept out." She described a very close staff; they weren't "at each other's throats or in competition with each other as other staffs were known to be."

The second philosophy is the importance of ethical behavior. Jane believes there is a lot of unethical behavior in politics and government. She worked to get her first Speakership without making commitments, stating, "Usually they want an arm and a leg if they are going to support you." She said that she always struggled with the "give and take atmosphere" in politics, as there is "an awful lot of vote trading going on down there." She has always felt that much of that kind of behavior had ethical implications. She always wanted to do her best to be honest in her work. Jane also felt that ethical behavior included a strong work ethic. She said her staff would say that she was a very hard worker. "They would say I was there both physically and mentally." She spoke of the difficulties she had as she worked to continuously set boundaries. Jane said that she had to be very careful not to run herself ragged. Yet, Jane was very focused on the issues at hand, which sometimes made sleep a challenge. When she was Speaker, she would get up in the middle of the night and start worrying about things. She explained,

> *In the morning, my chief of staff would get this long yellow sheet, "Reflections of Jane." He would say, "Oh no, she didn't sleep again!" By the time I became governor, we were computer literate, so he'd come in and find an email with lots of my reflections about how we should be doing things.*

Overall, Jane demonstrated a strong belief in her own ethical behavior and that of her staff and others.

ADVICE

At my request, Jane shared some advice that she gives to women with an interest in future political and public leadership. Her first piece of advice is that interested individuals need to get involved, study the issues, and network early. She said,

> *Get involved in party politics. Get involved with a school board. Get involved in your community, in your city, and in your state. Prepare yourself by reading the local and regional papers and the Wall Street Journal. Be aware of the is-*

sues of the day and try to find out both sides of some of those issues. You need to be able to argue your side, but you need to also understand that there are people who feel differently. Begin networking early. I always say if you want to run for office the first thing you get out is your address book.

Jane believes that unpaid opportunities, such as those mentioned, can provide valuable leadership experiences that can be helpful in politics and government service.

Her second piece of advice was that women need to obtain an effective education to prepare their lives for future leadership. A positive educational experience in secondary and post-secondary settings is vital for acquiring the critical thinking and communication skills to lead effectively.

A final piece of advice Jane provided is that young women should become as competent as possible throughout their lives so they are prepared to accept opportunities that may come naturally from being "in the right place at the right time." Yet, they should also learn to be assertive enough to "make and take" opportunities, not necessarily wait for them to come. She explained that women need to know that many leadership skills that are naturally developed from motherhood and service actually provide them with the unique characteristics needed in today's society. These skills and abilities can help women make a true difference on a large scale. Women need to believe they can make a positive impact and influence important changes that are critically needed today in communities, states, and nations.

FINAL THOUGHTS

Today Jane is in her 70s, looks great, and continues to be physically active. Jane plays golf and said that she plans to "drop her handicap below thirty sometime." Although she still likes to keep up with the issues of the day in her state and the nation, she enjoys the quiet of her life and loves her role as a grandmother. She also enjoys having the time to spend with her husband of fifty-two years and to read mysteries from time to time.

Jane has found that her professional career as a politician and public servant has been very rewarding. Her passion to accomplish important work throughout her life has led to years of leadership that have made a difference for the state and the people of Arizona. Her steadiness, perseverance, and commitment to education, her family, and the public good have resulted in a life that has impacted thousands. Whether through her one-on-one work as a teacher, friend, neighbor, and parent or through her leadership in providing positive changes in legislation and policy, her legacy will continue to be felt for decades to come.

Chapter 5

Governor Jane Swift

Through the years, I have had both wins and losses. My involvement in sports during my youth helped me develop the ability to take risks without being afraid of losing. I love to win, but when I lost in sports, I learned to deal with it. I soon understood that losing wasn't the end. . . . Being graceful in defeat is a very important (although hopefully little utilized) and a necessary skill for successful leadership. . . . In fact, all the lessons I learned from sports were very helpful in politics.

~ Governor Jane Swift

On November 21, 2005, I interviewed Governor Jane Swift at her family farm in Williamstown, Massachusetts. She was elected to serve as the lieutenant governor of Massachusetts in 1998 and then became governor when Governor Cellucci resigned to become the U.S. ambassador to Canada. She served in that role from April 2001 to January 2003 and focused her efforts on stimulating economic growth, imposing fiscal discipline, and enhancing the quality of life for working families. In addition, her passionate commitment to public education was the primary focus of many of her efforts during her service. Prior to these positions, she also served as a Massachusetts state senator, assistant minority leader in the senate, and director of the Office of Consumer Affairs and Business Regulation. Although she was only forty years old at the time of my interview, she had already been involved in political service in some way for most of her life. In our interview, on the back patio of her home, Jane shared stories, experiences, and insights about how, through the years, she developed the leadership knowledge and competencies to become the political leader she became.

HOME AND FAMILY BACKGROUND

Jane Swift was born in North Adams, Massachusetts on February 24, 1965. She has three siblings, a brother who is thirteen months older, a sister who is two and a half years younger, and a brother who is six years her junior. Jane lived in the same North Adams house, neighborhood, and town for her entire upbringing, and her parents continue to live there today. Both of Jane's parents were also born and raised in North Adams, so she has a rich family heritage in that area. Jane believes that there were about 23,000 people living within the city boundaries when she was growing up. She described North Adams as a "blue-collar mill city with tough socioeconomics." She described her family's financial situation as follows:

> We were not rich, and we were not poor. For North Adams, we were doing pretty well, but you have to understand North Adams. In the broad context of the country, we would have been lower middle class; in North Adams, we were probably upper middle class.

She knew her parents worried about money, but the children never went without.

Jane was raised in a devout Roman Catholic home and believes she "grew up with privilege" because her "parents' entire life was focused on raising their children." She was taught all of the basic values for good citizenship "such as being nice to others, being honest and ethical, and giving and keeping your word." She also remembers learning the importance of not burning bridges because "a person completely against you today may be the individual who can become your best ally tomorrow." She believes these values provided an important foundation for her eventual role as governor.

Jane's parents raised her to have a "strong core," which she believes has helped her endure the challenges and difficulties that leadership has brought. She feels her core was further developed by a committed family and the opportunity to be involved in a "highly engaged and tight community." According to Jane, "This connection to community helped me develop strength and peace of mind." She feels this connection provided the confidence she needed to reach out to others and to listen and learn. She explained,

> This tight community was important to me because I knew if I screwed up as a youth that, by the time I got home, my parents would know about it. I knew that everyone in my community knew what was expected of me at home by my parents, so they had the same expectations for me as well.

Mother

Jane described her mother, Jean Swift, as her best friend during her childhood and youth. Jean was a stay-at-home mom for most of Jane's upbringing, and Jane described her as "an amazing woman in many different ways." Jean was a Girl Scout leader, Cub Scout leader, and PTA president. She was involved in the community, and primarily focused her time in activities and efforts that had to do with her children. Jean had graduated with a four-year education degree from the local college, and as both a mother and trained educator, she focused her efforts on the positive development of her children. She worked very hard with all four of her children to ensure they had positive experiences with their schooling and a wide variety of developmental activities. Jean believed that the "greatest gift she gave all of her children was the capacity for and love of reading." As an educator, she went to great lengths to ensure all of her children read well and often. Jane explained,

> *I remember years when my mother would give us five words every Sunday night to look up in the dictionary and learn. At the dinner table that week, we would have to work those words into the family conversation. She worked really hard at being a great and involved mother.*

Jean occasionally substituted in the schools when Jane was in middle school, and when Jane was in college, she went back to teaching full time. She was a strong and powerful influence in Jane's overall development and growth.

Father

Jane's father, John (Jack) Swift, grew up as one of six children in North Adams. He received a two-year degree in architecture from Wentworth Institute in Boston and then decided to work with his two brothers and manage the family plumbing business. Jack was very involved in the community in politics and governance. For example, he was active in serving on the housing authority in their city. Jane also remembers that he was a Republican political volunteer and, in fact, actually ran a few Republican state senate campaigns when she was young. He was involved in politics for years, and instead of leaving her mother home with all four kids, he would often take Jane with him to political events, since she was the best behaved. Jane remembers riding in parades and putting stickers on envelopes. In fact, she knew the state senator personally from the time she was six or seven years old. Jane recalls thoroughly enjoying the relationship she had with her father, which she believes was enhanced by her involvement with him in these activities through the years. Jane said, "Commitment to community and contributing back by volunteering in the community was a very important part of my life growing up."

Jane described the interesting style of communication that existed in her home. Jack enjoyed discussing political and current issues of the day at the dinner table and in other settings with his wife and children. He enjoyed and encouraged open conversations and debate. Jane said, "If you came to our house and weren't used to us, you may be horrified. We talked and discussed and had lots of arguments and debates. It's a hard hitting kind of thing to get used to for some, but we absolutely loved it." Jane and her family had lively dinner table conversations on politics, current issues, and a variety of other topics. Jane's father taught her to "disagree without being disagreeable," which is a skill she has used throughout her political career.

Extended Family

In addition to her parents' positive influence in her life, Jane was also raised with a large extended family nearby. She said that her maternal grandparents were very influential. Her grandmother emigrated from Austria to the United States when she was nine years of age, so she was a first-generation American.

For over forty-five years, these grandparents worked at the town mill, which employed most of the people in North Adams and dominated the economic life there until about the mid-1980s. They worked every single day in a factory line doing the same exact thing. She stated,

> I can remember my grandmother (Nonie) saying that she got her satisfaction basically by breaking the curve. They got paid by the piece, and then if they outperformed the piece by a certain amount, they'd get a bonus. She was very disliked by her peers right on the line because she'd always be pushing the curve outward. She didn't care what they thought, and she wanted to be twenty or thirty percent above every time. I have a lot of my Nonie in me. I was very close to her. My mother always said that the role of "grandmother" was what she was born for, and she was wonderful at it. My grandfather was her steady counterpoint. They were very influential and taught me that, if I worked hard enough, I could be successful.

Jane said, "I think I get my industriousness gene and competitiveness from my grandmother." Jane recalls visiting her grandparents every Saturday evening and going to church with them on Sundays. Jane's mother was an only child, so Jane and her siblings were the only grandchildren on her mother's side of the family.

Jane's paternal grandparents lived very close as well. Since her father had many siblings, Jane still has many aunts, uncles, and cousins in town. She said, "To this day, the cousins all get together a lot." She remembers that most of her father's family used to come to their house on Thanksgiving evening. She grew up with a feeling of belonging because of the shared values the extended family held. Jane felt she had many positive influences that helped create a stable environment for her to learn and grow during her upbringing.

CHILDHOOD AND YOUTH

Personality

Jane described herself as a "very competitive child from day one." She also recalls always being very achievement oriented and task focused. She told the following story to help illustrate these traits:

> I was always in a hurry to get things done. Apparently, when I took my first grade assessment and placement test, I turned two pages at once. Therefore, I ended up not being in the class that I should have been in. When I started the first grade, my mother was called in by the principal, and she was asked why she had taught me to read over the summer. My mother explained that my older brother, John, was reading and that I made him show me what he had learned. The principal and teacher said, "According to the placement tests, she's not capable of having mastered reading." That's when they uncovered this snafu. However, instead of moving me to the other class, my teacher wanted me to continue and she would help me one-on-one. She was not letting me go once she had me in her class. I remember that my teacher had a program with stars,

stickers, posters, and public recognition for reading books. My mother was terribly embarrassed when she came into the school with the other parents. The other students had five or six stars on the reading poster, and Mrs. Douglas had to put an extension onto her poster for me after I reached forty. I'm sure the other parents thought I was a show off. I just really loved reading, competition, and stickers.

Jane said she thrived on activities that brought both external and internal rewards. Jane also said she typically had a good attitude about most things and was a happy child. For example, although she didn't have the most innate athletic ability, she was the one on the basketball team who always hustled. She always put her "whole heart" into whatever she did.

Jane was always good at being a social leader and had lots of friends. Yet, her mother said she was always the benevolent one as well. Her parents would not allow her to be mean to anybody. She said, "I had to go to every birthday party I was invited to, which included some that none of my peers would go to. Yet, I understood and actually have the same rule today for my girls. I learned that being nice is important."

Activities and Involvement

Jane spoke about many of her school and non-school related activities as a child. She was always expected to do well in school and "typically earned As and Bs." As a young child she developed a deep love for reading, and she described herself today as "a voracious reader."

Jane enjoyed being involved in every activity she could find. Although competitive sports weren't available for younger girls, the YMCA did offer some basketball, which she absolutely loved. For a time, Jane's mother also put her in a dance and gymnastic program that was in a neighboring town quite a distance from her home. However, when North Adams built a new YMCA close to her home, her mother "successfully, single-handedly lobbied to add a gymnastics and dance program." Thereafter, Jane remembers going to the "Y on Saturday mornings and doing three dance classes in a row and then gymnastics." In the fourth grade, Jane also started chorus and band. She did admit, however, that she was "not particularly musically talented." In band, she started with trumpet and then moved to the French horn by middle school. Jane believes all of these activities helped her develop important competencies she continued to strengthen later in her life. Each gave her the opportunity to enjoy the learning process and gain additional confidence in her own abilities. She learned that she loved being involved, busy, and active, and that "when you register for or commit to something you must attend, support, and follow through."

One activity not yet mentioned is most likely Jane's favorite as a child. Jane explained,

> *I remember coming home from first grade one day with tears in my eyes because I couldn't join Girls Scouts unless a mother volunteered to be the leader. I wanted my mother to do it. Although she was busy with other siblings and re-*

sponsibilities, my mom agreed. However, she made me commit that I would never quit Girl Scouts once I started. I loved Girl Scouts, and to this day I've never left. At eighteen, my mother gave me a lifetime membership to Girl Scouts.

She recalls that during her youth, when it was not "cool" to continue Girl Scouts, her mother would find ways to keep them involved even when it was only one activity a month. One of her most important developmental experiences, while a young teenager, came through the Girl Scout program. When Jane was nearly thirteen, she received a brochure on a Girl Scout program called "Cadets on Horseback" in Worland, Wyoming. Although she had never ridden a horse, she completed an application in pencil, collected letters from references, and sent it in without any help. Jane's mother was nervous, but when she called a staff member at the Girl Scout regional office with her concern, she was told that the program was so competitive that there was little chance her daughter would ever be chosen. Jane told the following story:

In January or February, the letter came with the news that I had, in fact, been accepted into the program. My mother was beside herself and called the Girl Scout office to tell them she couldn't let me go. They convinced her that they'd never lost any girl before and things would be okay. My mother found that there was an almost sixteen-year-old girl from Baltimore going, so that diminished her fears a little. All I had to do was to fly to Baltimore from Albany and then this girl and I would fly to Denver and then to Worland. Everything went great on the way there. However, after leaving her in Baltimore on the way home, I had to fly through JFK and was delayed for quite some time. My parents had already left for the Albany airport, and I called my older brother and told him I was stuck at JFK. I found a bookstore and bought The Thornbirds, which was completely inappropriate for me to read at that age. I ended up reading the whole book before I could get home and my mother could take it away from me.

Jane believes the whole experience was very good for her. It definitely gave her new experiences and confidence in her own independence and abilities. She said, "I think all my life I have not been risk averse; but I don't have a death wish and am not reckless. Yet, I would always push myself out there like I did with this trip." When she returned from Wyoming, she did a presentation on her trip at the Girl Scout Council and in other settings. These experiences helped her continue to strengthen her speaking and presentation skills at a young age.

Jane also had other wonderful leadership opportunities through the Girl Scout program during her later teenage years. She remembers running the Western Massachusetts Girl Scout Council's senior planning board, which was comprised of two or three girls from each county, during her junior and senior years of high school. She enjoyed the leadership experiences and said, "planning and organization was a huge part of her Girl Scout program." She remembers as a high school junior being an unofficial assistant to her mother in planning a whole field day for groups of Brownies, as well as planning and running a summer camp and leading a Brownie troop one year. Jane liked being in leadership positions because she believed she had "good plans to accomplish good things." She also understood early on that she was very organized "in terms of realizing where I wanted to be and what I needed to do."

During her middle and high school years, Jane continued to be heavily involved in various school-related activities and organizations. In addition to Girls Scouts, sports were particularly important in her life. She played on the girls' high school basketball team and also ran track. She believes that playing competitive sports taught her many competencies and skills that are essential in leadership today. She said,

Through the years, I have had both wins and losses. My involvement in sports during my youth helped me develop the ability to take risks without being afraid of losing. I love to win, but when I lost in sports, I learned to deal with it. I soon understood that losing wasn't the end. Sports also reinforced the work ethic I had learned from my parents and grandparents. Because I wasn't the most gifted athlete on my high school basketball team, I had to work very hard to be successful. In fact, all the lessons I learned from sports were very helpful in politics.

Jane said that although playing sports was her central focus during those years, she was also a homeroom representative and was on committees, such as the prom committee and ring committee. She also enjoyed being on the staff of the school newspaper and yearbook. She admitted she was a little nervous about running for student body office in a formal election so she did not, but she "definitely jumped off the deep end later on!" Jane enjoyed being very busy and involved during her youth. This included her strong involvement in her church, which she believes benefited her greatly, as church taught her the same values she received in her home. Jane believes that these engrained values are an important part of her leadership today.

Employment

Jane had her first paid job when she was ten years old. Her parents had a core philosophy in their home that there was no quitting once anyone joined or started something: "Quitters never win, and winners never quit." Although her parents strongly discouraged her, Jane decided she wanted to earn money and took on a Penny-Saver paper route for a free local advertising paper. She quickly discovered that it was a terrible job as the ink would bleed all over and her route was in the low-income housing area, which was a little scary for a young ten-year-old girl. She said,

When everyone else was playing in one hundred degree weather, I was lugging these papers. After two weeks I wanted to quit, but my parents would not let me. They made me finish out the entire summer. Yet, I do think it was probably good for me. Sometimes you have to do stuff that's hard. I had days in politics where it would have been much easier to quit. But that core philosophy was deeply ingrained in me. Staying is sometimes harder than leaving.

Jane actually mentioned that her parents wouldn't let her quit a number of activities that she eventually "became pretty good at" and that benefited her life.

Jane had a few different jobs during her teenage years, her first being babysitting. One summer she "babysat almost forty hours a week and saved up a lot of money." Next, she worked at a couple of "fast food joints," and she often worked two jobs at a time. She recalls being employed at her father's plumbing business, and she shared the following humorous story:

During the afternoons when the guys weren't around to run errands, my father would occasionally need a part and send me to pick it up. I remember one time driving from North Adams to the big city of Springfield, which was probably about a one-hour-and-twenty-minute drive. I had to pick up a part that was desperately needed back in Richmond. Now there was always a very old, awful truck that was hard to drive. I did well once I made it to the freeway, but I didn't drive a stick shift all the time so it was rough. When I got to Springfield, I started up a hill and knew the minute I got there that I was doomed. The street had a series of lights, and I knew there might be trouble. Fortunately, I hit lots of green lights, but I did have to stop at one red light. I tried to get the truck going after the light changed, but I couldn't. I went through a whole cycle of the light changes still sitting there. Finally, this African American man and his wife came and knocked on my window. He said, "Are you having trouble? Since we have to carry these groceries all the way up this hill, we're going to make you a deal. If we help you get this car up the hill, will you give us a ride?" I said, "Fine." He didn't drive. He just talked me through it, and I got to the top. I had panicked and didn't want to have to call my father and tell him I was stuck at a light!

Jane learned that listening to others who had more experience could help her become more successful. She loved challenges and, although this experience was a little traumatic, when Jane got back to the business that day she immediately asked for more opportunities.

Influential Individuals
Many individuals had a deep influence on Jane's development. However, outside her immediate and extended family she provided only a few examples. She recalls a freshman English teacher who noticed that she wrote run-on sentences. Jane was one of her better students and so this teacher found an outdated instruction book and gave her independent assignments on sentence construction. Although Jane was a good student and earned As in this class, she was impressed and thankful that this teacher recognized her potential and wanted to assist her in improving her skills. This teacher not only took the time to give Jane those assignments, she also corrected them and then worked with her before and after classes. Jane said, "I've always thought fondly about her because of how she helped me improve." During her junior year of high school, she had another

English teacher who was "really big into creative writing." This was a new experience for Jane, and she loved it. In fact, she went to college thinking she would be an English major because of her positive experiences with English teachers and their classes.

College Plans
Jane always planned to attend college. It was not just an expectation from her parents, but she always had the innate desire and motivation to graduate from college. Because North Adams was a blue-collar town, not many people from her community left to take other opportunities. She didn't have strong advising from her high school counselor. Jane was told that she should attend the University of Massachusetts. However, Jane figured out on her own that she wanted to go to Trinity College, which she did.

COLLEGE

The fall semester after Jane graduated from high school, she attended a small, elite liberal arts college in Hartford, Connecticut called Trinity. Jane believes that the demanding, high-quality liberal arts education she received at Trinity was very good for her. Jane planned on majoring in English when she started college, but she hated her first-year literature course and decided to major in American Studies instead. Trinity also helped her suddenly broaden her view of the world, which became very helpful in politics later in her life. Interestingly, the college was located in a bad neighborhood, so she saw a level of poverty that she had never seen before. Yet, what was really shocking to her were the levels of wealth and privilege that she had no idea existed. She said,

> *Some of the students at Trinity were driving BMWs that they got when they turned eighteen. I'll never forget the first day I showed up at my freshman dorm, the girl across the hall had one of these completely coordinated name brand comforter and pillow sets with a matching chair. She had nicer furniture and linens, better than my parents ever had or have had to this day.*

College was an eye-opening experience for her in many ways and was important in helping her see other perspectives and circumstances so she could broaden her understanding of society. Jane attended Trinity for four years and graduated with a degree in American Studies in 1987 at the age of twenty-two.

Activities
Jane soon realized at college that she could be "socially competent and a leader on a much bigger playing field." She explained that she had the "full college experience" at Trinity. Yet, she struggled at first because she didn't have a place to fit in. Initially, she felt "way out" of her "comfort zone and league." She also had to extend more effort and time academically, which was a new experience

for her. By the time she was a sophomore, she could pledge a sorority. Fraternities and sororities dominated the social scene at Trinity, but they didn't dominate the membership of the college. There were only two sororities on campus, and a few of her friends encouraged her to join. Jane said, "It was nerve racking to go through the whole process of rush and so forth." But Jane felt it was worth it because she saw the benefits of a Greek association and wanted to be involved. She said,

> *The sorority probably appealed to the part of me that was missing not having the Girl Scout outlet. I have to admit that there is a lot more drinking in sororities though. There was no drinking in Girl Scouts. That's a big change! I enjoyed and even yearned for organizing and being in groups. I believe I got into my very competitive sorority by the strength of my personality.*

Jane joined the national sorority, served in a leadership role, and received "a lot of really good planning and leadership training for officers." Jane's chapter was assigned a "master's student" who worked with Jane on delegation. This individual taught Jane that she needed to trust other people and nurture their ability so the organization would be in better shape when she left. Jane didn't become the president because she went international for a semester, but she ended up doing much of the job without the title. She did become the social chair and put her "heart and soul into every event." She was involved in introducing new programs and even changing some national policy. She believes that all of the sorority experiences helped her prepare for running for office (planning, fundraising, social activities) and serving in the legislature.

Jane also played rugby at Trinity, but said it wasn't really a big deal on her campus. She admits it was actually more of a social outlet than a competitive sport. She said, "It was more about the beer than about the sport, but I enjoyed it." Jane's participation on her high school basketball team was a prominent part of her identity during her youth, so rugby helped in some small way to keep her connected to her athletic and competitive needs.

Profound Experiences
Jane shared three profound experiences that she felt were important in helping her develop certain leadership competencies. First, she recalls an "academic crisis" during her junior year of college that profoundly influenced her confidence, self-esteem, and life in general. She was taking a demanding seminar where the students had to read novels that spanned American literature and then write three- to five-page papers about each of them. She had previously been told that she was a relatively good writer, but these assignments took a great deal of time, and she was only earning Ds on them. Although she had "skated through" many of her classes, she hadn't "cut corners" in this one, yet she was still getting poor grades. She explained,

> *This was a notoriously tough course, and I had to get at least a C in the class to keep my major, and I was scared. The seminar instructors told me that I*

couldn't write and couldn't think well either. This was my first real memorable crisis of confidence. It was the first time somebody had really pushed me to perform to a higher level and to analyze my thoughts. Fortunately, I passed the class, but it had shaken me up and gave me doubt about my capabilities.

The next semester, Jane went to Rome to study abroad and had a "great professor of Italian history, a very cool, sophisticated woman, who was very impressive and brilliant." During one particular class, this professor "completely reamed out our entire class for being unprepared." She basically told Jane and her classmates that they were "privileged and because of that they were not taking things seriously." She told the students that they had opportunities that most people in the world would never have and that they were not taking advantage of them. This experience had a "huge impact" on Jane because she had never thought of the privilege she had been given and obligation that came with it.

After Jane returned from a semester in Rome, she decided to stay at home for the summer to work at the family business. The two experiences (being told she could not write or think well and being told she was privileged and wasn't taking the responsibility that came with it) had caused her to engage in great reflection. Because she was concerned about her writing and wanted to understand how she could improve, Jane registered for a writing class at North Adams State College. The teacher gave each student individual writing assignments and met with each student one-on-one. He quickly discovered that Jane was more advanced than most of his other students. She explained,

During our first meeting, he asked me why I was there. I told him about the bad experience I had with my instructors in the seminar. I told him I had to take another seminar my senior year and that I needed to improve. He told me to bring in all my graded papers from the seminar I had taken the previous fall. I brought them in and, bless his heart, he started working with me. He worked with me on rewriting two or three of those papers. He talked me through what I had done. We discussed where the original criticism from the seminar professors was fair because my logic and writing was faulty, and we talked through where they were just trying to shock me and were not being fair. He didn't need to do this for me. It wasn't in the syllabus. Yet, he found himself with a student who had talent and the desire to learn, and he chose to become involved in my growth and development.

This was a profound learning experience for her. It also helped her increase her confidence related to writing. When Jane entered her senior seminar, she ended up having a wonderful teacher and did very well in the course. She said, "Although I had strong thinking and planning skills before this experience, the art of learning to write concise thoughts was very helpful. It required discipline and focus of thought, and I believe I improved from this difficult and challenging experience. This sequence of experiences also helped her develop her analysis and critical thinking skills, which are vital for strong leadership in politics.

The second profound experience really helped Jane fully appreciate, for the first time, what a strong base of faith can do for individuals. When she was in high school, her older brother, John, pledged a fraternity; Jane became good friends with his friends and roommates. During Jane's freshman year of college, her brother and his roommate Brian were in an accident, and Brian was killed. She said,

> *This was probably the first tragedy that was close to me. I was very close to Brian and, in fact, I had a hero worship crush on him, largely not returned. Brian had spent weekends at my home many times. My brother was in the car and luckily walked away, two other kids were really critically hurt, and Brian died. I'd never had loss. I'd never had trauma. It impacted me for a long time.*

Yet, this experience taught Jane that she was stronger emotionally than she thought. She learned that the faith she had always taken for granted was meaningful and helpful in her life. She said, "It was the first time I felt like I was drawing out instead of inputting." As a youth, she wasn't cognizant of how big of a role spirituality had in her life, but she started discovering how central it really was because of this experience. That faith provided strength that she has used throughout her life.

The final experience Jane shared was related to an internship she had the summer after her sophomore year of college. Her father had helped the state senator in his campaign and was able to help Jane get a great paid internship in Boston. He convinced Jane that this was a wonderful opportunity and would look great on her resume. It was a great experience for her, and she was surprised by how much she enjoyed the work. Although she hadn't planned on having a political career, she said,

> *During my internship, I learned a lot about the political process and about current events. The woman who was the leader of the senate internship program was a real dictator about process, so we learned. I was really excited about the experience and ended up making lasting relationships from that two-month experience. In fact, I stayed in contact with the woman who was the number two person in the office.*

The interns not only worked in the office, but also had weekly seminars. This was great both socially and educationally. Jane was exposed to many different ideas, perspectives, policies, processes, and rules. The internship also included working with constituents, and Jane had an experience that really got her excited about public service as a career:

> *A young woman from my hometown had decided to transfer colleges during the summer, and her paperwork got screwed up. She found out in July that they were going to pull her state scholarship, which meant that she wouldn't be able to go back to college. I had empathy because I knew it could have been me. I was heavily dependent on financial aid and had to work hard to make ends meet. My parents struggled even with the extensive financial aid I received. I can still remember wondering if I would get the checks in time. I got on the phone with the bureaucracy about the situation, and it turned out that it was*

just a snafu. Because I called representing the senator's office, they said that she just needed to submit the paperwork again and they would reinstate her grant. If fact, she would actually get $200 more than she thought she was going to get. It gave me a feeling of empowerment I can't describe. To this day, I remember that experience and the feeling. This was the first time I felt the joy that comes from having that kind of influence in someone's life. I had actually made a real significant difference in someone's life through the political system. I did it, and it was huge for me. When I called her to tell her the news, at first she didn't believe me. When I told her it was a larger amount, she was shocked. Her mother was also listening on the other line knowing that her child might not be able to go to college. I could hear the gratitude in her voice. This was incredibly rewarding for me.

Because of this internship, when Jane returned to school, she took a course in public policy administration. She became very engaged in the class, and the male professor ended up being her advisor and overseeing her senior project. In fact, through the years he has always sent her a $5 or $10 check with a letter of support during each of her campaigns.

Employment

Jane worked during college to help support herself. Although she ended up having some great work experiences, her first was "just plain awful." She had received a full financial aid package that included work study, which meant she had to work with food services in scraping dishes and racking trays. Although "it was horrifying," she did it her entire freshman year. She doesn't believe she learned anything particularly helpful other than realizing she didn't want to work in food services again.

The summer after Jane's freshman year of college, she and some friends decided to be camp counselors in the Poconos. She believes this helped her strengthen many skills she had started developing in Girl Scout leadership. She organized, directed, disciplined, and motivated others. She became more skilled in conflict resolution and managing. Yet, the most memorable element about the whole Pocono experience was that she had the most "gorgeous hot boyfriend in my whole life—except for my husband of course." Her father wasn't excited about the relationship and didn't want her to go back to the Poconos the next summer; hence, his efforts at lining up an internship in Boston—something that "trumped the Poconos."

The next fall Jane had figured out how the work-study system worked, so she looked for early postings. She obtained a position as the assistant to the administrative assistant in the Religion and Philosophy Department. They had never had a student intern, and she heard later that there was a lot of debate about whether it would really work. She remembers making copies of handouts for classes and other maintenance tasks. Although it was mindless work, she gave herself goals to get a lot done in a short amount of time. This job pulled her out of "that sort of drinking college atmosphere" back to what she had in high school. The woman she worked for, Gay Weidlich, became her campus mother in a way. Gay soon got to know Jane well and had high expectations for her. Jane explained,

> All of a sudden, I had to be a little more careful. Since I hadn't really bonded at that point with any professors, Gay was a big influence in a sort of moderating way. I was also having success in that position. It was the first time any professors got to know me. Because of this position, my experience at Trinity changed. Someone discovered the high achieving, committed, responsible, and good me.

The department even took up a collection when Jane went abroad and gave her about $400. She felt part of "a little community in that department." She worked for this department during the rest of her college experience.

Influential Individuals

Jane was positively influenced by many individuals during her college experience. Previous sections of this chapter have already highlighted the master's student assigned to her sorority, her Italian professor in Rome, the teacher from her writing class at North Adams State College, her brother's roommate (Brian), the woman who headed her internship program, the woman in the senator's office who befriended her, her public policy administration professor, and Gay Weidlich in the Religion and Philosophy Department.

In addition to these individuals, Jane said that some of her friends were influential in her development as well. One particular friend helped her deal with the traumatic experience she had during her freshman year when her brother's roommate had died. This friend's college roommate had an aneurism over Christmas break and didn't come back for that semester. They both had difficult experiences and bonded because of it. Having someone to talk to about difficult challenges was critical for Jane during that tragic time. Jane and this friend also went through some other experiences as well and have stayed friends through the years. The experiences bonded them, and they learned to listen, support, and provide helpful feedback and encouragement to each other. In fact, when Jane was governor, she asked this friend to move to Boston for six months to be her interim assistant when her regular assistant went on maternity leave. This became a true, lasting friendship.

EARLY CAREER

Retail Manager

Right after college graduation, G. Fox was recruiting on campus, and Jane decided to accept a position in retail. Her father desperately wanted her to go to law school, and she remembers him asking, "Are you really going to sell perfume after four years of a good education?" G. Fox was a division of the May Company and had one of Fortune's highest-rated management training programs in the country. Jane was able to take part in this eight-week program and believes she learned a great deal from it about conflict resolution, business and people management, and spreadsheets and financials. She managed a department and had thirteen people working for her. She said, "It was good for me, and I was also good at it." Jane had some very challenging work assignments that year, and she believes those experiences, although brief, were very helpful as she moved on to running a senate office and managing staff. During this year at G. Fox she was also introduced to women who struggled with balancing work and family issues, and Jane became conflicted about some of the choices she saw them make. She saw the intended and unintended consequences from their choices and decided she needed to interview for other jobs.

Legislative Aide

After Jane decided to start interviewing for a new job, she happened to stop by Senator Peter Webber's office to say hello to Susan, the woman she had worked with during her internship program. Susan was now the chief of staff and asked Jane to consider taking a job as a legislative aide. Jane was surprised and pleased by such a wonderful and exciting opportunity. She said,

> *I loved being an aide and was able to design my own job. The senator had actually known me as a young girl because I had helped on his campaigns with my father. He gave me a ride home one day and asked me how the office could run better. I told him about the disconnect I saw between district cities and towns and his legislative office. The people in the district office didn't understand what was happening with legislation. He told me that he was really concerned about thirteen towns in three new counties that had just been added to his district. He said he didn't think these counties had the level of service they needed. So, somehow jointly we concocted this new position for me where I would spend two days a week in the district and three days a week in Boston.*

When Jane was in the district, she would be the liaison to those thirteen towns. She loved this assignment and went to each town a few times a month to meet with the selectmen so that she could understand their issues, needs, and concerns.

This position was wonderful for helping Jane continue her political and leadership development. She was only twenty-three-years-old at the time and was given excellent developmental opportunities. She also enjoyed living in Boston while also coming back to the district where she could be close to her family. She liked being "in charge of making relationships and building something new in these new areas." Although not by design, this position prepared her nicely for her next career move.

State Senator

Senator Webber had decided not to run for reelection in 1989 and suggested to Jane that she run for his seat. He knew she had built some strong credibility and connections in the thirteen towns where she had been working. She decided to

110   *Chapter Five*

take on this challenge, and her capable and motivated father helped to manage the race. Jane worked all of the time during this first campaign. She moved back home, raised money, and made new contacts each day. Because she was a Republican in a predominantly blue-collar Democratic area, winning the seat was challenging. Yet, because of her youth and college experiences, she discovered that she was able to relate to people across a broad spectrum. Jane and her father rallied support from past senators. Bright young women wanted to get involved and worked hard in the campaign. Her aunts, uncles, and cousins had Friday afternoon bake sales in front of the office in Pittsfield to raise money. There were many people who wanted to get involved. Campaigning gave Jane practice in motivating others and bringing people together for a common cause, which became particularly important skills as she became lieutenant governor and governor.

Jane had many interesting experiences during her campaign. One story illustrated some of the competencies that helped her succeed:

> *I was running against a man who was a popular state representative from Williamston. He had this reputation of being quite articulate and very ambitious. I was the underdog, so I would take debates anywhere. He agreed to a series of debates, and then was committed. I had never debated before, so I was pleasantly surprised to find out I was good at it. My opponent was surprised as well. We debated often, and I gave him a terrible time about an issue that related to a tough budget situation. He had voted "Yes" on the floor of the House on an issue that was important to the cities and towns locally. It won by only one vote in favor of the cities and towns, which was the position he took. Someone requested a revote, and he was in favor of the revote, which opened the issue back up, seemingly almost voting both ways on the issue. Then when the vote came up again, he was miraculously out and didn't vote. I had worked in the senate enough to know exactly what was going on. Well, I was torturing him with this vote throughout the campaign, and I was getting under his skin. At one debate, one of my people planted a related question, and he started getting mad. So, I started into talking about what he did in changing his vote. I couldn't have scripted what happened next any better. He interrupted me in his anger and said, "Jane, you don't know what you're talking about because you weren't there." I just looked up at him in this sweet little-school-girl voice and said, "Neither were you, Sherwood. Neither were you." Everybody went crazy, even people who were there to support him. He got even angrier and jamming his finger toward me like, "You silly little girl," while I had this look on my face like, "You weren't there either. That's the point." It was a great moment, and I think it was a turning point in the campaign.*

This and other successes gave her continued confidence in her speaking, debating, reasoning, critical thinking, visioning, and general communication skills.

Jane won the race by about 1200 votes, which was about her margin of victory in those hill towns. She said, "It was a close race, but in those hill towns I kicked butt." She noted that it was not her plan to run for a seat in the state senate. She said, "Things just came together to make it possible." She believes that "the key was being willing to take risks and being able to see opportunities where others may not." Although she was only twenty-five when elected and looked even younger than that, she said, "I knew my arguments cold because I had grown up with them."

Jane served in the Massachusetts senate for six years. Through networking and connections she developed many good relationships. A Republican was elected governor, and she was able to develop good relationships with individuals in his office. There were more Republicans in the senate than ever before. She said, "I was the known commodity of all these new faces, because I had worked in the building while most of my freshman colleagues had no idea where anything was." Jane was immediately training others. Because the incumbents already knew her, she "became sort of a liaison" to her freshmen colleagues. Within one year, she was put on the Ways and Means Committee, which is the most coveted committee in the senate. She also had a good reputation with the governor's office. She loved being a senator because she could see how she was helping others and felt a direct connection to the public. She was reelected twice and was able to secure a leadership position her second term in the senate.

MARRIAGE AND MID-CAREER

Jane dated on and off through the years, but found it particularly challenging as a senator. She said, "The senate would not be the place to go looking for a husband!" Jane was having career success but admitted she was somewhat lonely during those years. She did have bright, talented women in her office to interact with at work and, on occasion, social events. Although they were wonderful and supportive, Jane said, "As I've heard said many times, it is lonely at the top. And, it gets lonelier the higher you go." She spoke about how isolating it was to become a public figure and how it made normal interactions with others challenging. However, things would soon change.

Charles (Chuck) Hunt had moved back to Massachusetts in 1989 to be the interim athletic director at Mount Greylock High School in Williamstown—the adjacent community to North Adams. He had seen Jane out campaigning, at a wrestling tournament, and "on a street corner waving one morning during the campaign." He had no idea who she was and asked someone. When he found out that she was a state senator and single, he started paying attention to the media to find out more about her. Months later, when she was running for reelection to the senate, he came to the Williamstown town hall to talk to her about a particular political issue—or so he said! When he was preparing to leave, he handed Jane a handwritten card asking her out. They dated for a short time, but were engaged for nearly three years. They married in February of 1994 when she was twenty-nine-years-old and a Massachusetts state senator.

U.S. Congress Race

In 1995, Jane decided she "wanted to do something different." Although she enjoyed being a state senator, there weren't many more achievements and accomplishments that she could look forward to if she stayed in that role. She had been able to be involved in many of the changes she had been focusing on already. That year she attended a variety of national workshops focused on women in public service, mostly legislators, who wanted to advance their careers. She said,

> I wasn't entirely sure, at that point, what I would do next. I knew that I was not going to stay in the senate for much longer. The Women's Campaign Fund was doing seminars for women legislators interested in advancing their careers. It was how to transition from being a legislator to a statewide or federally elected official. They did things like media training and fundraising, and I attended several of those kinds of seminars. They were extremely helpful and helped me make connections to people that were very critical to my long-term success. These workshops also gave me the confidence and the organizational strength that I needed to make the leap to becoming a congressional candidate in 1996.

So, in 1996 Jane decided to forgo another run for her state senate seat and decided to run against an incumbent congressman. At the start of the race, she was "given no shot of winning," but a few months before the election, the consensus in Washington and western Massachusetts was that Jane was actually very close to unseating the incumbent. During this campaign, she learned a great deal about strategy, media, public relations, motivating volunteers, and fundraising. She lost by only a few thousand votes in a devastating year for Republicans in Massachusetts. Yet, her race had attracted an enormous amount of attention from statewide press and leaders. It was this campaign that she believes put her on the "soon-to-be governor's short list of running mates in the next election." When I asked her if the experience was good for her, she said,

> Although it was incredibly painful and it's hard for me to say this, it was good for me. However, if you could find ways to grow and be a better leader without losing an election, I suggest those instead! I do think that my participation in high school competitive sports helped me the most getting through this loss. Being graceful in defeat is a very important (although hopefully little utilized) and necessary skill for successful leadership.

Airport Authority

Jane was only thirty-one when she was defeated in her congressional race. After the election, she sought out the counsel of quite a few people to try to decide what she should do next. A woman in New Jersey who had been very successful professionally, was enormously supportive of Republican women running for office, and had supported Jane's campaign was instrumental in summing up the advice Jane was hearing. This woman gave her probably the best advice Jane received:

> She told me that any private sector job that I went into directly out of legislative service was likely not going to be as challenging as I wanted it to be. But because I had very little private sector service, I would get slotted probably somewhere that was less demanding than where I thought my skills would take me. She was of the opinion that I should accept an appointed position in government that would bridge into the private sector by allowing me to develop close private sector contacts and capabilities. This is what I did. I took a job working for the state's airport authority on regional airport issues.

Jane worked in this position for only eight months and learned a lot, particularly from her mistakes. She didn't enjoy the work very much, but did admit the experience broadened her perspectives and provided learning in new areas, concepts, and issues.

Director for Consumer Affairs and Business Regulation
While Jane was serving at the airport authority, the governor resigned to become an ambassador, and Paul Cellucci became governor and offered Jane the cabinet position of Director for Consumer Affairs and Business Regulation. She had some other opportunities to move closer to her home, but she and Chuck decided this would be a good political move and possibly a "much better bridge back to some kind of full-time job in the Berkshires down the road." So in 1997, Jane went to work for the governor. She enjoyed the position, which provided new opportunities and insights for her continued growth and development.

Lieutenant Governor
Interestingly, six months prior to Jane's accepting the position as Director for Consumer Affairs and Business Regulation position, Governor Cellucci had called her to get a feel for where her political career was going. She described the phone conversation as follows:

> The governor asked me whether or not I was considering another run for Congress. I told him that I didn't believe it would be a good choice for me at that time. He then asked me if I would ever consider running for another office. I told him that since I was from western Massachusetts and didn't have a huge base of support, I couldn't think of another position I would consider. He then mentioned the idea of me running for lieutenant governor with him. I knew there was an opening and that he was looking for a running mate, but I was still very surprised. I said, "I am very grateful and supportive of you, and so I would consider serving in any role that would help you to win a full term in your own right."

Jane then spoke to a good friend who had worked for several governors and was advised to keep the governor's inquiry confidential. Jane told this friend and her husband, and that was it. Then her phone rang again in December, and she was asked to take the cabinet position. She explained what happened after the call:

I went in to meet with the governor in his office for the formal ask. He said, "Do you want to do this?" I said, "I told you months ago on the phone, if you think this is the best role for me to play in order to help you secure a full term in office, then absolutely. I think it's a great personal experience." He said, "I do." I assumed at that point that I was not in the plan for lieutenant governor. This position fit much more where I thought my life was headed. In fact, my husband and I started to really focus on starting a family, and that was something that I needed to—how do I say this carefully—apply some effort and focus toward. So, although I had this great new job, I was also family-focused as well.

I loved this new job from the first day I started. However, within six weeks of taking that job I got another call from the governor's top political person. He said, "If the governor asks you to be his running mate, will you say yes?" I said, "I told Paul that I would do what I could, but I haven't really thought about it because I assumed I wasn't on that list anymore." This individual asked me to come down to his office, and we talked about the issues where the governor and I disagreed. He told me I had the weekend to think about it. I had already mentioned to the governor that my husband and I were trying to start a family, and I didn't want to put it off. The governor said that wasn't a problem. My husband and I spent a lot of time that weekend thinking about the opportunity and decided that it was the chance of a lifetime. The interesting thing is that within the week of telling the governor that I would run my husband and I discovered that I was in fact pregnant.

According to Jane, "The governor was terrific and supportive regarding my decision to run for lieutenant governor being pregnant. In fact, he defended me throughout the campaign." In some ways Jane's pregnancy was helpful because they were seen as family-friendly and interested in defending women's right to work.

Jane spoke of a few of the related challenges she faced during the campaign. She remembers saying to her mother, "This will be a short campaign compared to the fifteen-month congressional campaign. How hard can it be?" Then she started throwing up every night, which continued for nearly the full nine months of her pregnancy. She was expected to deliver her first daughter, Elizabeth, about three weeks before the elections. Although initially it didn't seem a hard decision to run for office during her first pregnancy, in the end she said "it was more monumental than I realized at that time." Jane's life changed dramatically during the campaign and, to her surprise, the fact that she was pregnant was a major issue to the press. She explained,

My pregnancy attracted national press attention and criticism. In fact, a woman in Washington actually said, "Women who are deciding to work versus staying at home to take care of their children are our generation's Vietnam. Some of us choose to serve and some of us choose to shirk our responsibility." In her mind, not staying home to take care of my children was shirking my mothering responsibility. I obviously had to start dealing with a level of public criticism during this election that I had never experienced. I soon realized that I couldn't make everyone happy. In fact, it became clear to me that the higher you rise in leadership the more likely you are to make more people unhappy. Although I developed thicker skin, I think that it is very hard for most people to be completely okay with being attacked, particularly in the most personal ways. I also had become convinced that the kinds of people that probably are totally okay with harsh criticism are not necessarily the ones we want in leadership positions.

She and Governor Cellucci won the election, and the governor gave her a "huge amount of internal responsibility." She loved this role and learned a great deal about another facet of politics and leadership. She was strong in some areas that were particularly useful for this partnership, particularly in managing staff and saying "No," when needed. Although she loved the responsibility, it was a disadvantage because it was then easy for people to blame her. Because she had a new baby at home, she chose to focus on parts of her position that she was already comfortable with and enjoyed. She said, "In retrospect, I should have stayed more focused on the kinds of things that might allow me to advance to the next level." However, because she wasn't focused on becoming governor, she wasn't doing the "kinds of things that you needed to do if you wanted to be governor." She said,

When I had publicity and media challenges, the places that you would go to sort of circle the wagon to get support, weren't the places I was spending time cultivating. In my political career, I was at the point where I decided that I had sort of reached the level I was going to reach. If the governor ran for reelection again and wanted me to stay as lieutenant governor, I was enjoying the work and would probably do that. It was five rungs higher than I expected to get in politics anyway.

Yet, she admits she should have been focusing more as a lieutenant governor on the political and media side of her role; however, she said, "Being the lieutenant governor gave me the best preparation for the management and policy issues and responsibilities I confronted as governor."

Governor

Jane and Chuck made the decision during the middle of that four-year term as lieutenant governor that it was a good time to start thinking about having one more child. Jane said, "We agonized because life was busy, but we wanted to make a decision we would be happy with the rest of our lives." The great irony, of course, is that they were not sure if they could manage one more child, and she ended getting pregnant with twins. She described her meeting with the governor when she told him she was pregnant again. She said,

We actually found out I was pregnant with twins right before the 2000 election, and Governor Cellucci was working very hard for then Governor Bush. I had not yet told him I was pregnant and was trying to keep it quiet, which was not an easy thing to do. When I was three months along, he and I set a lunch date that I actually thought I had initiated and he thought he had initiated. So we

> had this hysterical lunch in this private room in a restaurant in Boston. Both of us were sort of preparing to tell each other why we had set up the lunch. He went first and informed me that he was fairly certain that if Governor Bush won the election the next day, he would be leaving his post and would appoint me to be governor. At this point in the conversation, I needed to tell him my news about being pregnant with twins. He reacted better than my father did. He was a little shocked, but he recovered quickly.

So, less than two years into Jane's role as lieutenant governor, Governor Cellucci resigned to become the U.S. ambassador to Canada, and Jane was inaugurated as the governor of Massachusetts on April 11, of 2001. Her twin daughters, Lauren and Sarah, were born a month later on May 15, 2001. She served in her role as governor through January 3, 2003.

Governorship included many new responsibilities and more media challenges. Although she didn't serve long, she believes that the skills she possessed were the "most important and relevant for the commonwealth at that time." Jane was in office during 9/11 and led the efforts in the aftermath. Because two of the airplanes took off from Boston, that harbor had the second highest level of security alert for the longest period. For many reasons, there was a lot of post-9/11 intelligence chatter about Boston for some time. She dealt with the U.S. attorney general and others on serious threats and various security issues. Massachusetts also had "probably the worst fiscal fallout in its history" resulting from 9/11. Interestingly, those were the issues Jane was most prepared to deal with. She stated, "I already wasn't particularly popular and had some controversies. At the end of the day, however, I had the capabilities to do the job. The issues presented themselves, and I handled them."

CAREER PATH AND ISSUES

Jane obviously did not have a formal career path focused on becoming a state senator, lieutenant governor, or governor. She believed in working hard and doing the best job she could in the positions in which she served. She also believed in constant preparation so that she could take opportunities that arose.

Jane believes that she has confronted gender barriers throughout the years, but she likes to "focus on how to break through barriers rather than their existence." She feels that this is an important criterion. She explained,

> I'm not of the opinion that we should deny that there are barriers and differences. But we should also recognize there are also some advantages to getting ahead when you're a woman. I think that my philosophy has always been to recognize and identify the barriers, challenges, and opportunities. Then it works best to exploit the opportunities while figuring out how to overcome the barriers.

Being realistic and seeing both sides of challenges is an effective strategy that most successful women leaders take. Jane believes that a unique barrier for women as they become public high-profile leaders is the emphasis on their physical appearance. She noted that the press is very critical of how women look and that when she decided to "adhere to the norms of what was expected, a lot of that attention went away."

Jane made an interesting observation about her upbringing. She said,

> *For some reason, I was raised in this post-Title IX false sense of equality that most women my age did not have. During high school and college, I think I could make a pretty good case that this type of equality existed. But then I discovered that something was amiss. When I made the announcement I was running for my first office, I was interviewed by a grizzly old veteran reporter who asked a series of intrusive questions.*

Jane was single at the time, and he asked questions about marriage and boyfriends. He asked her what she would do if she had children while she was serving as a senator as well as other seemly irrelevant questions. The questions made her uncomfortable, and she realized that running for office as a woman would be much different from running for public office as a man.

VALUABLE DEVELOPMENTAL INFLUENCES

Jane spoke of three additional development influences she believes have helped her develop leadership through her professional and personal life: influential individuals, motherhood, and support systems.

Influential Individuals

During the interview, Jane mentioned a number of individuals who were important in developing leadership throughout her professional career. First, she mentioned Peter Webber who she credited with being a mentor. He was the senator she had worked for as a legislative aide. After he decided not to run again for his senate seat, he joined the governor's administration and was in a commissioner's role for environmental management. When Jane struggled with "gray issues" as a senator, he was nearby, and she could still rely on him for advice even when they disagreed. Second, because of a few connections, one of the Democratic senate leaders helped Jane quietly due to the loyalty he felt to a mutual friend. Third, she also felt her senate colleagues were helpful and were "pretty amenable." She watched and listened to those she respected, many of whom were supportive and served as role models for her. Fourth, Jane said she learned something from many individuals she served under. As a senator, she learned from the senate leaders and committee chairs. As a cabinet member and lieutenant governor, she learned from the governor. Finally, Jane had many people who gave her advice and counsel through the years. Although she didn't always follow all of it, Jane believes these individuals were particularly influential at decision-making moments in her life. They helped provide new perspectives and insights that were especially critical at times. She had a well-developed network and leveraged it through the years by drawing on this advice.

Jane spoke of her struggle with the notion that everyone needs a strong mentor to progress in their careers. She said,

> *So many women's leadership books and strategies lately focus on this whole idea of having a mentor and having role models. I've probably been asked a thousand times who my role model is, and I just can't think of one specific individual. I think that when you're charting your own course and perhaps breaking through barriers that other people haven't broken through before, there may not be one particular mentor or role model. That is true in my case. However, I did watch and listen to many people through the years and picked up some good behaviors, strategies, and practices because of their positive influence.*

Jane believes that when you are able to see your own shortfalls and capacities, you can figure out how to move forward by looking at others' examples and by using your own abilities and those of the people who provide support. She believes that this is what she did.

Motherhood

Motherhood has been an important developmental influence for Jane. Although she was having her children while already in office, she believes they have taught and continue to teach her about leadership. First, her children have definitely helped her learn more patience, an important leadership quality. Second, motherhood has also taught her how to better recognize and nurture an individual's unique gifts and capabilities. She said, "I think you learn a lot about human nature and how to get the best out of people by being a mother." Third, children also helped her realize how central her faith was in her life. She wasn't cognizant of it throughout her childhood, but motherhood has helped her focus on incorporating faith more actively, although quietly, in all dimensions of her life. Fourth, being a parent has provided her with opportunities to continue developing her ability to organize and multitask. Since having children, she has used an integration strategy to balance her work and family responsibilities. She's had to integrate both to be effective in each, and it takes continual multitasking to be effective in both her family and work domains. Along with multitasking, her planning and visioning skills have improved, as she has needed to understand in a more concrete way what is ahead. Finally, motherhood has helped her learn to set broad parameters in her life so that she can empower others.

Support Systems

Although much of Jane's support system has already been discussed throughout this chapter, it is important to note that this system has been imperative to Jane's development of leadership. The individuals who have provided valuable support include her husband, parents, siblings, cousins, neighbors, co-workers, staff, friends, leaders, and others. For example, Chuck was particularly supportive during her congressional race. During this time he was running a small business, but took time off to drive her to events. He listened and shared his observations and his advice, which has often been some of the best she's received. His mental and emotional support has also been invaluable in her development and growth. Of course, through the years her parents, siblings, and relatives have provided all types of support, which has given her the confidence and resources to become the leader she has become.

LEADERSHIP STYLE AND PHILOSOPHY

Jane described her leadership style as "collaborative, empowering, and probably demanding." She has always had very high expectations for herself and others. She likes to give people lots of responsibility and believes that talented women sometimes underestimate their own capabilities and often need encouragement to step forward. She believes that it is "really important to nurture talent" and feels that was one of the things she was best at. She enjoyed putting people in positions and then helping them develop. In fact, she gave many individuals opportunities that they might not have thought they were capable of doing at first. When she gave them developmental position, she also thought ahead to areas they might find challenging and then provided them with the right kind of support and strategies they needed to overcome the difficulties that would arise. Although Jane said she was reflective, one of the leadership style areas she wants to improve on in the future is her self-reflective abilities. She noted that one of her flaws in office was her lack of self-reflection. She said, "I always felt I was too busy to be self-reflective, but now I see it is critical to continue my personal growth and development."

Jane spoke of two of her leadership philosophies. First, she believes that it is critical to have a staff of people who share similar priorities and who are committed and loyal. She said, "Some people perceive loyalty as never disagreeing with your leader. I actually see loyalty as having the courage to raise their objections or points of view." She believes that is how leaders are best served. She likes being challenged on certain issues and plans so that she knows she and others have "fully thought through every potential view of decisions and their ramifications." Her second philosophy is that, although sometimes difficult for her and many other women, it is important to move beyond one's comfort zone to "more readily take credit for successes," because "that's where you get the fuel of support to tackle new challenges." Although it is noble and important to share the credit, Jane believes that women politicians must take credit so they can continue their effectiveness.

ADVICE AND FINAL THOUGHTS

Jane believes that young women interested in leadership in government should find leadership opportunities in a variety of activities and organizations applicable to their stage of life. She said, "I think high school and college, in particular, offer organizations that are focused on developing leadership in youth and young adults." She believes these opportunities can be very helpful just as Girl Scouts and her sorority work were for her. She encourages young women to take opportunities to be involved in organized team sports and other competitive activities so they can learn about success and failure. She also advises young women to become involved in politics and other community efforts early in their lives. Each opportunity provides experiences and insights that help develop the skills needed to be a successful and effective leader.

Jane's motivation for leadership continues to focus on her desire and drive to make a difference for those around her. Although she continues to be involved in community and politics, she is enjoying more time with her children. She enjoys being her daughter's Girl Scout leader and looks forward to coaching her girls' basketball teams in the future. Jane is still young and looks forward to getting back into formal political office when the time is right. Her desire to serve in public office and to lead important change is still as strong as ever. Jane has already made a difference for many others in years past and intends to continue her efforts for years to come.

Chapter 6

Governor Jeanne Shaheen

I have this theory that some people are born with a political gene. . . . In some ways, I think I got that gene from my father. He was always interested in politics and current events. He would quiz us on the state capitols and who's who. . . . We all watched the news every evening and had discussions about it around the dinner table. If we had a different perspective or disagreed with my father, that was okay. We were encouraged to have our own opinions. . . . When we traveled, we would always stop at the state capitol buildings and historic markers so we could learn. It was exciting to us.

~ *Governor Jeanne Shaheen*

I interviewed Governor Jeanne Shaheen in her office at Harvard University in Cambridge, Massachusetts on January 18, 2006. She is currently the director of the Institute of Politics in the John F. Kennedy School of Government. She was elected as New Hampshire's first woman governor in 1996 and served three terms, from 1997 to 2003. As governor, she successfully fought to strengthen education, improve health care, build the state's high-tech and international economy, and maintain a fiscally responsible state budget. Before serving as governor, Jeanne was elected to the New Hampshire state senate in 1990 where she served three two-year terms. I spent a few hours with Governor Shaheen as she shared insights, stories, and experiences related to how she developed the knowledge and competencies in leadership throughout her life to eventually become a successful governor. This is her story.

FAMILY BACKGROUND

Jeanne Bowers was born in St. Charles, Missouri on January 28, 1947, and was the second of Ivan and Belle Bowers' three daughters. Her sisters are three-and-a-half years older and eleven years younger than she is. Jeanne lived in Missouri until she was thirteen but "moved around a fair amount in the southern and northeastern parts of the state." For example, she described in detail the town of Sikeston, Missouri (a town of about 10,000 to 12,000) where she lived during part of her childhood. It was in the boot heel of southeastern Missouri, and she described it as "very much delta-country where farmers raised cotton and soy beans." She also remembers that another small northeastern Missouri town was very different and had a "very northern culture." She felt that living in several types of communities at an early age provided her insight into the differences between cultures and people. In eighth grade, she moved to Reading, Pennsylvania; she then moved one last time as a youth, during her sophomore year of high school, to the small town of Selinsgrove, Pennsylvania where she eventually graduated from high school. In discussing these various moves, Jeanne said that relocation was very difficult for her. She said,

> *It's always difficult, I think, when you're growing up to have to move and make all new friends. But I think, as I look back on the kinds of things that helped shape my ability and what I've done, moving around has been one of the most important preparations for leadership. As hard as it was, I learned to tough things out and developed a real appreciation for other people's differences. There were different perspectives and different ways of doing things. I think it also helped me learn tolerance.*

Jeanne felt that she was raised to believe that she had different options in life. She believed that she had opportunities to be successful. Yet, she also had "awareness, even at that age, that girls were treated differently than boys." Because there were only girls in her family, she didn't really get that perspective from the family but knew it existed.

Father

Jeanne's father, Ivan, graduated from high school and then served in the army during World War II. After he finished his service, he went to business school for a few years but never graduated. She knew that he valued a college education and noted, "I think that one of his regrets throughout his whole life was that he didn't go back and get a college degree."

Jeanne's father worked in a shoe factory throughout much of her upbringing; he "started out on the floor and worked his way up to management." She remembers that he was promoted to superintendent at the factory when she was in middle school and continued in that role through her college years. She thinks her father was probably a workaholic. She said, "He spent most of my childhood and youth working very hard, as most men in that generation did." She also described her father as "one of the most honest people" she has ever known. She said that he would not take as much as a pencil from his office if it belonged to the company.

Because of his jobs, Ivan belonged to the Rotary organization but wasn't involved in local politics or community issues. Yet, Jeanne attributes some of her political interest to her father. She remembers that throughout her upbringing he was very interested in both politics and current events. She said,

> *I have this theory that people are born with a political gene, like you're born with musical ability or artistic ability. In some ways, I think I got that gene*

from my father. He was always interested in politics and current events. He would quiz us by way of games on the state capitols and who's who. He had a very deep interest in history. Because my mother's family lived in Washington State, we did a lot of traveling when I was little to visit them. My father always got a week or two off work for a summer vacation. When we traveled, we would always stop at the state capitol building and historic markers so we could learn. It was exciting to us. I thought it was very interesting to get the history as we were driving around the country.

Jeanne also said that her father spoke about politics and current events nearly every evening at the dinner table. She explained,

My father would watch the news every night, so it was on during family dinner. In those days, you didn't have a lot of different channels, and you had only one TV in the household. So, we all watched the news every evening and had discussions about it around the dinner table. If we had a different perspective or disagreed with my father, that was okay. We were encouraged to have our own opinions. I remember having family discussions where everyone could voice his or her opinions. I also remember my father taking out the encyclopedia, reading, and then discussing different aspects of people or history with us.

Jeanne actually doesn't remember disagreeing in any major way with her parents on these issues until she went to college in the 1960s. During that time, she said that they disagreed over Vietnam, politics, and "just about everything!"

Mother

Jeanne's mother, Belle, was a "very strong woman" from the state of Washington. Neither of Belle's parents could speak nor hear, and she was the oldest child of three in her family. Jeanne described her mother's upbringing as follows:

My mother was very much in charge even as a child. Her mother didn't drive, so as a youth, she was the one who drove her mother where she needed to go. She had always planned to attend college, but her father died when she was eighteen. Because she needed to help her mother, she wasn't able to attend college as planned. However, my mother figured out a way to attend the University of Washington for two years. She lived with and took care of a family to pay for college. She didn't graduate, but had some college education. She clearly had dealt with a lot of issues that made her very strong and was always committed to the importance of a college education for her daughters.

Belle worked in a church for a few years while Jeanne was growing up. After Jeanne's younger sister was born (when Jeanne was eleven), Belle became a full-time stay-at-home mother for the rest of Jeanne's upbringing. Belle was always very involved in her church. She took her children and went to church every Sunday and participated in church activities during the week. Jeanne's mother was also involved in PTA and "other like organizations" but not in local politics. However, Belle believed that it was always important to vote.

Extended Family

During part of Jeanne's upbringing, she lived fairly close to her paternal grandparents in southern Missouri. She would see them nearly every weekend, as they lived less than an hour away. She remembers that she did not get along with her grandmother. Jeanne was a tomboy, and her grandmother felt this was "not a good thing." However, Jeanne was "really crazy" about her grandfather. She said,

> *He had a farm that he ran and maintained for years. I always wanted to go with him to the farm to see the animals. He raised pigs and cattle and had horses. I was especially crazy about horses and loved go with my grandfather to see them. Those were the days when family farms could still make a living.*

Two of her grandmother's sisters (Jeanne's great aunts) lived out in the country near her grandparent's home. They were also influential for her as a child. They lived on a wonderful "real family farm" and were quite poor, although she never thought of them as poor. In fact, they didn't have indoor plumbing and still used wood burning stoves. She remembers that they didn't have a television, so they had to find other ways to occupy themselves. These sisters had a few cows, pigs, sheep, and chickens. One great aunt was a schoolteacher who never married. She taught school for forty-nine years, and she lived with her sister and her husband on this farm. Jeanne loved visiting these aunts as a kid and was influenced by the environment and her relationship with them. She said,

> *It was great fun to be able to go visit with them and occasionally stay overnight in a feather bed. Every spring there were always baby lambs for me to feed because the mothers would reject them. My great uncle still plowed with a horse drawn plow. The house was up on a hill, and we had to drive up through a rocky creek to get to it. When the creek was dry there was no problem, but there would sometimes be rainstorms and the creek would rise. We had to wait until the creek fell before we could get back out. I loved it.*

She remembers her great aunt, the schoolteacher, was "very particular." She pushed Jeanne and her sisters to use words correctly. Jeanne said, "We had an ongoing debate that 'ain't' wasn't a word. I looked it up in the dictionary and said, 'Yes it is!'" She would play scrabble and other games with Jeanne for hours. Importantly, this aunt encouraged her to do well in school and to continue her education.

CHILDHOOD AND YOUTH

Personality

Jeanne described herself as "mostly obedient." She was generally outgoing, particularly with her peers, and a self-proclaimed tomboy. She said that she didn't like spending a lot of time with most adults because she found them boring. She was a fairly responsible child as she loved pets and had to care for them throughout the years. She also described how much she enjoyed observing people and her surroundings. She believes she became fairly good early in her life at reading situations and behaviors because of these observation skills.

School and Activities
Jeanne was "very good in school" and generally received excellent grades. She remembers attending segregated schools as a child. Growing up through the integration period in the public schools provided her opportunities to observe and think about differences and similarities between people, groups, and races.

Jeanne spoke of her childhood activities. Jeanne liked being out on farms and enjoyed the outdoors and nature. She loved animals and spoke of having lots of pets around while she was growing up. She recalls bringing pets home, and her parents letting her keep most of them. She had two dogs, a cat, a baby chick, parakeet, fish, turtles, and tadpoles. She said that one of the dogs was specifically her responsibility. She got this dog when she was seven and remembers feeding her and taking her for walks for many years. Jeanne also mentioned that there weren't recreational or competitive sports for girls in those days. She loved sports and said she would have loved them as a child had she had the opportunity. She also loved to read and did so often. Jeanne remembers taking art lessons and also participating in Girls Scouts, her mother was the Girl Scout leader for her and her sisters for many years. Jeanne remembers playing a band instrument in the sixth grade and continuing to play the clarinet through most of high school.

During Jeanne's teenage years, she continued to love school and became much more involved in all kinds of activities. Although she enjoyed studying and being challenged intellectually, she loved high school primarily for its extracurricular activities. Jeanne played girls softball and was a cheerleader. She was in the drama club and performed in several productions. In fact, she felt drama helped her learn to present herself well in public. She not only enjoyed it but also felt that being part of working with others on a major project helped develop camaraderie and held her responsible for her "integral piece of a bigger whole." She was also in the National Honor Society and was very involved on the yearbook staff. She said she would have enjoyed working on a school newspaper if her school had had one. In addition to being on student council, she also remembers being the prom queen one year.

Jeanne's favorite and most time-consuming activity in high school was playing women's high school basketball. They played half court basketball in those days with two rovers who were allowed to play full court. She was a rover and loved it. Fortunately, by the time she played in college, all of the girls were playing full court basketball. Jeanne loved basketball and felt it was extremely helpful in her development of leadership. She said,

> *I think there were several things about basketball that were very helpful. It was competitive, which I liked, and it was good training for politics. I was forced to take some risks. I can remember having a young woman coach who was only a couple years out of college; she was very good. We really loved her. We had camaraderie, that sort of team spirit that I enjoyed very much about basketball. We learned to win and learned to lose. Now when I look back, I realize that learning to win and lose gracefully are important qualities to have in politics.*

Jeanne was the co-captain of the basketball team and felt this leadership position was beneficial for her. Overall, she said, "I enjoyed being involved in many different extra-curricular activities."

Participation in each activity taught Jeanne leadership in different ways. In fact, she believes all of these activities helped her continue to build her self-confidence. Each activity provided the opportunity for her to learn to work with different people. She said, "It wasn't only learning to work with them, but it was developing an appreciation for people's different talents and abilities." She also learned the importance of finishing what she started and always trying to do well in everything she did, so her work could benefit others.

It is important to note that Jeanne also spoke briefly of Kennedy's assassination occurring during her junior year of high school. She said it "definitely had an influence" on her life and that it "clearly had an impact on all of us." She believes that it affected the sense of security people had within the United States. Yet, she felt stability around her and open discussions at home provided a foundation that helped her learn to cope with such events.

Influential Individuals

Jeanne didn't remember many influential individuals during her childhood other than her family members. She got along well with all of her teachers. She remembers her first-grade teacher very well because this woman was born without a hand on one of her arms. She ended up falling off a horse and dying a few years after Jeanne had her as a teacher. Jeanne remembered her positive influence more vividly than her other elementary school teachers in part because of her disability and death.

Jeanne's English teacher was very influential during her senior year of high school. He had an amazing ability to describe literature, and he also taught her to write, which she says has been very helpful throughout her life. In addition to "just being in his class, talking to him one-on-one had a big impact" on her during her last year of high school. He wasn't even an advisor or mentor; she said it was just "the way he was able to present the material and talk about literature." He brought literature to life and clearly had a passion for his subject. She provided additional insight into his style and influence:

> *He was somebody that most students felt comfortable joking around with. One very funny and memorable high school incident happened in his class. Several of us had older siblings who had taken him in years prior. The older siblings had talked about an incident in class where he swore there was a dog in the*

classroom, but there was not. He made the students pick up the imaginary dog and put it out. When I had him for English, one of our friends had rabbits. We had her bring a rabbit to class one day, and we got all the students to pretend like the rabbit wasn't there. We let the rabbit hop around class. It was so funny because he saw the rabbit, and he refused to acknowledge the rabbit was there. We finally told him, and it was very funny. You couldn't do that with many teachers. He gave us a safe environment, and we enjoyed learning.

Jeanne's basketball coach had a positive impact on her life as well. Jeanne not only liked this woman's coaching style, but she felt this coach provided an enriching environment that, according to Jeanne, "pushed me in a certain way that was beneficial." This coach was also very supportive. Jeanne remembers her saying, "She who hesitates is lost. Pass the ball!" Even as governor that phrase came to her mind many times, as she needed to make decisions carefully and quickly.

Some of Jeanne's friends were also influential in her life during her teen years. Jeanne had a very good friend in middle school and several good friends in high school that became lifelong friends. Jeanne said that one particular friend in high school "probably had the most impact because of our connection and openness." They were in drama and band together and enjoyed being around each other. She learned that making deep connections with people can bring support in future years.

College Plans
Jeanne always planned to attend college and, in fact, it "was never questioned." Belle told Jeanne later in her life that her father didn't feel as if there was a need for his daughters to go to college; he thought they would "get married and that would be it." However, Jeanne's mother was always committed to making sure her girls graduated from college, and all three daughters did. Jeanne believes that college graduation was important to both of her parents at some level. It was "never an issue about whether we were going to college; it was when and where."

COLLEGE YEARS

Background
Jeanne went to college the fall after she graduated from high school. Her parents moved to West Virginia, and she stayed in Pennsylvania and began attending Shippensburg University in 1965. She chose Shippensburg because it was a state college and more affordable than a private college. Before her parents moved, she thought she was only going to be about two hours away from home, but because of the move she wound up about ten hours away from her family. Despite this distance, Jeanne felt ready and excited to attend college. She enjoyed high school and clarified that she wasn't going to college to "get away from everything," but she was ready to move forward with a "new phase" of her life. Al-

though she knew a few other students, she didn't go to Shippensburg with any of her good friends. After attending Shippensburg for two years, Jeanne's parents wanted her to transfer to West Virginia so she would be closer to them. Although hesitant, she agreed and transferred to Marshall University in Huntington at the beginning of her junior year. She found that it had a very different culture, so she transferred back to Shippensburg after one semester. Jeanne attended college for four years and in 1969 graduated from Shippensburg with a bachelor's degree.

When she started college, Jeanne had no idea what she wanted to major in. She began as a French major and thinks her original interest in French had to do with her initial desire to travel internationally. She later changed her major to political science and then English, which allowed her to graduate in four years despite transferring colleges. She still enjoyed politics and finished college with a minor in political science.

Involvement and Employment
During her freshman year at Shippensburg, Jeanne immediately became involved in extracurricular activities. She played on the women's basketball team and ran for a position in student government. She loved basketball, but after a few years, the coach told her she needed to make a choice between basketball and student government; she chose student government. Jeanne was also very involved with a sorority but said she became too busy with other activities after her sophomore year and was never involved in its leadership. In fact, after she transferred back to Shippensburg her junior year, she went inactive in the sorority for the remainder of her undergraduate college experience. She said it was good to do as a freshman because it helped her meet lots of people and gave her an early connection with the college. But after a time, she said,

> *It felt to me like too much of the discussion was about what color the napkins were going to be and not enough about things that really mattered. I realized that I was much more interested in student government and more substantive endeavors.*

Jeanne was involved in lots of other activities on campus as well. College was the first time she was involved in actual change efforts. As a junior, she ran for president of the Women's Residence Association and was elected. This was an important leadership position for her. The 1960s were "turbulent times on college campuses," and college students began having more interest in taking responsibility. She explained,

> *When I started college, women had dorm hours [curfews]. We had to be in at 9:00 p.m. during the week and around midnight on weekends. My friends and I didn't think it was fair that women had dorm hours and men did not. I believed that I had the ability to help get this changed. I was involved in the residence association during all my college years, and during my senior year, we changed the hours. We didn't get everything we wanted, but we changed it.*

Jeanne said it was "thrilling to be part of making a difference for others." She spoke of a few other changes she was very involved with on her campus. For example, Shippensburg had a requirement that off campus students could not be visited in their apartments by any members of the opposite sex. She remembers arguing that it wasn't the college's responsibility to regulate this and helped convince the administrators to make a change. These change efforts provided Jeanne with opportunities to articulate her position and speak out, while representing the views of others.

During the summer before her senior year of college, Jeanne attended the National Student Association Congress in Kansas. She remembers attending a particular workshop on how to successfully lead change on college campuses. She found it fascinating, thought about what she learned, and then took the principles back to her campus to use in future change efforts.

Employment

Jeanne didn't have paid employment during high school because her family was always traveling to visit relatives during the summers. The summer before her first year of college she obtained her first paid job working as a waitress. During other college summers, she worked on the line in a shoe factory (which she described as "quite an interesting experience"), did an internship in the Missouri welfare department, and worked retail in Hawaii because her boyfriend was in Vietnam and she wanted to be there when he came for "R&R." She doesn't believe any of these jobs provided real opportunities for leadership, yet she felt they were helpful in her general development. She felt that her intern program was probably most helpful as it expanded her understanding of the welfare system and the needs of many struggling community members.

Influential Individuals

Jeanne mentioned a few individuals during her college years that influenced her deeply. When she was a sophomore in college, she had an American government college professor, Richard Beckner, who was "wonderful." She said, "It was after I took his course that I realized, 'Gee, I could actually major in this!'" She then took a number of courses from him and decided that she really wanted to be a political science major. However, because of her semester transfer she lost credits, and she could graduate with an English major in less time, so that's what she did. She did, however, receive a minor in political science. In reflecting on this particular professor's influence, she said,

> *We had one-on-one conversations every once in a while, but just attending his class was important for me. He had high expectations for me and other students, and I was motivated to work hard because of these expectations. He also taught us an interesting lesson about expectations that I have always kept with me, particularly as governor. He spoke about the passing of the Civil Rights Act and how much progress was occurring. Yet, he challenged us to think about why, after the passing of the Act, there were now more riots in cities and why the real agitation on the part of black leaders and black Americans at the time*

happened after it had passed. He said, "Well it's the rising expectations. People think things are going to be different and things are not. That's when people get upset." It was a very important lesson for me.

Jeanne also remembers this professor talking about the Vietnam War. There were hundreds of thousands of people demonstrating against the war at that point. The students in the class asked him why the government hadn't yet listened and changed. She remembers him saying, "Well, because that's the way democracy works. When enough people get upset enough about what is happening, you're going to see the policies of the country change." She learned that he was right. He was a significant influence in her thinking at that time, and he was the first one that helped her discover that she could have a career in government.

Another individual who had a positive impact on Jeanne during college was her basketball coach. Quinn Baker was a very interesting woman. She was single and had been coaching for about twenty years. She was an example of a woman of strength, character, and independence.

Jeanne was a good student and was on the dean's list; she felt this was one reason she had good relationships with nearly all of her professors during college. She believes that all of them, including the men, made some kind of impact in her intellectual and general development. A few even took a specific interest in seeing her succeed. In addition to the political science professor just mentioned, she remembers a psychologist on campus who was involved with student activities. He was very helpful as she and other students were trying to figure out how to make some changes on campus in a way that was productive and not disruptive. She felt this man was very important in helping them think through options and opportunities.

Graduate School

Two years after graduating with her undergraduate degree, Jeanne went back to school at the University of Mississippi for a master's degree in political science. By this time, she had married (see next section for details) and was very focused on doing well in school and getting her degree. Therefore, she wasn't involved in extracurricular activities.

Jeanne started out majoring in international relations and then changed her focus to political science after the first year. She said,

To get the international relations degree, I would have had to write a thesis. I did all the research for the thesis, but took extra coursework and wound up switching my degree. I didn't have to write the thesis, which was what I wanted at that point. My advisor was a man from India, and most of my research was on the India/Pakistan conflict.

She enjoyed the research in general and believes it did enhance her "appreciation for individual and world differences." Her political science degree in general broadened her perspectives. She said, "I think the world view was what was important about my master's degree—getting a different view of the world." She had courses in European diplomacy, Latin America studies, and "learned a lot of information about what was going on in the world." She felt that this provided insights and knowledge that became helpful throughout her political career. She successfully graduated with her master's degree in 1973.

FAMILY AND CAREER

Jeanne married Bill Shaheen during the fall of 1967 after she graduated from college with her bachelor's degree. Within one year, Bill got accepted to law school in Mississippi, and so they moved and then spent three years in Oxford. They began having children in 1974 when Jeanne gave birth to their first daughter, Stefany. Jeanne eventually had two more daughters, Stacey and Molly, with the first two being three-and-a-half years apart and youngest being born eight years after the second. Jeanne's desire to be heavily involved in raising her children, framed each of her decisions to move into various paid and non-paid positions for many years. This section is organized around Jeanne's various positions and includes applicable information about Jeanne's non-work life so the reader can understand Jeanne's career choices.

Teaching School
Jeanne and Bill both taught school for a year in New Hampshire during the first year they were married. After moving to Mississippi for Bill to attend law school, Jeanne was immediately hired to teach at the newly integrated high school. It "was a fascinating experience" for her to work with the students as they dealt with the challenges of school integration.

Although Jeanne taught high school full time for only two years in total, she felt it was definitely beneficial in many ways. She believes that "just being in on the other side of education" was very helpful for her, as she later dealt with so many educational issues as a state senator and governor. This experience helped her understand concerns and issues around education "probably as much as anything." She believes it gave her a deeper understanding of what is important to families with children. Teaching also helped her strengthen and develop many skills important for leadership, such as speaking, presenting, observing, listening, and evaluating. Jeanne also explained that teaching was key in helping her think through discrimination issues. She said, "I learned a lot from dealing with issues around integration, and this had a big impact on my later involvement in politics." She left teaching after two years to return to school for her master's degree.

Retail Business Ownership
After they were married, Jeanne and Bill went to Maine every summer for eight years to manage a seasonal retail business they owned with Bill's sister and brother-in-law. Jeanne quickly became involved with the details of "running the business and learning the ins and outs of budgeting and managing." They hired

and managed various employees through the years and "did everything small business owners do." Jeanne ended up managing the business for three of those years and said,

> I learned a lot. I learned about managing people, figuring out schedules, what works in retail and what does not, how to handle various issues that arise, and how to work with the public. All of these are important competencies that a good politician should have.

University Senate Secretary

After Jeanne and Bill finished graduate school, they moved back to New Hampshire. Jeanne wanted to go back to teaching but couldn't get hired in the same school because she now had a master's degree, which meant they would have to pay her more. So, instead of teaching, she ended up accepting an administrative job at the University of New Hampshire (UNH) as the administrative assistant to the university senate—the senate secretary. She explained, "At that time, UNH had the only unicameral governing body in the country at a college or university. Our senate had faculty, students, and staff—all part of the same governing body." Through this job, she gained more insight and perspective into educational systems, particularly higher education. She held this job for a year, and then she got pregnant. At this point, she decided that it made more sense for her to run their retail business during the summers and then "have the year off to spend with her daughter."

Political Campaign Work

Jeanne remembers being interested in political work immediately upon graduation from college. While teaching school, she clearly recalls having an interest in Jimmy Carter, who had been elected governor of Georgia that year. He took his strong stand against segregation in the south and talked about the need to work together. His message was very different from what she was hearing from the leadership in Mississippi where she lived at the time. She listened carefully to the debate and thought a great deal about the issues of the day. She decided that she liked Carter's message and philosophy, and she and her husband began thinking about becoming more involved in political work once they were able to finish their graduate degrees.

Jeanne did become heavily involved in campaign work. First, Jeanne and Bill got very involved in Carter's 1976 campaign after their first daughter, Stefany, was born in 1974. Because Jeanne had decided to stay at home with her daughter during much of the year, she had more time for political involvement. In addition to Carter's campaign, Jeanne also became involved in other campaign work. In fact, after her second daughter, Stacey, was born in 1978, Jeanne worked on a gubernatorial campaign for Hugh Gallen, who was elected New Hampshire's governor in 1978. During 1979 and 1980, after she finished her work with the governor's race, Jeanne accepted a paid nine-month position to run Jimmy Carter's presidential primary campaign in New Hampshire. Later, in

1984, Jeanne was asked to manage Gary Hart's New Hampshire presidential primary campaign and loved that opportunity to continue strengthening her campaign management skills. This work provided learning opportunities as she gained new perspectives, had new experiences, and received opportunities to practice her leadership skills. She oversaw the recruiting and deployment of hundreds of volunteers, the hiring and management of paid staff, and fundraising efforts. She also developed a network of people around the state, all of which were beneficial.

In 1985, Jeanne gave birth to her third child, and when Molly was about six-months old, Jeanne received an offer and decided to run the gubernatorial campaigns of Paul EcEachern in 1986 and 1988 in New Hampshire. Unfortunately, the campaigns were not successful, but she recalls learning as much from losing as from winning. Overall, Jeanne believes her campaign work was very helpful in her development. She not only enjoyed the work, but these political experiences also taught her how campaigning and politics worked. She believes these were wonderful opportunities for personal growth and development.

Women's Commission Vice-Chair

After Jeanne worked on the campaign in 1978 for the newly elected governor of New Hampshire, Governor Gallen appointed her to serve in a volunteer position as the vice chair of the state's Commission on the Status of Women. During these years, she became very involved in a number of women's and family issues. In addition to serving as the vice chair, she also chaired what they called the Employment Taskforce. She led efforts to research women's employment issues in the state, holding a series of public hearings and producing a final report. As chair, she wrote most of this report, which generated a lot of interest among the press and policymakers. These positive outcomes led her to think about her future options. She said,

> *Being involved with a group of committed, interesting, and energetic women provided me a lot of support as I thought about future options, developing my capacity, and believing that I could do anything I wanted to do.*

She believes that her work on this commission was also very helpful in developing leadership capacity. Regarding volunteer work in general, Jeanne believes that her non-paid experiences were incredibly helpful for her. Each provided opportunities for her to strengthen and/or learn new skills. She explained,

> *I think for women, particularly in my generation, the challenge was to figure out what we could do that was engaging, that we liked to do, and that would also allow us to have the time that we needed for the children. Volunteer work filled that gap, and I loved it!*

Co-Director of Children's Festival

After she ran Jimmy Carter's presidential campaign in New Hampshire (1979–1980), Jeanne job-shared a position with a friend. They managed the Somersworth International Children's festival—a celebration to link the city's ethnic heritage to some of the downtown restoration issues. It was in a neighboring city, and her friend's husband was the mayor at that time. When this friend asked her if she was interested in job sharing, Jeanne thought it sounded like "great fun" and accepted the offer. The position was about organizing, mobilizing, and engaging the community, which Jeanne loved. She co-directed the festival from January to June for two years. Because she wanted a flexible schedule with her young children, Jeanne felt this was a good position for her at this time in her life. She said, "These were all of the same kinds of activities and responsibilities I had already had while involved in campaigning. It helped me keep these skills sharpened and also let me continue to develop them."

Director of Parent's Association

After Jeanne finished working on the festival, she decided that she needed to find something that would pay her, still be somewhat flexible, but would not be "quite as crazy as a campaign." So, she accepted a part-time position at the University of New Hampshire as the director of the Parent's Association. She worked three or four days a week, but had the flexibility to set her own schedule. The Parents' Association provided additional opportunities for her to work with different constituencies and further develop her organization and communication skills. She worked as director for four years and then took a leave of absence in 1983 and 1984 to run Gary Hart's presidential primary campaign in New Hampshire.

State Senator

After finishing her work with the 1988 gubernatorial campaign, Jeanne decided to take most of 1989 off to decide what she wanted to do next. Her youngest daughter was about three-and-a-half at that point, and Jeanne thought it was a good time to spend with her children. She had been so busy for many years with campaign work, volunteer positions, and other part-time paid jobs, that she wanted to take some time to reflect and make some new career plans and decisions. During this year, she decided that she was going to run for the state senate.

So, in 1990, Jeanne ran for the senate where she successfully beat a three-term incumbent, and then spent the next six years serving as a state senator. She learned a great deal about state government during these years. Other than some experience on the women's commission dealing with women and family issues, she hadn't had a previous opportunity to learn about state issues, challenges, and solutions. Although she had a lot of campaign and political experience, she didn't yet have the substantive experience she needed for future state leadership positions. She said,

> *Being a state senator gave me a real understanding about government that was important, not just in terms of understanding state government and what was going on with issues, but giving me the confidence that I knew what needed to*

be done. For women, I think it is often about the realization that you can do this. I don't think that is as much an issue for men.

The senate position gave her confidence and a political agenda. When she ran for governor, she knew what she wanted to do because "a lot of that had to do with spending those six years in the state senate." She remembers learning to deal with being attacked by others during her senate experience and said, "You only want to deal with that for so long." She definitely developed a thicker skin during those years.

The senate also gave her "a whole new group of people and contacts." She developed an appreciation for the importance of working "across the party aisle." She learned that she needed to work with Republicans to "get things done" and make the changes that needed to be made for the state to become more successful. She felt like she had some wonderful Republican colleagues. She developed a lot of good relationships with people that "then carried over into getting things done as we dealt with issues." She explained,

> One of the best pieces of political advice I received came from a former Democratic leader in the New Hampshire House. He was a very colorful figure named Chris Spirou. After I got elected to the senate, Chris said, "Now remember: What's important isn't that you're a Democrat or a Republican. It's your relationships, so develop those relationships." This was very good advice!

Governor

At the end of her three terms as a state senator, Jeanne decided to run for governor of New Hampshire. She said, "I thought I could do it, but it took me about a week of having an uneasy stomach before I settled down and said, 'Oh yeah. I know I can do this job!'" The person who was governor at the time had stepped down, so it was an open seat. He announced in April that he was not going to run again, so Jeanne and her supporters "got a campaign geared up very quickly." She said, "We made a decision, announced in May, and had a very short campaign season." New Hampshire hadn't elected a Democratic governor in sixteen years and had never elected a woman governor. She won fifty-eight percent of the vote, was reelected twice, and left office at the end of her third term in 2002 after losing a close race for the U.S. Senate.

CRITICAL SUPPORT

Jeanne believes that being married to a spouse with a full-time job that would support the family gave her the flexibility to pursue a variety of different volunteer and paid positions. The family didn't depend on her income, which made her more available to take on new roles and learning experiences. Jeanne spoke of her husband's positive influence throughout the interview. She said that he "has always been very supportive." He loved politics as much as Jeanne and they were both involved for many years. In 1977, Carter appointed Bill to be the

U.S. attorney in New Hampshire, a position he held until 1980 when he stepped down and was quickly given a judgeship by New Hampshire's governor. Because of these positions he could no longer be involved in political activities. Yet, Jeanne said he always provided her encouragement and support to pursue her interests and passions.

Jeanne's girls were also very encouraging and supportive as they grew and understood more about what their mother was doing. In addition to their support, Jeanne believes that her experience as a mother has helped her develop certain competencies that became helpful as she moved into leadership positions. Motherhood helped her learn multitasking, which, according to Jeanne, "is one of the most important skills in successful leadership at high levels." Motherhood also helped her strengthen her skills in mediation, organization, listening, patience, reasoning, motivating others, and holding firm to decisions that have been made.

Bill's family was very important in helping with and watching the children when they were young and Jeanne needed to be away. His family lived close by and her in-laws would pick up the kids from school. In fact, they'd often take the girls home for a few hours after school when Jeanne needed to be working. Bill's sister lived fairly close and was very helpful with the girls as well. Jeanne never wanted her girls to feel as if they were abandoned, but she also wanted to continue the work and projects she loved. She said that she would have had difficulty working if she had not had the support of her husband's family, especially because of the hours involved during her campaign work.

Jeanne explained that, because she worked part time during many of these years, she was able to keep up with the kids and housework "up to a point." However, she also hired a student who lived with them and "helped out for about a year." In addition, after her third daughter was born, Jeanne hired a Chinese woman (whose husband was a post doc student at UNH) to come in during the days to do childcare and housework. Jeanne remembers that this woman was wonderful with her girls.

Through the years Jeanne has been asked how she was able to juggle her family responsibilities and her work duties. In fact, when Jeanne was in the senate she remembers being asked to give a speech to a group of women on that very topic. She said,

> *They wanted me to write this speech on work/life balance. I sat down to try and write it, and I worked on it for a couple of days. Finally I realized that I couldn't write the speech because I don't have a real strategy. My idea of work/life balance has been learning to live with the guilt!*

Jeanne believes that she learned to compartmentalize her two roles most of the time. When she was home, she would try to focus on the family and household tasks, and when she was at work, she would try to focus primarily on her job-related responsibilities. However, she said that this didn't work well when she was running campaigns; even though these were temporary positions, they were "all encompassing."

CAREER PATH AND GENDER

There is no question that Jeanne had an informal career path. She had no idea that she would get involved in politics to the extent she did, and she had absolutely no idea that she could or would become the first woman governor of New Hampshire. She made her career choices based on what she found interesting and exciting or where she felt she could make the greatest difference and impact. She never approached an assignment or position consciously considering how it could lead to a future position or role. In fact, she didn't even start thinking about becoming governor until she was well into her state senate experience. She explained,

> *When I was a state senator, I remember thinking that we really needed a governor who would do something meaningful in the state. I knew things weren't going the way they needed to be going and remember thinking that we desperately needed someone strong that could help change that. One day I thought, "I could be that someone."*

Jeanne certainly always understood that there were more career obstacles for women than for men in professional life. She remembers that was very clear in college when she found that the dorm curfews were different for men and women. Yet, with this understanding Jeanne has been careful throughout the years not to take a victim stance in her work. She has always been willing to acknowledge inconsistencies, but she has been more interested in using a rational and productive approach rather than complaining.

VALUABLE INFLUENCES

Jeanne felt that many different influences helped her learn to become an effective leader. She felt that being in positions that provided her with experience and insights were central forces in her development. She stated, "Personal experience is always the thing that has the most impact on developing my intellectual knowledge and leadership competence." She also said that reading, listening, and observing have also been powerful personal growth mechanisms.

Jeanne also mentioned a number of influential individuals who made a difference in helping her learn and grow in her political skills and leadership competencies. While Jeanne was employed as the senate secretary for the University of New Hampshire (UNH), one of the benefits she received was being able to work with a man named Bob Craig with whom she became close friends. Bob was the chair of the senate at that time and was a political science professor at UNH. He later worked in Washington for a congressman and was very involved in politics. He was "kind of a mentor or a coach" to Jeanne. When she was trying to figure out what she wanted to do in politics, he was one of the people she would talk to about it. He encouraged her by listening and responding. She said,

> *I can remember going to see him when I was trying to decide if I was going to work for Walter Mondale or Gary Hart. He said to me, "Well Mondale runs an army and Hart's got a gorilla operation. It depends on what you want." He helped me think through things but didn't try to give me all the answers.*

Other influential individuals included the women in the senate. The year that Jeanne was elected to the state senate, nine (over 1/3) senators were women. There were a number of other women who were elected that same year and the women in this group, in particular, provided each other important support and encouragement. She described this group as "a real force!" She felt fortunate that a lot of women in politics at that time were supportive and wanted other women to succeed. Although Jeanne didn't attend any formal leadership training, she met almost daily with women in the senate to talk about state and political issues. She frequently felt these often-informal meetings provided a "training and development" environment for her to learn and strengthen her skills. She also spoke of one particular woman in this group:

> *There was a woman in the state senate, Susan McClain, who was very well known at the time. She was a Republican who had run for Congress. She was very supportive of other women in general and was very supportive of me. Knowing I had this support gave me additional confidence in my competency and work.*

During these years, the senate members in general were also very supportive of both Republicans and Democrats.

Although Jeanne doesn't remember specific individuals telling her that she had strong capability and skill, she said people simply asked her to take on new responsibilities or assignments. For example, the individual she worked for on Carter's campaign in 1976 called her again in 1979 and said, "You are the best person to run his campaign in New Hampshire. We really need you to do that." She remembers people approaching her through the years in this way.

LEADERSHIP STYLE AND PHILOSOPHY

Jeanne believes that part of her leadership style is deliberate, whereas the other part has always been somewhat intuitive. She believes her staff would say that she is a good listener and observant. She believes that both these skills are critical in successful leadership today as it helps individuals keep abreast of what is happening around them. She also spoke of the importance of learning from observing the responses and reactions of others to her own behaviors, decisions, and actions (self-monitoring skills). When she has received negative responses from others, she has always tried to learn from them and not repeat the behavior, if indeed she determined there was a better way to respond. Learning from her mistakes has been an important characteristic of her leadership style throughout the years as well. These competencies (e.g., listening, observing, self-monitoring, and learning from mistakes) are all elements of a reflective leadership style. The ability to consider, analyze, and evaluate actions (self and others) is the basis for reflective and critical thinking. Yet, she believes that political leaders in general do not have a lot of time to be reflective. She said,

> I think that, particularly in a political environment, you don't have a whole lot of time to reflect. It's not like an academic setting where you're writing an article, thesis, or dissertation and you really have time to reflect. In a political environment, there is not time to sit around and think for thinking's sake. You have to make decisions and something actually happens as a result of those decisions. Hopefully, you are going to analyze the decision and then, if needed, try to do better next time, but you don't get a lot of time for reflection.

Jeanne said her staff would also say that she has a collaborative leadership style. She likes to gather lots of opinions on most topics and situations. Although there were some things she took early positions on, she would nearly always listen to different people on most issues. She typically wanted to acquire as much information and as many perspectives as possible before making decisions. She explained,

> I like to have other people collaborate with me, and I like to try to reach consensus and compromise. I wasn't usually an "in your face kind of leader." I didn't pound my chest saying, "This is the way it is going to be." I tried to bring other people into the decision making, sometimes even to a fault.

Jeanne's leadership philosophy focuses around hiring great people, helping them learn and develop, and "hopefully keeping them for many years." She believes in finding people she can trust, which were often people she had already known. Having a trustworthy staff is critical to effective and ethical leadership. She was the first Democrat elected governor in New Hampshire in sixteen years. She brought in a new political team that included people she had worked with for many years in other positions. She hired individuals she trusted and who had a strong work ethic, had solid political understanding, and were very smart and capable. She said, "I wanted to have people working for me who were smarter than me. I don't threaten easily." As governor, she also believed it was important in leadership to get rid of people who were not effective in their posts. She received some advice from existing governors during an orientation at the beginning of her service. They said, "If someone is not performing or if there is a major problem like ethics or honesty, the best thing you can do is to get rid of them, get rid of them fast, and make a clean break." Although she didn't like to fire people, she learned that it was an important leadership responsibility so that ultimately more positive work and changes could be made for the state.

Many years earlier in her life she had learned some important lessons that have become part of her philosophy as well. One of her advisors (the psychologist) in college once said to her, "Did you ever stop to think that everyone on campus may not be as responsible as you and may not have the capacity to deal with this change in the same way that you and others do?" This was the first time she had ever really thought through this concept. From this, she began to learn that there are at least two points of view to everything. She said, "It's important to learn that you aren't always right. Most of the time when you're taking action, you're probably convinced you're right, but don't assume you are." The same individual also helped her discover that political change is not generally revolutionary, but rather evolutionary. She said, "It's usually better to bring people along with you in the change effort by helping, developing, and supporting them. Once they're involved and supported, then you can make the changes that need to happen." She believes that involving others throughout the change process is the only way to lead positive change efforts. These were important lessons for Jeanne.

ADVICE

Jeanne has given career advice to young women for many years. First, she tells them that they don't have to make "the decision tomorrow about what they're going to do fifteen or twenty years from now." Second, she tells them that they need to both enjoy what they are doing and do it as well as they can so they can make an impact or difference. Third, young women need to "develop good relationships along the way." In political leadership, having a reliable network of people who "look fondly on what you've done" can be very helpful. Fourth, experience is the best way for someone to learn about leadership. Instead of getting impatient, it helps to remember that "whatever they are doing now is not what they will be doing for the rest of their lives." They need to learn to appreciate the journey instead of thinking they "need to get to the end tomorrow." She believes that future leaders should take time to "get some life experience." Jeanne explained,

> *Everything you do in life counts. Get life experience not just because it's going to be good on your resume, but also because you can learn so much from it. Having true empathy with constituents goes a long way. You need to understand what it's like to have to work all day, pick up the kids and go home at night, cook dinner, and then get them through their homework and to bed. You need to learn what it's like to make a payroll in business. You need to do whatever it is you need to do so you get those personal experiences that help you identify with others.*

Finally, Jeanne believes that being honest and ethical in all one does is "critical no matter what you do." Young women should think deeply about what their personal principles and values are so that they are better able to understand their own core, which will ultimately guide their future decisions.

FINAL THOUGHTS

Jeanne's leadership development journey is unique. She didn't plan to become a political leader but continued to prepare herself by accepting interesting and intriguing opportunities she was offered. She used her flexible schedule throughout the years to harness a wide variety of experiences that eventually led her to becoming a state senator and ultimately the governor of New Hampshire. She feels fortunate now to be able to continue using the governmental, political, and leadership abilities she has developed as she now directs the Institute of Politics at Harvard and speaks often to a variety of audiences throughout the country. Although she has clearly made a difference for the residents of New Hampshire already, she continues to look for ways to improve the world around her. She says that this desire never ends for political leaders who really care.

Chapter 7

Governor Madeleine May Kunin

My political life was so rich in experience and emotion. Like art, political action gives shape and expression to the things we fear as well as to those we desire. It is a creative process, drawing on the power to imagine as well as to act. The driving force is a vision of an ideal. As governor, I had the incredible luxury of being able to dream on a grand scale. And this sense of infinite possibility gives politics its romance.

~ Governor Madeleine May Kunin

I interviewed Governor Madeleine Kunin at her home in Burlington, Vermont on December 19, 2005. She was inaugurated as Vermont's first woman governor in 1985 and served in that office for three terms, finishing in 1991. While governor, she was recognized for significant achievement in education, children's services, and the environment. Since her governorship, she has also served as the deputy U.S. secretary of education (1993–1996), U.S. ambassador to Switzerland (1996–1999), a scholar in residence at Middlebury College, and is currently a visiting professor at the University of Vermont. She also serves as president of the board of the Institute for Sustainable Communities, a nongovernmental organization which she founded in 1991. Governor Kunin has lived a fascinating life full of remarkable accomplishments. She spent a few hours with me on a cold winter morning in Vermont speaking of influential people, events, circumstances, and opportunities all of which helped her to develop leadership knowledge and competencies throughout her life. She also gave me permission to use information and excerpts from her 1994 book titled *Living a Political Life: One of America's First Woman Governors Tells her Story*.

BACKGROUND

Madeleine Kunin was born in Zurich, Switzerland on September 28, 1933. Although her parents lived in Germany the first few years of marriage, they moved to Zurich before having children. She has one sibling, a brother four years her senior. Her father died when she was only three years old, so she essentially grew up in a single parent family. Her father's death left her mother (who was thirty-six at the time) "restless and in search of something she never quite found." The family lived on a small inheritance left from her father's business and her mother's uncertain income. After his death, the family began moving from place to place for a number of years. Madeleine's mother then moved the family to London to live with her sister. However, for some unknown reason, within the year they had moved back to Zurich and eventually moved into a home outside of Lucerne. In 1940, when Madeleine was six and a half years old, they immigrated to the United States. Madeleine believes her mother did this for two reasons. First, her mother had concerns that Hitler would march into Switzerland. Second, Madeleine believes that her mother left Europe to get away from the memory of her husband's death—a suicide. The United States was also a reference point in her mother's mind as many relatives had moved to or visited America during previous decades. Madeleine remembers that it was not easy to get visas to the United States during those years, and she remembers her mother going down to the consulate often to check on them. According to Madeleine, they were very lucky to get them, because the United States didn't issue visas the following year, and it became unusually difficult for Jews to leave Europe after that time.

After moving to the United States, Madeleine's family settled in Forest Hills, New York, but after only a year her mother decided to move them to California. Madeleine's mother had cousins in both places. They hadn't lived in California long before her mother moved them back to New York to be closer to that part of the family. Madeleine was about eight years old when they moved back to New York, and fortunately, they remained there until her junior year of high school. Before leaving home for college, however, Madeleine and her mother moved once again, this time to Pittsfield, Massachusetts. She said, "My mother was always looking for something—something different than we had. She somehow thought life would be easier or better someplace else."

Throughout the years, the children were "never deprived, but never had money either." Madeleine was raised in a very modest home. Her mother didn't drive, so they didn't have a car. The family had food and shelter, but Madeleine was "aware of financial insecurity." She knew her mother worried about money but "didn't have the education to have a full-time job."

Parents

Madeleine's father was born in Germany. He became a successful businessman in Zurich by importing and exporting shoes and boots. Although he wanted to be a lawyer, he never went to college. He could have been a lawyer but was running a big, successful business and was financially successful; hence, there was no justification for him to continue his education. In fact, Madeleine believes that he may have actually only finished elementary school.

Madeleine has no recollection of her father except through photographs. When she was young and would ask her mother what happened to him, her mother would tell her that he died of a heart attack. Madeleine did not learn that her father had actually committed suicide until she was in college. She spoke of the difficulty this incident was for her mother:

> *The pain of his death was unspeakable. Each time I asked my mother to tell me more, I felt I was picking off a scab. She pulled away. Its silent legacy accompanied us always, enshrouding us in embarrassed, deprived silence. My father's death made my mother a widow as other people might become a teacher, a doctor, or a nurse. Underneath every bright outfit, I spied her mourning clothes. She did not remarry.* (Kunin, 1994, 328–329)

Madeleine's mother, Renée, was born and raised in Switzerland. She went to a finishing school in the French part of Switzerland during high school to learn the language. It was a boarding school and a good experience for her. After high school, she continued her education by taking a few courses at a university in Switzerland.

Although Renée had to be independent, Madeleine said that "she wasn't terribly happy being independent." She suffered from loneliness, and Madeleine felt, as the daughter, a sense of obligation that she should try and help her through these years. Renée did various kinds of part-time and temporary labor to support the family. They had a boarder that Madeleine "sort of resented," because she had to give up her room. Her mother babysat, gave French lessons, did sewing piecework, and was an Avon lady. Renée was still a stay-at-home mother as she was able to do all of her work from home.

Madeleine's mother read the New York Times daily and was well informed. She believed that people must be attentive to the issues, so she was very aware of what was happening. At home, the family talked about the political and social issues in the nation and world. Renée was intelligent and knew about the holocaust. Madeleine attributes her strong sense of social justice to her mother.

Madeleine explained that her mother whole-heartedly knew that "Anything is possible in America." Renée had a typical immigrant's vision of life in America and believed that it was truly a land of opportunity. Madeleine and her brother also believed it without question. Their mother gave them optimism, a sense of wonder, and a feeling of gratitude about this country. Madeleine said,

> *Despite the tragedy of her life, she refused to be defined by it. Her faith in America was infectious; never would I be able to be cynical about this country. It had saved us not only from war, but also from self-denial. We could grow up to become anything we wanted to be. This was not fantasy; this was America, the country in which the old restrictions of social class and religious bias did not count.* (Kunin, 1994, 326-327)

Extended Family

Although Madeleine had an extended family in Switzerland, she was too young at the time to remember any real influence they may have had on her development. As mentioned, some of her relatives had traveled to and/or lived in the United States, and this provided some hope for Madeleine and her family that in

America they could be safe and successful. After immigrating to the United States, they lived close to various extended family members throughout her childhood and youth. These family members generally provided support, encouragement, and stability in Madeleine's life. Her mother told her many stories about her relatives and their lives. For example, Madeleine heard stories about her maternal grandfather who ran for office in Zurich. Although he didn't get elected, she spoke of many of the ideas he had for social improvement. As Madeleine became older, she also heard stories of her relatives who died in the holocaust. Although extended family members may not have been directly influential on Madeleine's leadership development, she knew of their lives and challenges, which provided her an understanding of her own history and a sense of self.

Influences on Political Interest
Madeleine spoke of thinking back in her life more deeply to try to determine why she became so interested in politics. She attributes her interest primarily to two events: 1) her immigrant experience and 2) the holocaust. She explains:

> *First, the immigrant experience gave me a sense of optimism, a sense of "anything is possible in America." This is what my mother taught us growing up. Immigrants need to believe that. We learned that we could change, transform ourselves, and really become someone. This was an important optimism for me. Second, I think the holocaust experience somehow influenced my political interests in the way that we never articulated; we didn't talk about the holocaust because my mother didn't want me to know. She had the theory, as others also did, that it was bad for children to know about these things. I discovered the holocaust in high school in a book titled, "Blessed is the Match." It was much later that I found that very close relatives of ours (including my father's sister, her husband, and a number of other members of my family) had died in the holocaust. The holocaust kind of gave me the sense that I could do something—that just being passive is no protection. I guess in a way my mother's story taught me that too, that being passive doesn't work. You've got to protect yourself, and you've got to speak up. Something can be done, and something must be done.*

Madeleine said that in some strange way it made sense to her. She stated, "It just made me a person who felt engaged both in my own life and engaged in the world." She began believing that individuals can make a difference. During times of deep reflection, she came to believe that the best way she could honor the victims of the holocaust was by using the opportunities she was given. She explained,

> *As a woman, I could do things my mother couldn't do, my aunts couldn't do, and my grandmother couldn't do. As a Jew, I could now do things that previous generations couldn't do. It somehow became almost an obligation that I become successful so that I could contribute in ways woman and Jews couldn't previously have done.*

CHILDHOOD AND YOUTH

Personality

Madeleine described herself as being very shy as a young girl. She said,

> *I am told that I suffered from unusual shyness as a child. My aunt had worried whether I would be able to cope. I arrived in the United States with my mother and brother at the age of six and half, not speaking English. . . . My first day in public school was traumatic: I was placed in the second grade and asked to read the five-digit numbers chalked on the blackboard. I could say nothing, so the teacher put me back in first grade.* (Kunin, 1994, 61)

During most of her school days, it was easier for her to be a silent observer rather than to risk being a misfit participant. Looking back on these days, Madeleine believes her low confidence as a child was not a lack of skill, but a lack of courage. She said,

> *Silence was safe. Speech was not. Being the courteous listener, for so long, I became adept at keeping the other person's flow of words moving, interjecting a nod here, a word there, to make my presence known but not heard.* (Kunin, 1994, 62)

Madeleine remembers as a child being very self-conscious as she was trying to learn English and was also concerned about her mother's heavy accent. She explained,

> *Like all immigrant children, I wanted to be as American as possible. I was conscious that our house was different, our furnishings were different, and we were different. I really would have liked to have been more "normal" or at least what I idealized as normal.*

Yet, she had confidence in herself in other ways. She said, "I think I had kind of a strong inner light, but I didn't have confidence to speak up." This inner light led her to feel the need for self-sufficiency in her own life. She watched her mother's lack of self-sufficiency and knew she had to do better. Because she was both an immigrant and a fatherless child, Madeleine felt that increasing her self-sufficiency would lessen the sting of feeling she was an outsider.

Madeleine described herself as a dreamer, in some respects. She had many dreams of what she wanted to do when she was older. She imagined herself doing something very important. For example, the family had a plot of land that her father had purchased in Israel. For a long time, she dreamed of going to Israel to start a wonderful school that would help many children. It was a school that could make a difference. She also dreamed of being a famous violinist for a few years during her teens.

As Madeleine became more comfortable with the English language and U.S. schools, she began to be competitive in school. However, this trait didn't emerge strongly until she was in high school. During these years, she remembers that she had a "strong desire to compete intellectually with others." Although she wasn't "the smartest," she was in the top group of academic students and describes herself as "very strong academically." She was also competitive with herself. She wanted to learn and do well in whatever she did. She felt driven to excel and achieve.

School and Activities

Madeleine remembers relocating and transferring to new schools a number of times as a child. She always loved learning and was very excited to start school. One of her first memories from Europe, before the move, was living in a small town outside of the Lucerne. She was supposed to go to kindergarten, and they didn't start kindergarten until a year later. She remembers being terribly upset because she desperately wanted to go to school and could not. She enjoyed grade school but has few memories of influences. She doesn't remember even playing with children during those early years, so she believes that she "must have just spent a lot of time" with her mother.

After moving to the United States, Madeleine remembers being involved in a number of activities during her childhood. She absolutely loved reading. In fact, she was often profoundly influenced by the stories she read, as "reading was a wonderful escape." There were no organized sports for girls at this time, but she does remember roller skating and playing sidewalk games. She also recalls being in a dramatic production. Although she was shy, she felt these activities where helpful for her in developing social and interpersonal skills.

Madeleine began being recognized by others for her academic strengths during high school. She went to two high schools, moving just before her junior year. Her first high school was a very strong academic high school, but the second was "academically disappointing." Academics were important to her. The move before her junior year was particularly challenging, as she had to "get used to a whole new set of students and learn to fit in again." At first it was hard, but then she made some very good friends. This gave her confidence that she could adjust to new experiences and surroundings. It provided practice for her to adapt and develop flexibility. She and five of her good friends were known to be more "intellectual" than the rest of the students, and they read books and met to discuss them. In fact, she remains in touch with some of these friends even today. Although this school "had a real hierarchy as to who was popular, like cheerleaders and the captain of the football team," she felt it was a good formative experience.

Madeleine spoke of two activities in which she participated during high school. First, she said she took violin lessons because she had read a book by Jean Porter, where the father of the main character had been a great violinist before he died. The main character had her father's violin, and when she picked it up, it magically played beautiful music. Madeleine said, "I had very romantic feelings about playing the violin. I thought I would be able to play it beautifully like the main character in this book. It didn't quite happen that way." She also wrote poetry and essays for a literary magazine in high school called the "Student Pen." She always enjoyed writing and believes this experience provided important developmental experience in strengthening her writing and articulation skills.

Influential Individuals

Unlike other governors, Madeleine didn't mention many influential individuals during her childhood and youth. Certainly her mother continued to be very influential, and her older brother, Edgar, was as well. He was the star in her family. He was very entrepreneurial, even in high school, selling magazines, delivering meat for the butcher, and so forth. Their mother was very proud of him. In fact, Madeleine never felt that she was expected by her mother to do great things because "that was her brother's job." Even without expectations, Madeleine said that she just "absorbed the ambition anyway." Edgar became one of her role models, and she wanted to be like him. She wanted to be independent and strong and "couldn't see why she couldn't do that."

Madeleine also mentioned being positively influenced by two friends and two teachers during high school. She had two particularly good friends, and they'd walk to school together, eat lunch at each other's houses, and spend a lot of time together studying, talking, socializing, and dreaming. She believes these friends helped her begin to "step outside her shell." They were honest with each other and provided candid and helpful feedback about many issues, concerns, and stresses. She also remembers being positively influenced by a history teacher and a French teacher. She was excited intellectually in their courses. She said she "enjoyed the courses, not necessarily their styles." Unfortunately, she missed the "good English teacher" and was put in the wrong class, which was a big mistake. Some of her friends were in the other English class, and this teacher helped them get major scholarships to private colleges.

College Plans

Madeleine didn't think much about pursing a college education until she was in high school. Because her mother and extended family members hadn't graduated from college, it wasn't a priority in her family. Her mother did not encourage her to go, yet she didn't discourage her either. She did know, however, that her mother didn't want to be left alone. Madeleine was the "daughter and the dutiful one," while her brother could go off and do what he wanted to do. Her high school teachers spoke to her of college and a few began encouraging her one-on-one to consider attending.

Madeleine did not know how she would ever get to college, as "there wasn't money for that." However, she did decide to go and resigned herself to commute to the inexpensive state teachers' college. Fortunately, she received a $100 scholarship from the Merchant's Association in Pittsfield, and it "opened up a new world of possibility." In fact, this was a turning point in her life. Although she still needed to work part time, the scholarship money was exactly enough to pay for tuition for one year at the University of Massachusetts. She also earned $800 the summer after high school as a waitress, so she could pay for her other school expenses. So instead of attending the teachers' college, she was able to attend a university. She noted how interesting it was that such small moments can change the course of lives.

COLLEGE YEARS

Madeleine believes that "probably the most important decision" she made was to go the University of Massachusetts. It was not only a better school, but she felt liberated. She loved her mother but needed to move away. In 1952, Madeleine moved into a dorm on the campus of the University of Massachusetts and instantly loved college. She consciously decided that she did not want to join a sorority. She would have been accepted into a Jewish sorority, but she didn't want to segregate herself. She said, "The whole idea of a sorority just didn't appeal to me. I was nineteen and decided it would confine and limit me. I wanted to find friends from different places." Her high school friends went to different colleges, so she went alone. However, she made many good friends during these years. When she started college, she still planned to be a teacher until she took her first education course, hated it, and knew she didn't want to teach as a career. She loved history and decided to major in it. She also had a passion for English and took various English courses as well. She also recalls taking one political science course that she found "somewhat interesting." She was a good student and believes she received a good college education.

Although the 1950s weren't highly political times on campuses, she did get interested in politics. Her mother continued to keep up with the issues and spoke to Madeleine by phone about what was happening around the country. In fact, her mother read Eleanor Roosevelt's column every day, and they'd talk about it often. Eleanor became an important role model in Madeleine's life through her mother.

It was during college that Madeleine blossomed and really started developing leadership and other important competencies through a variety of experiences and opportunities. She became very intellectually stimulated because of the teachers she had in courses she loved. She started speaking up and voicing her ideas and opinions. She explained that because students were "kind of unengaged during the 50s, if you became engaged at all the professors paid attention to you in class and gave you individual attention." She felt her professors, mostly men, were very good and encouraging. She enjoyed films and joined a film society. She was nominated to a women's honorary society and also recalls being a co-chair for an international weekend on campus where they invited dignitaries to come and talk about foreign affairs. During her childhood and youth, one of her weaknesses was speaking in public. She describes her feelings as she began conquering this fear:

By the time I was in college, though, I had begun to express myself by writing for the college newspaper. In my senior year, I became editorial-page editor. Rarely, however, did I have to face an audience. I ask myself what it was that enabled me to learn to speak in public. Speech is more than a tool of politics; it is essential to the political life. Without articulating a view of the world, political action is impossible. I had no choice: I had to learn how to project my inner self onto the public stage. The constriction in my throat that once silenced me is as difficult to diagnose as it is to say what cured me. Now that I look back at it, it was not skill that I lacked, but courage. Silence was safe. Speech was not. . . . I learned how to speak because, after a time, keeping silent became more disturbing than the fear of public exposure. I lost self-consciousness when I focused less on how I was saying something and more on what I was saying. As I learned to trust my beliefs, I learned to speak. I discovered courage because cowardice became unbearable. I could no longer bear the chastisement I inflicted on myself for not speaking the lines I had rehearsed. (Kunin, 1994, 62)

During her senior year, she was surprised to receive many student honors, including the "Woman of the Year" for her class. College in general was a "rich experience" for Madeleine and provided her many leadership developmental experiences.

Employment
Madeleine was employed as a waitress every summer before and during college, and said it was an important experience for her. Her mother gave $50 for her first year of college but, other than that, Madeleine had to earn her own way. As a waitress, she practiced multitasking and interpersonal skills, as she had to "be friendly toward and relate to these people in order to get a tip." She believes this job actually helped her become much more social and get over some of her shyness, and it put her in touch with working people. She believes this experience was important in helping her understand and empathize with other people.

Graduate School
During Madeleine's last few years of college, people (e.g., a German professor and a history professor) encouraged her to continue her education after she finished her undergraduate degree. Because of this encouragement, she explored opportunities for scholarships and graduate programs. After graduating with her bachelor's degree, Madeleine received a "wonderful open-ended scholarship from the Massachusetts Association of Women's Clubs for $1,000, which at that time was a lot of money." This made it possible for her to go to whichever graduate school she chose. She wanted to go to Europe to continue her studies, and one of her professors advised her to apply to the London School of Economics. However, because she was interested in journalism, her brother (a journalist who won a Pulitzer Prize later in life) advised her to go to the Columbia School of Journalism for a one-year journalism master's degree. Her mother desperately wanted her children to stay in the United States, so Madeleine decided to attend

Columbia. Interestingly, that same year her brother took off on a long tour of Europe.

The scholarship she received paid for her tuition at Colombia, and then she worked part time in New York as well. It was a wonderful year and very exciting. She enjoyed moving back to New York and saw it in an entirely different way. She doesn't remember specific professors as influential, but she enjoyed her coursework in general and was involved in typical campus and academic activities. Her journalism coursework provided her an opportunity to continue strengthening the communication skills she needed for future leadership.

EARLY EMPLOYMENT AND FAMILY

Finding a Job

After Madeleine finished her master's degree at Colombia, she knew that she wanted to be a journalist. Yet, because she was female she knew that finding a job would be difficult as her choices would be limited. She explained,

> I got an interview at the Washington Post and was so excited because I really wanted to work in Washington. After the interview, they called me back and said, "Are you still available for the job?" I told them I was. They said they were considering three people, and I was one of them. However, when they called back that afternoon, they told me they had decided to give the job to a man. I was mad, but I didn't say anything. I didn't know I could or should. Interesting, at our recent 45th Columbia reunion, a man came up to me and told me that he was the one who did that. That's just the way it was.

She also described an interview she had at the Providence Journal.

> I remember this like a scene from a movie. When I entered the editor's office for an interview, he was looking out the window at the parking lot. He glanced at me and said, "The last women we hired got raped in the parking lot." I knew instantly that he was telling me that he couldn't hire me. Although that's the way it was, I never forgot this experience.

In fact, these experiences became "pivotal moments" for some of her future leadership motivations and decisions. Madeleine did get a job offer at the Newark Evening News on the women's page, but she turned it down because she knew she didn't want to write about bridal veils and weddings.

Finally, Madeleine received a job offer she accepted. She secured an interview from the Burlington Free Press in Vermont. It was a small town newspaper, but her brother advised her to take it, and she did. She remembers taking a Greyhound bus to Vermont for the interview. Although Burlington was a lot less interesting then and was a totally different world from New York (which she loved), she decided that this position would give her some experience. She figured that after a year or so she would get a job at the New York Times and move back to New York.

Newspaper Journalist
Madeleine immediately began enjoying her work at the Burlington Free Press. She romantically envisioned herself making a wonderful difference.

> *Journalism promised to be the means of my transformation. The power of my words would propel me into an imagined life. With pencil and pad in hand, I could walk into any room as my brother did. Life would open up to me like a book resting on its spine. I imagined my byline, black and bold at the top of the story, a new medal earned each day.* (Kunin, 1994, 164)

When she started as a journalist in Burlington, she wasn't particularly interested in writing about politics. Another reporter covered the legislature and would engage in political conversation with his friend about what was going on, but Madeleine said she didn't find their conversations particularly interesting. She was assigned the school beat, so she covered local selectmen, city council meetings, and school board meetings; she also started a regular column about schools. She explained, "I liked covering community issues, and at that time, the legislature seemed too complicated." Yet to be successful as a journalist she had to learn a little about nearly everything. She said,

> *I learned how to plunge into new and unknown areas of knowledge. . . . The first meetings of the Winooski Board of Selectmen, which I covered as a twenty-three-year-old reporter . . . were conducted partly in French by Mayor Armand Rathe; but it was not much easier for me to follow the English-language version of these small-town political skirmishes. Only when I followed the selectmen into the diner across the street for late-night coffee did I begin to discern the battle lines of the debate and get the information I needed to write a story.* (Kunin, 1994, 70-71)

Madeleine believes that she learned a great deal from journalism that helped prepare her for political leadership. In fact, she believes these years provided the foundation of "a political education." She learned to understand the community by attending school board and selectmen's meetings. She learned about power and who had the right to exercise it. She said,

> *With pencil and pad in hand and a deadline to meet, I had to sort out the relevant facts and identify the key players, essential skills for a journalist and excellent training for a politician. No field of knowledge was off-limits. Everything had to be described and understood. Curiosity and the urge to satisfy it are the driving forces in both journalism and politics. One of the surprising rewards of political life is the intellectual pleasure one derives from discovering new ideas and information and from analyzing problems. . . . I learned not to be intimidated by expertise.* (Kunin, 1994, 71)

She also learned to "make a quick study of issues and problems to be able to size up the situation." As a journalist, she had to continually try to "get to the heart of the matter to actually write a story." She became skilled at gathering information, asking questions, and being put in different situations. She learned to look at both sides of issues objectively.

Marriage and Family

While writing for the Free Press, her husband-to-be was first intrigued by Madeleine's byline. He wondered what her real name was, not believing there could be a person named Madeleine May. They met at a dinner party, and then he asked her out when they bumped into each other a few days later. However, shortly after they met she had a chance to go to Europe for six months, which she took. In 1958, after working for only one year at the Free Press, she left and became a guide for the American Pavilion at the Brussels World's Fair. This was the opportunity to go to Europe that she had been looking for.

In 1959, six months after she returned from Brussels, Madeleine and Arthur were married and settled back in Vermont. At the age of twenty-five, she struggled with taking this traditional route, "possibly abandoning a part of her"; yet, she had wanted to be married and to be rooted in family and community. She said, "How to create separate and shared existences that encompassed two careers and one family was a question that few people then asked, and no one seemed to answer" (Kunin, 1994, 165). Yet, within the next eight years, she gave birth to four children: three sons and one daughter (Daniel, Adam, Peter, and Julia). For about ten years, she was primarily a homemaker engaged in volunteer community activities, except for two years when she was a part-time graduate student. She received a second master's, for pleasure, in English literature from the University of Vermont in 1967. Although she occasionally wrote for the newspaper, she was immersed in motherhood during these years. Madeleine was generally content and wove a life centered on the family. She bottled fruit and vegetables, watched her children play, sketched, read, and sewed. For intellectual diversion, she and her friends met at the League of Women Voters and gathered in one another's living rooms for a book club.

In 1964, they moved to Boston where her husband became a postdoctoral fellow at Harvard Medical School for two years. While he worked in the laboratory, Madeleine cared for their first child and anticipated the birth of their second. During this time, she decided to form a book club to give her and the other doctor's wives some social and intellectual stimulation, which "they badly needed as none of them worked outside the home." And in 1966 she and Arthur returned to Vermont.

In 1970, Arthur had an opportunity to take a sabbatical from the University of Vermont to go to Bern, Switzerland. Madeleine had just started teaching at Trinity, but with the exhaustion, a new baby, and the recent death of her mother, she was excited to return to Switzerland to be close to an aunt whom she loved. This year became the most family-focused year of her life and, because she could now see Europe with American eyes, she described it as having a profound impact on her political growth. This time allowed her time to read, think, and redefine herself. By the end of that year, she felt more independent. She began thinking about running for office when she returned to the United States, which she did a year later.

COMMUNITY INVOLVEMENT AND ACTIVISM

During the period of Madeleine's community and family involvement, she was unknowingly preparing for a political life. She said,

> *The difference between community activities and political action is merely one of scale. . . . When I was eventually elected to public office, I discovered that I was far better prepared than I had anticipated. I had underestimated the enormous amount I had learned in the community and was unaware of my ability to transfer my knowledge into public life.* (Kunin, 1994, 74)

Early in her marriage, she attended a New England regional meeting of the League of Women Voters and joined. She said, "In my era, this organization was a great political educator." Through the League, she started getting involved in community issues and volunteerism.

In 1961, when she was a newly married young doctor's wife, Madeleine remembers that there was a debate about the role of doctor's wives. Wives were expected to dedicate themselves to their husbands' careers. The Vermont Medical Society Auxiliary existed for that purpose. At that time, each state auxiliary was asked to hold neighborhood teas to lobby against legislative bills that were forerunners to Medicaid and Medicare. However, Madeleine actually supported the proposed legislation. She enlisted a group of her friends, also married to doctors, and formed an organization they called the Study Group for Medical Care for the Aged. She intended that the group would present both sides of the issue. They arranged a public forum on the issue with two well-known individuals, and she had her first encounter with the press when she did an interview with the local paper to publicize this forum. She had no idea that their sessions would cause the uproar it did among the other groups.

Soon after returning from Harvard in 1966, Madeleine started a volunteer organization to bring professional children's theater to the state. She wanted her three children, now one, three, and five years old, to have access to live music and theater.

She also became involved in an effort to stop the demolition of the beautiful Bishop of Burlington's house, as someone wanted to make a parking lot. She doesn't remember how she got involved to try to save it, but they didn't succeed. It didn't discourage her, however, as she became involved in other memorable efforts.

Madeleine's early community efforts provided opportunities for her to test herself in "small ways without fear of failure." She wanted to learn to speak more confidently in public. She felt she was in a "continuous state of becoming, which is where the real adventure is."

Concern for her children's safety enabled Madeleine to "span the distance between mother-wife and public person." This is how her political involvement actually began and then continued. She shared the following story:

When my children were young, there were no sidewalks in our neighborhood. I remember being so nervous when my daughter started kindergarten because she was not walking on a sidewalk and had to walk on the road or grass. Of course because of the snow she had to walk on the road during the winter. Cars would whiz by and almost touch her. I started campaigning to get sidewalks and actually found out a lot about how my neighbors loved their lawns. They didn't want to give up an inch for a sidewalk. I did a lot of work on this effort with petitions and so forth. I turned for help to our alderman who encouraged me to bring the question before the Board of Aldermen. I testified at the public hearings and worked with men who were very helpful. I didn't succeed in this effort, but it helped me learn about the process of community change. I also learned that it is hard to achieve change with divided forces. It also taught me that I could stand up and speak before an angry crowd, and that I could say what I believed.

Because of safety concerns, Madeleine and her husband moved the family to another home in Burlington but soon there was another issue that needed to be addressed. Her children had to cross unmarked railroad tracks on their way to school every day, and there were no warning lights. Again, she was worried about their safety. She explained,

After raising the question with my neighbors, I discovered that a number of parents agreed . . . in the laboratory of my neighborhood, I learned that defining the problem was the first and most important step. I didn't have to know all the answers in order to begin. There are advantages to being a political newcomer. . . . I got a petition from my neighbors, and I had to appear before a public service board. As a newcomer, I was unfamiliar with the obstacles and refused to take no for an answer. I gathered facts and rounded up neighbors to come with me to the hearing. This effort taught me how to do these things, and I was successful! After two failed attempts at leading change in the community, this success was very important to me. For the first time, I became aware of my potential political effectiveness. In fact, it was life changing. The ability to build an arc between my maternal role and a public one was an essential part of my political development. Not only did it give me a sense of purpose, but it gave me permission. The next fall I ran for the legislature. (Kunin, 1994, 79, 82, 83; also portions of the interview were incorporated into this quotation)

Madeleine developed a belief that a single individual could have an affect on an entire political system. The experience made her believe that she "could change the world" and step over the line from "private citizen to public advocate." She vowed to pay attention to everything that was going on in the city and in the state and knew that she was no longer the same person. By this time, she was the mother of four children, and her husband was an assistant professor of medicine at the University of Vermont

Because of her previous success, she became increasingly proactive in her involvement in the community and political advocacy. For example, she recruited four or five neighbors to come with her to the local Democratic caucus, where she made a short speech pointing out that there had never been a woman elected to the Burlington Board of Aldermen. She also joined the Women's Political Caucus in Vermont and later developed Lilliput Children's Programs where she learned how to build an organization, a skill easily transferred to politics. When she learned how to "meld information with conviction and emotion," she discovered her "true public voice." Because she was a volunteer, she could proceed as she wanted, "unintimidated by rules or experts." She said,

> *This is why volunteer activities can foster enormous leadership skills. The nonprofessional volunteer world is a laboratory of self-realization. . . . There is a tendency to dismiss the value of such work done for no pay, something voluntary, squeezed between routine obligations. . . . But those years, I see now, offered a time of leisurely exploration. I could devote time to different projects without having to decide my life's work.* (Kunin, 1994, 78)

When Madeleine didn't know how to do something, she asked for help or advice. When one course of action did not work, she tried another. All of these experiences increased her desire to become involved in the political process and were also helpful in developing leadership.

CAREER

Writing and Teaching
After she started having her children, Madeleine continued her career in journalism by occasionally writing for the local newspaper. This helped her continue to keep abreast of some of the local issues of the day. Later, after her fourth child was born, she also started to teach at a local college. She explained,

> *I accepted a job in 1969 at Trinity College in Burlington, to be a part-time instructor in freshman English. . . . Teaching taught me to clarify my ideas, a helpful prerequisite for politics. Through teaching, I also discovered the excitement that comes from connecting with an audience.* (Kunin, 1994, 65)

She was supposed to be part time but had three classes of fifty students each, so it ended up being very full time and very exhausting for her. She felt that teaching provided her the opportunity to become more comfortable speaking in front of an audience and gave her initial practice in responding publicly to questions.

House of Representatives
At this time, the women's movement and the environmental movements were

becoming important issues in the State of Vermont and in the nation. Madeleine started feeling a responsibility to speak out on these issues because she believed they were important. During this time, there was a women's political caucus formed in Vermont with the specific purpose of encouraging women to run for office. So, Madeleine decided to do just that. She had the support of the women's caucus, and she notes that it was helpful that there were already women in the legislature at that time. At the age of thirty-nine, Madeleine was elected to the Vermont House of Representatives. She immediately loved it.

One of the first lessons she learned while serving in the legislature was that lots of people "run around thrilled to be elected, but there are only a dozen people who really run the show." Right off she decided that it was going to be important for her to be in a leadership position because she wanted to influence policy. She also learned early that it would be important for her to be on the Appropriations Committee. She wanted to make an impact and was able to move into these leadership roles after her first term.

Democratic Whip and Appropriations
Madeleine ran for Democratic whip her second term and defeated an incumbent. She was the first women in Vermont to hold a leadership position in the legislature. This position taught her how to function in a legislative leadership position. She also spoke of how she obtained her seat on the Appropriations Committee and continued her effectiveness,

> *I was now the Democratic whip and there was also a Democratic Speaker for the first time in the House. As a result, I was able to get appointed to be on the Appropriations Committee. I spoke very carefully during these years, and I didn't speak on every issue. I think I became recognized as somebody who could "do things." I did my homework on a lot of issues and became very engaged in the process. There was a lot to learn, particularly about process. Yet, I absolutely loved learning new ideas, concepts, and processes. I was very excited about it, but I must admit that it was totally exhausting.*

She established her place as an important member of the Appropriations Committee, although at first, she felt inadequate, as math was her weakest subject in school. However, after only a month she had learned to "read budget numbers like words and find meaning between the lines." She learned to compare one budget with another, one year with the next, and to look for trends and aberrations.

During her third term, Madeleine became the chair of the Appropriations Committee, which was very important preparation for governorship. She said that it equipped her to be governor because it helped her become very knowledgeable in critical areas. She received "an advanced degree in government from that position," learning how to keep a statewide perspective and gain an overview of state government in general. She learned that no matter how skillful she became, she could never avoid controversy. Interestingly, as the chair of the Appropriations Committee she had to argue from time to time with the governor about the appropriation bill. In 1977, after one of these sessions, she realized that she knew as much as he did and decided she could run for governor. She had learned what she could from the legislature and was ready to run for a higher office.

Lieutenant Governor
Madeleine decided to run for lieutenant governor of Vermont and was elected and served for two terms, four years. She believes that it was necessary to serve in this position so she could get recognition through a statewide campaign. In Vermont, the governor and lieutenant governor run on separate tickets. She was a Democratic lieutenant governor serving with a Republican governor. As expected, the job was frustrating in many ways because she didn't have the power or influence she desired. The governor wouldn't give her more responsibility because he felt threatened. Even with these challenges, she said it was a very good learning experience. During her last term as lieutenant governor, a variety of people gave her encouragement to run for governor.

Governorship
Madeleine had already had experience with campaigning, but this time she learned more about fundraising. She had always struggled with asking people for money, but now she learned to do "fund-raising without blushing." She learned to separate her campaign from herself. She won the governor's race and became governor of Vermont in 1985. She spoke of how much she enjoyed the experience of serving in this position and also how much she learned from the opportunities and challenges it created.

INFLUENCES AND OBSTACLES

Madeleine spoke of a number of career and family influences, challenges, and obstacles that were helpful in her development of leadership. These include balancing work and family, support systems, gender, training and development, influential individuals, motherhood, and internal challenges.

Balancing Work and Family
Madeleine said that those who are looking for the formula to combine marriage and career would be disappointed by this statement:

> *I have no expert advice. Each day we reinvented our lives together and apart as we moved into different stages of marriage, children, careers, and children growing up. Sometimes we happily succeeded; at other times, we painfully failed, and then our lives would diverge, creating a frightening chasm between us that politics widened as it scourged our separate sides. During long periods, we were uncertain of the right course, prompting us to look for new ways of accommodation, again and again.* (Kunin, 1994, 166)

Madeleine believes that "some sense of conflict remains for every woman who has obligations outside of the home." She acknowledged her conflict openly by relating it to the experience of all working women. She explained,

> *Successful women were expected to work out the conflicts between home and work completely, in their own way and on their own time. Only by preparing the next day's dinner at midnight, if need be, did we believe we could obtain permission to lead our daytime professional lives. If we failed, that was our fault. I accepted that bargain without questioning. Later, I had to learn to change, to allow my husband to take over more of the mothering role, which in time [when the children were in high school and college] he did. I had to take the risk of being called a bad mother, and he risked becoming a new kind of father, who cared for the daily needs of his children.* (Kunin, 1994, 260)

Support Systems
Madeleine said she was able to meet the demands of multiple roles by having a spouse who supported her financially, emotionally, and physically. She said,

> *What I gladly share is that my husband was unusually giving of his support to my career. Few other men could have been as generous as Arthur was, not only in rearranging his own life to ease mine, but in taking genuine pride and pleasure in my achievements. . . . He let me run, not by granting his approval, but by giving me courage when I grew afraid, by urging me forward when I wanted to retreat, by cheering my victories and mourning my defeats, and by doing all the small things that made it possible for me to create a political life. His largest gift was his inner strength, which allowed him to be the companion of a strong woman.* (Kunin, 1994, 166)

She admitted that she couldn't have been involved in politics if her husband hadn't been supportive. In fact, she stated, "I probably couldn't have done it without a husband to support me. That's the irony of it!"

Her children were also supportive and patient with her pursuits. Their networks became her support network as they got older. When she was a legislator, she termed herself as a part-time mother. She had lots of responsibilities and felt that "getting good help" was particularly helpful. She said, "I was fortunate we could afford to get help." She had a wonderful woman who babysat her children when they were young. Madeleine said, "I couldn't have done things without her." She also had some housekeeping help, which was important.

Overall, she found that trying to be a "good" mother and having a political career was very challenging. She said,

> *I went through a lot of times of doubt, conflict, and guilt through the years. I guess the bottom line is that I think I would have been worse off if I hadn't had a career. I needed it in my life. In fact, I think in the long run I was a better mother for having gone in this direction. I love being a mother and grandmother. I loved having babies, but it wasn't enough for me.*

Gender

When I asked Madeleine if she thought things would have been different in her political career if she would have been a man, she said "Yes." However, she enjoyed the challenge and motivation of being a "path finder, path breaker or whatever it is called!" She felt a thrill in being in unknown territory for herself and other women. Being a pathfinder both took courage and inspiration and also gave it to others. She believes that woman in leadership today are still watched more carefully and evaluated differently by both men and women. She also felt that it was harder to get elected as a woman, and it was harder to govern in some ways. Yet, she said she didn't feel discrimination:

> *I don't feel I was discriminated against as a woman at all. I was treated equally in the political game. Of course, you have to learn not to be too ladylike. You have to appear like a lady, but you've got to fight like a man. "Worse than a man," Arthur said, but I don't think there could be much worse.* (Kunin, 1994, 59)

A few times she felt herself slip into the trap of victimization, which she worked very hard to avoid. She had to quickly evaluate herself and her actions. She said, "Gender in politics counts for everything and nothing all at the same time." As a woman, she continued to feel the need to prove—to herself and others—that she was qualified to hold the positions she did.

As the governor, Madeleine said that although she functioned as any other governor, she felt gender made her different from the start although the "differences faded somewhat." She said, "It was impossible to draw a line between my womanhood and other inherited characteristics. Being a woman was a part of my being, but it was difficult to say which part" (Kunin, 1994, 352). She explained that most gender generalizations are "inevitably flawed," because (like all generalities) specific experiences will frequently contradict them.

Training and Development

Madeleine recalled going to conferences that were very energizing after she became involved in political leadership. She remembers attending national conferences—like international women's year conferences and women's political conferences—that were very motivating and exciting experiences. She belonged to groups like the Women's Campaign Fund, which taught her more about a variety of topics around politics and leadership. In fact, this organization sent her a consultant when she ran for lieutenant governor, and she felt he was helpful. Madeleine spoke more about women-only training or groups than those offered with mixed genders. She believes that women still need more encouragement than do men. She thinks that the bonds in these women-only groups are very powerful and can be particularly motivating. However, she does believe that leadership training programs should be a combination of both mixed-gender and women-only trainings, and acknowledges that both can be helpful.

Influential Individuals

Madeleine said that she was positively influenced during her adulthood by many individuals. Although she didn't have a formal mentor, she said that the closest she came to having one was in the legislature. It was an unlikely person—a Republican who chaired the Appropriations Committee. She had been appointed to a seat on the Appropriations Committee, and this man had a lot of confidence in her. He was influential because he respected her and showed that he trusted her by giving her responsibility. He, as a Republican, ended up recommending her—even though her own party was more apprehensive—to be chair of the Appropriations Committee when he completed his term. This man could see that she had strong leadership and political skills. She said, "I supported him, and he supported me. I was a loyal member of the committee too. I respected him even though our views on a lot of things were different. So we had a very good relationship. That was important."

Madeleine spoke of female role models in the Vermont legislature. One woman, Esther Sorell, cheered Madeleine by her encouragement. Esther was a great teacher and understood politics well. She taught Madeleine how to love politics and had unshakeable faith in the system. Esther gave her the courage to plunge ahead. She mentioned three other women who were also supportive and influential. She was able to watch these women who had more experience in politics. Other politicians and community members provided important support through giving Madeleine opportunities and encouragement. Although they weren't mentors, knowing others respected and trusted her was important in her personal and professional development. In fact, she said that many individuals were influential in her life because of this.

Madeleine's mother and brother also remained important influences in her life throughout the years. In fact, her brother also became a politician later in life, and she always valued his opinions and counsel.

Motherhood

Madeleine believes that she learned a number of skills through motherhood that were helpful in developing leadership. In fact, sometimes she jokes and says, "Anyone who has had children and settled arguments around the dinner table knows a great deal about negotiation and mediation." She also said that motherhood pushes one to continuously learn and look for new solutions and creative ideas. Because her children had so many connections to the community, Madeleine also developed and strengthened these connections. She also learned more patience and humility as a mother. She noted that the best legislators must have humility and patience to be effective. She explained,

> *While I may have longed for the peace and quiet of uninterrupted professional life, those split-screen years were important . . . motherly skills I learned at home have extraordinary public usefulness. Counting out strawberries one by one to make certain that exactly the same number of strawberries went into each child's dessert dish taught me how much people care about fairness and*

how to mediate an argument. Cleaning up the third glass of spilled milk in the course of one meal taught me a great deal about the art of self-control. And where better to learn patience than watching a child learn to tie his shoe? (Kunin, 1994, 78)

She also learned multitasking, as she spent many hours talking on the telephone and cooking or baking in her kitchen. She said she perfected the skills of cleaning the kitchen and caring for her children while, at the same time, talking on the phone and sounding as if she was in a "navy-blue suit behind a polished desk." She spoke of how valuable the multitasking skill is as a governor. A governor must have a quick pace for everything and move from issue to issue very rapidly.

Internal Challenges

Madeleine also believes that a variety of challenges, including many already discussed, have been important in developing political leadership skills. However, she stated that her internal struggles were often the most important challenges or barriers she had to overcome. She believes her greatest challenge was that of fear and self-doubt, but through practice, she gained the capacity to keep them under control. Each time she had a successful experience she felt a sense of accomplishment. At times, she had the "most chronic symptom of female insecurity: feeling like a fraud" (Kunin, 1994, 11), which she worked to confront. Overcoming this gave her more strength and stability. Another challenge she had to overcome was finding a connection between her inner life and outer persona. She noted, "One adds intensity to the other and keeps them both at a highly synchronized pitch" (Kunin, 1994, 29). She understood earlier in her life that she needed to have a sense of courage, and she did. Courage was essential, as "It was an inner fire that had warmed and comforted me whenever I felt besieged and isolated in public."

A final challenge Madeleine spoke of was her internal drive. This drive is similar to many women who also have deep desires to achieve, accomplish, and make a difference somehow and somewhere—and then chose to have children and stay home for at least part of their lives. The following quotation summarizes Madeleine's feelings (and possibly those of other driven women) as she felt blessed and sometimes cursed with these drives and ambitions:

This is the drive I never understood; why could I not be content, as most people seemed to be, with a smaller circumference to my life? At times, I envied people whose lives were more self-contained, who did not need outside approval to affirm their personal validity. From this perspective, those of us who lived public lives were not more courageous, only more fearful of confronting ourselves, turning to others for confirmation of who we are. This assurance and reassurance becomes increasingly necessary, because a public figure is constantly in a state of becoming, learning to play new roles on strange turf, needing feedback in order to stay on course. The process of self-invention is creative but also dangerous. Mistakes are made. Then delight of new discovery gets the upper hand and sets caution aside once again. *This cycle of risk taking, followed by fear, followed by euphoria, followed by new risk taking, must be akin to what a gambler experiences each time she rolls the dice. There was a part of me that thrilled to the game, but another part felt trapped by the addiction.* (Kunin, 1994, 31)

LEADERSHIP MOTIVATION, STYLE, AND PHILOSOPHY

Motivation

Madeleine's true motivation for leadership through the years has been to make a difference. In fact, her children tease her saying she should start the "I made a difference" museum. Other motivations include her desire for "accomplishing things" and her "thrive for achievement." She also believes that change is good for society and has always desired to be part of it. She said, "I guess I'm restless with the state of the world, and I can't simply accept the status quo!" For many years, Madeleine said that, although she could not bring herself to acknowledge it, another motivation for leadership was the need for power. She said, "It was not a desire I could articulate even to myself." As an adult, she said she has always been ambitious and probably wanted some kind of "power" even though she termed it as "wanting to have an impact, get something done, or carry out my new responsibilities as effectively as possible."

Style

Madeleine described her leadership style and philosophy through the eyes of her former staff. She was known for her "consensus-oriented" style. She asked for a lot of input from her staff and wanted to create a collegial environment. Sometimes she would lead staff and leadership retreats with a pretty ambitious agenda so they could learn, plan, and strategize. She wanted to carefully plan and accomplish things that could help the communities and state. She has strong self-monitoring skills, important for both men and women, which allowed her to continually learn and improve how she acted and reacted. She liked to think ahead on issues and determined beforehand how much to initiate and then how to react. She tried very hard to step back and put things into perspective giving her a reflective leadership style as well. When in office, she consciously reflected on what had happened and what needed to occur on various issues. Interestingly, this reflective ability was useful in helping her learn to take criticism, benefit from her own mistakes, and take and give effective feedback. Madeleine believes that it is critical that women learn to take criticism well. Although never pleasant, no individual will become a good governor or leader unless he or she learns to do this and develop thick skin. Madeleine spoke briefly of criticism,

> *The hardest part was feeling like I was misunderstood or that my motives were questioned when they were really straightforward. The only thing that helps is that you have to move on. You can't brood about things because there is always something ahead. It's hard, but you just keep moving. I don't think women are*

as armored as men are, even still. We still have thinner skins. For some reason, we are still more vulnerable. The press was tough sometimes. I do think the criticism is the hardest thing about having a public life.

She said that her staff would also describe her style as having a "toughness" element. Madeleine said, "Women have always been carefully examined for their ability to be tough. 'Is she tough enough?' is always the subtext in an executive position." Part of her toughness may have been developed through her innate competitiveness. Madeleine believes she has always been competitive in some ways. She said, "I think you have to be competitive to run for office. If you run, then you typically don't want to lose, so you become focused and work very hard to win."

Philosophy

Madeleine's primary leadership philosophy is based around the importance of finding and hiring competent individuals who cared about the work, shared her vision, and were loyal. She said that she probably appointed and hired differently than a man would have in the same positions. She expected that women's resumes would be interrupted and unique; yet, this difference doesn't mean that they were unqualified. She felt it was important to appoint and employ women, and the women she hired were very qualified—"just in a different way." For example, she appointed a woman to be head of the Forest, Parks, and Recreation Department. This individual had a degree from UVM in forestry, but she didn't have management experience. The previous director had actually recommended her, and Madeleine took a risk in appointing her. She turned out to be excellent and ended up later working in the Clinton administration as head of Fish and Wildlife. Madeleine said that ninety-eight percent of all her appointments were very good.

Madeleine also has a philosophy that developing others is a critical role of leaders. She believed that it is "important to nurture and support others in their positions." In fact, she has served as a mentor to many through the years, and said, "Mentoring has been a very important in my life." She went out of her way to provide opportunities for others, women particularly, such as "going back to school, supporting their decisions, boosting them up, and encouraging them."

ADVICE

Madeleine has some important pieces of advice for young women who are interested in becoming political leaders. She currently teaches a political science course at the University of Vermont and gives the following advice to her students:

Dream big and envision yourself doing something that you really want to do. Envision the changes you would like to create. It is better to live an engaged life than a passive life. You probably have more leadership skills than you think you have, and you can learn the others. Read the paper, watch the news, and stay informed.

Madeleine believes that young women today need assurance that they can achieve something—"that the system isn't as rigged, corrupt, or as hopeless as it is seems to be." They need models of success that they can pattern themselves after. She advised,

Take the risk, but start locally and start slowly. Public and community service can be a good start, but women need to think beyond that to understanding the deeper issues: Why am I helping the homeless? Why are they homeless? What social and political policies have created this situation? Women need to be able to understand the root causes. They need to think of themselves as having power as individuals or working in groups. Women can in fact have an impact. They need to believe this.

Finally, Madeleine felt that all of her work experiences—paid and unpaid—were "critical" in her development. All of her volunteer and community activities were important. Each provided her with a new perspective and new experiences. She suggests that women participate in these types of activities and remember they can develop strong leadership from everything.

FINAL THOUGHTS

Even in her 70s, Madeleine works to make a difference and enjoys community involvement. She has no interest in running for office again, but remembers well her love for and the excitement of politics—"the drama, the theater, the people you meet, the diversity, the slices of life you in encounter." She remembers how much she loved going through factories, shaking grimy hands, and trying to connect to people who were very different from herself. She said,

One reason I love politics is that the political life is so rich in experience and emotion. Like art, political action gives shape and expression to the things we fear as well as to those we desire. It is a creative process, drawing on the power to imagine as well as to act. The driving force is a vision of an ideal. . . . As governor, I had the incredible luxury of being able to dream on a grand scale. And this sense of infinite possibility gives politics its romance. (Kunin, 1994, 266, 12)

As she looks back on her life, she truly believes that all the work and experience she had throughout her lifetime helped prepare her for a successful life in politics. As a child, she learned that "anything was possible in America" and that she needed to do something with her life that mattered. She feels peace in knowing that she has done just that.

Chapter Eight

Governor Martha Layne Collins

The first philosophy my parents taught me is that I was put on the earth to make a contribution, and I'd better have an answer for my time here on earth. This makes me want to accomplish a lot and do it quickly. The second one is that I always need to do the best I can in whatever I do.

~ Governor Martha Layne Collins

I interviewed Governor Martha Layne Collins in Lexington, Kentucky on March 23, 2006. Martha Layne was elected in 1983 as the first woman governor of Kentucky and served a four-year term from 1984 to 1988. She is known for her achievements in education reform and economic development. Before being elected as governor, she served as lieutenant governor from 1979 to 1983, chair of the Democratic National Convention in 1984, and Supreme Court clerk from 1975 to 1979. Prior to this, Martha Layne was a junior high and high school teacher until 1970 and assumed the role as coordinator of women's activities in a number of political campaigns, which ultimately lead her into public office. The purpose of my interview was to discuss how she developed the knowledge, skills, and abilities throughout her life to become the leader she became. Hence, this chapter will share many of her thoughts and experiences related to her lifetime of developing leadership. Although the majority of this chapter was written from information obtained in the interview, a few stories from the book *The Little Girl Who Grew Up to Be Governor: Stories from the Life of Martha Layne Collins* (Smith, 1991) were also included with permission.

FAMILY BACKGROUND

Martha Layne Hall was born on December 7, 1936, in Shelby County, Kentucky to Mary and Everett Hall. She was raised in a middle-income family with a strong work ethic and commitment to family, church, and community. She was an only child and explained, "My mother had raised a lot of her own siblings, and so one child was enough for her." Martha Layne lived in the small town of Bagdad, Kentucky until she was in junior high when her family moved to nearby

Shelbyville. She said, "I was the hick. I was the country bumpkin who had come to town." She believes that growing up in a small town helped her learn a lot about leadership. Since Bagdad was a town of only 250 people, everyone knew each other, and they also looked after one another. She remembers having many good neighbors and friends who taught her in various roles and settings throughout the years. She also remembers being taught two primary philosophies as a child. She said,

> *The first philosophy my parents taught me is that I was put on the earth to make a contribution and I'd better have an answer for my time here on earth. This makes me want to accomplish a lot and do it quickly. The second one is that I always need to do the best I can in whatever I do.*

These philosophies have guided many of her behaviors and choices through the years.

Mother

Martha Layne's mother, Mary, was the third of ten children and was raised in a rural area of Kentucky. Although she desired a college education, she did not have the opportunity. After her two older siblings went to college, her father died, and she was left to help her mother raise the other children. Mary had a heavy load. She became the disciplinarian in her home, and that role continued in her own home with Martha Layne. Interestingly, when Martha Layne was born, her mother's youngest sibling was eleven, and her aunt was more like an older sister for many years.

Martha Layne's parents met when her father was the principal and the women's basketball coach and her mother played on his basketball team. After they married, Mary and Everett became very active in church-related activities and continued this heavy involvement throughout their lives. Martha Layne remembers her mother taking her to church as a very young child. She remembers going with her mother to women's groups that studied the lives of missionaries. She said,

> *At an early age, I got to know about the world and different countries through going to church with my mother and listening to the women study missionaries. I now believe that this is one of the reasons that I always liked international relations. I've always enjoyed learning about the cultures. Although I was in a small town, I was introduced to larger issues and perspectives.*

Although Mary was a stay-at-home mother, Martha Layne also remembers her mother always being "at task and busy." The house had to be cleaned, and Martha Layne couldn't bring friends home very often. She remembers her mother being a "no nonsense kind of person who liked her surroundings orderly and controlled."

Father

Martha Layne's father, Everett, grew up in the Lexington area and was one of five children. They owned a grocery store so his family had more financially than did her mother's family. Unlike Mary, Everett did have the opportunity to attend and eventually graduate from college. He majored in education, but also planned to become a funeral director. Everett enjoyed helping people and felt he could do so in both occupations. Therefore, Martha Layne grew up in the funeral business. Yet, Everett also became a teacher and a principal. She also remembers that her father ran his own ambulance service in town. She explained,

> *My life was one of twenty-four hours a day seven days a week in the ambulance service. We had calls in the middle of the night. It made an impression on me because I grew up in a service-oriented family, and so for that reason, I've done service-type work all my life.*

Martha Layne described her father as a "tall fellow of about six foot six inches and over 200 pounds" and a "very likeable man." In fact, when he died, many people said things like "Your daddy told me that I shouldn't marry this guy, and I should have listened to him." She said, "Many years ago my father was one who started telling girls that they could do whatever they wanted to do. He told them that they needed to get an education and do something with their lives. He was a little ahead of his time." Everett was very active in industrial and economic development in Shelby County, and Martha Layne remembers him chairing a committee on improving the quality of life for others in the county. He was always progressive in looking at issues and situations and was not afraid of change. He was never set in his ways, and she always respected and valued that trait.

Extended Family

Martha Layne doesn't remember being particularly close to her grandparents. Her maternal grandmother worked a lot and had many children and grandchildren. Although she lived in the same town, Martha Layne didn't see her very often. She remembers visiting her paternal grandparents in Lexington from time to time but doesn't remember them being particularly influential. She does remember many family gatherings with her mother's brothers and sisters and their children. She said that one of her uncles and a few aunts were somewhat influential in her life. She explained,

> *I remember one aunt and uncle who lived on a farm in Bagdad. I got a calf, and my uncle took me to the fair to show the calf at a 4H event. They had one daughter who was about nine years younger than I was. I also had an aunt—that was kind of a favorite in a way—who was the youngest of my mother's siblings. I loved her personality, I guess. I remember her "drive," her "get up and go," and her travels. I admired who she was and what she did. She was always dressed great. I remember that she was pregnant at the same time I was with*

my first child. I know she didn't tell anybody at first because she didn't want to take away from me. I admired her thoughtfulness.

CHILDHOOD AND YOUTH

Personality

When describing her own personality as a child and adolescent, Martha Layne said that she always loved achievement and was very accomplishment-oriented. In fact, she has always had strong accomplishment and achievement needs throughout her life. She recalls always feeling driven to make a difference and to achieve certain goals and objectives even while young. Martha Layne was also competitive during her upbringing. She explained, "I love competition. I've just always wanted to win." Martha Layne said that she has always been her "own worst critic." She was tough on herself when she knew she could do something, and she has always been competitive with herself in many respects. In fact, Martha Layne said that she has continued to be tough on herself throughout her life and her employees would attest to that. She believes this helped her staff understand that when she was tough on them, she was actually helping them improve themselves. Martha Layne was a pretty observant youth and enjoyed studying people. Yet, when I asked her if she was reflective she said,

> *I've never done a whole lot of that. I'm more of a fast-paced person because it was part of growing up in the funeral business and with an ambulance service. You're always on call. I'm more of a visionary. When making a decision, I try to think of what it's going to do five years or ten years from now and how it's going to impact a larger number of people. I have very poor recall.*

Martha Layne's stories and experiences also demonstrate a tendency toward problem solving. She also seemed to thrive on learning new concepts and skills and found learning rewarding. In fact, she sought new activities and experiences particularly so that she could learn from them. She also had a deep desire to be helpful and was generally obedient and respectful. She enjoyed working hard and having interesting challenges. She remembers many incidences where she was nervous or scared to do something new but had the courage she needed to learn and expand her skills.

Martha Layne remembers always enjoying interacting with people of all ages and situations. For example, as a child she remembers watching her elderly neighbors and understanding that they were lonely. She used to visit them, and they would give her coffee, "which was actually more cream than coffee." She also remembers intentionally waiting in her front yard to say "good morning" to another elderly man who she thought needed to have interactions with others. As a youth, she remembers enjoying interactions with adults, peers, and children. She remembers always being interested in helping others develop themselves. Martha Layne's love of people has continued throughout her life.

Influential Individuals
Outside her parents and extended family, Martha Layne doesn't remember many influential individuals during her childhood or youth but did briefly mention three. The first was a woman named Sally who was a "big influence" in her life. Sally was Martha Layne's Sunday School teacher and had no children of her own. She would sometimes take Martha Layne home with her after church, which Martha Layne believes caused a little jealousy in her own mother. Yet, Martha Layne's parents and Sally and her husband would double date all of the time and were close friends. Martha Layne was close to Sally all through her childhood and remembers making popcorn balls and candy with her. Because her own mother raised her younger siblings and was the disciplinarian, she used the same firm parenting style with Martha Layne. Sally was important in helping Martha Layne feel loved in a soft and gentle way. Sally was the one who would find time to read books and listen to her.

The second and third influential individuals were both public school teachers. Martha Layne started first grade in Bagdad with a teacher named Mrs. Francis who she recalls being the "sweetest woman in the world." Mrs. Francis cared about her students and was a strong educator. In fact, when Martha Layne was campaigning for governor years later, Mrs. Francis would sometimes make appearances with her to help demonstrate the importance of a teacher in a child's life. Martha Layne also mentioned a high school algebra teacher who was particularly influential in a unique way. She loved math and really learned in his class. She said,

> *He was very critical and sarcastic. He was one of those who made you feel small. Yet, I worked really hard in his class. His approach worked well on me. It was a positive experience because it was a challenge. He pushed us and challenged us. We all worked hard to make him happy.*

In addition to being her math teacher, he was also the basketball coach. Because she was a high school cheerleader, she was in contact with him and enjoyed interacting occasionally with him one-on-one. His personality and teaching style somehow challenged her to stretch herself by learning and seeking to improve herself.

School and Activities
Martha Layne remembers that she and her parents spent most of their time during her childhood at church. She said, "Whenever the church doors were open we were usually there." She also grew up with a deep love for reading. She recalls that she wanted to be a teacher even when she was young. She said,

> *Before I could even read, I would get a book off my mother's bookcase, and I would pretend I was reading to students sitting on the steps in my house. I spent hours doing this. I liked to read. I read the Bobbsey twins and those kinds of books. I read quite a bit.*

Although she doesn't recall participating in very many organized activities as a child, she does remember how much she enjoyed being in the outdoors, playing outside, digging in the dirt, and spending time with neighborhood friends. She also recalls going to Sally's home often to feed hens and remembers being "sent to the garden to get green beans for lunch." Sally lived on a farm, and Martha Layne "loved everything about the farm." She rode on the tractor and hay wagon, helped Sally take food to the men working in the fields, played in the piles of straw, and watched the farm animals. She remembers helping with calves, although it made her nervous. She even had some regular chores on the farm. She believes that these early farm experiences taught her courage, risk taking, and other leadership lessons. For example, farm experiences taught her for the first time that some jobs and tasks require groups and teams of people to make them work successfully. In fact, Martha Layne believes that practically everything she participated in during her upbringing—including piano, dancing, and swimming—helped her prepare in some way for leadership.

Martha Layne has vivid memories of her first year in school. She enjoyed her first-grade teacher and loved school the first half of the year. However, during the second semester she had to go to a school in Shelbyville (twelve miles from Bagdad) and had a tough teacher. The teacher often got irritated at her, as she was often late to school because her mother was not a morning person. She also admitted that she "sometimes talked at inappropriate times," which the teacher did not appreciate. The other children had already developed their groups of friends, so Martha Layne had a bad attitude and didn't have a good experience the rest of that school year. Her parents allowed her to return to the Bagdad grade school during her second grade year, and she stayed in that school through sixth grade.

Although Martha Layne doesn't remember her parents being particularly involved in politics, she does remember one childhood experience that became memorable and somehow inspired her to begin becoming at least generally aware of politics and related issues. She explained,

> *When I was eleven years old, my father took me out of school to see the President of the United States. President Truman was arriving by train, and I remember getting to the railroad station in Shelbyville and seeing many people already gathered. When Truman arrived, I remember looking around and seeing people so excited to see him. I remember listening to his speech and then hearing people clap and cheer. I loved the anticipation and excitement of that experience.*

In fact, Martha Layne was deeply moved by this experience and remembers thinking how wonderful it would be to be a political leader that people would enjoy seeing and listening to.

Martha Layne lived in Bagdad until she was in junior high when she and her parents moved to the nearby but much larger town of Shelbyville (around 10,000 people). She remembers that move being particularly difficult as she was the "hick" and the other youth didn't accept her at first. This was difficult for her because she yearned to be involved and serve in leadership positions, but many of these jobs were peer-elected positions. For example, although she wanted to be a class officer, she ended up in positions, such as the publicity committee, clean-up committee, or stagehand. She always had jobs but not necessarily the ones she wanted. She remembers going home devastated one time and explained,

> I came home one time in tears because I didn't win an election. My mother said, "Martha Layne, if you do the best you can at this job, then next time you'll get a better job." Although I didn't see many results from her advice for awhile, I did finally get the female lead in the class play my senior year. Although I wasn't always certain about this advice growing up, I now give this same advice to young women today and believe it is true.

Not getting the positions she wanted became somewhat frustrating for a time, although she does believe now that it did help her learn more about change and understanding the perspectives of others when they are in new settings and surroundings. Even with the relocation struggles, Shelbyville was a larger town and offered more opportunities for her during her adolescent years.

After she transitioned to Shelbyville and made new friends, she quickly became involved in many activities. She continued her heavy involvement in church during these years and recalls being involved in many goal-setting programs like memorizing scriptures and other tasks that could help her "earn the top step in the program." She was always willing to help at church when she was asked and would even volunteer for assignments. She loved accomplishing tasks and working "toward earning awards and rewards." She described other activities as follows:

> During junior high and high school, I became a cheerleader and also participated in marching and concert bands by playing the flute, colored flute, and flute-piccolo. I also enjoyed being involved in drill team and dramatic productions—both behind the scenes and on stage. I remember being involved in so many clubs during those years as well.

She also took the two foreign languages that were taught at her school. She enjoyed learning and trying to understand more about people from other countries, and she feels now that learning other languages helped her deepen her understanding of international issues.

Martha Layne mentioned her involvement in a few additional activities as well. She was involved in debate and, although she never claimed to be a wonderful public speaker, she felt the instruction and practice she received in her debate activities and competitions were important in helping her develop speaking and critical thinking skills. She was also quite involved in 4H throughout her adolescence. She enjoyed doing various kinds of demonstrations, which also provided her opportunities to be in front of groups and often speak and present. For example, she remembers demonstrating how to pack luggage at one event.

She also prepared animals by "washing their ears and tails and then flattening their tails and shining their hooves and horns," and then she'd show them at 4H events. She loved it and was good at it. In fact, other people asked her to show their animals as well. She believes that these continuous opportunities to present and speak helped her become comfortable and confident in front of individuals and groups. In high school, she was involved in contests and remembers being the Tobacco Festival queen and the Maid of Cotton. She had to answer questions in these contests and feels that these may have been "somewhat helpful in her development."

Martha Layne had many friends during these years. She knew everyone in her class and was somewhat popular, but wasn't one of the five or six "in girls" during those years. Her friends were not the cutest girls or the most popular and were the "girls on the outside of the clique." She remembers struggling with these groups and boundaries. Yet, she knew everyone and had plenty of friends. The one major challenge she had, however, was that her mother was very strict. This meant that she couldn't do all of the social activities the other girls did. She had to be in earlier and couldn't go many places they were allowed to go.

Martha Layne had both formal and informal leadership positions during her youth. She recalls sometimes having ideas not related to a formal position she held, but she would recruit people informally to help with projects. Although she didn't always want to be in a leadership position, she always wanted to accomplish goals. It was clear that she liked putting together teams to work toward goals even during her youth. She was always willing to help school groups in whatever way she could and continuously looked for ways to make things better. For example, she recalls during high school helping to start a teen center so young people would have a place to go after school. By the time Martha Layne graduated from high school, she was clearly a leader and well liked among her peers as well as school faculty and administrators.

Employment

Martha Layne began working at a swimming pool in the summers as a youth. She taught lessons, was a lifeguard, and also worked with clothing baskets, money, cleaning, and concessions, depending on what was needed at the time. She learned some important leadership competencies from this job including responsibility, organization, assertiveness, teamwork, and firmness. She also worked at a jewelry store where she was a sales clerk and did gift wrapping, and then worked for a department store in Louisville the summer after she graduated from high school. She believes retail work was helpful in her competency development because these jobs facilitated her continued development of people skills, responsibility, punctuality, hard work, and doing a good job. She didn't want to disappoint her bosses and always tried to be an ideal employee. Because of this, her employers have always trusted her. She thrived on feeling trusted and knowing others depended on her.

College Plans

Martha Layne spoke of the lack of good advising and counseling during her high school and college years. She exclaimed, "They were not doing their jobs!" She knew she was going to college because it was expected by her father, and she didn't believe she had any other options. At that time, "women could be nurses, teachers, or secretaries." Martha Layne's father didn't want her to be a nurse because he had seen what a difficult job it was when he was running his ambulance service. He made it clear that "he didn't want his daughter doing that." She decided against being a secretary because she was not good at shorthand. Her father was a teacher and that is what Martha Layne knew, so she decided to major in education.

COLLEGE YEARS

The fall after high school graduation, Martha Layne began her first year of college at a girl's school named Lindenwold. At Lindenwold, she studied radio and television and even had her own fifteen-minute radio talk program on campus. She explained,

> I would travel to St. Louis to look at the new trends and fashions, and then report them on my program. I believed that the media should be used to inform consumers about new inventions and discoveries that would make their lives better. I always loved new products, services, and experiences. This experience helped me continue to become more comfortable in speaking to an audience.

Although she enjoyed her first year, she quickly realized that she didn't want that "all-girl experience for four years." The college was not only expensive, but she had decided that she "really wanted to major in home economics with a teaching certificate," and Lindenwold did not offer that degree. Although she planned to teach, her ultimate goal was to do demonstrations on new equipment.

Martha Layne transferred to the University of Kentucky (UK) in 1956 for her sophomore year of college. UK had a strong extension program and offered a degree in home economics with a secondary-education teaching certificate. She spoke of the number of difficult labs she had to take with her courses in chemistry, biochemistry, anatomy, physiology, and bacteriology. It was a rigorous degree, and she noted that some of her courses were with pre-med students. She said, "When we got out of those classes we almost had a minor in science and a minor in math." She mentioned that she enjoyed her anatomy and psychology classes the most. Near the end of her coursework, she spent a semester as a student teacher. She believes this experience was important in her development. She was assigned to teach home economics at the junior high and high school levels. Her supervising teacher was very influential in many ways. Yet, Martha Layne decided during this experience that she didn't want to teach like most of the home economics teachers were doing at the time. She wanted to teach it a more pragmatic and realistic way. She explained,

> *Shampooing your rug once a week is not what the average housewife does. Now we had to learn how to do it, and I understand that. When we had to prepare meals, everything had to be made from scratch. We had to figure out how much each meal was going to cost. For example, we had to prorate a tablespoon of flour back to a whole bag. I didn't have a choice and had to do it. But I clearly remember the night I was supposed to cook in the home management house, and I had forgotten dessert. So I picked up a box of cake mix. I got a major lecture. I decided then that I preferred to be realistic.*

She decided she wanted to teach students what they really needed to know to be successful. She decided she wouldn't give busy work just to keep students quiet.

While a student at the University of Kentucky, Martha Layne became involved in many extracurricular activities on campus. She was a member of Chi Omega sorority and was even going to be president. However, she missed it because her G.P.A. was one-hundredth of a point too low. She had taken bacteriology that semester, which was particularly difficult and got a lower grade than she had hoped. Her roommate ended up becoming the president of the sorority. Although Martha Layne was disappointed, she knew her rigorous college schedule would take most of her time, and therefore realized it was better she wasn't president that year. She was also involved in "a little politics on campus and even ran for an office." She also entered and won beauty contests and was chosen to be the queen of certain special events—like the Kentucky Derby.

Martha Layne worked for Colombia Gas during her junior year of college. She demonstrated Caloric gas ranges, which meant that she went to the state fairs and other events. They had put in a new little burner that was very sensitive, and so she demonstrated the use of the range and thoroughly enjoyed it. She remembers making donuts at the state fair with hot grease, cans of biscuits, and sugar and cinnamon. The kids loved the treats, so it was a big attraction. She recalled receiving an award and recognitions as well as winning contests because of her work. Again, she strengthened her speaking and teaching abilities through this work.

Martha Layne loved her college years and felt they helped prepare her in many ways for leadership. She continued to love learning new things, keeping busy, and challenging herself. In fact, she was known as a "change agent of sorts in college." She also learned more about herself during these years. This self-discovery process during college helped her realize that her leadership strengths focused on "getting along with people and putting them together to get things accomplished."

MARRIAGE, FAMILY, AND TEACHING

After Martha Layne graduated from the University of Kentucky, she and Bill Collins were married during the summer. She had met Bill at a Baptist Church summer camp during college when he was a lifeguard and she was a camp counselor. They immediately discovered they had a lot in common, including both of his parents being teachers and his father a coach. Bill had also graduated and had been accepted to a dental school in Louisville. They moved to Louisville so Bill could continue school, and she immediately obtained a teaching position.

Martha Layne's first teaching position was at a "middle school teaching core, which was everything but science." She said,

> I started out teaching history and other core classes. I was putting together lesson plans and teaching primarily the freshman class. I was also the cheerleader sponsor, so I worked with the JV teams and cheerleaders. I got very attached to my cheerleaders. I was there for just one year and then got transferred to another school in Louisville, but it was a wonderful experience.

Her second year of teaching was at a different kind of school in the suburbs. It was in a primarily manufacturing area and was "very blue collar." The students had a whole different background than her first set of students whose families either belonged to the country club or were poor African Americans. At this new school, Martha Layne taught home economics and "absolutely loved it!" She decided to design the first home economics elective class for boys, which became very successful. She wanted her classes to be realistic and applicable so she had her home economics students become involved in major school productions. She said,

> When the school did the production Oklahoma, the home economics department made the costumes. This was a way to teach the students harder skills and lessons. We also made the decorations, the trees, and even the clay flowers. When we were learning to bake cakes, we had bake sales. The students took great pride in their desserts. They were motivated to make them well because they wanted them to sell. The students wanted the money, so they were much more attentive to the details. The money went into the home economics department for future needs and wants.

Martha Layne loved the challenge and complexity of these endeavors. She said that she believes in leveraging things, which became a useful skill to have in politics later in her life.

In her second year of teaching, Martha Layne got pregnant with her first child (Steve) and had a lot of morning sickness, which made teaching somewhat challenging. Her second child, Marla, came along three years later in 1963. By that time, Bill was out of dental school and the family moved to Versailles, Kentucky where Bill set up his first practice.

Chapter Eight
CAREER

Martha Layne had her own unique career path as have each of the women governors I have interviewed. She believes that the wide variety of paid and nonpaid positions she has held helped her network with people throughout the state, which became very important when she decided to run for a state office. She was able to "pull support with many groups," but "struggled with organizations that wanted to hear promises" she was not willing to make. She also believes that each position helped her develop and strengthen the various skills needed for political leadership. Each gave her valuable insight and experience that she used as she rose through the ranks to become governor of Kentucky. Throughout her career, Martha Layne remained involved in her church, belonged to several clubs that were involved in community activities and service, and volunteered to help in other efforts.

Teaching
The previous section has already included information about Martha Layne's first few years of teaching while her husband was in dental school. After moving to Versailles and giving birth to her daughter, she decided to take some time off to recover and be with the children. However, she did plan to go back to teaching after her recovery. The school district in Versailles wanted her to work for them because they were in great need of a middle school math teacher. She accepted the position and began working full time again. In all, Martha Layne taught public school for eleven years. She believes teaching is a wonderful career to prepare one for political leadership. Teachers can continue to hone leadership skills and abilities in presenting and articulation, listening, innovation, critical thinking, multitasking, organization, trustworthiness, ethics, and diversity awareness.

Campaign Work
Martha Layne always seemed to have an interest in political issues and current events. Through the years, she had always enjoyed listening to candidates' speeches and debates. After her children were born and she was teaching school full time again, she occasionally began volunteering on campaigns. In 1970, when her children were six and nine, Martha Layne was asked to work on Wendell Ford's gubernatorial campaign as his sixth congressional district chairperson responsible for twenty-two counties. She was immediately successful in this assignment and "learned about politics and making the contacts, networking, and strategizing." She visited many counties, met lots of people, and listened to community members' concerns. She enjoyed the work and used everything she had learned about contests, radio and television, networking, and public speaking in this position.

Because Martha Layne did very well working in Ford's campaign, other politicians began asking her to work on their campaigns as well. For example, she decided to work on Dee Huddleston's U.S. Senate campaign and was put in charge of organizing women all over the state. To her surprise, Martha Layne found this assignment to be a rather difficult challenge. Most women were not involved in politics at this time and some were even forbidden to be so by their husbands. Many women did not understand why their involvement was so important. Yet, she felt that her efforts "definitely helped make headway in getting women involved." In 1968, after a number of years of campaign work for many candidates, she decided to give up her teaching career and work in politics full time.

Democratic National Committee and Convention
In 1973, while she was still teaching school, Martha Layne took a year leave of absence to work at Democratic headquarters as a Democratic national committeewoman in Kentucky. She was elected by the state committee to serve in this four-year position. There are 120 counties in the state to work with, and she had been to all of them many times through her prior positions and assignments. She felt it was important—when writing legislation, making policy, or making decisions—to understand that what is good for the larger cities may not be good for the rural areas. She also wanted to help change the level of involvement of women in politics and explained,

> *As a committeewoman, I worked hard to get women involved. They would have bake sales or do some teas, but I wanted to help them learn more about politics. At that time, the county executive committees had no women in leadership, even as secretaries. I helped establish a policy that women had to have a role in that local leadership, and it was implemented at the state and county levels. Along with others, I worked hard in seeing that passed in every one of 3,000 precincts in the state.*

She believes this position was helpful in her development as she had the opportunity to meet with people from all over the United States. She was eventually asked to preside over the 1984 Democratic convention in Kentucky.

Court of Appeals Clerk
After working on other's campaigns for many years, Martha Layne described the following event:

> *In one lieutenant governor race, there were fifteen candidates who had announced that they were going to run. Several of them asked me to run their campaigns because of my reputation of working hard and making contacts. In the evenings, Bill and I would talk about it at supper. Bill finally said, "You've put in enough miles yourself. I think it's time. It's either time for you to run yourself or come home." He knew I wasn't coming home, so I chose to run.*

Martha Layne was still teaching school when this ultimatum came. She decided to enter the race for clerk of the Kentucky Court of Appeals. She was interested in the courts because of their purpose and focus on fairness to all citizens. So, in

1975, Martha Layne ran her first statewide race on $30,000. She was elected and worked hard in this position for years. She continued to develop her ability to look for better ways of doing things in the state.

Lieutenant Governor
During the last year of her term as court of appeals clerk, she decided to run for lieutenant governor. Her campaign was of course successful, and Martha Layne became lieutenant governor of Kentucky in 1979. She enjoyed being lieutenant governor more than anything she had done up to that point. She said,

> *I worked hard to find out what people needed and to ask them how the government could help. I had opportunities to speak often and attend ribbon-cutting ceremonies and so forth. I obtained a reputation for listening and figuring out who could help. During this time, however, I also received criticism, and I had to develop a thicker skin and continue to move forward with what I felt was right. Because I didn't take sides with particular groups, I believe many critics came to believe that I was at least fair.*

During her term, she traveled throughout the state to towns and schools to find out what citizens needed from the state government. She toured coalmines to learn what it was like to work there. She visited older people in nursing homes and spoke to the unemployed to understand their struggles. Because of these efforts, many people in the state believed that she wanted to help them, so they trusted her. Interestingly, she actually went from being a schoolteacher to governor in only twelve years.

Governor
Martha Layne then decided to run for governor and did so near the end of her term as lieutenant governor in 1983. She worked hard in the campaign but credits one particular event for "giving her the edge in a very difficult race." She was running against baseball giant Jim Bunning and participated in a televised debate. Martha Layne knew her material well but was concerned about making sure she expressed it appropriately. She explained:

> *Here's this big tall guy over here talking, and I could see all the athletes and everybody watching him with interest and awe. He was a baseball pitcher and had won all these games and been quite popular. My father had always taught me to really think carefully before answering questions. So they asked me a question, and I paused. He jumped in and started talking, and I looked at him and said, "You answer your questions, and I'll answer mine." I won the debate.*

Voters apparently saw strength and feistiness in her response. She was unwilling to tell people what they wanted to hear when she knew it would be impossible to actually follow through with it. Because of this she struggled with endorsements from some organizations that should have provided support. For example, the teachers association did not endorse her because she would not say what they wanted to hear. Although many people did not think she would win the race, she won despite the odds. On November 8, 1983, Martha Layne Collins was elected as the first woman governor in the state of Kentucky, and she served from 1984 to 1988. During her term as governor, her two children were teenagers and lived with Martha Layne and Bill in the governor's mansion. Interestingly, even with her challenges with the teachers' association, she eventually became known as "an education governor."

Martha Layne continued to learn and develop leadership as governor. She had previously learned a lot about the counties because she had worked with them in her other positions. She said,

> Some had good leadership and some did not. Some had certain resources and some had certain problems. As governor, my staff and I were able to analyze all of the data. Yet, sometimes they wanted help and sometimes they did not.

At times, she struggled with the competition between city government and county government. She remembers one particular instance when a company wanted to build a plant in Kentucky, but because of conflict they decided to build in another state before she even found out what was happening. There had been a feud between a county and city, which the company did not like. She explained,

> I said to my staff, "This will not happen again. We are going to have some programs where the city and the county in some of these problem areas would begin conversations." At the time, they didn't like each other or speak. I helped create programs that assisted them in starting these conversations.

She developed toughness through the years in part because of all her experiences. Through her leadership roles, Martha Layne continued honing her skills in figuring out ways to improve situations and relationships. For example, she learned strong leveraging skills because Kentucky doesn't have a lot of money, and leveraging was a necessity. She focused on helping others see that figuring out solutions to improve the situation was what needed to happen. Sometimes she was not successful, and she learned from those experiences as well.

CAREER SUPPORT AND ISSUES

Martha Layne knew she would teach school but had no idea she would end up in politics. She said,

> I definitely did not have a formal career path targeted at becoming the governor of Kentucky. I had no clue I would even become as involved in campaigns as I became. I just prepared myself by learning everything I could in what I was

> *doing at the time, and then I took opportunities as they came. People asked me to take on new assignments and challenges, and I did.*

Martha Layne had prepared herself through the years by learning and developing her skills as she embraced new opportunities. She also listened to people she respected, and they encouraged her.

Martha Layne spoke of the supportiveness of her husband throughout their marriage. She believes his support and encouragement was integral in her development and success. He really wanted Martha Layne to run for public office and enjoyed being active through the years in helping with her campaigns. He was also a "true family man and was so good and wonderful with the children." As a dentist, he also had a flexible schedule and could often take off from work when she needed to be gone. Bill was one of the most important support systems she had throughout her political career.

Martha Layne responded to a question I asked regarding her perceived gender barriers. She believes there are different glass ceilings for different people. She stated,

> *I've never paid much attention to gender barriers through the years. Yet, I do believe that there is a double standard. I know that I had to work harder than many men. A man can walk through that door, and he's automatically considered a businessman. Women have to prove themselves. In fact, I get tired of proving myself, quite frankly. I get really tired of it.*

She has often wondered why this is the case. She admits that the "men thing is always going to be there, but I don't dwell on it. I just try to do the best work I can and let things be." Yet, Martha Layne does believe that there are still things that need to be done for women, and that's one of the reasons she hasn't slowed down even though she is now seventy years old. She admits that she occasionally gets irritated with some women because they don't seem to appreciate what has been done for them through the past decades.

VALUABLE DEVELOPMENTAL INFLUENCES

Martha Layne also spoke of three additional developmental influences through her adulthood that she believes helped in her development of leadership: influential individuals, motherhood, and leadership training.

Influential Individuals

Martha Layne mentioned only two non-family individuals who were particularly influential in her leadership development. The first was Wendell Ford who she had worked for in his campaign for governor. He was charismatic, popular, and a people person. She appreciated his straightforwardness. He became an important role model for Martha Layne. He ran for governor and then the U.S. Senate. Although she didn't have a close one-on-one mentorship with him, she learned from watching his behaviors, decisions, and style. The second person she mentioned was "J.R. Miller, who was more of a strategist." She said, "We called him Papa Bear, because when I worked at Democratic headquarters, he would fly in from western Kentucky as chairman and in two hours he could give us a month's work." He gave Martha Layne assignments to see how well she could do the tasks. Martha Layne quickly earned his trust and was given more responsibility and leadership. He became her mentor. She remembers J.R. taking a group of them out for dinner many times to listen to their ideas. She gave him an idea at one of these dinners that he liked, and he made it happen through the state governing committee. She said, "It was amazing and invigorating to see my ideas implemented!"

Motherhood
Being a mother helped Martha Layne develop a number of competencies that were useful when she became governor. She said that motherhood helped her "learn to make all of her time quality time and to use it wisely." She learned to make choices between important commitments. She explained,

> *I worried about the fact that I might be ninety, sitting in my rocking chair and regretting the fact that I didn't get to go to every school play or every ball game. Yet my children were part of my life and a part of the campaign. They made their own choices and were often on the campaign trail with me. When I was working on somebody else's campaign, they would have the choice if they wanted to go with me to an event. They often decided they would. I would give them choices, and they did well. Letting others make choices and then respecting those choices are important in effective leadership. I learned this from motherhood.*

She remembers many times finishing her teaching day and then picking up the children. They would do homework and eat snacks in the car. They loved some of the events, listened to the speeches, and met lots of people. They noticed when candidates changed their speeches from one event to another. Martha Layne believes it enriched their lives. All of this taught her multitasking. She said that "time multiplication was important during these years."

Leadership Training
The final category is leadership training. Although Martha Layne doesn't remember ever attending any specific seminars or programs on leadership, she did mentioned a few helpful conferences she attended later in her career that she believes helped her strengthen her leadership abilities. She became the chair of a lieutenant governors' conference and also attended all of the governors' conferences. She said,

> *All of those conferences were very important. It is important to see what is happening in other states and to hear about their challenges, which by the way*

interestingly sound very similar to our own. These interactions gave me ideas of possible future challenges and solutions.

LEADERSHIP STYLE AND PHILOSOPHY

Martha Layne spoke of her own leadership style by telling me what her staff would say if I asked them. She believes they would first speak of her strong work ethic and the way she helped develop others. She explained,

When I was campaigning, I had a lot of young people who helped me. What happened was we'd leave the headquarters with a crew of young people at six-thirty or seven o'clock in the morning. At about two or three o'clock in the afternoon, I'd see another van pull up with a fresh new group of kids. I continued working. The first group would go back to the office, follow up, and prepare for the next day. Many of them have become very successful. When I worked with them, I wasn't flowery, meaning that I never praised someone a lot for their job. The way they knew that they had done a good job was if I gave them more responsibility. I liked developing others by giving them opportunities.

Martha Layne has enjoyed developing others through the years. She finds satisfaction even today in hearing that past employees or volunteers now have wonderful, influential jobs. She credits some of this to the development they received while working for her. Although she admits that developing others takes time and energy, she believes it has "definitely been worth it."

Next, Martha Layne's staff would say she believes in being open, candid, and honest. In fact, she admits that one of her shortfalls at times is that she likes to "tell it like it is." She said, "You'll never have to worry or wonder where I am." Although she did have to soften her words in various situations, she prefers to say things candidly and honestly. She said, "I did not and do not tell untruths."

The third leadership style category Martha Layne mentioned was that, because she had "only four years to accomplish assertive goals for the state," she "didn't have time to do a lot of fence mending and explaining." Therefore, she decided as governor to lead with a "consensus-building and team-building approach." She often asked others what they thought of her ideas and listened to their ideas as well. She said, "Sometimes they'd take my idea and add to it, and then somebody else would buy in and say it was their idea." She was fine not getting credit as long as good things were happening. She enjoyed working with teams of smart and committed individuals in making efforts and events successful and told the following story to illustrate her point:

We landed Toyota when I was governor, and I did it with a team. I started going to Japan and calling on Toyota even before they said they were coming to North America. They finally announced that they were going to come. There were twenty or more states competing, and it was eventually narrowed down to

Kentucky and Tennessee. I had little strategies all the way through. I was only one of two women governors, so I believed that helped people remember me. As women, we got their attention, and they remembered our names. The male governors would announce at home that they were going to go do economic development and they would bring back jobs, so they pushed too hard. I walked in and smiled, and we had a great time. The Toyota team would come with an idea, and I'd candidly tell them what I thought about it.

She worked closely with her cabinet in these types of efforts. She'd pick out the members who were very important for economic development, such as budgeting, human resources, natural resources, and transportation. A company would come to visit with their project people to do research and then give recommendations to their CEOs. The previous governor would visit with the CEOs but never thought about connecting with the project people. She said,

I had a philosophy that my cabinet and I needed to connect with these project people, secretaries, and even the maintenance people in some cases. I believe that these were the people who could make a difference in the decisions. When we met with corporations, I took cabinet secretaries with me so they could promptly answer all of the questions the project people had. Other states did not do this. When a project team left Kentucky, they had answers.

Although Martha Layne didn't have to operate this way, she believes her team was successful in recruiting businesses because of these methods.

Martha Layne continued her story about working with Toyota in convincing them to build their plant in Kentucky. The following detailed story demonstrates a number of important elements regarding her leadership style and philosophy that provides important insight:

A major corporation from Japan was going to build a facility in North America and well into the process had narrowed their options to either Tennessee or Kentucky. They told me they were going to visit Tennessee first. I preferred to be first, but I had no choice. My cabinet and I started talking about all the things that we were going to do when they were in Kentucky. My advisors argued that it needed to be a serious business dinner. Yet, I thought we needed to do something more interesting, because it was our last chance to convince them to choose our state. Finally, I had to pull rank and mandated what we would be doing. They didn't argue with me too much. The corporate representatives went to Tennessee and were shown a site that they didn't like. So the Tennessee folks kept trying to convince them, which made them late for our appointment. Now, if you study the Japanese culture, you know that they don't like to be late. Tennessee played right into my hands by making the Japanese late for our visit. They were very embarrassed to be over two-and-a-half hours late.

I had decided to meet them at the airport, although I didn't need to. I went to the airport to meet them and an individual from their team had come in advance. He came back to update me on how late they were going to be and so forth. He said, "Go back to Frankfort and we'll meet you there" as he was bowing and so forth. I told him not to worry about it and that I would wait.

Since I was at the airport anyway, I greeted every flight that came in by saying, "Welcome to Kentucky. We are so glad you're here."

Two and a half hours later they landed two private jets with three vice presidents plus the project team. I could tell that they were very uptight. We got them in our vans, and I started giving them a tour of the city all the way to the hotel. We had radioed ahead so somebody came out and gave the translator all the room keys and they could go directly to their rooms where we had left a little gift. I told them that I'd meet them back in Frankfort. I immediately flew back to Frankfort and did not have time for the leisurely afternoon I had planned to prepare. When I arrived, I had to meet with all of the different people—university presidents, attorneys, and bankers—I had invited to sit at separate tables to talk to the Toyota representatives about how wonderful Kentucky was. These people were already there, so I had to entertain them immediately.

Finally, the Toyota people came and we had a reception with food I knew they would like. Then we went to dinner. I had done my homework. I insisted on having baked Alaska, and we had them on white teacarts. When the formally dressed waiters rolled them out, the lights were dimmed. We had stuck sparklers in them and it was wonderful. I heard our guests "ooohh and ahhh." I also knew they studied folk music, so I had the Steven Foster Singers from "My Old Kentucky Home" come to sing at the event. Everyone was singing along and having fun. Finally, we took the group out on the front porch of the mansion, and I had people behind the annex shoot fireworks over the capital. Although it was late, the Japanese loved the fireworks. We definitely showed them that we cared about them and that we were interested in building a real partnership with them. It didn't take them long to make their decision to come to Kentucky.

This story illustrates that effective leadership qualities may include studying, being prepared and flexible, listening to others but being willing to make the final decision, respecting others and treating them well, paying attention to small details when needed, and being willing to go the extra mile. The ability to plan ahead and discover options are also attributes she believes were important in her success.

Martha Layne explained that one of her top leadership philosophies is that hiring good people can make the difference in any administration's success. Trusted individuals can make up for areas the leader is weak. She said, "Leaders should hire people smarter than themselves to really be successful." Martha Layne is not as impressed with titles as she is impressed with people. Attitude has always been very important to her. She said, "If an employee has a good attitude, I'll overlook some of the challenges or some of the problems they may have. If an individual has a desire to do well, learn, and cooperate, he or she will be successful in working with me." Martha Layne believes that great employees need to have strong skills in many areas but that there must also be a good working chemistry among team members. She also believes that actions are stronger than words. If a member of her staff "didn't do what they needed to do, they didn't get another assignment and usually knew the reason why." She didn't have to say much for them to make the needed changes.

ADVICE

Martha Layne is often asked for her advice to girls and young women who might be interested in future political leadership. She often tells children and youth how important it is for them to study and learn everything they can possibly learn. She reminds them that at their age they don't know what they're going to become and that they need to be ready for any opportunity to contribute in the future. Each individual can play so many important roles and should be prepared to make the difference that needs to be made. She said,

> When the window of opportunity opens, you want to be able to go through it quickly because a lot of times it won't stay open for very long. If you are prepared and willing, then you don't need to be afraid. You are going to have to take risks; sometimes you are going to win and sometimes you are going to lose. Sometimes you are going to be right, and sometimes you are going to be wrong. However, if you are prepared and courageous you can make a powerful difference in a variety of ways.

To make this difference, Martha Layne believes the top skill individuals need to develop right now in the United States is problem solving. She encourages students of all ages to work assertively to understand and develop this skill.

When Martha Layne speaks to college-aged women, she warns them to carefully consider their actions. For example, if they are caught on film partying during spring break, nowadays they'll have trouble later in life if they are interested in running for a political office. She encourages students to live their lives now in such a way that they won't need to explain or apologize later when they want to run for political office. She also encourages these young women to learn professional skills. She said, "When women complain, gossip, dress inappropriately, and display other nonprofessional behaviors, they don't reflect well on themselves and other women."

Martha Layne spoke of the importance of women being comfortable with themselves. They need to work toward understanding themselves to be able to obtain this comfort. She doesn't suggest that young women try to become like any one specific leader. Each women needs to become the best she can become and not try to "put a round peg in a square hole," as it's "very uncomfortable for everybody." Women also need to become comfortable with each other. Through the years, women have been their own worst enemies. She believes women should do all they can to support and strengthen each other.

Martha Layne believes that getting involved in other people's campaigns will not only teach women how to campaign but also what is important in campaigning. She said, "By helping someone else, you learn both the good strategies and the things you definitely don't want to repeat." She believes that campaigning can help women understand how to decide on issues and set policy. Women can also learn "a lot about the media and how to handle it" from other's campaigns. She also spoke of what good women can do for their communities and states by serving in volunteer and elected positions. She stated that "volunteering is very important for the community as well as the personal development of women." Regarding elected positions, she understands that many women are not interested in stepping forward because "politics have gotten so ugly, so nasty, and so dirty and expensive." Yet, she believes that women must be involved in decision-making positions in their communities and states. She said, "There are so many things women can do for their communities, states, and country by becoming leaders of all kinds for a multitude of efforts and causes."

FINAL THOUGHTS

Since her governorship, Martha Layne has served in the following positions: president of St. Catharine College, executive-in-residence at the University of Louisville's School of Business, and director of the International Business and Management Center at the University of Kentucky's Carol Martin Gatton College of Business and Economics. Today, she is an executive scholar in residence at Georgetown College, serves on several national boards, and is the chair and CEO of the Kentucky World Trade Center in Lexington. She also mentioned that she loves being involved in individual school efforts that motivate children to read. Yet, one of her most favorite activities now in her life is being a grandmother to her five beautiful grandchildren. Her family continues to bring her great joy and provides her with continued support and encouragement in her life. To this day, Martha Layne remains driven to continue to make a difference to those around her. She is passionate about improving the quality of life for others and supports leaders she believes can make that happen. She has left a legacy in Kentucky of a woman of strength and action who cared about those she served.

Chapter 9

Governor Nancy Putnam Hollister

We are here on earth for a miniscule period of time. People shouldn't make government their entire life's work. Individuals need to enjoy their lives in so many other ways. They need to be broadly and continually learning and developing themselves. The worst mistake that politicians and public servants sometimes make is thinking their jobs are their entire life's work. There's always something more to do, there's always something more to learn, and there's always something more to become.

~ *Governor Nancy Putnam Hollister*

I interviewed Governor Nancy Hollister at her home in Marietta, Ohio on February 23, 2006. She was elected as the lieutenant governor of Ohio and served in that role from 1995–1998. At the end of her term as lieutenant governor, the governor resigned to become a U.S. Senator. Nancy was then inaugurated and served briefly as the first female Governor of the State of Ohio between late December 1998 and early January 1999. Throughout her state leadership positions, Nancy became a tireless advocate for economic development, job training opportunities, local education, and health programs. She has received many honors from community and professional groups for her service and influence. I interviewed Nancy about how she developed leadership through her life, and I asked her to reminisce about important events, influences, experiences, and opportunities that may have influenced this development. These are her thoughts.

FAMILY BACKGROUND

Nancy Putnam Hollister was born in Indiana on May 22, 1949, but when she was two months old, she moved with her parents to the small town of Marietta, Ohio where she was brought up. She is a descendent of one of Ohio's first pioneer families and takes great pride in her heritage. She spoke about the Putnam family and how one of her "illustrious ancestors was part of the founding of Marietta, Ohio in 1788." This heritage provided her a "sense of who I was," which has served her well. Growing up as a Putnam in Marietta, her paternal grandfather taught her that she had "a history, a legacy, and a responsibility to the community." She described herself as a "child of history," as history has always been a passion for her. She fervently believes that "if we don't recognize where we came from and understand our history, then we'll destroy ourselves in the future." She was also taught by her family that, "You are no better than anybody else, and you do have a responsibility to participate and treat people with dignity and respect."

Nancy felt that she was raised in a fairly stable home with lots of privilege. However, in 1964 her "family fortune fell apart." Troubled family finances and her father's alcoholism led to the loss of their home and the unraveling of her parent's marriage. The family then moved to the "Second Street Slum." Although difficult, Nancy felt this situation helped her experience "the good, bad, and ugly" during her upbringing, broadening her understanding of others' struggles and challenges.

Nancy is the oldest of five siblings and said that she was, along with the housekeeper, the "chief cook and nanny to four siblings." She has sisters who are two, four, and six years younger than she is and a brother who is ten years her junior. She said that they (the girls) used to tease their little brother unmercifully saying, "I don't know how he survived with all the mothers and all the pounding that he took."

Parents

Nancy's mother, Betsy, grew up in Clendenin, West Virginia. Betsy's parents were college graduates. Her mother was employed as a home economics teacher, and her father was an engineer throughout his career. Nancy's mother grew up with parents who taught her that "education was the key to her kingdom," so Nancy grew up with that theme central in her life. Betsy became a college graduate with an undergraduate degree in teaching (physical education) and a master's degree in guidance and counseling. However, she didn't teach until after her children were born. Nancy was in junior high school when her mother went back to teaching and to school for her master's degree.

Nancy explained that her mother was very active. The family had a housekeeper to help with homemaking responsibilities so her mother could be physically active and civically involved. She played golf and was very athletic throughout her life. Nancy said, "My mother was everywhere, and my parents traveled. So I actually had two mother figures in my life—my mother and our housekeeper."

Nancy remembers her mother always saying,

> *You can be anything you want to be. Don't ever let anybody tell you that you can't do something. You are an individual of intelligence and strength. You understand who you are and where you are going, so don't ever let anybody tell you differently. You will make mistakes, but that's life and you must keep going.*

Because of her mother's strong influence in her life, Nancy grew up with a sense that she had choices and options in her life.

Nancy's father, Ben, was also very active. He completed three-and-a-half years of college, but didn't quite finish his degree. He was in banking as well as the oil and gas industry. His family was heavily involved in the early exploration for oil, gas, and coal in the region and had continued working in this industry. Ben loved politics and was very involved in political activities. Nancy explained,

> *During the 1950s and 60s, my father was involved with the congressional delegation and the Republican Party structure in Washington and Ohio. He raised money; he ran for Congress and lost, and he served on city council. He was in the Electoral College when Eisenhower was elected. He loved politics. He loved to be involved. When I was nine or ten I started going with him to political events like dinners. I was the only child in our family who was interested, and I thought it was pretty neat.*

She remembers her parents wearing their formal attire to attend the presidential swearing in for Eisenhower. Nancy was raised believing that it was just natural for parents to be involved in politics.

According to Nancy, her father spoke about his political involvement and issues of the day at the dinner table with his family. She said,

> *We always discussed things at the table like what we were doing and why we were doing it. We were encouraged to ask questions. We would read newspapers and talk about the issues. I remember being very aware of President Eisenhower and what was happening in the country.*

Nancy and her siblings were always encouraged to share their views at home, and they "argued about issues like crazy." Nancy's parents loved to cook, and they instilled that passion in all their children. Everyone enjoyed the preparations, loved to eat, and thrived on the family conversations.

Extended Family
For many generations, Nancy's extended family on her father's side were all born and raised in Marietta. It was a tradition that all of the relatives met each Sunday for dinner. Everyone was at the table including great grandmothers, great grandfathers, grandparents, aunts, uncles, and cousins. They were major gatherings, and Nancy recalls the lively conversations about what was going on in their lives and why. She remembers listening to and interacting with her paternal grandfather who "instilled in her the sense of history." Nancy also said that her nearly six-foot tall paternal grandmother was "an incredible woman." She had Parkinson's disease for eighteen years, and Nancy was eighteen when she died. So, Nancy saw her with the disease her entire life. Nancy explained, "I saw her as a determined, passionate individual with a spark about her that I admired." These relatives provided stability and support through this phase of her life.

Nancy also spoke of the influence of a gay uncle (her mother's youngest brother) who she spent a lot of time with in New York City. She saw and did many things with him, like the Guggenheim, nightclubs, museums, Central Park, and Broadway plays. She explained that her parents had no idea "the world she was introduced to in New York." Nancy remembers going to Fire Island with her uncle when she was about sixteen and "sitting on the beach surrounded by many gorgeous men with no interest in her." This was in the 1960s, and "it was a startling revolution." Having a gay uncle seemed like no big deal to Nancy, and as a youth she knew the gay community and developed an appreciation for differences. As a teenager, she saw diversity and started understanding its complexity.

CHILDHOOD AND YOUTH

Personality

Nancy described herself as bossy, candid, and opinionated during her childhood. For example, when Nancy and her siblings were young, they produced musicals in their living room. She remembers her sisters calling her "bossy" and getting mad on occasion because she always had to be the director. Nancy was also candid, which got her in trouble on more than one occasion. She was taught to have a sense of politeness, and she knew the line that was not to be crossed. But at home she was encouraged to challenge, so occasionally she challenged others outside the home environment. She explained,

> *I have incredible memories of growing up in a very New England congregational church. I took the classes to join the church, and I asked questions. I was immediately told not to ask questions because it was disruptive to the class. So, I said I wouldn't join. Then there was a meeting at the house with the minister and my parents. I still said I wouldn't join if I couldn't ask questions. My parents accepted my decision but said I had to go to the Sunday service and acknowledge my peers who were being inducted into the church. I went, determined in my decision, but it was a difficult morning. As my mother said, "You made your bed so now you have to lie in it!" I did.*

Nancy was also an instigator. For example, religious education was required in her grade school, and she thought it was "not necessary and a waste of time" since she already went to church on Sundays. She told the teacher she was Jewish so she could get out of it, and of course, the teacher knew better. Nancy's parents were not happy with her. She remembered telling them that she didn't think it was appropriate to be teaching religion in school. Since the children in her family were allowed to express their opinions at home, she occasionally got into trouble expressing such opinions at school.

Although Nancy was a fairly confident child, she clearly remembers an experience that shook her self-esteem for a short time. When Nancy was in third grade, she went to the city museum with her grade school class. Her classmates saw pictures of her relatives in the museum and knew she was related to them. For the first time in her life, she remembers thinking "they are awfully funny looking." The teachers and other students told her that she looked like them. She was horrified and remembered wearing her raincoat over her head for the rest of the tour.

Referring to her adolescent years, Nancy said, "I was who I was. I didn't run with a particular group of people." She knew and liked everyone, but she wanted to "hang out with any group" she cared to. She felt that she didn't need to belong to a specific group. Nancy believes that her adolescent peers were not major influences in either her life or her development of leadership. She spent most of her high school years with her husband-to-be, Jeff Hollister. He was very much a central part of her life.

Nancy described herself as "extraordinarily competitive, when I wanted to be." She enjoyed pushing and challenging herself to become better at doing things she hadn't done before. She was very competitive in debate and in her leadership roles with Girl Scouts. As a camp counselor, she enjoyed the challenge of taking a group of young kids, teaching them, and then "helping them create a home in the woods." She enjoyed the challenge of helping children work together to have fun. She described a particular situation where she and other counselors had to keep dozens of children calm in the outdoors during a tornado warning. She forced herself to keep focused on the children so they were not afraid.

Activities

Nancy loved to read and was passionate about what she learned. Her mother challenged her to think deeply and broadly through reading books. She remembers her mother giving her a copy of *The Diary of Anne Frank* when she was nine. She recalls being particularly emotional and upset after reading it because Anne died. Her mother responded by taking time with Nancy to have a "discussion about Hitler and WWII." When she was eleven, her mother gave her and her sister a copy of *To Kill a Mockingbird*. Again Nancy was angry after finishing the book as she had grown to love the characters. After her sister also finished, mother and daughters went to see the movie. Her mother was an incredible reader and passed along that habit and passion to Nancy and her sisters. She said that she started "devouring books as a child" reading National Velvet, Nancy Drew books, and others. She described her experience in more detail with one of these books:

> *After reading National Velvet, my dream was that I was going to be the first female to win the Irish sweepstakes with my horse. I was National Velvet, and I loved horses. My horse was my best friend. When I stopped growing up and started growing out, my plans sort of went out the window. However, my fascination with horses has always continued.*

Nancy also remembers reading the Little Colonel books published in the 1900s, which her godmother, an English teacher, gave to her. Nancy believes that this love of reading throughout the years has enhanced her "life lessons" by expanding her knowledge, perspectives, and insights.

Nancy was very involved in Girl Scouts during her childhood and early youth. Her mother had been a Girl Scout and a troop leader so "By gosh all of us girls were going to be Girl Scouts, too." Nancy grew to love scouting and eventually became a counselor. She liked being in the woods and enjoyed the challenge of creating a campsite out of nothing. In fact, she had an important experience with Girl Scouts when, at the age of sixteen, was able to attend the last international Girl Scout Round-up in Idaho. She was chosen along with two others from about one hundred girls in her region to attend. They traveled with hundreds of girls from other regions across the country on a train. At the Round-up, she had opportunities to lead events and activities, yet she said, "I just had fun. To me I never thought of it as leadership. It was a sense of getting things done."

Nancy also remembers being involved during her childhood and youth in many family activities, such as dinners, parties, vacations, and outdoor activities. Her family had a boat, so they water skied often on the river. She kept very active during these years. She attended political events with her father and sometimes both parents. In fact, she specifically remembers wearing a button for Barry Goldwater and getting into an argument with her best friends during seventh grade over politics.

Nancy spoke of her involvement in plays, dance, and church activities. Nancy was voted best actress in her class because she was in most of the productions. She noted that acting taught her to memorize more effectively and to bring words to life for others around her. It provided her with practice in understanding another individual or character in a deep way by becoming them. She believes this was helpful in improving her ability to see different perspectives. She remembers that her mother wanted her to take ballet, but she "was a klutz." She sang in choirs, but didn't excel in that area either. She became very active in church events and enjoyed being involved in the youth group activities.

Debate was one of the most helpful activities Nancy participated in with regard to helping her develop leadership skills. She was the only girl on the debate team at her high school for several years. She enjoyed debate, and people encouraged her to continue. She was never shy about public speaking. She told the following humorous story about one of her debate experiences:

> *During my tenth-grade regional debate finals, all of the debaters came prepared with their briefcases and card files. Our opponents came in with their glasses, suits, and the judges. I quickly noticed I was the only female in the room. My partner, now an attorney in Mississippi, was a character. Now it is important to insert that I had gotten ready very early in the morning and couldn't find a slip. Remember this is 1962 when you had to wear slips. I grabbed an old one and stuck a pin in it because the elastic was all gone. So we started the debates and were giving wonderful speeches on the proliferation of nuclear weapons or something. I got up to give my speech and was doing a great job. Suddenly, I felt the pin pop and it stuck me. I thought "Oh crap!" I*

knew I needed to continue, so I did. While standing at the podium in the middle of the room, I could feel the slip sliding down. My partner was sitting there, and I could see his face getting ashen so I knew he could see my slip. I just kept talking, and when my slip hit the floor, I gracefully (at least I like to remember it that way) stepped out and kicked it under the desk. I just didn't have any other choice. Our two opponents just sat there with their mouths open thinking, of course, how inappropriate it was. I definitely unnerved our two opponents, although I didn't do it on purpose. I was so embarrassed that I didn't even retrieve my slip until everybody left the room. We won the debate, and the judge wrote on our form, "Nice trick with the slip. Don't do it again!"

Nancy loved debate and spoke of how it helped her develop skills in quickly articulating her arguments. It strengthened her critical thinking abilities and provided practice in working with a team—all important leadership skills.

Influential Individuals

Nancy spoke of developing an understanding of diversity when she was young, in part because of the influence of their housekeeper, Valerie. Nancy described her as "one of the most incredible woman on the face of the earth." Valerie was an African American widow with eight children. Nancy told the following experience,

> When I was ten or eleven, I remember coming in from playing one day and seeing Valerie ironing with tears running down her face. I asked, "What's wrong?" She was watching Doctor King's march on television, and it showed dogs and fire hoses attacking people. So Valerie talked to me about Doctor King. I was stunned that people would teach dogs to attack good people and was shocked at the violence. I went upstairs, gathered some belongings and the little money I had saved, and I went to the bus station on my bike to buy two tickets for Valerie and me to go to Alabama. Of course, this was a small town and everyone knew my name. My mother was called, and by the time I got home, Valerie and my parents were there and wanted to talk to me. One of the messages that I got from Valerie that day was that although it is good to feel strongly about the way people are being treated, the best way I could honor Doctor King was to treat all people the same—to always have a piece of your heart that will love and accept people of all races and colors. I've never forgotten that; it was powerful.

Valerie was influential during many years of Nancy's early life.

Although Nancy's godmother (Grace Marie) died when Nancy was only ten, she was also very influential. Grace Marie was a "tiny, beautiful lady," and she had been her mother's English teacher years prior. Nancy described her as an "unbelievable life force." This woman encouraged Nancy to read and to think critically. She allowed Nancy to dress up in all her amazing clothing, which made Nancy feel like a princess. She listened to Nancy and encouraged her to learn.

Nancy didn't mention any specific influential schoolteachers during her upbringing but felt she learned at least something from each of them. Schoolteachers kept her busy and involved, even during her challenges and struggles. She thought grade school was fabulous. She enjoyed most of her secondary school experiences, but because of challenges in her family, she struggled with some courses that she wasn't interested in taking. She remembers a guidance counselor looking at her and saying, "I just don't understand you. You are so intelligent, and you just don't work to your capacity." She was most influenced by teachers who were excited about their subjects.

Challenges and Struggles

During Nancy's early teens, her father's battle with alcoholism began. As the oldest child, she helped take care of him during these years. He would disappear and then reappear without notice, which took an enormous toll on the rest of the family. Nancy said that she learned a great deal from this difficult time. She knows the horrible heavy feeling of losing everything. When she deals with individuals or groups who are dealing with problems and have very little economically, Nancy says that she can empathize. She understands the "psychological darkness that can put you in a hole that is difficult to get out of." She said,

> *I understand it is easy to be angry and stay in that dark place. I learned that anger and frustration are venomous and infectious. I learned that you need to just keep putting one foot in front of the other sometimes, and that you must keep hope. Keep moving forward and look ahead. I learned that it's okay to scream, yell, and cry sometimes. However, I learned you must then pick yourself up and keep going. Everyone has something of value.*

These experiences helped her learn many lessons early in her life. Nancy spoke of the interesting role she had of being a caregiver and caretaker for her father as she told the following story:

> *Mother had taken the rest of the siblings and gone to the east coast because she couldn't deal with my father and needed a break. I stayed behind because I had to be a counselor at Girl Scout camp. I remember my future husband, Jeff, driving me to camp with my dad very ill in the backseat. All the parents and grandparents were delivering their children, and I was frantic about leaving my father, and yet I was also embarrassed. He told me that day that he would never drink again. Jeff drove him four hours back to Marietta and right to the hospital. I received a phone call at camp from my Dad a week later. He told me that he was okay and that there would be "no more living life upside-down." My father had been sober for forty-two years when we lost him in June of 2007.*

Nancy had a relationship with her father that none of her other siblings had. Her mother counted on Nancy to shoulder tremendous responsibility in raising the four other siblings, and because of this she also developed "a powerful relationship" with her mother as well. Importantly, during this same time her grandmother was also dying of Parkinson's disease, which was also very difficult for the family.

Because of the family challenges, Nancy found high school somewhat disconcerting. Jeff, her boyfriend, was her stability during high school. She didn't get involved in the "petty issues of the day" (what to wear, who was driving, who was dating whom) that teenage girls seem to do; however, she did enjoy going to sporting events,ced dances, and parties. No one had a clue that her family was imploding, except for Jeff.

Nancy's mother started teaching during these years and also went back to school for her master's degree. This was a pivotal time in her mother's life, as she had to step into a different role. Betsy had to deal with her husband, teenagers, and lots of complexity. Nancy remembers seeing her mother take on this new role with determination but also with some anger and not always confidently. But, Nancy could see new strength and courage in her mother that she had not previously seen. She learned firsthand that women need to be prepared to lead their families through dangerous times and that anger and frustration can accompany love. Nancy herself learned to handle lots of complexity because of all of the family and personal issues she confronted during her adolescent years. She said,

> *My parents and I had numerous arguments and angry words. However, I had received such a positive foundation from both of them that we all—father, mother, and daughter—emerged whole individuals who survived a difficult experience with love and respect for one another.*

Employment

As a teenager, Nancy had a job handing out literature for political campaigns. She also worked as a waitress during both high school and college and enjoyed it because she made "fabulous money." She explained that working as a waitress helped her strengthen her people, multitasking, and problem-solving skills. Nancy said her greatest motivating challenge at work was to get a table full of difficult people "eating out of my hand by the time they went out the door." It was the type of challenge she loved.

COLLEGE YEARS

After high school, in 1968, Nancy went straight to college at Kent State University; Jeff went to the University of Virginia on a football scholarship. During her first year at Kent, Nancy met a roommate who would become her dear friend for life. She valued this friendship greatly. Nancy majored in speech communications, as it was natural for her with her background and experience in debate. She had some excellent speech professors but thought they weren't tuned in to the circumstances and environment of the day. She earned As and Bs in all her speech classes but didn't do well in many others. Her parents were frustrated with her poor grades, but Nancy felt there were too many other issues to care about during these years. She worked two jobs to help support herself at college, with the challenges and complexity in her life continuing even after she moved away from home.

College Environment
The year 1968 was a volatile time on campuses throughout the United States, and Kent was particularly tumultuous because it was known as a "suitcase and party school." She described the situation:

> *In 1968, women were starting to assert themselves. Drugs were becoming part of the college culture, and LSD and marijuana were everywhere. It was a wide-open environment, and particularly strange for me. I saw kids, who had lived in cocoons all their lives, go crazy. Young women were starting to burn their bras. Most of these kids were just starting to see discrimination for the first time, while I had known it existed most of my life. Personally, I liked my bra and hadn't felt personal discrimination. I started paying attention to Vietnam. I would describe myself as the only Republican at Kent State University who became an anti-war person during that time period. So between the drugs, feminism, Vietnam, and family issues back home, I was distracted and didn't find my coursework very motivating.*

Nancy experimented with marijuana and alcohol and "had a ball for a short time." Then she started getting nervous when she saw people "dropping speed." She quickly decided it was all "crazy and insane" one night when she had to help get a female peer "out of a tree, and then had to deal with her as she come down from her high." Nancy exclaimed, "It was total madness."

The political situation continued heating up during this time. Nancy provided the following description of the environment and one specific situation:

> *Young men that I had danced with at the prom were dead in Vietnam. I could see no reason for this, so I became angry. I remember the night of the national lottery for the draft. Young women sobbed as the numbers were drawn. The Kennedy and King assassinations made us feel like the world was ending. Looking back, I would never wish those circumstances on anyone. It was the angriest and most volatile time I remember. Fringe anarchy was alive and well. I remember being called in to the dean's office, because there was going to be a peaceful demonstration. That's when I first learned about mob psychology. We ended up having 3,000 people walk. I learned that it takes only one idiot to turn it into a mob. It was peaceful, but boy did we have to work hard to make sure it was. The dean was right, and I didn't realize until halfway through the march what **could** have happened.*

Nancy learned that she needed to listen to others who had more experience and insight. She learned that people and groups are unpredictable and that she needed to think ahead at the possible unintended consequences of the behaviors of herself and others.

Dorm Presidency
Nancy became the president of her dorm, which housed 500 women. She first

ran and won a seat on the house council and then became president. She said, "it wasn't planned, it just happened." She decided originally to run for the council because of concerns about dorm hours. Women had curfews, and men did not. She said, "It didn't seem right that we had to be in at 9:00 or 10:00 p.m., when the boys could run around all night." Because she felt it was an important issue, she decided to become involved; she believed that she could help make the needed changes. As the president, she actually violated the rule herself to make her point. Of course, she got into trouble; however, she and others were able to get rid of unfair dorm hour regulations.

Life-Changing Moments
Nancy had two additional incidents during her college years that became life changing in a number of ways. She learned a great deal from both. She described the first one as follows:

> *In the midst of all these larger issues and challenges, another life experience provided opportunity to help me put some type of perspective with some common sense and dignity. One night, a group of students said they were going to take over the Speech and Hearing Fair. It was such a dumb thing to do, but they were very serious. They captured the building at KSU, and the riot police from Cleveland came in. Although I was not part of it, I went with everybody else to the curb. I saw a police officer split a kid's head open because the officer was frightened. Then it happened; I picked up a rock to throw. After I pitched the rock, I immediately stepped back and thought "You idiot! What are you doing?" The whole thing erupted into massive disaster that frightened me to my core. I understood the mob psychology first hand—the anger and the frustration. I knew immediately that I'd better step back and get my friends out of there.*

Nancy was reflective in the sense that she immediately began thinking of consequences to actions. She explained that it was obviously self-preservation, as she knew she would either get arrested or get hurt. Yet, the experience pierced her soul, as she could see consequences of the actions she and her friends could have taken if they had continued that night. The second experience was just as serious and dramatic:

> *The black panthers came to escort the black women out of the dorm on campus so they could set up a university off campus. There are dozens of young men, many armed. At nineteen years of age, I was president of a dorm with 500 young women. I requested that everyone stay in their rooms. I went to the black women in my dorm, and I was able to keep half of them there while the other half walked. I asked them not to do anything to anyone and not to call the riot police. I knew I had to be strong in front of everyone, but after it was over I went to my room, sobbed, and probably drank an illegal beer or two.*

Marriage and First Pregnancy
Nancy got engaged in December at age twenty, and her mother was not happy

because she wanted Nancy to finish college. Nancy got pregnant in January, and she and Jeff were married in March. After three years at Kent State, she went to the University of Virginia to be with her husband; she never finished her college degree. This was a sudden and shocking transition. She had been at Kent State dealing with people, guns, riots, and drugs, and now she was pregnant and married. Jeff was a football player, and they moved into married student housing with others who had children. It was an international student community with a focus on families and education. Married student housing was a "comfortable adventure." Yet, for all the "idyllic grandeur of UVA, other events were always pushing in." For example, she spoke of her husband coaching a basketball team in 1969 of little black children who lived on the street with no running water or plumbing.

Nancy settled into her first pregnancy and waited. She stayed updated and aware of the national issues. She made friends with other new mothers while she and Jeff transitioned into marriage after dating for six years. In October, at the age of twenty-one, her first child was born. Jonathan was incredible, and she quickly discovered that she loved having babies. This was quite a dramatic change in her life, but she felt comfortable in her new role as a mother. She did worry that Jeff was going to end up in Vietnam, so they made plans for him to enter military service and attend law school. He didn't pass the physical examination.

Law School Years
After Jeff graduated from UVA, the couple and their one child moved to the slums of Cleveland so that Jeff could attend law school at Case University. They moved from "lovely historic Charlottesville to the gritty bad neighborhood of Cleveland," so once again, it was time to "buck up and jump into another situation." Nancy spoke of the Hells Angels being their neighbors and numerous graduate students and many other folks being on all forms of public assistance. Jonathan, with his blue eyes and blonde hair, was often the only white male on the nearby playgrounds. She told the following story:

> *Originally, I said that my son couldn't play with guns of any kind, so I wouldn't buy him any toy weapons. Then I discovered he was playing guns with a broken beer bottle. I immediately put him in the car, went to Woolworths, and told him he could pick out any toy gun he wanted. That was the beginning of quite a collection.*

Nancy learned to be flexible based on her situation. Living in this new environment provided many important learning experiences for her. She explained, "I saw and lived a whole different side of life. I lived next to people who didn't have enough food to eat and whose kids didn't have coats." The living circumstances provided an interesting mix of very poor people who were never going to leave and then students of all nationalities who were temporary residents. Despite a few tense times, everyone got along well.

Jeff worked during these years, and Nancy babysat. Jeff's parents also helped financially since Jeff had received a full scholarship during his undergraduate years and didn't have one for graduate school. Even so, the couple still had to be very careful with money to get by. Nancy continued to read and keep up with what was happening around her in the community, state, and nation. During these years, she got pregnant with her second son. She told of a situation that occurred during her pregnancy that became pivotal in her perspective of feminism:

> *I will never forget when three female law students came up to me and said, "What are you doing? Why are you pregnant? Why is your husband in law school and not you?" I was surprised and angry; I then responded, "Do you know what true feminism is all about? Well you're not it." I told them feminism was about women supporting women in the choices they make. I told them that I was doing what I wanted to do at that point in my life and that they should support and respect me for my choices. They did not want to understand my choice.*

Nancy gave birth to their second son, Jeremy, while Jeff was still in law school.

CAREER AND FAMILY

When Jeff finished law school, he had a job offer in Marietta and an interview in Chicago. Jeff, Nancy, and the two boys decided to move back to Marietta. Nancy and Jeff didn't want to move back to their hometown but thought it best to have their children surrounded by relatives during their upbringings. Nancy said, "Although I was ready to go to Chicago, coming back here was the best thing we ever did. It has been an incredible place to raise children."

Community Involvement and Campaign Manager
Once Nancy moved back to Marietta, she immediately became involved in the community. She began working on a levy to build a new school for mentally disabled children and adults because she felt very passionate about the issue. She believed that there was a real need in the community for this type of facility—a "huge hole in the community fabric that needed to be finished." She immediately began looking for other "gaps in the community" and wanted to be a change agent for improvement.

Shortly after moving back to Marietta, she became pregnant with Justin, her third son. During this pregnancy, a friend from high school called and asked Nancy to run her city council campaign. Nancy had always loved politics and quickly agreed. She had worked on campaigns with her father when she was young and knew generally what this entailed. She had decided that she would rather "organize behind the scenes than ever be in front of the camera herself." The campaign went very well; her friend won, and Nancy became very excited about politics.

City Council

After Nancy's third son, Justin, was about seven months old, a member of the Marietta City Council resigned. Nancy, at the age of twenty-seven, received phone calls from some council members requesting that she fill the unexpired term and serve on the city council. Nancy declined over the phone but agreed to talk to them in person about it. Because she had three very young children at the time, she did not think it would work. However, after meeting with them, she decided she wanted to do it and was appointed to fill the unexpired term. Nancy spent ten months on city council and loved the work.

After Nancy finished the term, she stayed involved. She told her husband that she wanted to run for city council at large. Jeff reminded her that she wanted to have another baby, but Nancy wanted to run and did. She filed her petitions and then got pregnant, thus running her first official race "very pregnant" with her fourth child, Emily. During this time, Nancy had lots of complexity in her life. Her three-year-old son was "diagnosed with a disintegration of the hip socket, was in horrible pain, and had to wear dreadful leg braces." Jeff was serving on the school board and dealing with a teachers' strike, the first in the community's history. Her daughter Emily was born on Labor Day, the strike was settled, Justin adjusted to his brace, and Nancy won the council race in November. Because of her experience with complexity earlier in life, she had learned to thrive in unusual circumstances. She said, "Those were truly the best and worst of times. There were tears, laughter, a large family of support, and lots of stubborn determination."

On the city council, Nancy became the first female chair of the Police and Fire Committee. She told the following story:

We had an old police chief who wanted more policemen. He was not happy with a female being chair of the committee, and he informed me of that. I just smiled and told him that I couldn't be an advocate for more police officers unless I spent time in the cruisers. At that time, I had no idea what they did. So, I rode at two o'clock in the morning, and Jeff was beside himself. Although he had always been extraordinarily supportive, two o'clock in the morning was kind of pushing the limits. I didn't want to go during the day because I needed to see what they really had to deal with. I told the police chief that I could represent them well if I understood what they did and needed. Riding with them was a useful experience.

I also ran up against my first in-your-face prejudice. As a woman, I'd never ever had a problem before with this. In fact, I never paid a bit of attention to it until I got on city council. While riding in the cruiser, the captain said to me, "You just need to understand that I do not approve of you being in the cruiser." I said, "Do you not approve of me being in the cruiser because I'm a female or a civilian?" He almost swallowed his tongue and said, "I guess I don't approve because you are a woman." I told him that if he wanted to get more officers, then he'd better learn to work with me. I knew where he was, and he knew where I was. We ended up having mutual respect for each other and worked together well.

She also spoke of riding in a cruiser another time with an officer who decided to chase a suspect at high speeds to try to scare Nancy. Years later, he told her that she looked totally calm, and he didn't even see her blink. Little did he know just how scared she was.

During her city council terms, Nancy was assigned to various committees and had to learn everything as quickly as possible. She believes that this local committee work was very helpful in preparing her future positions in government. She said,

> The knowledge was incredible, and applying the knowledge was particularly helpful. I worked with all different kinds of people including police officers, fireman, trustees, and business people. I worked with the water and sewer department, so I could talk about sludge all day long. Being in local government was the best education in the entire world. In fact, it should be a prerequisite for anybody that goes into state or federal government. I've run into many people who have never served in local government that are missing a huge piece of practical application of real life—of what it feels like to govern. Local government is where you spin straw into gold.

She explained that local issues are very similar to state issues; they are just at different levels. She believes that when individuals understand the issues at the local level, they can quickly learn the same issues on a statewide or federal level.

During her last term on city council, Nancy gave birth to Kate, her fifth and youngest child. In fact, the entire city council (mostly men) came to the hospital to see her after the delivery. The council had come to know Nancy's children through the years as she occasionally brought them to meetings and council members helped entertain them. She mentioned that it was amazing to see how small children could defuse tense situations.

Mayor

In 1984, Jeff told Nancy that since she was working nearly full time with her city council work that she might as well run for mayor. There had never been a female mayor in Marietta, and "a woman mayor with five small children was unheard of." Marietta was going to be Ohio's first bicentennial city, and Nancy was a "Putnam with 200 years of history." She decided to run for mayor. People knew Nancy was competent and could do the job, but some were concerned that with five children she would not be able to do the job well. In fact, most women in the city did not support her in the race because they felt she should be home with her children. Being the mayor of Marietta was a full-time job as it was the chief executive officer of the city. She explains:

> I was shocked that the women did not support me. No woman had ever been mayor. There were letters to the editor about diapers in the mayor's office and pink curtains. I never questioned my ability to do it. I never questioned that it wouldn't be an absolutely incredible adventure. My biggest horror was that

women were negative. I won, barely won, by about 500 votes. My opponent was an incumbent councilman who had been there for years. I decided that I wouldn't stand up and **tell** people that a woman can do this job; I'd just **show** them.

I put together a wonderful team of people who would work **with** me, not **for** me. We worked together and had incredible things happen. The gentleman who wrote about the pink curtains ended up volunteering for my reelection campaign.

Nancy told of a humorous, yet particularly powerful learning experience she had when she first became mayor. During the first month of her mayorship, she said that she "felt pretty important." The governor of Ohio was coming to Marietta for one day, and she wanted to impress him. She told the following story about his visit:

I wore a gorgeous red hat and a beautiful gray suit, and I bought new shoes for the event—four-inch black pumps. I had only been in office for a month, but I was determined to show him what an Appalachian woman was all about. He was a big man and very charming. Halfway through the day I realized that my hat had given me a headache and that my feet felt like they would probably need to be amputated. My feet hurt so badly that I doubted I was ever going to be able to get my shoes off. I was in true pain from my head to my toes. I was at the senior center where the governor was speaking and because of the pain had to slip out the back door into the secluded alley. I quickly took off the hat and discovered, of course, that I had hat hair and a large dent in my forehead. I then took my shoes off and my feet immediately went from size 7 to 12. I soon realized that I would never be able to get my shoes back on my feet as they were so swollen. So, I threw my hat back on my head, picked up my shoes, and was hobbling down the alley probably uttering some really interesting words.

Suddenly I heard a voice behind me: "Oh now we see what women in southern Ohio are made of!" It was the governor and the entire press core. I was standing there with shoeless, swollen, enlarged feet, a large dented forehead, holding my beautiful black four-inch high heels in one hand. The only thing I could think of to do was to laugh and say, "Well perhaps you should try and put these heels on yourself!" We laughed as he helped me down the alley with the press taking lots of pictures. I crawled into the car and someone took me home to change, and I was able to finish the day with a different pair of shoes tightly fitted around my bandaged feet.

The next morning one of my sons came running upstairs, jumped on my bed, and said, "Mommy, your bare feet are in the newspaper." The kids were laughing, giggling, and jumping, but I was so enraged because I thought I was so important. I learned two very valuable lessons that week. I realized that I really wasn't that important and that a position shouldn't change someone. I also learned that I wasn't going to make it in politics if I couldn't learn to laugh at myself.

She became known by some as the barefoot mayor. In fact, over the years she has received at least 150 pairs of shoes—from combat boots to ballerina slippers.

Nancy had a number of other learning experiences during her two terms (nearly eight years) as mayor. For example, she led the plans for a bicentennial celebration and her office raised over a million dollars locally. The energy and enthusiasm on the committee and in the community were amazing. Nancy worked very closely with the governor on these events. One day the Ohio State Development Department called her and said they had a delegation from the Hubei province of China who wanted to come to Marietta and discuss a Sister City partnership. They came, discussions went well, and city leaders had a great time hosting the delegation. At the end of the delegation's visit, Nancy was delighted with an invitation she received:

I was sitting in my office with the local chamber director when the leader of the delegation asked me if I would be willing to lead a delegation to the interior of China to represent Ohio. I was flabbergasted and then of course accepted. After months of planning, it was a great honor to lead a delegation of ten people from the business and agriculture community into the interior of China. It was an unforgettable experience. I learned so much as I observed the protocol and listened to the different languages. Making comments, asking questions, and giving speeches through an interpreter were quite an education in public presentation.

Nancy said they she learned so much from this three-week trip to China. She told of one particular amazing experience on this trip.

Because I was a mayor, I was never "off" and never allowed to leave the public stage. There was always a microphone in my face and somebody watching me. It was exhausting but exhilarating as well. I remember walking into their civic auditorium one night and being so tired with swollen eyes. I was totally surrounded by people touching me. This was their big civic event planned specifically so they could welcome us. We pulled up in front of the auditorium and there are hundreds of people with cameras standing in front waving. I got off the bus, waved, and greeted the group. I went into the auditorium and found 3,000 Chinese people with American flags singing God Bless America. We walked down the middle of the auditorium and smiled. Everybody watched us throughout the program, which included the Shanghai acrobats and opera. At the end of the program, one hundred young children dressed in incredible costumes sang an American song to us. After they finished, everyone looked at me, so I got up and walked on the stage. I stood in the middle of the children and asked my entourage and the host to join me. Of course, I was hoping I wouldn't do anything wrong and cause an international crisis of some kind. It got very quiet, and all I said was "Sha Sha," which is "thank you." The audience cheered loudly. Then we sang with the children on stage. It was an unbelievable experience.

During this trip, Nancy received reinforcement regarding her ability to listen. She was able to generally figure out what people were saying when they spoke in Chinese. She learned to watch people's expressions to understand what was happening around her. Although she was in a different environment and didn't speak the predominant language, she was able to refine perceptions and abilities in ways she had never done before.

Director of the Governor's Office of Appalachia
Near the end of her second term as mayor, Nancy was running for reelection. Her mother had become ill and spent four months in a coma, eventually dying from surgical complications in September of 1990. During that time, George Voniovich was running for governor, and Nancy knew him when he was the mayor of Cleveland. They had agreed and disagreed on a number of issues both rural and urban, but she liked and respected him. After he became governor, he called Nancy and asked her to be the director of the Governor's Office of Appalachia. Because of her family situation and the reelection, she declined. He called her again and told her that he really needed her to take this position, and she declined again. Then he asked her to meet with him in person, and Jeff and her children encouraged her to go. After meeting with him and having multiple family discussions, Nancy ended up accepting the position which included twenty-nine counties and the federal A.R.C. board. She drove back and forth to Columbus (a two-hour drive) and stayed in a hotel a few nights a week. She traveled throughout twenty-nine counties and was on the road every day for three years. From the mother of five, wife, and former mayor of a city—to the politics of state government, twenty-nine counties, federal policies, governor's representative, and weekend mother—those three years proved to be a difficult challenge. The work was exhilarating, but the guilt of being wife and mother by phone (a situation I refer to as 'teleparenting') was painful. Although there were some difficult times, Jeff and the children did well and provided Nancy with an important source of support during those years.

Lieutenant Governor
As the director of the Governor's Office of Appalachia, she occasionally traveled with the governor to events. On one occasion, the governor told her that his lieutenant governor was going to run for the Senate, and that it was time for a female to be lieutenant governor. Nancy explained,

> *I had no idea he was talking about me, so I told him I was proud of him and said, "It's about damn time! Do you know how many women would be phenomenal?" After offering to give him a list of qualified women, the governor told me he wanted me to be his running mate. Surprise was the least of my reactions as I said, "Let's talk."*
>
> *His office ended up talking to many women, while he and I met several times to look at our options. My name was not mentioned in the press speculations about possible running mates. He called the house on a Thursday evening, and Justin answered and informed the governor that "Mom wasn't home. She was busy at the grocery store buying lots of food." About two hours later, Justin casually said, "Oh, I forgot to tell you that the governor called, so you better call him back." We had a big discussion with the children before I called him back. We decided I should accept the invitation to run with the governor.*

The announcement of Nancy being Governor Vonovich's running mate was quite a surprise. People wondered who this female from rural Ohio was and what she was all about. Because the opposition was minimal, choosing an unknown female was safe for the governor. However, he informed Nancy that she needed to meet and "get to know all of Ohio." So, Nancy spent the next ten months in every single county in the state introducing herself and talking about policies. Nancy believes she had many opportunities during this time to hone her leadership skills. She learned to deal with statewide and federal policy and security issues. Although she knew twenty-nine counties, Ohio has eighty-eight counties, so she spent her time traveling and speaking to most of them. She had a schedule of where she was going to be and during the summer, when her children weren't in school, they could pick and choose if they wanted to go on the road with her. Campaigning was exhausting for her, but she learned that "it is good to have a lot of adrenaline."

All of her children were in attendance when she was sworn in as the lieutenant governor of Ohio in January of 1995. She served for the next four years as lieutenant governor. The governor felt strongly that his lieutenant governor should be a working partner, so Nancy was the director of the cabinet and, with a staff of eight, had extensive responsibilities with agriculture, development, and employment services. The governor gave her other critical responsibilities during her term as lieutenant governor that were helpful for her growth and development. She had responsibilities that she felt she was able to use to make a difference. Nancy had another interesting and helpful international experience when she spoke at the U.S. Midwest-Japan trade conference in Tokyo representing the governor. During her time as lieutenant governor, she had the opportunity to travel to foreign countries, such as Mexico and Italy, and also met with the Nation Guard troops in Germany and Turkey. Each of these experiences provided valuable development experiences for her.

Governor
At the end of 1998, near the end of her term as lieutenant governor, the governor needed to leave office eleven days early at the end of 1998 to be sworn in as a U.S. Senator. Hence, Nancy became a "little piece of history," becoming the first female Ohio state governor. She only served until the newly elected governor was sworn into office, but she did serve as governor for these eleven days. The day the new governor was sworn into office, she was also sworn into the Ohio legislature.

DEVELOPMENTAL INFLUENCES

Nancy said that the primary developmental influence she had was the opportunity to serve in various positions (paid and non-paid), growing in knowledge and competence from each. Nancy spoke of two other categories of developmental influences beneficial in her career progression: support systems and motherhood.

Support Systems
Nancy clearly stated that her husband provided more support in her life than anything or anyone else. He was encouraging, yet challenged her ideas so she could carefully think through opportunities and consequences. Once she made a decision, he was behind her one hundred percent.

Another important and critical individual was a naturalized citizen from the Philippines, named Carmen. Before Nancy was mayor, she hired regular babysitters and used the children's grandparents to help with childcare. However, once she became mayor, she needed full-time care for her children and home. Carmen worked in their home for seven and a half years, and Nancy said that "she was a gift." Carmen was married, but lived only a few blocks away. She worked five days a week, while the boys were primarily in school. Nancy said, "She cared for the two girls and herded the boys around. If it hadn't been for Carmen, I couldn't have served as mayor." Carmen became an important part of the family during those years providing the support that Nancy needed to work effectively as mayor. She gave Nancy the peace of mind she needed to know her children were well cared for.

Nancy's flexible schedule provided the ability to balance her work and family roles. If she needed to go to school plays, parent-teacher conferences, or another programs, she was able to adjust her schedule accordingly. It was a small town and had a culture such that Carmen could easily bring the children into the mayor's office to see their mother and go out to lunch together. If Nancy needed to be home, she could get there in five minutes. Although the phone never stopped ringing at home and the kids had to deal with "irate crazy people" sometimes, Nancy, Jeff, and the children learned to "weave it into their lives." Life was busy, but Nancy always made time to enjoy her children. She believes that her children provided a foundation and support system for her work that has helped her be successful through the years. She described them now as "wonderful well-seasoned adults, who lead lives of adventure and promise."

Motherhood
Nancy believes that motherhood was a critical developmental influence in her pathway toward learning how to lead. She was able to develop many new skills and strengthen existing competencies through her experiences raising children. First, she noted that motherhood taught her to "go with the flow," which is a crucial skill in political and governmental leadership. Second, motherhood helped her develop and fine-tune her listening skills, which is "an incredibly important skill in politics." Third, Nancy attributes her increased empathy and communication skills to being a parent. Finally, she "definitely learned a lot and strengthened" her abilities in the "arts of multitasking and balancing multiple responsibilities." For example, sometimes she had difficulty hiring babysitters and had to take her children with her to city council committee meetings. Fortu-

nately, her colleagues were comfortable with that and the children were "pretty well behaved so they didn't interfere too much." She practiced her teaching skills with her children, as she had to work with them to help them learn to behave. She said, "They knew they had to color and play games, and couldn't cry and yell. They knew that when we were there, it was a quiet time." She learned to be fairly proficient at handling multiple demands and complexity from being a mother.

CAREER DEVELOPMENT AND CHALLENGES

Nancy obviously did not have a formal political career plan. Her life plan was to bear and raise children while contributing in some way to the community and its citizens. Nancy stated, "My career just evolved into what it became. It just happened." In fact, she mentioned some previous conversations with other female politicians who felt that most women of their generation who ended up in politics didn't have a plan to do so. It just happened.

Nancy shared a few stories where gender became "an issue." For example, she "wore a chocolate suede pant suit to be sworn in as a legislator in the House." A male colleague approached her on the floor of the House and informed her of a dress code that said women could not wear pants. She said to this gentleman, "well not any longer" as she laughed and walked away.

It is important to note that Nancy called them "challenges not necessarily barriers," because she doesn't believe that she had a glass ceiling in her situation. She explained, "I can't say that I fully understand the glass ceiling concept, as I didn't feel it in my situation. In some circumstances, my gender actually opened doors for me." When asked whether she felt things would have been different or easier if she'd been a man, she said, "No" and that "It wouldn't have been nearly as much fun either." She did not feel barriers because she was always in positions "where no one was going to push" her around. She did "hit a few walls," but they again became "challenges rather than barriers." In fact, she enjoyed a "wall" from time to time; she explains,

> *Walls sometimes helped me go through a self-realization phase. I would take some time to reflect and figure out if and why someone had a problem with me or my actions. I tried to understand if their issue with me was related to my gender or something else. Sometimes it was a gender issue, but this became an interesting challenge for me, and I don't believe it ever thwarted my progress.*

LEADERSHIP STYLE AND PHILOSOPHY

Nancy spoke about how her former staff would have described her leadership style. Her first response was that they would say that no one really "worked for Nancy; they worked with her." She believes that her staff always felt they were part of a team. Because of this, she feels that her staff would also say they felt accepted by Nancy and their own colleagues. She mentioned that she also enjoyed socializing with her valuable team and their families.

The staff always felt that Nancy was particularly driven to "leave some footprint" through making a difference. She wanted her staff to do "some extraordinary things" while she was positioned as their leader. To do this, she wanted to hire competent, self-starting individuals who "could pick up and run with whatever task they were given." She wanted to hire people who could manage themselves and did not want to be micromanaged. To help make this difference, she desired and believed in the importance of hiring up. She always looked for smart people who could effectively be part of her team. She wanted individuals who didn't feel like they had to always ask permission. She wanted bright and intelligent people who were willing to spend the time needed to learn and were not afraid to challenge her. She believed that it was then her role as a leader to help her staff continue to learn and develop themselves individually. Speaking of the satisfaction she felt in seeing her former employees succeed in other roles, she said,

> *I wasn't offended when individuals took the new skills they'd gained from working with me, and used them as stepping stones for more development. For example, I recently spoke to two individuals who worked with me a number of years ago; one is now in law school while another (chief of staff) is finishing his Ph.D. at the University of Michigan. They'll both become very influential individuals. I enjoyed challenging my staff to get as much knowledge and education as possible.*

Overall, creating the best team was critical in "leaving the footprints" she yearned to leave.

Nancy enjoyed facilitating meaningful discussions and had her own style to accomplish this. Her team had countless conversations and always knew that Nancy would ask a variety of questions like, "Why are we doing this? What's the benefit in this?" If she had a contingent problem or challenge, she would ask six or seven questions like "Have you looked here? Have you asked a question about this? Have you done that?" She believes that her staff members felt comfortable with her leadership style and were able to be candid with her.

ADVICE

Nancy provided insightful advice for women interested in political leadership. First, Nancy believes that government, volunteering, and general community work at the local level can be very powerful preparation for leadership. She explained that volunteerism is particularly helpful as one needs to have and feel a "sense of place" and understand where one has come from. Nancy also believes that it is important to know regional politics and history. Second, Nancy explained that each individual should "build his or her base of knowledge and needs to spend time and earn dues. Only then "can you try to get the ticket punched." Third, she said that it is very important for women to keep their sense of humor, which, she acknowledges, is sometimes difficult to do. She advised, "Learn to laugh and find humor in yourself and others. Learn to enjoy all of the things around you." She said,

> *If you don't keep your sense of humor, you will start taking yourself way too seriously. I know this from experience. The people (men and women in this profession) take themselves way too seriously and think they are so bloody important. They're not. They might have their fifteen minutes of fame, but there is so much more to life than politics.*

Finally, she suggested that all young women learn to listen and absorb what is going on around them. Learn from everything that is happening including all opportunities and challenges; this also helps people keep everything in perspective. Women should learn to be reflective and enhance their ability to step back and constantly look at their surroundings and circumstances, saying, "If you can't step back and look at where you've been and then look ahead at where you're going you'll surely fall into a deep hole."

FINAL THOUGHTS

Nancy believes that politics should never become one's whole life, because "sometimes you win and sometimes you lose." Although difficult to keep in perspective at times, she has always believed that it is the family that keeps one focused on what is truly most important in life—spouses, children, grandchildren, friends, and service. Nancy concluded our interview with this "basic but absolute philosophy about government":

> *We are here on earth for a miniscule period of time. People shouldn't make government their entire life's work. Individuals need to enjoy their lives in so many other ways. They need to be broadly and continually learning and developing themselves. The worst mistake that politicians and public servants sometimes make is thinking their jobs **are** their entire life's work. There's always something more to do, there's always something more to learn, and there's always something more to become.*

Nancy has served in the community and state for many years. She has felt driven to make a difference in many domains of her life, and she has. She believes that she has developed leadership from every dimension of her life, and that all these experiences and opportunities have been integrated to become her life's work.

Chapter 10

Governor Olene Walker

I learned a great lesson from being a PTA president one year. If you want things done, you don't tell people it won't take much time. Instead you say, "This is so important that it will take time!" You have to get people to buy in before they will be willing to put forth the time and energy to make a difference.

~ Governor Olene Walker

I interviewed Governor Olene Walker at her home in Salt Lake City, Utah on May 10, 2005. She was sworn in as Utah's fifteenth governor on November 5, 2003, and she served as Utah's first woman governor until early 2005. Walker spearheaded many important initiatives including education programs, healthcare reform, workforce development, and tax reform. Her peers recognized her leadership ability and elected her to chair the National Conference of Lieutenant Governors. Olene was also elected as the president of the National Association of Secretaries of State, the only lieutenant governor ever to be elected to that position. Prior to becoming governor, Olene Walker was a leader in the Utah House of Representatives where she served as majority whip and assistant majority whip. Using her strong academic background, she led Utah toward improvements in education and literacy throughout her decades of public service in a variety of roles. This chapter will share Governor Walker's insights, stories, and experiences, helping us understand her lifelong leadership development journey.

FAMILY BACKGROUND

Olene Smith was born on November 15, 1930, in Ogden, Utah and was raised on a family farm west of the city. During that time, she lived in the same house her father lived in from his birth to his death. Olene was reared in a stable, modest middle-income home and felt secure and loved. Coming from a rural, hardworking background, Olene was instilled with a strong work ethic and a desire to help those in her community. As the second of five children, she was also taught the importance of family and the need to work together to accomplish the task at hand. She has three brothers (not quite two years older, twenty months younger, and six years younger than she) and one sister (fifteen years her junior).

During Olene's upbringing, she doesn't remember her parents differentiating between the "boys and the girls regarding education and general work expectations." Although the boys typically milked the cows, Olene said she could "milk a cow just fine." All of the children learned to work hard by fulfilling a variety of tasks and responsibilities. She said,

> *I don't know whether my father was an educator so he could farm or if he farmed so he could be an educator! We lived on a farm with dairy and beef cattle, and we also grew crops like tomatoes, potatoes, sugar beets, alfalfa, grain, and corn. We really learned to work hard. I remember spending days thinning and topping beats, planting tomatoes, and digging up potatoes. My dad use to call the farm his "golf game" and we all learned to play.*

Olene doesn't remember any discussion about whether or not she and her siblings would go to college. She said,

> *It was just assumed that we would attend college. Both of my parents had gone on to college and to receive higher degrees, so we all just planned to go to college when we finished high school. The question was not **if** we were going, but **where** we were going.*

Education was clearly an important value in the Smith household.

Father

Olene's father, Thomas O. Smith, graduated from college with his bachelor's and master's degrees during the depression, and the only available job at that time was to "round up and teach the kids who were sloughing school." He did well and quickly moved into administration. He spent many years as a principal of an elementary school, junior high, and a high school. He was then appointed to be the superintendent of Ogden City Schools and remained in that position for nearly twenty-five years until his retirement. Olene and her siblings attended Weber High School, the archrival of Ogden High School, so there were many debates on who would win football and basketball games at the dinner table.

After Olene's father became an administrator, he eventually received his Ph.D. from the University of Southern California by going to school during the summers. She remembers piling into the family car each summer to make the long journey to California so that he could finish his degree. Olene said, "I've often wondered what motivated him to get a Ph.D. It was definitely not typical, even of educators for that time, but he felt obtaining the highest levels of education to be an extremely important goal." Both of her father's parents had only eighth-grade educations because that was what was required at that time. They had a very small farm, which was their meager livelihood.

Thomas was also very involved in church and community work. He served for twenty-five years in a non-paid leadership position in his church. He was involved continuously in community work, and Olene remembers him serving on community boards that were instrumental in building a new hospital in town and also bringing the symphony to Ogden. When she was young, Olene remembers her family attending the symphony whenever it played in Ogden.

Mother

Olene's mother, Nina Hadley Smith, started teaching elementary school after she earned her associate degree at the early age of eighteen. She ceased her teaching career when she got married, but later returned to the classroom when Weber School District became "desperate for teachers during World War II." She then continued her schooling and obtained a bachelor's degree in education from Utah State University. Olene knew that her mother was a wonderful teacher because years later "people remembered her for her caring nature and willingness to give special attention to those who needed it." They said she would stay in during recess and after school to help struggling students. Although it was unusual for the time, Nina taught school most of the time Olene was growing up. However, Olene remembers her mother taking "some years off," particularly after her younger sister was born.

Although both of Nina's parents only had eighth-grade educations, she and her three sisters all pursued careers in education, teaching school. Olene finds this situation "amazing and ironic" as her mother's parents were farmers and had limited resources for most of their lives. Yet, somehow Olene's grandparents stressed the importance of a college education to their children, and education became one of Nina's core values. Nina also learned to work hard growing up on a family farm, and she continued that tradition after she married. In addition to the farm work, her mother planted an acre-and-a-half garden for family, neighbors, and friends. As a child, Olene spent countless hours working in her mother's garden. It was a way of life and Olene felt that it was important to teach her own children the necessity of hard work. She would bring them from Salt Lake to her mother's farm to "give them the opportunity to experience farm life." Many important lessons were taught while weeding, pruning, and harvesting that garden. Nina also left an important legacy for her children and grandchildren. Olene said, "Even when she passed away at seventy-nine, my mother still had an acre garden that she meticulously planted each summer. She loved working hard and sharing the bounty of her garden with family and friends."

Olene's mother was also very involved in their church and had various service positions throughout the decades, including being the president of the women's organization for many years. Nina was also Olene's 4H leader and, later in life, a school volunteer. Olene also described her mother's efforts in other community work:

> We were probably better off than most families because we were a two-income family and had a large farm. My mother, being very industrious and frugal, sewed the clothes for my family. When she had extra fabric, she made clothes

for others in need. I kept saying, "Why do you sew for other people?" She would say, "Well, it would be nice for this family to have something extra."

Extended Family

Both of Olene's grandparents lived close to her in Utah. She remembers going to one grandparent's home on Christmas Eve and the other on Christmas day for many years. She said, "I was very close to my grandparents, and they were certainly an influence in my life." She spent time with relatives on holidays and other special occasions. Her father had lots of aunts who were her mother's age, and "they'd get together on everybody's birthdays." Olene feels that she had a "very close extended family" that provided stability, support, and encouragement for her to develop throughout the years. One important value she acquired from her family and extended family was that everyone has an obligation to contribute to society. She has kept this with her throughout her life.

CHILDHOOD AND YOUTH

Personality and Schooling

Olene said that she was quite outgoing as a child. She remembers having lots of friends her age as she was growing up, more girls than boys. She also enjoyed being involved in many different activities. She believes she was fairly courageous as a child, which she illustrated in the following story:

> *I remember one time, when I was about eight or nine years old, I was supposed to give a 2 ½ minute talk in church. I remembered arriving at the chapel and someone asking about my talk, and I realized that I had totally forgotten about it. I rushed to my mother, told her the situation, and asked her to tell the people in charge that I wasn't prepared and couldn't give it. She asked me whose responsibility it was that I took this assignment, and I answered that it was mine. Then she told me she would help, but that I must give the talk. I remember sitting down with my mother for a few minutes and coming up with some ideas. She said, "I think if you could find a song you could talk about, then you could use the words as part of your speech." I remembered I liked a song about prayer and took the words up with me to speak. I got up, read some of the words, and then talked about the importance of prayer. I did pretty well and felt good about it. When I look back on that experience, I think that I must have been brave. I also learned from my mother that I needed to take responsibility for my own assignments.*

Olene remembers people telling her that she had given a great talk and how they appreciated that she hadn't read the whole talk like others did. This gave her some confidence in her speaking ability as a child and may have led to her interest and involvement in debate and extemporaneous speaking later in her youth.

Olene shared a few more insights into her childhood. First, she told the following humorous story about her limited vision as a child:

> *I remember having a sleepover when I was ten or eleven one time in our big front yard. We decided to see who could come up with the best idea of something that could actually happen in our lifetime. One girl came up with the idea that a man would walk on the moon. The rest of us wouldn't let her count it, because we knew it could never happen. To this day, she still accuses me of being the one that wouldn't let her count it.*

When men actually walked on the moon, Olene was reminded that even unimaginable events can occur and that having lofty goals and dreaming about the future can be helpful. The second insight she shared was that she was always a little afraid of heights. Her friends used to ride up to the top of the haystack holding on the forks of the derrick, and she remembers doing it a few times and hating it. She recalls being aware of this weakness and wishing she wasn't afraid. She began acknowledging her strengths and weaknesses during these years, which is an important characteristic of successful leaders. Finally, she remembers her strong desire to attend school as a young girl and some struggles she had that also demonstrate her childhood personality:

> *When I was five, we didn't have a kindergarten; however, I was able to go to school in a first grade class for about three days with a cousin. Somehow I could read pretty well so the first-grade teacher told my mother that she could put me in second grade. Of course, my mother wisely said, "No." I later stayed with an aunt that year and was able to go to full-day summer kindergarten, which was great. However, after lunch every day, the teachers wanted us to go to sleep on a mat. I had trouble holding still and never went to sleep. They picked the children to go do crafts by how fast they went to sleep, and I was always last. It probably warped my whole psyche!*

Olene described herself as a good student, but quickly mentioned that she was one of many good students in her schools. She said she definitely didn't stand out in art and music (singing). Yet, she remembers that she must have been viewed by adults as somewhat influential to her peers. For example, in sixth grade the school administration called four or five girls into the office and asked them to help some of the others who were being left out and struggling. She remembers doing a "fairly good job for a while." She recalls having a cognitive awareness of the fact that she should be inclusive during this year, and that commitment to inclusiveness stayed with her throughout her career.

During high school, Olene said she was academically strong but said there were several students who "competed for top honors." She was sufficiently competitive that getting good grades was important to her. Olene felt she was in one of the outstanding groups in her school. This was a group of about fifteen girls with a lot of different personalities. Olene and three others were more of the "tight group," but she always felt a burden to try to make sure people didn't feel left out. Regarding dating she said, "Although I was asked out more than anyone should be, there was always some very popular boy who wouldn't even look my way." Looking back she wishes boys hadn't been that important and that she would have just focused more on studies.

Activities and Employment

Olene enjoyed keeping busy and active as a child. She remembers spending a lot of time working on the farm and in the home. When she and her siblings had time to play, she recalls "riding horses and bikes a lot." Olene and her friends also used to make up stories and act them out among the farm equipment on the property. She also recalls a lot of evenings playing "kick the can, hide and seek and Red Rover, Red Rover" with both siblings and friends. She remembers swimming in the canal that ran close by her home, even though today it would have been considered unsafe. She recalled having numerous sleepovers with friends, especially during the summertime. Olene also spoke of being very involved in her church throughout her upbringing. She and her family went to weekly meetings, attended banquets and other activities, and participated in service projects. She also liked playing sports with her brothers and provided the following delightful description:

> *I used to play football with my brothers. I wasn't especially well coordinated, but I was pretty tough. I remember one time my mother saying, "Olene, I don't care if you want to play football with the boys, but you can't force your friends to play because they always get hurt and come in crying." I grew up with brothers who were kind of rough and tumble, and I loved playing football with them. Two of my brothers ended up playing football in high school and one played at the University of Utah.*

Olene also spoke of the importance of reading in her life. She said her family frequented the library when she was a child and youth. It was common for her family to meet at the library after shopping on Saturdays, where they would get new books for the week.

As Olene became a teenager, she was interested and involved in leadership. She was elected as student body president of her small junior high, but her parents felt that the ninth-grade teacher did not provide the educational opportunities that existed in the school where her father was principal, so she changed schools. However, in high school, she had plenty of leadership positions. Olene admitted that she and several other friends were chosen probably more than their fair share for these responsibilities because they had good organizational and management skills. She was president or had a leadership role in several clubs. She served as a youth group president in her church and had various responsibilities in that role. She said that she never looked at these responsibilities as "more than routine and what was expected." She and other close friends were often in charge of assemblies and other high school events. She recalls being elected as an officer in Pep Club. Now, as she looked back on that experience, she said, "Why in the world did we waste our time decorating football and basketball player lockers and doing other Pep Club activities? It seems like we should have been doing more substantial work."

During her youth, she also became involved in 4H and orchestra. She excelled in 4H and in fact won a state award for sewing a suit with a blouse, skirt, and jacket. Because she won the state competition, she had the opportunity to travel to Chicago for the national event her senior year. She said,

> The conference organizers asked me to be on a panel at the national event. After I presented at the panel, the head of Kraft Foods asked me to chair a large forum two days later that would have 4H leaders, business people, and others participating and attending. Although I panicked a little because of the magnitude of the assignment, I conducted the session, and it was a great experience. I felt very good about it. I think about what an incredible experience that was for a seventeen year old.

Olene played the violin for the orchestra for many years and enjoyed developing her musical abilities, but felt that her "true talents lay elsewhere." She said, "I don't know why my parents wasted money for so long on lessons." She was always the second violinist, not the first. However, from this experience she learned the importance of contributing to a group or team even when she wasn't the best or the leader.

Olene also loved physical activity and played lots of informal sports. She was "capable and adequate" but reminded me that she was never the superstar. She was always one of the first five or six chosen and remembers playing lots of dodge ball, baseball, and other "gym games" but not basketball or football, as "girls couldn't play organized basketball or football during those years." She mentioned that their junior and senior high schools didn't have formal sports programs for girls. In high school, she was president of the ski club and was a reasonably good skier. She believes that participation in sports helped her develop skills like teamwork, toughness, dealing well with conflict and loss, and "working together with people who are different from you for the common good."

Olene absolutely loved debate and believes it was good for her development in many ways. She did extemporary speaking and said that this was "probably the best developmental activity" she had to prepare her for service in the legislature. She learned to think clearly and quickly on her feet. Speech and debate gave her practice in presenting in front of people, using logical information, and putting together rational arguments. She always had the same debate partner, and they learned to work as a team. She believes this experience was "critical" in helping her prepare for future leadership roles. Debate, speech, and other similar opportunities helped her continue to build self-confidence during these critical years. Olene said, "I probably felt as much at ease in communicating and speaking as anyone I knew." The school "always touted us as the top debate team." Years later, Olene's debate partner told her that she felt it was unfair that Olene spent less time preparing for their debates and always seemed to receive the higher marks from the judges.

Last but not least, Olene admitted that one of her favorite activities during high school was dating young men. During her adolescent years, she remembers being a little "boy crazy like teenage girls become." She explained that in her dating days kids just didn't "hang out" like they do today. When she was in high school, she could occasionally work in two dates on certain Saturdays. She said, "I was the queen of getting those dates in." Looking back, she said she wasted "way too much time" in that area.

Olene's main job during high school was still unpaid work on her family farm and in her home. However, after she graduated from high school, she worked at a little restaurant during the summer. She said,

> My folks tried to talk me out of working at the restaurant as there was a lot of work to do on the farm and the family had only one car. The restaurant was probably 4 ½ miles from home, but I was determined to work there. Often I walked there and walked home. It took me about an hour and twenty minutes to walk to work if I went fast. Sometimes I caught a bus part way but that still took more than an hour.

She believed this work experience was good for her in a number of ways. It gave her the opportunity to manage money and the experience of working for someone other than her own family.

Influential Individuals

Olene had a "collective appreciation" for many individuals during her youth but remembers a few teachers and a coach that were particularly influential. First, she spoke of a fourth-grade teacher whom all of the children loved. This teacher, Charlotte McGrath, had a "tiny little store down in west Weber," and during the summer, Olene and her friends would ride horses and bicycles down to this store to see her. She remembers this teacher having a positive, happy disposition; they always felt accepted by her. When Olene and her peers moved on to fifth grade, the students were disappointed to be assigned a teacher who was going to retire and would actually fall asleep during class. She remembers that when the students returned from Thanksgiving, their former fourth-grade teacher had been reassigned to their class. The students were thrilled and enjoyed the rest of the year. This teacher was passionate about what she taught and also had a way of helping the students find joy in learning and education.

Christian Graves, Olene's high school debate coach, was also influential in her life during these years. This coach "really urged and encouraged" Olene in speech and debate. Olene believes that she was able to excel because of the influence of the coach. Although she remembers several other teachers being influential, she only mentioned one other by name. Harold Brown was influential because he "was a great teacher and treated me with a great deal of respect." All of these people gave Olene general encouragement and support. She felt because they all knew her parents as outstanding community leaders that they expected and anticipated that she too would excel.

Life Expectations

As a child, Olene doesn't remember contemplating whether she had various options in her life. She remembers at one time thinking she would love to be a great symphony orchestra director, but she quickly realized she didn't have the musical expertise to do that. She also recalls wanting to be a librarian because she loved to read. Although her mother and other women she knew taught school, she didn't have women role models in leadership positions. As a young girl, she doesn't remember even considering most professional occupational options because of the lack of these role models or mentors. Yet, as she entered college, she knew that she did not want to be a secretary, a nurse, or even a teacher in the public schools, the job opportunities that most girls considered in the early fifties.

UNDERGRADUATE COLLEGE YEARS

Olene received a scholarship in debate from Weber College, now Weber State University, so she started her college career in her own hometown. During her freshman year, she became involved in debate and extemporaneous speaking. At Weber College, she lived at home but was in a sorority. Social pursuits continued to play an important role in Olene's life. She said, "I think I was the only one that got rushed by every sorority at the college. Although it seems so insignificant now, it was important to me at the time." She also worked part time in the Athletic Office, which was a busy and exciting place to be for a freshman student.

Olene visited Brigham Young University (BYU) campus for a week during the summer after her freshman year of college to visit her brother who was going to school there. She said,

> *I quickly discovered there were more boys than girls attending BYU, so I immediately decided I should transfer there for my sophomore year. I hate to admit that now, but it's true. Of course when I got down there in the fall, all the girls returned.*

When Olene transferred to BYU that fall, she moved into an apartment with two close friends. While attending BYU, she took eighteen to twenty credits every semester and didn't have paid employment. She majored in political science and minored in history. She also decided to earn a secondary-education teaching certificate because her father kept saying, "Now, what is it you are going to do with a political science degree?" She believes political science and education were helpful fields for leadership development with their focus on applicable topics and skills related in part to political leadership.

During these years, Olene was inspired by two excellent BYU professors, Gaylen Caldwell and John Bernhard, who helped shape her thinking about politics. Because their classes were interesting, politics and government became very exciting to her. She actually decided to major in political science because of the influence of these men. She remembers having some very tough classes with only a few females in each, but she appreciated the academic challenge the courses provided. She also had an influential history professor, Richard Paul, who went on to become a university president. She ultimately decided to minor in history after taking his course. She said, "If I had to pick academic mentors in my whole progression, it would be those four." She not only enjoyed attending their classes, but the classes themselves provided the encouragement she needed to eventually begin graduate school.

Olene clearly continued to have a strong desire to achieve and accomplish her goals. At BYU she quickly became involved in several clubs and organizations. As a sophomore, she was elected to the legislative body of the school. She was also selected first attendant to the homecoming queen her junior year. As a senior, she was elected as the BYU student body vice president. In fact, she was first vice president in charge of all the student assemblies on campus. In this position, she used to attend campus and faculty leadership meetings to represent the students. She remembers one particular experience:

> *I remember attending one particular leadership meeting when the president of the university was attending. He just lit into the football coach about how terrible the football team was that year. The football coach said, "You know, I can't recruit good players because other schools are offering scholarships to football players and we are not." The president said that is was against the rules to offer football scholarship, so that couldn't have been the case. The room was quiet for a minute, and then I courageously raised my hand and said, "President, I have a brother who just got a great football scholarship at the University of Utah." After the meeting, about thirty faculty members came up to me and thanked me for saying that. I must have had some confidence to defend the football coach like that.*

Although she didn't realize she was doing so at the time, Olene believes she was practicing many leadership skills in these roles. Olene did not join the debate team at BYU, but continued debating occasionally "whenever they needed somebody." Therefore, she ended up attending a lot of debate meets and kept involved. When she graduated with her bachelor's degree (cum Laude) from BYU she received the outstanding graduate award which was based on leadership, academics, and service.

During her college years, Olene learned to prioritize her activities. For example, Olene was involved with a ROTC-sponsored drill team for women that met at the same time as a committee over student assemblies, which she chaired. She explained,

> *I missed a lot of ROTC drills because of student government commitments. Also, I had trouble with left and right (I could handle east, west, north, and south very well). They finally told me that I could remain one of the top officers but that I didn't have to come to drill practice any more. I thought, "Great!" By that time, I was beginning to question all of the female appendages created for the adoration of the males. I thought, "Why are we doing all of this marching when the boys are training for something real. We're just wasting our time marching up and down the field."*

This humorous story provides a good example of how Olene was able to keep things in perspective and move quickly on when she discovered her personal weaknesses and inabilities. She set priorities to allow herself to do everything she wanted to do. She came to rational realizations and then moved forward.

During her college years, Olene became aware of important social issues. She saw the need for women to become involved, and as a result of this, she organized additional social units on campus to encourage more young women to participate. She was asked to reach out and encourage the creation of new leadership groups on campus. All of these activities helped her continue to learn to work with different kinds of people. She doesn't remember leading any crusades, but learned to work within the system fairly well. Overall, Olene said that her college experience was "remarkable." She enjoyed every element of her courses and extracurricular involvement. However, she still says that, "In retrospect, I would have focused more on studies and less on social elements."

GRADUATE SCHOOL AND MARRIAGE

During Olene's junior year of college, she met Myron Walker. The first time she saw him he was directing the parade lineup for homecoming and she was on a float. Her first impression was "what a good-looking guy." He was a student body officer at BYU, and shortly afterwards she formally met him in the student council. They dated, but after Myron graduated, he went into the army, and Olene was busy with academics and student activities her senior year.

When Olene graduated in 1953, she realized that her educational pursuits were not over. She absolutely loved learning and wanted to continue her formal education. Olene had debated back and forth whether she should go into law or get a master's degree in political science. She had been heavily involved in student government and enjoyed leadership roles. She said,

> *I wasn't very conscious of the fact that I enjoyed leadership, but I guess a pattern was beginning to emerge that I could and would be a leader. However, after graduation, I certainly made a conscious choice. If I had applied to law school, I would have gone to the University of Utah. Instead, I applied to the political theory program at Stanford. I made a conscious choice because I had decided I wanted to become a professor.*

Olene was accepted at Stanford and entered a one-year master's degree program on a scholarship. She loved her program and had very good professors. She was "thrown in with a lot of people from all over the country." She said,

> *It probably broadened my horizons a great deal. I had to seriously study for the first time. I couldn't get by with cramming the night before as I had done so often throughout my college career. I got As and a couple of Bs at Stanford, so I wasn't at the top of the class; but I found that I could still compete and do well in this new environment. It gave me a certain degree of confidence.*

She remembers two particular professors at Stanford asking her to correct papers for undergraduate classes. This also gave her a degree of confidence that the professors liked her work and acknowledged her intellectual value. Although she did have a scholarship, she worked as a resident assistant in one of the houses on campus. She met with the dean of women on a regular basis to discuss issues and policies.

Olene's earlier involvement in leadership during her undergraduate college years was motivated by her desire to "get things done." Although at Stanford she wasn't involved in student government, she continued to become aware that women needed to and should emerge as leaders. She was beginning to see the "bigger picture regarding what women could do." In her political theory education at Stanford, she began thinking about the role of women in becoming critical policy makers. She said, "Somewhere along the road, my experience was beginning to nudge me in that direction."

Myron was at Fort Ord, which was relatively close in proximity to Stanford. Olene always knew she would get married and have children, but she wanted to do certain things first. They continued to see each other during her year at Stanford, but then she decided that maybe she wanted to do a Rotary fellowship to Italy for two years. Myron finally grew impatient and gave her an ultimatum. Olene explained,

> *Myron finally said, "This is it. If you go to Italy, our relationship will never work out." He called my bluff, and we ended up getting married between winter and spring quarters while I was a student at Stanford. It was the best decision I ever made.*

After they married, Olene drove from Pacific Grove to Stanford during spring semester, ninety miles each way, which was no small task. Myron was going to attend the business school at Harvard for his M.B.A. the next fall, so they moved to Boston and began living as "very poor married students."

EARLY PARENTHOOD AND RELOCATIONS

In Cambridge, Olene obtained employment at Polaroid Corporation and was in charge of new accounts. She felt it was good for her to work in a for-profit company, so she could have some business experience in a professional setting. She said, "In those days, women didn't work while they were pregnant, but I did." She worked until just before her first child was born, "a little less than one year after she was married." She then chose to become a stay-at-home mother.

Myron had a scholarship that paid for tuition, but they struggled to make ends meet with living expenses. They couldn't afford student housing, so they found rent-free living situations where they could manage and care for apartments and a home. They enjoyed Boston and had a wonderful group of friends who were also in school. She said, "We were all poor, but we all played Monopoly. On Friday nights, we had parties after our husbands handed their papers in at midnight." Olene remembers that she and Myron had the most inexpensive season symphony tickets and occasionally went to plays and musicals before they hit New York. She recalls "having a remarkable time there because of the academic environment and great friends." Myron finished his M.B.A. at Harvard after two years, just before their second child was born.

For the next thirteen years, Olene was a full-time stay-at-home mother and had little time for community involvement outside her basic church attendance and service. She and Myron had all seven of their children and moved thirteen times within a twelve-year period. Most of the moves were across the country or to a different state. Olene explained that living in a variety of states and cities helped widen her perspectives on community issues and needs. Her social circles were often within her church group, and she recalls having "a lot of great friends" in various places during those years. She said, "It also made us more self reliant, because we couldn't run home to anyone if we had an argument." She also believes these moves and continual transitions helped her become more independent and learn to adjust to change. Finally, Myron decided that if he was going to work sixty hours a week, he might as well start a business of his own and move to Utah near extended family. So, after thirteen years of moving around a great deal, they moved back to Utah and have lived there for over forty years.

SERVICE AND VOLUNTEERISM

Olene's professional career actually began as a school, church, and community volunteer. Because her decisions regarding her participation in specific efforts were dependent on her family, this section will include elements of both her family life and community involvement so the reader can more clearly understand her career pathway. This will also provide a more comprehensive picture of how she learned and practiced leadership.

PTA
After Olene and Myron moved their family to Utah in 1969, she quickly began getting involved in a lot of community activities including the PTA in her children's schools. In fact, she eventually became the PTA president of every school her children attended. She believes that she acquired some very valuable leadership experiences in this role throughout these decades of service.

In addition to working with a wide-variety of people in organizing events and efforts, Olene also remembers some particular lessons in PTA work that were helpful later in her political positions. She said she actually learned more from the year she felt most ineffective as a leader than from the years she had many successes. She explained,

> *One of the greatest lessons I learned was from an experience when I felt that I was most ineffective as a leader. I was PTA president at a high school, and everybody was so busy. The school leaders said, "Oh, you just need to do the minimum." I talked other people into doing the same. We'd hold meetings over the phone and cut corners. As I look back on all my leadership roles, I've been chairman of so many things. I feel that was the year that I was probably most ineffective. It taught me a great lesson. You have to get people to buy in to whatever you are doing before they are willing to put the time and energy in it to make a difference.*

She realized that her own expectations were pivotal to the PTA doing the minimum that was required that year. She learned that she didn't like leading with no major purpose in mind. She didn't get the unity and support because she had no "cause to lead." They did the regular required duties and people assumed she was successful, but she knew there was more that could have been done. She learned, "If you want things done, you don't say it won't take much time. Instead you say, 'This is so important it will take time!'" After this experience, Olene became PTA president at another school. She and other parents got passionately involved and ended up making a true difference in many ways. She remembers involving other people, delegating a lot of the work, and really having great success. She said,

> *We were able to accomplish so much. We brought volunteers into the school to help children. We implemented important programs in the school that had some of the richest and poorest in the state. We were committed to making a difference, and we found the time and energy to do so.*

Church Service
Olene spoke about her leadership experiences in doing church service, particularly after she became established in the community. She was asked to serve in many roles that became helpful in her development in a variety of ways. For example, she was the president of the young women's organization in her church for over eight years. She explained,

> *By then, I was smart enough to say to the bishop, "I'll do it if you'll appoint Barbara Gibbs as my administrative assistant." I knew from my past experiences that I had to work with the right people to get the right things done. The bishop said, "But, Olene, that isn't a specific position or calling we have in our church." I told him that I thought we could be creative and make this new position, because I knew by then Barbara and I were a great team. She was so organized and detailed. And, I was kind of a big picture person wanting to get things done. This is the reason I was never asked to serve as a secretary in any organization.*

Olene spoke about how well they did as a leadership team. She'd get great ideas for outings and adventures, and Barbara was the one who made sure they had rides and food. They each loved their own roles and complemented each other well. In this and other church positions, she strengthened her skills in organization, communication, listening, and motivating others.

Other Volunteerism
In addition to her PTA and church service, Olene continued her involvement in other community service efforts throughout the years and remembers serving on many boards. She continued to do this even after starting her paid positions and throughout her Ph.D. program. She served as the chairperson of a committee to revitalize a section of downtown Salt Lake City. She served on various state and local task forces, as well as boards and committees for the United Way, Ballet West, Red Cross, Girls Village (a home for girls who were having problems with parents, school and law enforcement), the League of Women Voters, and the Utah Homeless Committee.

Olene served as the community council chairperson of a high school and a junior high and felt they made positive changes that "really benefited the children." She believes that being involved in these change efforts helped her understand public education in more detail. These efforts led her to become involved in some political elements of the educational systems as well. She said, "I absolutely benefited from my K–12 volunteer work. When I look back on my experiences, I believe that I had many opportunities to write, speak, and expand and strengthen many skills important for leadership."

DOCTORATE EDUCATION

Shortly after Olene and Myron moved to Utah with their children, Olene went to the University of Utah and talked to a professor who was "sort of the guru political science professor at that time." He advised her not to pursue a formal degree, but just to take a few classes. Because she had been out of school for about thirteen years at that point (she was thirty-seven at this time), he told her that the GRE would just be too tough and that she should "just enjoy life." She took an evening class in mid-eastern politics and absolutely loved it. However, shortly after this she began working part-time and didn't take additional classes until she formally commenced working on her degree years later.

Olene started actually working on her doctorate degree in 1976. She found that she needed that intellectual stimulation, and her husband was "very cooperative" in helping with the children so she could do this. Although she remained interested in political science, she decided to get her Ph.D. in educational administration because she still felt that she wanted to either teach at the university level or become a superintendent of schools. Olene was working in the schools at this time and was "heavily connected with both disciplines." So, she basically took classes whenever she could manage them, typically in the evenings. The University of Utah did require her to attend school full time for one year sometime during her doctoral program so she took fifteen to eighteen credit hours for two semesters so she could fulfill this requirement. During this year, she also worked thirty hours a week and took care of her family and community obligations. She explained,

> I merely set aside time from ten or eleven at night until three in the morning to study and eventually do my dissertation. I'm a night person. I do not require more than four or five hours of sleep. That's still about what I sleep at night. I wish I could get more. I really do. But that is when I have been able to accomplish what I have needed to get done in my life. During those quiet moments when everyone else was sleeping, I was able to study uninterrupted.

During these years, Olene remembers three influential individuals. A professor named David Sperry, dean of the department, was her first chair. She remembers him primarily for his strong encouragement and support and his dedication to improving the educational system. She also remembers Gene Jacobsen who took over as chairperson of her committee after the departure of David Sperry. He too took a special interest in her work and making certain that she completed her Ph.D. She took a challenging class from Professor Sterling McMurrin. He gave the students a reading assignment of forty books that they were to be tested on. Although she had seven children at the time, she still enjoyed a good challenge. There were fifty students in his class at the beginning of the semester and only a dozen at midterm. Olene recalls being the only student who showed up to take the final examination. She found great satisfaction in finishing and conquering those kinds of challenges.

It took Olene three years to complete her coursework for her Ph.D. and then two more to do her dissertation. She was fifty-one and a Utah state legislator when she finished her Ph.D. in education administration with an emphasis in law and policy. When she received her Ph.D., two of her children and a son-in-law and a daughter-in-law graduated the same day: one with a medical degree, one with a master's degree, and two with their bachelor's degrees.

CAREER/PAID POSITIONS

Olene had a paid professional position at Polaroid Corporation for six months after she graduated from Stanford. However, she did not have paid employment for nearly fourteen years as she gave birth to and raised children. As already noted, after giving birth to all seven children and moving to Utah, Olene immediately began her involvement in community work, which eventually led to paid employment offers.

Educational Consultant
In 1973, Olene was chairing a task force of an elementary curriculum analysis of the Salt Lake School District (just for fun), and she was working with a consultant who had been hired by the district to do the overall staff work. He quickly discovered Olene's capabilities and asked her to work full time with him as an

educational consultant. She turned him down because she had seven young children between the ages of three and fourteen and knew it would not work. He then proposed that she work only a few hours a day while her youngest was in preschool, and she decided to accept the position. So, she began working for an education-consulting firm analyzing the skills necessary to read and do math and developing materials.

After the completion of the contract with Salt Lake School District, the firm had a contract with the United States Department of Education evaluating Title III projects that were innovative and creative. She said, "I ended up being gone Tuesday through Thursday one week, to visit a project, and then I spent the next week analyzing and writing." Olene quickly discovered that the position took too much time away from her family even though she enjoyed the work. Her family needs always would be her first priority. This experience did strengthen her time management skills and she certainly learned more about the educational system. She met with the top people in education in the state and networked with various people that later became supporters. Olene also "certainly learned the process of education in terms of curriculum and curriculum development."

Federal Program Director
Olene then began working for the Salt Lake School District administrating a federal program and explained,

> *I negotiated time instead of salary in this position. In hindsight, I should have negotiated both, but I wanted to be able to go to my children's football games, basketball games, tennis matches, swim meetings, dance concerts, and all of that!*

Olene ran the federal program for four years and worked with at-risk schools to develop programs that would help students stay in school. She learned more about the responsibility all community members have for all of the socioeconomic groups and ethnic populations in the state. She worked with educators, parents, and students, and acquired new insights into the issues of poverty and diversity. It broadened her perspectives and gave her the connections she still has to this day with ethnic communities within the state.

Director of Salt Lake Education Foundation
After working on the federal program for a few years, the superintendent of the school district asked Olene to form a foundation that would bring in additional money for the schools in that district. So in 1984, Olene became the full-time, paid director of Salt Lake Education Foundation. She had done some fundraising as a volunteer with other groups, but this was a challenging new experience. She quickly learned about fundraising saying:

> *First, I tried to raise money for education in general and found it was impossible. Then I decided to narrow it down to one specific school and that kind of worked, but I knew there must be a better way. I learned that we had to raise*

money by talking about something concrete. I needed to raise money for a specific school to meet a specific need—for example, a new violin program for a specific central city school. I learned that I needed to know the costs of bows and sheet music. I discovered I could get people to donate money for books for a specific library but not books to help education in general. I discovered that people would contribute if they could see the specific needs and knew that their contribution would help individual students in a specific way. I learned that people need to see the result of their efforts.

Olene learned a lot about fundraising from this position. She also continued to develop a sense of "what works and what doesn't." She became very successful and later helped other school districts set up their own foundations. Again, she was also involved in boards and other community work during this time.

Legislator and Majority Whip
By 1980, several people had approached her, encouraging her to run for the legislature. With her political science background, she had always been interested in government. She continued to have a desire to "make a true difference to her community by trying to make things better." Although she still had children at home, which meant that she was "driving carpools and going to a lot of sporting events," and was writing her dissertation, she decided to get more involved in the state politics by running for a seat in the Utah House of Representatives. She soon discovered that she was a Republican in the third most Democratic district in the state. She started campaigning by going out and knocking on doors every night after work and every Saturday. Her children were "a great asset in helping" her run. Many of the people she met had children who were friends with her children. They were also helpful in distributing campaign materials.

Olene was elected to be a legislator and then served for eight years between 1980 and 1989. When she was first elected, she was one of only seven female legislators among a total of 104 in the state. Yet, she said, "I was treated very well in the legislature." When she was first elected, the Speaker of the House told her to "get to know the budget." She took his advice and "got to know it probably as well as anyone." In fact, many male legislators would come and ask her questions about the budget. She learned it was important to understand where the money went, what the revenues were, and what the tax policies were. Although "rather unusual," she was made chair of an Appropriations Committee during her second term. Despite the fact that hardly any females had been in leadership in the Utah legislature, Olene was elected assistant majority whip in her third term and then was elected majority whip in her fourth term. The legislature only met forty-five days a year so she continued employment as director of the Salt Lake Education Foundation during these years. Of course, she had interim meetings and continued her involvement in legislative committee work and other projects throughout the year.

To this day, Olene gets credit for the Rainy Day Fund in Utah. That particular bill took her two years to get passed. She felt strongly about it because she'd looked at the historical trends of the revenues for the state, and it became "very obvious" to her that there were times when the state had to cut programs and raise taxes with the downturn. She figured that if money was put away for these times the state would be far better off in the long term. At the time it passed in Utah, only one other state had this fund. Now, nearly all states have a similar fund. One year she sponsored and was successful in getting more bills passed than any other legislator. She quickly determined that was not necessarily what she wanted to be known for and was more selective after that. She sponsored many critical pieces of legislation including the Utah Consumer Credit Code, the Insurance Code, the Juvenile Corrections System, and Human Services Legislation.

Olene said that serving in the legislature gave her continual practice in speaking, writing, negotiation, compromise, budgeting, problem solving, and taking criticism gracefully. She said,

The legislature is a great education; better than any other kind of training for government leadership because it helps you see how the state runs, get to know the budget, and learn about different programs. It's a great training ground!

She also received a lot of practice in analyzing data and trends and finding solutions. Running a campaign also gave her practice in gaining support, obtaining funds, and rallying the troops—all important competencies needed as governor. She said, "I enjoyed the legislature and found it remarkably informative and challenging.

Director of Community Development
After eight years of serving in the House of Representatives, Olene was defeated. She knew she was always a target being in such a Democratic district, but the defeat was still very traumatic for her. However, she had "a lot of amazing offers," so she was able to move on fairly quickly. She accepted a position as the director of community development for the State of Utah and worked in this capacity for two years. She was over libraries, the art council, history, state fairs, housing, services for the homeless, community service, and more, and she "thoroughly enjoyed it." She also said it was great preparation for her future positions.

Lieutenant Governor
In 1991, Olene decided she wanted to serve in elected office again. She explained,

I decided to run for Congress because I got angry with the federal auditors over housing. However, while I was running and doing well in the polls, I was asked by the governor [Mike Leavitt] to run with him as lieutenant governor. Although Congress sounded interesting and challenging, Myron was still involved in his business endeavors and had no interest in moving to Washington. Our family was in Utah, and it would have been terribly difficult for me to relocate. I understood Utah's issues and problems from the legislature and other experiences. In Washington, I would have been one of 435. It didn't take me too long to figure out that I was better off staying in Utah.

Olene ran for lieutenant governor with Mike Leavitt three consecutive times and served in this role nearly eleven years. She enjoyed this position and said they worked together very well as a team. In looking at the nation, she believes they "got along probably better than most any other lieutenant governor and governor in the United States." She said, "He had a great deal of respect for me, and I for him."

Olene was able to use all of her previous experience and knowledge to perform effectively in her position as lieutenant governor. As lieutenant governor, she chaired the Health Policy Commission for seven years, developing critical health care policy. She spent three years chairing the Workforce Task Force, which created legislation that moved twenty-six different programs from five different departments into one unified department. This basically changed welfare to a process of gaining employment. During these years, she was also part of the budgeting process and usually sat in on all judicial appointments. She also established the State Volunteer Office. She noted, "If you don't care who gets the credit, you can get a lot done as lieutenant governor." As previously mentioned, Olene was recognized by peers in others states as they elected her to chair the National Conference of Lieutenant Governors and to serve as the president of the National Association of Secretaries of State.

Governor

Olene said that she never had plans to become the governor, but that "it just happened." She always knew as a lieutenant governor that there was always the possibility of becoming governor if something happened. During his last term as governor, Mike Leavitt was asked by President George W. Bush to accept a post to head the Environmental Protection Agency (EPA). He accepted the invitation, and Olene was sworn in as Utah's fifteenth governor at the age of seventy-two on November 5, 2003. She was excited about the challenge and the opportunity to accomplish many important initiatives.

Six weeks before she became governor, she and her staff immediately began to strategize on what they could get done in the fourteen months she would be in office. She carefully considered which issues would have the greatest impact on the State of Utah and how to implement effective change in such a short time period. Olene and her staff decided on sixteen initiatives they wanted to move forward in fourteen months—more than one each month. She believes that starting her governorship with a plan of action and deadlines helped her become a successful governor. She also believes she was successful because of her ability through the years to learn from a wide variety of paid and non-paid positions and experiences, each contributing to important skill development and intellectual insight needed to understand the complexity of running a state government. Several of her initiatives that she is particularly proud of are the reading initiative that encourages families to read with their children twenty minutes every day, tax reform principles that would give greater stability to the state budget, and the program that helped foster children become integrated into society as they entered into adulthood. She left office with an eighty-seven percent approval rating.

CAREER AND WORK-LIFE ISSUES

Career Path
Olene never became a university professor or school superintendent as she had originally envisioned. Her life obviously moved in other directions. She did, however, teach a few college classes but ultimately decided that she "could have a greater influence" in her role as legislator, lieutenant governor, and governor than she would have had in the classroom. In serving in such a prominent position, she felt she had a hand in making important changes that have benefited many Utah residents throughout the years. She obviously did not have a formal career plan targeted at being a state legislator, let alone the governor. In fact, she doesn't remember ever thinking about becoming a lieutenant governor or governor until she was well into her legislative service. Yet, she believes she has had many different avenues throughout her life to develop the leadership competencies needed for successful service in prominent positions. Olene has been honored by having the Utah Affordable Housing Fund named after her. She received the National Points of Light award. She has received numerous awards for her legislative work, her community service work, her human service work, as well as her work in education. She has also received honorary Ph.D. degrees from three different universities.

Gender
Olene spoke for a few minutes about the gender issues she faced. She remarked that she did not like to dwell on gender barriers but does admit that being a female in the political environment was sometimes challenging. She didn't even consider many career options throughout much of her life because she had no female role models in those arenas. In fact, she actually felt a "real burden as the first female governor," because she believes that she needed to change the image for young women growing up today. She admits she has confronted gender issues from time to time and told the following humorous story to provide one example:

> *I've had issues from time to time, but I don't dwell on them. I remember when I was leading the youth organization for young women in my church group; I was sitting in a leadership meeting with the men who lead the scouting and young men's program. The man in charge of the young men wanted to take the boys on a rafting trip down the Snake River. And I pitched in and said, "Great. I think our young women would enjoy that as well." He said, "Oh, why don't you just consider doing something on the Jordan River?" Now you have to re-*

alize that the Jordan River is a small, very slow river that runs through town. I think I threw my lesson manual at him. There were moments.

Work-Life and Motherhood

Even with occasional gender-related challenges, Olene believes that her role as a mother and volunteer gave her the flexibility to pursue interests that she might otherwise not have pursued. In fact, many people have asked her through the years how she was able to accomplish what she did. She feels she was always very fortunate to be in a position where she was able to pursue her interests. She explained:

One of the things I have learned is that in the workplace, in the political arena, and even in community service, it is important that if you have constructive opinions or creative ideas, you express them, even if it means taking risks.

Although Olene's primary focus for many years was caring for her family, she stayed involved with community efforts, part-time paid employment, advanced education, and church service. She remembers "time being very precious during those years." She did struggle with the conflict that exists between work and family because she integrated them closely. In fact, she said that she sometimes felt guilty, but she decided not to dwell on it too much. She explained,

I've often felt that there are a lot of things that I just do to get by—housework, for example. I never had domestic help in the home, and we just kind of got by okay. When my kids were younger, we always thought they should be involved in housework. They helped a lot. When my kids were younger, I also did a lot of sewing. I made a lot of clothes and prom dresses. Finally, I reached the point and decided it wasn't worth my time. After that, we just purchased them. I just didn't have time to sew anymore. I had to prioritize my time, and being a mother helped me learn to do this well.

She chose to work part time for many years because she loved being involved with her children's lives and activities. She continues to see the value of part-time employment today.

Through various part-time positions there was no question that I gained important knowledge and skills that were definitely useful in my later leadership positions. Remember, these were the days we had to use typewriters and White-Out so things took longer. I really had to manage my time with my motherhood responsibilities of carpools, cooking, and cleaning, and I learned to multitask even better.

Olene also believes that motherhood taught her a great deal that has been helpful in her numerous leadership roles, including that of governor. She said,

I think it teaches you sacrifice. It certainly teaches you negotiation because you're always negotiating between children. It teaches you to prioritize, be-

cause I really did have seven children each with their own priority needs. My oldest was eleven when my youngest was born. I hit the tops of the icebergs. I couldn't always get everything done, so I had to prioritize. I think motherhood teaches you responsibility. I drove the carpools and attended so many events and games. When another mother couldn't drive, one son would often say, "Oh, my mom will drive." So, I think that my kids had the sense that I could be there and be responsible.

Overall, Olene believes that women can accomplish a great deal if they understand that they may not be able to do everything at once, but that there are various stages in life. She was able to make time to raise her children, make time to pursue an education, and make time to become very involved in community service and politics. She said, "Although challenging, it can be done."

LEADERSHIP STYLE AND ADVICE

I asked Olene how her former staff would describe her leadership style. She said they would first comment about her energy level and strong work ethic. They would also say that she understood policy as well as anyone in the state. They would describe her as committed, caring, and competent. They would say that she was also a good listener and preferred hearing various viewpoints from a variety of individuals and groups. Olene stated,

Although I may not be a truly reflective individual in some respects, I've always thought leadership was the ability to get things done. I look and say, "These are the things we need to do. Let's get them done." I've always had a hectic schedule, so I didn't have a lot of time to ponder.

Her staff would also tell me that she has a very ethical and honest leadership style. She also liked to use facts and figures to justify her positions and efforts because she believed that rational justifications would convince others to follow and support her work.

Throughout the past few decades, Olene has been asked to give advice to other women. She believes that women should take advantage of every opportunity they are given. Women must be willing to enter into new experiences, map out their goals, and pursue an education. She said, "While I didn't actually need a Ph.D. to be a legislator, lieutenant governor, or governor, the fact that I have those degrees opened doors for me." She encourages young women to get as much education as they can and get involved in their communities. She said,

If you have interest in being a leader at the local or state level, then volunteer to be on boards. Seek out opportunities to serve and have leadership experiences. Analyze what needs to be done in your community and come up with suggestions of how to accomplish things. Energize others to get involved in your projects, yet remember that when it's done it is important that they feel like it was their idea and their success!

Chapter Ten
FINAL THOUGHTS

After she left office, Olene served a full-time mission with her husband in New York City for her church. At the time of this writing, she has returned to Utah and continues to accept speaking engagements for many events. She also continues to serve on a variety of boards and advisory committees. Through the years, she has dedicated her life to her family and community, as she has served in various capacities and led many positive efforts that have benefited thousands of Utahans throughout the state.

Part 2

Themes and Overall Findings

Chapter 11

Family Influences, Childhoods, and Youth

Warren Bennis (1989), a well-known leadership expert and scholar, wrote that looking back on your childhood and adolescence is a critical element for developing leadership. In his book, *On Becoming a Leader,* he explained that reflecting on what has happened to you in the past can "enable you to make things happen now, so that you can become the master of your own life rather than its servant" (99-100). He taught that this is an important way to learn from your own experiences. He explained,

> *There are lessons in everything, and if you are fully deployed, you will learn most of them. Experiences aren't truly yours until you think about them, analyze them, examine them, question them, reflect on them, and finally understand them. The point, once again, is to use your experiences rather than being used by them, to be the designer, not the design, so that experiences empower rather than imprison.* (98)

He believes that "the process of becoming a leader is much the same as the process of becoming an integrated human being" (4). So, understanding how we became who we are is truly a journey that not only empowers us but also provides the self-knowledge needed to continue learning and developing leadership in our current life stage. Plato believed that the truest form of learning is remembering and recalling what is important. As I tell my college students from time to time, the greatest education that you can actually obtain in life is that of truly discovering and understanding yourself.

As I conducted the interviews of each of the governors, it became clear to me once again that we are truly products of our own experiences and circumstances, including our own family backgrounds, individual personalities, childhood and youth activities, interactions, events, challenges, and opportunities. Now that I have presented the leadership development journeys of each governor in the first ten chapters of this book, I will use the remaining three chapters to highlight the findings and themes across all of the interviews and to share some lessons learned. In this chapter, I will not only identify some basic themes but also some striking similarities and unexpected differences of the governors' childhood and adolescent years. Understanding the backgrounds of these governors can help us 1) learn about the starting points of the governors' journeys; 2) understand how we can help facilitate leadership development for others; and 3) reflect upon our own lives so as to further understand ourselves.

HOME AND FAMILY

Eight of the ten governors in this study were raised in two-parent homes and the other two by single mothers. Although all ten governors felt they were generally raised in safe, supportive, and loving environments, seven said they were raised in particularly stable homes. The remaining three experienced instability during part of their upbringings because of family relocations and alcoholism in the home, which created challenges for the rest of the family members. Most of the women described their families as being modest and middle income. They all seemed to have an American middle-class value system, mainly influenced by family, school, and/or church. They all had a real sense of possibility when thinking about future opportunities. For most, education seemed to be central in their minds to gaining access to these possibilities. In addition, all of the governors mentioned some kind of religious connection, with religion and/or spirituality playing an important developmental role in their upbringings. Some governors mentioned that their religious activities helped them learn how to listen, observe, set goals for improvement, and become interested in assisting in the development of others. Finally, as will be discussed in more depth later in this chapter, I found it fascinating to discover that all of the governors were reared in service-oriented homes with parents who were 1) involved in the community in some way, 2) politically active and/or interested in politics, and 3) mindful of and often passionate about contributing back to society.

Eight of the ten governors were raised in small towns in various parts of the country, most of which were farming and "blue-collar communities." They spoke many times of the value of being raised where everyone knew them and had high expectations for their behavior and potential. Small towns and schools gave them opportunities to be involved in lots of activities and leadership positions. A number of governors were raised on farms, or at least spent substantial time on farms, in these small communities. I was surprised to discover the profound influences the farm experiences had on their lives. They worked very hard for long hours during certain seasons each year. While growing up, they learned to love animals, nature, the outdoors, physical activity, space, and independence. Although they probably didn't appreciate it as much during their upbringings, the women attributed their appreciation for, commitment toward, and love of hard work to farm life. They also attribute their focus later in life on environmental protection issues and efforts to their farming experiences. Work experiences provided the governors practice with teamwork and a feeling of "working for the good of the whole." The governors felt all of these skills were essential for them to develop while young and were particularly helpful as they rose through the ranks to become governor.

A particularly striking finding of this study was the importance the women placed on their families' dinner table conversations. Their mothers and fathers read often and were well informed about the issues of the day. As children and teenagers, the governors were raised to voice their opinions and listen to others' points of view. Most said they enjoyed lively conversations about the current issues. They learned to listen, respect others views, and express their own opinions and insights. Most, if not all, felt their voices were respected, at least most of the time, by their parents and siblings. They learned to "find joy in the debate" and had "permission to respectfully disagree." Their families discussed current events, community issues, and/or the politics of the day, with these women being involved in dialogues as children. In fact, many of these leaders attributed the initial discovery of their own "voices" to these open, informative, and enjoyable daily family experiences. Again, the finding that the governors developed and strengthened a variety of leadership skills through years of engaging dinnertime conversations was one of most powerful themes in this study.

Siblings

There is a variety of birth orders in the families of this sample of women governors. Three of the governors are only children, two are oldest children in their families, four are second children, and one is fourth (a youngest child). Five of the ten had at least one brother, whereas two were raised with only female siblings. Two governors were raised in homes with five children, two had three siblings, one had two siblings, and two had one sibling. Although past research has touted the importance of being first in the birth order for optimal leadership opportunities or development, half of these women were not. Interestingly, some dated research (Hennig & Jardim, 1977) reported that all strong female business leaders in their study came from families with no male children. However, in my study the five women governors with brothers felt their own development was enhanced by being raised with males. They felt that they learned to work well with men because of experiences in their own homes. The bottom line is that there is no magic birth order or gender distribution in families that somehow provides a better environment for the development of leaders. Female leaders can and do emerge from a variety of family compositions and structures.

Mothers

The governors made loving, understanding, and relatively positive comments about their mothers during the interviews and described them as fascinating and interesting women. All of the mothers worked hard to be thrifty, productive, and effective in a variety of ways. Most governors spoke of their mothers as strong, steady, focused, capable, competent, and smart. In addition, these women were family-focused, hard working, dedicated, and determined. On the one hand, the governors described their mothers as giving, sacrificing, and service-oriented women; yet, on the other hand, they were innovative, independent, and determined. Interestingly, five of the governors spoke about the competitiveness of their mothers in athletics, board games, and other situations. In general, the governors have had very close relationships with their mothers through the years.

Eight of the ten mothers were full-time homemakers during much of their children's upbringings. Seven of these mothers were described as very busy and active as they were focused on running the household, assisting their children in school and activities, and participating in volunteerism efforts in their schools, churches, and communities. Four of these women either worked part time when children were younger or went to work full time as their children were in school, particularly once they were in high school. The two single mothers worked full time throughout the years, although one did various types of jobs that she could do from home so she could still care for her children. Four of the ten mothers of these governors had professional training and at one time in their lives were teachers, counselors, or dieticians.

All of the governors spoke of the powerful learning they received during their upbringings from their mothers. First, I found it interesting that the strong value of education for their daughters seemed to come more forcefully from many of the governors' mothers than their fathers. Although only four mothers graduated from college before or shortly after having children, three others did attend some college directly after completing high school. Interestingly, two of the remaining mothers had always planned to attend college but had family issues that prevented them from doing so. These governors said that their mothers yearned for the formal education they did not receive and felt a type of loss their whole lives in not having obtained a college education. Overall, the mothers had particularly strong, consistent, and resonant voices regarding college expectations for their daughters. The mothers believed that women need to prepare themselves for careers even if they don't choose to work after marriage. Second, their mothers taught them that they had an obligation to society and that they needed to reach out to others. Through example, these mothers taught their daughters that to be involved, active, and engaged in good works was important and, in some cases, an actual duty or responsibility. They were passionate about positively influencing their communities by helping people one by one. The governors remember being taught by their mothers that they should not give up on others that have had fewer opportunities. Third, the mothers helped instill in their daughters the love of reading and learning. In fact, the majority of governors spoke of their mothers teaching and challenging them to "read and think critically." Finally, many governors mentioned that their mothers gave them a sense of optimism and hope about the world around them as well as their own future choices and opportunities.

Fathers
Most of the women described their fathers as hard working, committed, dependable, honest, stable, strong, and encouraging. In most cases, they were good providers. Seven of the ten fathers went to some college, whereas only five received formal associate or bachelor's degrees. Only two attended graduate school with one eventually obtaining a J.D. and the other a Ph.D. Interestingly, unlike the

governors' mothers, the fathers with no college experience did not strongly encourage their daughters to seek more education after high school. Thus, the more educated fathers had higher educational expectations for their daughters. Of the ten fathers, two were educators (both were teachers and principals, whereas one eventually became a superintendent). One of these two men was also employed as a funeral director and ran an ambulance service in addition to his educational responsibilities. Three fathers were involved in management of small blue-collar type business. The remaining fathers had occupations that included a newspaper reporter, large business executive, business manager, and banker.

Of the eight fathers who were a part of their daughters' upbringings, most were involved in community service and/or politics. It was quite clear that these fathers stayed at least relatively up-to-date with current events and with local, state, and/or national political, social, and economic issues and challenges. They discussed many of these topics at the dinner table with their families. Five were involved in politics in some way. Most of these men seemed interested in improving the quality of life by being involved in such work as economic development, industrial development, housing authority, city council issues, new building creation (e.g., hospital), or cultural community enrichment (e.g., bringing the symphony to the area). A few governors also mentioned that their fathers were coaches for their recreational sports teams. Hence, the fathers were civically engaged in a variety of ways. Although some mentioned their mothers' influence in this area, more of the governors attributed their commitment to voting and their interest in politics to their fathers.

It is important to note that three of the women governors (including the two who were raised by single-mothers) spoke of serious problems with their fathers. Two of them spoke openly of the challenges and struggles with being raised with an alcoholic father or stepfather, whereas one mentioned a father's mental health issues as one of the difficulties they endured. The governors also spoke of other difficulties their fathers faced through the years with employment, war experiences, and unfulfilled expectations. These women, as children and youth, seemed to be very aware of their surroundings and attempted to understand reasons for certain behaviors, views, and situations. The governors spoke of what they learned from seeing their fathers' struggle, and they felt that observing and living through some of these challenges actually helped them in their development.

Another interesting finding that emerged from my research is that, in most cases, the governors' fathers had a great deal of respect for their wives. As children, the governors understood that their fathers knew that their mothers were competent and intelligent and, in some cases, encouraged them toward leadership roles. For example, one father encouraged his spouse to run for office. This governor explained that, although her mother never ran, she learned that her father believed his wife had the strength and competencies to do important work. These governors spoke of their parents having some type or level of partnership in their homes.

It is clear from this research that women leaders can emerge from a variety of backgrounds, support levels, and situations. These results support the notion that leadership can be learned within many different environments, particularly if individuals have opportunities to grow and develop in generally stable settings. Interestingly, this safeness even afforded the governors in my study the opportunities to learn from times of turmoil and struggle.

PERSONALITIES

As the governors described their personalities as children and adolescents, I discovered some interesting differences among the women. Although seven described themselves as fairly outgoing, three said they were somewhat shy, particularly during their childhood and early adolescent years. Although some were vocal and outgoing individuals in high school being deeply involved and in charge of everything—some were not as assertive. Some described themselves as "bossy" in their youth, whereas others stated they stepped forward to help facilitate when there was a need but that they were not necessary "bossy." Four said they were "show-offs" in some ways, whereas others were quite the opposite. Seven said they enjoyed getting in front of people and speaking or performing, whereas three were not comfortable doing that during most of their early years. Although all of the women described themselves as "somewhat to very popular," some governors said that they had lots of friends whereas others had a smaller group of very close friends. Half of the governors spoke of being risk takers during adolescence, whereas others said that their risk-taking tendencies emerged more strongly during their college years.

These women were naturally happy, friendly, social, and energetic as children and youth. They generally had a good attitude about life, school, work, and other activities and responsibilities. They kept fairly busy and maintained a fast-paced life particularly as they entered middle and high school. They enjoyed planning and organizing people and events. All of them seemed to have the ability to see the big picture, a possible start to being systems thinkers and visionaries. All were confident in at least some area of their lives. For example, although many said they were confident in a variety of situations, some believed their confidence was primarily based in their academic abilities. All of the women stated that they had confidence in themselves with regard to "getting things done." They knew they could help individuals or groups accomplish particular goals. They also seemed to have sense of who they were, and they were comfortable (although not totally and not in all situations) with themselves. Although they were very social, they were also task driven. They loved to achieve and accomplish. It is important to note that many women stated that they were not the most popular in their schools. However, many said they were members of groups who were known to be popular. Finally, all provided examples of themselves in situations where they demonstrated bravery and courage as a child and youth. They clearly had courage when they were young and continued to develop that throughout the years.

Five powerful personality themes emerged from my interview data. The first is that the governors were observant as children. A number of governors spoke of how much they enjoyed watching and studying people. They were fascinated with human behavior and complexity. They liked to figure out which actions and behaviors were effective and which were not. Secondly, as a whole they were generally good and responsible family members and students. They enjoyed school and worked to get good grades and do their best. They enjoyed challenges and complexity in its various forms. Third, they were competitive individuals. Many were involved in athletics whereas others participated in debate, public speaking competitions, and competing for cheerleading spots and royalty competitions. Although a few were not involved in these types of activities, they were nearly all very competitive academically. For example, the governors worked to be top academic students; they set personal goals and competed with themselves toward reaching them. Fourth, although all of these women were generally obedient as children, they did not blindly obey at times. Most were taught that it was acceptable to challenge things and to be candid and open. Their opinions were heard at the dinner table and in their homes, and they felt safe in expressing their views. Finally, these women were very smart, independent, self-directed, innovative, and generally logical and rational.

Before moving on, I need to discuss one more leadership characteristic that I have pondered about for quite some time. I now believe I have acquired insight that will provide some depth in understanding the theme of reflection. Let me explain. Successful leaders have been found to be very reflective individuals, however many of the governors in my study did not believe they were particularly reflective during their upbringings. Since this not only contradicts my previous research findings (on university presidents) but the findings of other leadership research as well, I decided to look deeper into the governors' stories and insights to discover any underlying themes. I now believe some governors did not respond positively to the word "reflection" because they associated being reflective with "sitting around and meditating." Yet their responses and stories showed somewhat unique reflective natures. I believe that these women somehow developed a more active form of reflection where they continuously, although probably subconsciously, thought about what happened, what they saw, and what they heard—and then considered those implications for their own behavior and actions. It is clear that these young women learned to alter and change their behaviors based on these rapid reflections. Change based on these observations and reflections helped them become more effective in how they thought and what they did, which resulted in more meaningful and successful outcomes. For example, these outcomes included results, such as making more friends, winning elections, recruiting more people to participate in service projects, rounding up more neighborhood kids for an informal softball game, and getting better grades.

In some of the governors' stories, it was clear that the governors began learning a type of reflection that I'm calling "reflection under fire," particularly during their late teenage years. They began learning how to carefully consider options under various kinds of responsibility and pressure. For a teenager, social pressure can be as powerful as the kind of pressure adults may feel later in life in visible leadership positions. Adolescent experiences in this arena (including what the athletes in this group explained about the pressure inherently found in sports during their youth) provided them good practice in eventually becoming comfortable with making important decisions under pressure. I would argue that this continuous, often successful decision making demonstrates reflective abilities in these leaders when they were young.

SCHOOL, ACTIVITIES, AND EMPLOYMENT

The governors' perceptions of childhood-adolescent school experiences and other activities provide important insights into what types of things may have influenced the development of these leaders-in-training. Interestingly, the same themes that I reported in my last book on the women university presidents are very similar to what I have found with women governors. Both support the notion that high involvement in school and other activities may be helpful in the initial development of future leaders.

The governors had positive feelings about school and education in general. They yearned to learn and found joy in intellectual growth. In fact, all enjoyed being challenged intellectually. Although two governors didn't necessarily get good grades in all of their courses all of the time, mainly due to personal or family challenges, they had similar academic characteristics as the other eight. Interestingly, even during times of difficulties, these two did well in those classes that related to their immediate interests. Overall, all ten women flourished in the school environment and seemed to "take it all in" and be involved in a "well-rounded secondary education experience."

Extracurricular Activities
These women were involved, moderately to heavily, in a variety of extracurricular activities during their teen years. They enjoyed being busy and involved. Some of the women wanted to lead activities, efforts, and/or organizations and easily stepped up on their own to take on such roles; others were asked by peers or advisors to take on such responsibilities and accepted the request or assignment. A few seemed content to be strong followers exhibiting influence without authority. When interviewed, the governors mentioned involvement in the following activities:

- *Athletics*: basketball, cheerleading, dance, drill team, field hockey, gymnastics, softball, swimming, track, volleyball

- *Clubs, organizations, and groups (non-athletic):* competitive speaking team, drama club, dance and event committees, debate team, Girls' Club, Girls State, Honor Society, horse riding club, Latin club, peer tutoring, pep club, royalty, school newspaper and magazine staff, service clubs, student body officer, student council, talent contests, yearbook staff
- *Groups (non-school):* 4H, church youth groups, Girl Scouts, Rainbow Girls, public speaking
- *Music:* choir, concert band, marching band, piano, orchestra, violin
- *Social events:* dating, dances, movies, parties, sporting events
- *Other:* biking, chores, informal sports (football, softball, baseball, dodge ball, tennis, golfing, skiing, hiking, boating), fishing, horse riding, library visits, picnics, reading, sewing, family activities, farm duties and activities, political events, outdoor activities

The governors believed that they learned from nearly all of their activities and related experiences. They all spoke (see individual chapters) about the leadership lessons they learned from specific involvement and efforts in a variety of domains. These experiences provided lessons in such areas as handling rejection and conflict; organizing and motivating people; being responsible, dependable, and committed to something; and listening and trying to understand the views of others. They were learning to lead in areas they enjoyed. There is a sense (as was also evident in my last book) that these women wanted to influence (possibly even control) their environment through some of the childhood and adolescent activities they chose. It appears that, for many of these women, when an activity no longer provided learning and developmental opportunities, they moved on to something else. These young women pursued different endeavors that provided new learning circumstances. They seemed to thrive on new challenges, and they were not satisfied to just remain "comfortable."

I would like to highlight six activities mentioned by many of the women that seem to have provided profound developmental influences for them. First, all ten women were (and continue to be) avid readers. Each started reading as a child with most being influenced by a parent or grade school teacher to develop the love for and enjoyment of reading. Second, all of the women spoke of activities related to communication skills, particularly writing and speaking. They were editors of papers or involved in journalism in some way, participated in debate and/or competitive speaking, and/or were members of the student councils or other groups that provided them with opportunities to speak, write, and articulate their opinions, ideas, and responses. Possibly because of the open dinner table conversations as children, these women developed a confidence that their opinions and thoughts were valuable and should be expressed. Third, many of the governors spoke of their involvement with formal and/or informal sports as important in their upbringings. They believed that athletics were important for them in developing and strengthening competencies related to leadership, such as competitiveness, teamwork, risk taking, maintaining a strong presence when things aren't going well, toughness, continually striving for improvement in self and others, recovery from loss, and dependability. Fourth, six of the governors spoke of being involved with and performing in dramatic productions during high school. They believe this experience gave them additional confidence in being in front of groups and also provided them with opportunities to strengthen their speaking and presentation skills, pay attention to their body language and posture, and perform under pressure—all being important skills useful in prominent leadership positions. Fifth, four of the governors were cheerleaders during their youth. All noted that this was one of the few opportunities during those years for women to excel and compete. Some used cheerleading as a way to become leaders in their schools as they used their organizational, motivational, and presentation skills in this role. Finally, all but one of the governors were Girl Scouts as youth. In fact, many of their mothers were their leaders, with a few of these women eventually becoming leaders for their own daughters' troops later in life. Girl Scouts not only gave them a group to have fun with, but also provided them with opportunities to manage and lead, particularly for those women who continued involvement into their teenage years.

Leadership Positions and Perceptions

While exploring the governors' school and activities during their formative years, I asked them to highlight their specific leadership positions and perceptions. These included

- 4H youth leader
- Academic and service club leadership
- Captain of the debate team
- Church youth leadership
- Community service leadership
- Editor of the school paper
- Girls scouts/Brownie leadership
- Head cheerleader
- Student government officer
- Yearbook editor

As girls, these women were open to assuming formal and informal leadership roles early in their lives. Many described this as very natural for them as they liked helping individuals and groups accomplish things. A majority of the governors spoke of having a deep desire to make a difference even as youth. Others spoke of having such accomplishment needs and driving desires to "get things done." Four mentioned specifically that they continually had ideas about how things could be done, changed, or improved, and intrinsically knew they were the ones that could make things happen. As one noted, "I knew I had the capability to get things done and accomplish things, so I stepped forward." Others also mentioned strong social needs during those years. Organizing and belonging to projects, activities, and clubs were ways to fulfill those needs. One woman explained, "I liked bringing people together and having a good time, but always getting something done."

Although most women mentioned that they were involved in typical youth activities and clubs, some explained that they were somehow drawn to activities or efforts that were either new or needed improvement or change. It seems they yearned to help make improvements, whether on sports teams, service clubs, or student councils. They were fascinated with how groups could be motivated and led toward a variety of goals or objectives. It was clear that both successes and failures in this area were particularly meaningful and helpful learning experiences for these governors.

Four governors spoke of incredibly influential opportunities they received because they were chosen to attend state or national events (Girl Scout, 4H, and Girls State) where they represented young women in their regions and states. The travel, exposure, responsibility, and overall experience opened up their minds to new ideas and motivations. They were given opportunities to lead during these events and now believe that these trips expanded their perspectives and insights about the differences and diversity across the country. The independence they felt as they attended these events seemed to empower them, and it also provided a setting that helped increase their self-esteem and confidence.

These and other leadership experiences provided these governors many opportunities to learn and develop leadership skills and abilities that they have used and strengthened throughout their lives. Some of the key skills mentioned include communicating, delegating, innovating, developing and involving others, encouraging and motivating others, listening, understanding issues, learning, trusting other people, respecting others, practicing self-development, having emotional resilience, adjusting quickly, taking personal responsibility, initiating new ideas, focusing on goals, and being an effective team member. The governors believed that these competencies gave them a firm foundation for leadership that they then continued to strengthen as adults.

Employment

The governors said that they developed some of the same skills mentioned in the previous paragraph from employment opportunities, even though many did not actually have specific leadership responsibilities. The following are jobs they had during adolescence:

- Assistant in a school for handicapped children
- Baby sitter
- Candy striper
- Cashier
- Farm worker
- Fast food employee
- Formal volunteer

- Gofer in father's plumbing shop
- Janitorial worker
- Jewelry store clerk
- Lifeguard
- Sales clerk
- Secretary
- Waitress

Being employed as a waitress seemed to be the most helpful developmental employment position mentioned. Through this the governors learned and strengthened such skills as multitasking, interpersonal communication, treating people kindly and respectfully, problem solving, decision making, working and serving diverse individuals/groups, responsibility and dependability, and work ethic. Retail work and fast food also had learning benefits as well as farm work and picking crops. Physically difficult work was helpful for many of these women to develop both physical and mental strength and endurance. Three were employed in their fathers' businesses and learned to work successfully in predominantly male environments, which they found helpful in future years. All of the governors preferred jobs that kept them busy and helped them feel like they were accomplishing tasks and were being productive. They also enjoyed positions that provided opportunities for them to learn new skills and knowledge. These women seemed to find ways to learn and develop themselves in all that they did. Some did not intentionally seek specific development from their activities and didn't intentionally choose them for their learning value. Although their choices were sometimes unconscious and random, they were able to learn and develop from many different avenues and experiences.

INFLUENTIAL INDIVIDUALS

The governors discussed many individuals that influenced their development during their upbringings. Each woman had fond memories of a number of people who made some type of impact on her life. The women used a variety of terms to describe these individuals: friend, role model, coach, counselor, advisor, boss, mentor, leader, example, supporter, and encourager. The governors mentioned the following individuals listed here in rank order:

1. Mother (10)
2. Father (8)
3. Good friends (7)
4. English teacher (6)
5. Grandparents (6)
6. Aunts (6)
7. Uncles/extended family/Godmother (5)

8. Political figures (JFK, Martin Luther King, Hitler, local leaders) (5)
9. Elementary school teachers (first, fourth, fifth, sixth grades) (4)
10. Math teacher (3)
11. Sports coach (3)
12. Boyfriend (3)
13. Siblings (3)
14. Debate/speech coach (2)
15. Teacher (1 each)—history, P.E., French, speech
16. Brother's friend, housekeeper, librarian, neighbor, school newspaper advisor, principal, and Sunday school teacher (1 each)

Parents and Siblings
All ten governors spoke of the profound influence of family members throughout their upbringings, and specific in-depth descriptions were provided in each of the previous chapters. These women seemed to have had fairly open relationships with their parents. The girls appeared to listen to their parents and often valued their advice. This is not to say there were no problems; however, overall the governors' parents remained very influential throughout their upbringings and into adulthood. Siblings also became influential in these women's lives, as some were close friends, examples, supporters, and encouragers. In some cases, oldest siblings set the expectations for the children who followed, both positive and negative. Yet, in a few cases this had a profound effect on these governors as youth.

Extended Family Members
The governors spoke of the individuals in their extended families that they considered important in their development of leadership. Many governors had a large family support system during their upbringings, and they spent time interacting with grandparents, uncles, aunts, cousins, and other extended family members. The governors felt they learned a great deal about leadership and personal development by watching and interacting with these individuals and groups. The governors observed their styles of interaction and support, watched how they dressed and spoke in public, and internalized how focused some family members were toward achieving certain accomplishments. As young women, these governors enjoyed listening and watching, but at times, they also enjoyed being the center of attention.

When responding to my inquiry about which extended family members were most influential in developing leadership, the majority mentioned grandmothers and aunts. Five of the governors spoke in detail about one of their grandmothers being very critical to their development of leadership. One explained, "She gave me a sense of who I was. She taught me responsibility and the importance of participation in the community." Another said, "She was incredible and was strong, upright, and had a spark about her that intrigued me." Others described their grandmothers as role models because of their strength, positive influence, and independence. A few told stories about admiring their grandmothers' competitiveness. Three had grandmothers who were "free spirits" and did what they wanted without fear of judgment from others. Six governors reminisced about their grandmothers' competence and intelligence. Five of them commented that their grandmothers spent many hours asking them questions and listening to them as they were growing up. All of these governors had an adult (other than their parents) in their lives that listened to them and valued their voices.

Six of the governors also mentioned aunts who were very influential. The influence came from admiring who they were and what they did. One aunt apparently cared for foster children and gave many children a home throughout the years. Others were schoolteachers who had strong desires to make a difference to their students. Two said they had aunts who encouraged them to do well in school. One aunt taught her niece "the ability to, every once in a while, just step back and enjoy life. To take a deep breath and relax." Another said she learned from just being around a female relative and "feeling her support." Spending time with aunts made a difference in many ways as they interacted, listened, and felt valued.

A few governors also mentioned their grandfathers as influential and admired qualities of steadiness and stability in these men. Two spoke of influential uncles who spend time with them, and one governor helped a disabled male cousin during the summers. She felt that the teaching opportunities and perspectives she gained from these experiences "definitely enhanced" her leadership abilities. Overall, the governors mentioned female family members as being influential more often than male family members.

Peers

Friends were also mentioned by many of the governors as influential. However, it is important to note that apparently not all friends were actually influential in developing the governors' leadership abilities during their youth. The friends who were most influential were those who provided the governors with open, candid, accurate, and honest feedback. The governors trusted and appreciated these friends, as they knew these individuals would tell them the truth. These friends were "not afraid to speak their minds" and "just said things the way they really were." This feedback was important in helping them better understand themselves. These friends were individuals the governors truly respected.

Teachers

The governors said that a variety of elementary and secondary teachers made an important impact on their development. Fourth, fifth- and sixth-grade schoolteachers were mentioned most often for childhood influences. These teachers 1) cared deeply about them, 2) taught them to love books and reading, 3) made learning interesting, 4) challenged them to do more or give more to the learning experience, and 5) had a passion for teaching. These were some of the most critical years for these girls to develop self-esteem.

These same themes continued over into their secondary school years as well. Interestingly, English teachers were specifically mentioned by six of the ten women governors. Learning to write well was important to the governors as youth. One governor noted the important connection between writing, thinking, and speaking, and how she felt she improved in all three of these areas because of the progress she made in writing with an English teacher one year. In some cases, the English teacher was also the advisor to the school newspaper on which they worked, so they had a one-on-one relationship that was very developmental in nature. Three governors described their English teachers as passionate. As one said, "He had an amazing ability to describe literature. He had passion and brought literature to life for his students" Another stated, "My English teacher helped me become intellectually stimulated. It was a new feeling and energy for me." A final governor mentioned, "She showed me that I could find excitement in learning and developing my mind."

Other teachers were also mentioned for their engaging teaching styles, one-on-one interactions, and encouragement. One governor said her "math teacher had an interesting, sarcastic, and pushy style" that motivated her to "work hard and learn well." The governors mentioned some teachers because of an additional responsibility that teacher had (e.g., athletic coach, speech/debate coach, yearbook advisor, newspaper advisor), which provided a second reason for interaction. The profound influence the governors felt occurred because these teachers' facilitated the students' engagement in the learning process during class and also one-on-one developmental interactions with them in extracurricular activities. Students had time and a forum to talk, listen, observe, and reflect on these interactions and grew in various ways because of them. These teachers held them to rigorous and demanding standards while making it possible for them to succeed. They showed confidence in the governors, provided a challenging environment for them, and gave them appropriate and accurate feedback. The most influential teachers were passionate about their topics and about the education of youth. They enjoyed teaching and made it an interactive and uplifting experience for the governors. And finally, these individuals provided critical encouragement and support for the governors when they were at an impressionable age.

SIGNIFICANT CHALLENGES

The governors felt that they learned great lessons and made substantial progress in their personal development through dealing with and rising above challenges. Their significant comments focused around two primary areas: 1) relocations and 2) family/close friend illnesses or deaths.

A number of governors mentioned moving during their childhood and/or youth years. These moves seemed to add some complexity and challenge in their lives that is somewhat unique compared to other struggles youths may encounter. Most felt that these experiences were helpful, although not always enjoyable. Relocation pushed them to strengthen their abilities in meeting new people, analyzing their environments, fitting in with new groups, adjusting to surroundings, adapting to changing circumstances, and moving forward with new opportunities.

At least half of the governors spoke of difficult family situations. Two spoke of the challenges they encountered with an alcoholic father/stepfather. They spent a lot of time thinking about the disease and its effects on others. They reflected and learned from their experiences as they watched how others reacted and coped. A few governors also spoke in detail about other illnesses of siblings or close family members or friends. These were difficult times that provided reflective opportunities for them to think about "life in all its complexity." Two governors spoke about a sudden death of someone they knew and how it "turned their world upside down" for a time. A young person's first experience with the death of a significant person in their lives is "particularly powerful, often challenging to the core." The governors spoke of the great lessons in life they learned from dealing with these situations and pointed out that, in different ways, they needed these skills while serving as governors. They had to deal with loss, recover from defeats, and remain strong in the face of difficulties.

LESSONS LEARNED

As I've traveled to various parts of the country speaking about leadership development, people tell me that my findings have helped them think back through their lives to determine what has influenced their own development. For example, many have shared stories with me about the influence of a grade school teacher or the specific things that high school sports participation did to prepare them for leadership. They tell me that they didn't realize the influence of these individuals or activities until now. I've also spoken to groups of parents and typically get asked the same questions over and over:

- What kinds of things can we do in our home to help our daughters develop confidence and leadership?
- What are important characteristics and skills for young women to develop that will help them truly make a difference through leading others?
- What types of activities and experiences would best prepare my teenager to be a leader?
- Who can positively influence my daughter toward developing leadership?

The findings and general themes of this study can provide possible answers to these questions for 1) parents, 2) others interested in the development of young women, and 3) emerging leaders themselves. These lessons learned and suggestions are categorized by home and family, important skills and characteristics, school and activities, and influential people.

A. Home and Family

1. *Stable and optimistic home environment:* Providing girls with a stable, safe home environment is helpful in creating an effective atmosphere for the development of all types of competencies. Family-focused parents and strong extended family units that provide children with a solid value-based belief system and a foundational belief in a higher power (spirituality) can also create positive developmental experiences. Mothers and fathers can pass on a sense of optimism and hope about the world around them that provides a feeling of possibility for children as they look to their future choices and opportunities.

2. *Service-focused homes:* Children raised in service-oriented homes are more likely to become involved in community efforts and societal issues throughout their lives. Parents' interests, beliefs, and behaviors are the most powerful examples for children of the importance of becoming involved in one's community and contributing back to society.

3. *Family conversations:* Family dinner-table conversations can provide a helpful, enriching, developmental, and safe environment for children and youth to listen to engaging discussions and also voice their own ideas and opinions. Mothers and fathers who encourage children to find their own "voices" by facilitating open and engaging dialogue on various topics (including the common good, politics, and current issues) can assist children and adolescents to increase their self-esteem by helping them feel their opinions and concerns are appreciated and respected.

4. *Family work ethic:* Children and youth will develop more leadership skills as they respond effectively to high family work expectations. When they learn to work hard and responsibly in various paid and nonpaid work environments, including household chores and family responsibilities, they will have more opportunities to learn various skills needed for successful leadership.

5. *Education and learning-oriented environments and expectations:* The desire and ability to learn is one of the fundamental elements of leadership development. Parents who have strong expectations for their daughters to become college educated most likely will produce children with a commitment to education. Children and adolescents benefit from parents who are lifelong learners and who provide opportunities for their children to find joy and excitement in learning.

B. Important Skills and Characteristics

1. *Awareness and reflection:* Children and youth who are raised to be aware of their surroundings and encouraged to understand reasons for certain behaviors, views, and situations become more reflective and engaged individuals. Emerging leaders should also seek to develop effective listening and observation skills. Watching and studying people and situations provides valuable educational experiences if young people are taught to reflect on what they observe. When appropriate, youth can begin altering their behaviors based on their observations and reflections, which facilitates the development of self-monitoring skills and an awareness of the complexity of human behavior—both of which are critical for effective leadership.

2. *Personality types:* Children with various types of personalities can grow up to become leaders. However, females who are achievement focused, accomplishment oriented, task driven, courageous, and competitive are those who may have the drive and ambition to become prominent leaders. These attributes should not be discouraged in young women. In fact, adults can encourage them by assisting and supporting young people in becoming involved in activities and events in which they can use these characteristics productively. Emerging prominent leaders typically thrive on challenges. Adults in various settings can provide challenging opportunities that allow young people to stretch themselves, which will also lead to the strengthening and development of related competencies.

3. *Confidence:* Strong confidence in one area can provide a foundation for building confidence in other areas. Young people must develop real self-esteem based on their own actions and accomplishments, not just from comments made by others around them. Although usually well intended, inaccurate feedback or reinforcement given by adults is not helpful. Emerging leaders develop more effectively when they trust that the feedback they are receiving is open, honest, and accurate—whether negative, neutral, or positive. Children need to be taught to find intrinsic satisfaction when they work hard, achieve goals, and accomplish assignments or tasks.

4. *Difficulties and challenges:* Failures, struggles, and hardships can often provide more profound leadership development opportunities than successes and times of ease. I believe, however, that this is only true if the individual is both self-reflective and generally reflective. Difficult times can bring out reflective opportunities that can help future leaders deepen their understanding of life, become aware of their internal emotions and struggles, discover their strengths and weaknesses, and gain

an awareness of their coping and self-management skills. During these times, future leaders can discover (and often develop) deeper resiliency and can explore their own core values and beliefs.

C. School and Activities

1. *Learning and education:* Effective leaders find joy and passion in learning. They enjoy most elements of their formal schooling and thrive within enriching educational environments. They yearn to learn and find joy in intellectual growth and love being intellectually challenged. Parents and other adults should encourage and help facilitate learning around the natural curiosity and interests of children and adolescents. Developing leadership is all about learning. A deep love for reading is a common characteristic of prominent women leaders. Adults can help facilitate and encourage the joy that can be found by opening up one's mind and learning from reading.

2. *Activities:* A variety of extracurricular activities can also provide many developmental opportunities for young women to practice using and developing competencies important for successful leadership. In particular, competitive activities can assist women in learning many specific leadership competencies. Formal and informal team sports can provide rich environments to learn about teamwork, winning and losing, strength and toughness (physical and mental), responsibility and dependability, resilience, and more. Competitive debate, speaking, contests, and other activities can also be beneficial. In addition, activities that provide opportunities for young women to strengthen written communication skills (such as the school newspaper, magazines, and yearbook) are helpful. Involvement in most clubs, groups, and activities can provide leadership development opportunities if 1) they are challenging and 2) the young women approach them with a desire to learn, do their best, and then reflect on their experiences.

3. *Leadership roles:* The same is also true for the formal leadership positions during their adolescent years. As mentioned previously, general participation in activities as members of teams or groups can provide developmental opportunities, but the growth opportunities increase as girls take leadership roles in any of these areas including school clubs, athletic teams, student government, church youth groups, community organizations, and so forth. These opportunities can provide fulfillment for young women who have internal needs to organize, administer, and lead. Leadership during adolescence can also give girls responsibilities to mentor and develop others, which is a unique hallmark of successful female leaders.

4. *Employment:* If girls and young women have developed an ability to learn effectively, they can increase leadership competencies from any employment experience. Important growth can occur in developing a strong work ethic, multitasking and organizational skills, customer service and people skills, supervision, delegation, and more. The best employment opportunities seem to be those that keep employees busy and provide them the chance to learn and cultivate new knowledge and skills.

D. Influential People

1. *Parents and relatives:* Adults (including parents and relatives) who listen and respect the voices of girls and young women can be powerful influences on the development of leadership in young lives. Girls can benefit from having one or more aunts, grandmothers, or other female relatives who are role models of caring, independence, professionalism, competence, and/or strength.

2. *Schoolteachers:* Emerging leaders are most often positively influenced by elementary and secondary school teachers who have passion in their subject, ask students to share their ideas and thoughts, challenge them to think more deeply and critically, have engaging teaching styles, listen to and respect the voices of their students, and provide support and encouragement.

3. *Other adults:* Any number of adults who respect and value youth and model positive traits and behaviors can positively influence the development of emerging leaders. These people can be in a variety of positions including school advisors, counselors, or administrators; church leaders and members; family friends, neighbors, and friend's parents; and bosses or supervisors at work.

4. *Peers:* Trusted friends who provide open, accurate, candid, and honest feedback are those peers who most often positively influence the development of leadership in young emerging leaders.

FINAL THOUGHTS

The governors in this study have shown that their lives are about learning, leading, following, and serving. Reflecting back upon childhood and adolescent experiences has been beneficial for these governors who continue to seek opportunities to learn and develop leadership. Understanding your past helps you understand yourself. It assists in providing a stable foundation on which to build so that you can "become the master of your own life rather than its servant"

(Bennis, 1989, 100). It is often the individuals who lead that make a memorable difference in homes, schools, churches, communities, and nations. In fact, I would argue that it is through making some kind of difference for others that we can find purpose in our own lives. And, to do this effectively we must become the most integrated, undivided, and competent human beings we can become. Importantly, I am not talking only about a gifted few—but about all girls and women. All can benefit themselves and others by seeking to develop the ability to lead. Therefore, these findings can in some way apply to all.

Chapter 12

College Years and Life Roles

Peter F. Drucker once said, "Leaders grow, they are not made" (HeartQuotes Center, 2007). As I interviewed ten United States women governors, their stories and insights described unique journeys of developing and "growing" leadership throughout their lives. I discovered this to be the case not only through their childhood, adolescence, and young adulthood, but also into all phases of their adulthood as well. From every life role they acquired critical perspectives and skills that helped them become strong, successful leaders. How did they do this? John F. Kennedy once wrote, "Leadership and learning are indispensable to each other" (QuoteDB, 2005a). My research supports this assertion and clearly illustrates that effective leaders are those who thrive on continuous learning and growth. Learning is the foundation for successful leadership. I have also found that remarkable leaders are those who can see the potential that lies within themselves and others. They believe, as Ralph Waldo Emerson (QuoteDB, 2005b) taught, "What lies behind us and what lies before us are tiny matters compared to what lies within us." These leaders discovered their own worth and potential and then sought to expand the role of learning and development in their own lives as well as in the lives of those around them. These women somehow discovered that there are lessons in everything, and they had the desire to develop the ability to learn from them.

In this chapter, I will continue to highlight some of the findings discovered as I carefully analyzed each of the interviews for themes related to how these women developed leadership knowledge, skills, and abilities during college and throughout their adult lives, particularly focusing on non-work-related roles. The college portion focuses on the leaders' overall experiences, activities, employment, influential individuals, and struggles. The life roles section of this chapter discusses the women's marriages, spouses, motherhood, support systems, work-life strategies, and related challenges. As in Chapter 11, the final section will then share some overall *Lessons Learned* from the interviews as a whole. My hope is that this chapter will help you reflect upon your own experiences so that you can acquire insights into your own development and help others do the same. Through this reflection, you may also be able to identify additional sources of future personal growth and create continued developmental strategies for yourself and others.

COLLEGE YEARS

Seven of the ten governors said that they had always planned to go to college and that they felt strong expectations to do so from their parents. Three didn't necessarily feel those expectations during their youth. Two of these three came from small towns where youth did not tend to pursue higher education. One was encouraged by her teachers to attend college, which she did. Another was also encouraged to attend college by friends and other adults and also eventually graduated. Eight of the ten governors in the study graduated from college with bachelor's degrees.

I asked each governor what they remember thinking, as a high school student, regarding possible college majors. Their responses included English, French (mainly because she wanted to travel), international government, journalism, pharmacy, teaching, and home economics. Only a few governors remember having strong opinions about college majors during high school, and many ended up changing majors during their first year of college. One governor said she attended college at eighteen years of age solely for the social life and had no idea what programs or degrees she was interested in. Focusing on a major was just not important to her during her freshman year of college. Interesting, but not surprising, was the finding that most of the governors were very socially focused when they entered college. In fact, they were much more socially focused than the women university presidents I interviewed for my previous book. Yet, even with this social focus, all had a deep love of learning and wanted to continue to develop their minds. Interestingly, it seems that the social interests of many of the governors led to numerous leadership development opportunities for themselves and others.

Nine of the governors went directly from high school graduation to attending college the next fall. They attended a wide variety of institutions from small liberal arts colleges to large research universities. A few attended women-only colleges, at least for a time, whereas most went to mixed-gender institutions. The women were full-time students and most lived in campus dorms or sororities. The majority had what is called the "full educative experience," meaning that they were very involved and engaged in their courses, campus activities, and the overall college experience. These women became very committed to college and had (or at least developed) a deep desire to obtain knowledge, develop skills, and graduate with four-year degrees. It is important to note that this desire was somewhat uncommon for women at that time.

Overall, these governors had good relationships with their professors; struggled with situations that shook up their confidence for a time, but were able to resolve them with support; received stimulating and demanding educations; realized (a few for the first time) that they were intellectually, emotionally, and socially competent; and discovered they could be leaders on a bigger playing field. As one stated, "It was a wonderful time, and it prepared me well for the political path I ended up taking." College was an important developmental time in nearly all dimensions of the governors' lives. These women loved being busy and enjoyed college life.

Significant Challenges and Events
Many of the governors attended college during highly turbulent times and spoke about their experiences during those years. Although a few attended universities in the 1950s, many lived on campuses during the 1960s right in the midst of the Vietnam war, John F. Kennedy and Martin Luther King assignations, civil rights unrest, and general political upheaval. Although a few campuses were protected from the effects of these events, most of these women felt and saw (directly or indirectly) the resulting conflict, fear, chaos, anger, injustice, discrimination, injury, isolation, elitism, and the devastating toll of death of others. Many of the governors have powerful memories of various events that changed their perspectives and understanding of life in some way during these years. These include:

- Attempted suicide of peers
- Campus riots, peaceful demonstrations, and protests
- Death of students, peers, or friends
- Dorm curfew discrimination—need for change on campuses
- Drug and alcohol influences
- Failure (academic, social, or leadership)
- Feelings of hopelessness around them
- Gender inequity—limited opportunities
- Involvement in various change efforts (e.g., discrimination, injustice)
- Peer pregnancies and abortions
- Political issues and current events

These challenging events and experiences were key in providing a firm foundation for the governors to experience transformative learning experiences during these impressionable years. In a variety of ways, these events facilitated a change in opinion, belief, value, perceptions, or role expectation—the hallmark of what Jack Mezirow (1991) termed "transformational learning." Many a student has felt overwhelmed and dropped out of college because of experiences like the ones these governors faced be it directly or indirectly. However, each of these governors used their college experiences, both positive and negative, to learn from and to become stronger. Failures seemed to motivate them to try harder and do better rather than stifle their progress—another hallmark of an emerging leader.

Activities
As college students, the governors were involved either as a participant or leader in various activities, such as athletics, beauty/talent competitions, change efforts, clubs, college newspapers, debate teams, film and honor societies, marching teams, musical or dramatic productions, radio shows, political volunteerism,

program panels or other special events, service activities, social events, sorority and dorm, student government, campaigns, and other extracurricular activities. In fact, seven governors were involved in the student government of their colleges or universities. Five women joined sororities and three became heavily involved in their leadership. For example, one governor became the president of a sorority, which provided her with positive and challenging experiences as she worked with over one hundred diverse women and their day-to-day problems. Through this experience, she learned to listen, care, counsel, advise, problem solve, motivate, and lead change. Another woman said sorority leadership gave her valuable leadership training as she served in positions developing new programs and organizing activities and events. One woman noted that the sorority experience provided a forum for her to "meet lots of people and make important connections." It is important to note, however, that some of these sorority women became disinterested in remaining involved as they grew tired of the environment or, as one noted, felt that there was "too much discussion about colors of napkins and other unimportant things."

These women learned from other activities and experiences during college as well. Four of the governors spoke of leading policy change efforts related to discriminatory dorm and sorority curfews. Another learned from putting together a speakers' panel and then meeting, hosting, and listening to diverse presenters. One spoke of organizing an international event in which she interacted with dignitaries while they were on campus. A number of governors learned many leadership skills (e.g., planning, fundraising, social activities, networking) that were helpful as they became involved in politics later in life by running for and serving in student body leadership positions. A few were in the organizing bodies of peaceful political demonstrations. All of these leadership, membership, and involvement roles provided opportunities for the governors to practice speaking, writing, organizing, planning, and strengthening many other critical leadership competencies. In fact, during these years, some governors realized they had strengths they had not previously discovered. I would also be amiss if I did not mention that most of these women were very interested in socializing and dating. They loved attending a variety of events on and off campus (e.g., parties, dances, sporting events, concerts). The women felt that social activities provided opportunities for them to enhance their interpersonal, networking, and general communication skills.

Overall, it seems that extracurricular activities provided important opportunities during college to practice leading and to build confidence. As mentioned, many were involved in student government and had substantial responsibility to organize and influence. For example, as a sophomore, one governor was elected to the legislative body of the school, and by the time she was a senior, she was elected as the student body vice president of her large campus. In this position, she was in charge of all the student assemblies and often attended faculty leadership meetings to represent the students. On one occasion, she spoke up in a meeting where the president of the university was present. She challenged him by providing applicable information, which ultimately led to a change in university practice and policy. Another governor was in a prominent student leadership position and interacted regularly with important visitors on campus. As one governor stated:

> *I was so involved in student government on my campus. I enjoyed leadership roles. I really did. I guess a pattern was beginning to emerge during these years that I could and would be a leader. I enjoyed and loved learning. College was such a wonderful time of learning and personal development.* (Governor Olene Walker)

A number of women said that their internships or student teaching were very powerful experiences. For instance, one governor was able to work in the political environment of Washington, D.C. Her work taught her that she could make a difference in people's lives by being an advocate for them. This was a very empowering experience for her, as she discovered that she wanted to work in government and politics. A second governor also worked as an intern in Washington, D.C. for a senator and remembers writing and rewriting a speech that the senator actually gave. She also visited embassies and was able to see some of the "inner-workings of the political process." Another governor had a meaningful student teaching experience that provided her a forum to refine her philosophy of teaching based on her experiences that semester. This philosophy then served to guide elements of her future life as well as her political work and decisions.

It is important for me to note that not all governors had these opportunities and experiences throughout their entire college experience. Two governors married within their first year or so of college and were not able to continue having the kinds of full college experiences discussed. Life changed for these two women as their family responsibilities increased, and one did not continue with her education. Three women gave birth to children by the time they were twenty years old. One of these did not attend college, one dropped out, and one continued with her education even with multiple children. The two who did not graduate from college did not see their full-time education as an option in their lives during those years.

Employment
The governors had a variety of employment experiences during college:

- Administrative assistant
- Assembly line worker
- Camp counselor
- Clerk typist
- Demonstrator
- Dorm president
- Food services employee
- Guest ranch employee (summer)

- Intern for a senator
- Newspaper editor
- Retail worker
- Waitress

Most said they learned from each position, although the influence varied substantially depending on the opportunities and experiences they had. A paid internship was one source of employment for some of the women and, as already discussed, one governor worked in the welfare department during her internship and saw societal issues that she had never seen or previously understood. Each of the internships seemed to have broadened the governors' views, helping to deepen the women's understanding of the influence that governmental processes and policy have on actual U.S. citizens.

These women also worked in a variety of other jobs. A few had already been employed as waitresses during high school and enjoyed the challenges, complexity, and good compensation it provided. They mentioned that this position helped them strengthen such leadership skills as multitasking, interpersonal relations, social abilities, responsibility, dependability, assertiveness, political (i.e., the need to be nice for good tips—similar to fundraising in politics), and understanding and empathizing with others. A number of women spoke of working in retail for part of their college experience and, as long as they were able to be busy and productive, found it enjoyable. One governor worked in an academic department on her campus and thrived in that environment as she had positive interactions with faculty and staff who held her to high standards. She noted that it was an "enriching opportunity" that changed her college experience. During her master's degree, one governor was asked by two professors to grade papers. Although they didn't tell her that she was doing well in their courses, these requests gave her confidence that they respected her intellect and scholarship. During this time, the same governor also worked as a resident assistant in one of the houses on campus and reported to the dean of women. This provided her important developmental experiences in advising, listening, encouraging, and organizing. One governor worked as a camp counselor one summer. She spoke of the skills she strengthened from that experience in organizing, directing, disciplining, and motivating others—all were important skills she continues to use in her political career. Another was able to do some work that ended up being a precursor to a career she was interested in pursuing in her future. She found she absolutely loved the work (demonstrating household equipment), and it provided the opportunity for her to continue strengthening abilities in speaking, people skills, responsibility, self-directedness, and self-motivation.

Influential Individuals
The governors spoke of a variety of individuals who were influential in their development during their college years. Of course their parents, siblings, and certain relatives continued to be (in most cases) positive influences in their lives.

Each governor continued to have a close relationship with at least one parent during these years and depended on his or her advice, encouragement, and support. In most cases, the governors' mothers were the ones who continued to have the closest communication with their daughters at college. However, those who had particularly close relationships with their fathers continued these relationships as well and sought specific advice and guidance from them.

College professors proved to be a very important source of influence. The women spoke of having their development positively impacted because of interactions with many of these men and women. The governors specifically mentioned professors in the following disciplines: speech, German, history, American government, Latin, and political science. The governors were not only positively influenced by attending classes, but they also felt a more profound influence as these teachers took one-on-one time to tutor, mentor, encourage, coach, and even challenge them. The women believed that the willingness of these professors to spend time on their individual development actually gave them a continued sense of intellectual and interpersonal confidence, helping confirm their perceived capability and potential. Some women noted that it was "easy to tell which professors really wanted us to succeed and which did not. Some were challenging to try to get students to fail, whereas some were challenging to motivate us to rise up to their expectations." In many cases, these professors challenged and pushed the governors (as young women) to learn differently—broader and deeper—and to improve their critical thinking and writing skills, which increased their overall intellectual competence. For example, one governor spoke of professors who "let students express their own opinions in class" and had a "passion for teaching." The governors responded well to professors who respected their students and "pushed in a good way." One governor had a professor die during the semester and only then found out that the professor hadn't known of his impact on so many students. From this experience, she learned that life was fragile and that she needed to become "more intentional about communicating others' value to them." For some, professors helped shape their thinking about society, politics, and government. A few professors were credited with the governors' interest in eventually pursuing politics as a career. A professor's encouragement seemed to be critical and, in a few cases, actually led to transforming moments for these women. It seems that encouragement that comes from a challenging, rigorous, and passionate professor is particularly influential for emerging female leaders. As mentioned, when graduate professors asked one of the women to correct papers for their undergraduate classes, she knew that they recognized her abilities, which served as "encouragement" without the actual words. Interestingly, "encouraging" and "challenging" were the two words used the most to describe influential faculty members.

In addition to professors, other individuals on college and university campuses also provided important influences for the governors as students. Those specifically mentioned included athletic and debate coaches, student teaching and internship supervisors, contacts made during internships, student activity advisors, college administrators who worked with them in student government or event responsibilities, on-campus work supervisors, school psychologist who worked with student leadership, and sorority/dorm advisors and mentors. In some cases, these individuals served as examples of individuals (often women) of "strength, character, and independence." These people helped them develop skills and competencies, such as accountability, being candid without offending, building relationships, creating and moving forth a vision, critical thinking, managing budgets, networking, self-discipline, and work ethic—to name a few.

Friends and peers were also an important influential source for developing leadership. It seems the friends who had the most developmental influence were those who were open and candid and provided accurate and honest feedback, reflecting the same findings mentioned in Chapter 11. The governors trusted and appreciated these friends knowing these individuals would always tell them the truth. This benefit was reciprocal as the governors also provided open and honest feedback for their friends. One governor spoke of how much she valued friendships in which both parties were "not afraid to speak their minds." It was important that the governors have others to talk to about their own thoughts, behaviors, and actions. These friendships were crucial as they could "give and received accurate information about themselves and the world around them"—at least through another set of eyes. I found that those who married early in their college experiences had husbands (instead of college roommates and friends) who became this source of friendship and openness. Strikingly, it was clear that all of the women had at least one friend or individual in their lives with whom they had this type of reciprocal, open relationship. This feedback became critical during these developmental years in helping these young women better understand themselves. In many cases, these college friends have remained close throughout the years.

A few governors were also profoundly influenced by the families of the close friends they made during their college experiences. For example, one of the governors who never knew her own father and didn't have a strong male influence in her home, became very close to one of her college friend's families. This friend's father became the "father she never had." She remembers "spending hours on end having wonderful arguments with him about current issues and politics." She didn't have an example in her own home of parents who were in a loving, strong, committed relationship. Her friend's parents provided this important example. They spent time with her and also listened, respected, and even challenged her. They were strong forces for good in her life and ended up contributing substantially to the cost of her graduate education.

Political figures of the day served as important role models for many of the women governors. John F. Kennedy was mentioned by four governors as being someone who had a great influence for good in their lives. It was he who fueled their desires to go into public service as a career. It was also he who somehow motivated them to continue their involvement (as already influenced by their parents during their childhood and youth) in community service and volunteerism of various kinds. One governor spoke of the influence that Eleanor Roosevelt had as an important role model in her life. Her mother loved listening to

Mrs. Roosevelt's radio show and would call her at college to tell her about the radio shows. State and U.S. senators and congressman were also role models for the governors. Some women had the opportunity to interact with legislators or state governors because of family contacts, college internships, or special events.

Finally, it is important to note that many of the governors mentioned influential "moments" that were facilitated by individuals who were not necessarily strong influential forces in their lives. Yet, these moments remain clear in their minds and hearts as they often provided clarity, encouragement, new ideas, or confidence. These moments were times when something was communicated in such a way (positive or negative) that caused the women to reflect as they tried to make sense of the statement or situation. Sometimes these moments ultimately resulted in a self-discovery phase where they would then obtain more clarity about themselves. Although some researchers would argue that personal transformation is a long-term process, I would argue that some of these "moments" play a critical role in leadership development. For the governors, some of these moments shattered previous assumptions and even previous biases, causing opportunities for deep reflection, critical thinking, sense making, rationality, and perceptive.

Degrees
Eight of the governors graduated with bachelor's degrees, with five receiving education degrees—four in secondary education and one in elementary education. All eight graduated within four or five years. One of the most interesting themes I discovered was the focus so many governors had on communication. Three women majored in speech communication, three in English with interests in writing, and one in journalism. Communication through speaking and writing was an important interest and passion for many of these women. Their majors and minors included the following:

- Speech Communication (3)
- English (3)
- Political Science (2)
- History (1)
- Journalism (1)
- American Studies (1)
- International Government (1)
- Home Economics (1)
- Elementary Education (1)

Importantly, the two who did not graduate, nonetheless took college courses at various times throughout their lives.

A total of four women obtained graduate degrees. Two of the governors went directly to master's degree programs after graduation, one started a master's degree a few years later, and the fourth went directly into a doctoral program (J.D.). Three obtained master's degrees in various areas including journalism, political science, and political theory. They were encouraged by professors and others to pursue their educations. One worked for a few years after receiving her undergraduate degree and then entered and graduated from law school. One of the women who received a master's degree, returned to school many years later after having children to complete a Ph.D. in educational administration.

During and after college, most of the governors had flexible career plans. Some did not expect to work after college; they expected to be married and begin having children. Some graduated with specific degrees and knew that it may take them some time, due to gender issues, to get the position they truly wanted. A few women knew they would need to teach school full time after graduating (even with young children at home) at least for a few years while their husbands finished their graduate degrees. Others needed to earn money while they had young children at home, but planned to do part-time work either from their homes (e.g., childcare) or while extended family members or neighbors cared for their children (e.g., teaching college courses). Most knew they wanted to do some kind of influential work in their lives, but were open and flexible to the paths and timing of this goal.

FAMILY AND LIFE

Marriage and Spouse
All ten governors have been in successful, long-term marriages. Three were married at eighteen or nineteen years of age. This included the two who did not graduate with college degrees. All of the others married after they completed their bachelor's degrees; they were either working or in graduate programs at the time. Only one of the ten is divorced, and this was attributed to the difficulties caused by the challenges of raising a disabled child. This governor remained single for many years, but did marry a wonderful man who had many of the characteristics of the other spouses I will describe later in this section. A few governors married in their late twenties, with one marrying after becoming a state senator. All of these women spoke of successful marriages, although none said their marriages were without inherent complexity and challenges. Their husbands' occupations through the years included attorney, dentist, medical doctor, healthcare investigator, private equity investor, legislator, athletic director, farmer, attorney general, judge, and businessman. A few of these men also served time in the military as well for part of their careers.

According to the governors, their husbands are remarkable men. The major theme mentioned over and over was their incredible capability to encourage and support (emotional, physical, and financial) their wives. Nearly all of the governors I interviewed spoke about these attributes and specific quotations are found in many of the profile chapters. However, a few are worth repeating here. For example, Governor Whitman stated:

> *What has made my career in politics possible was my good fortune in having a strong partner with whom to share the demands of political life, my husband, John. While politics provided a good fit for me as I was able to balance the demands of young children with part-time political office holding, having the support of my spouse was key. . . . None of it would have worked without him. He was also my chief cheerleader and supporter, urging me on even when I was ready to call it quits.*

Governor Kunin shared the following thoughts about her husband Arthur:

> *What I gladly share is that my husband was unusually giving of his support to my career. Few other men could have been as generous as Arthur was, not only in rearranging his own life to ease mine, but also in taking genuine pride and pleasure in my achievements. . . . He let me run, not by granting his approval, but by giving me courage when I grew afraid, by urging me forward when I wanted to retreat, by cheering my victories and mourning my defeats, and by doing all the small things that made it possible for me to create a political life. His largest gift was his inner strength, which allowed him to be the companion of a strong woman.* (Kunin, 1994, 166)

These remarkable men were not threatened by their wives' success, and they felt genuine pride in their spouses' accomplishments. These men had strong listening skills and were very willing to share their opinions and advice with their wives. For example, Governor Swift said, "He has always listened and shared his observations and advice with me. His mental and emotional support has been invaluable in my own growth and development—personally and professionally." Yet these men respected their wives enough to support whatever decisions they made—whether they agreed or not—even when they knew those decisions would mean that they would need to sacrifice and change their own lives in some way. All of the governors credited their husbands with being the most important element of their overall "support system." Some referred to their husbands as their "best friends" and spoke of how much they trusted their husbands and valued their advice. Most of the women also spoke of a portion of their married life being centered on their husband's careers and how, during later years, their own careers took forefront in their marriages, terming this as "trading roles." Three of the women also mentioned the unique relationships their children had with their fathers because of the time spent together throughout the years. The governors said these strong relationships ended up being a gift to all. Finally, at least half of the women mentioned that because their husbands worked full time and provided financially for their families, the women had "a great deal of freedom" to pursue their own interests. They also had more flexibility with their own choices and decisions. One said this circumstance also gave her the freedom to speak her mind openly, something she always appreciated.

Motherhood
All ten of the governors gave birth to multiple children. Four governors have

two children each (one has two sons, one two daughters, and two have one boy and one girl), two governors have three daughters each; two governors have four children (one with three girls, one with three boys); one governor has five children (three boys, two girls); and the tenth governor has seven children, including both boys and girls. Most gave birth to their children fairly close together (e.g., one had four children in eight years and another seven children in thirteen years). Children and families were (and continue to be) central in the lives of all ten governors. Most of these women chose to be stay-at-home mothers during at least a portion of their children's upbringing. They were heavily involved in all elements of their children's lives, yet they remained engaged in their communities and various volunteerism efforts. Governor Shaheen explained, "I wanted to be involved in my children's lives and this guided my decisions for non-paid and paid employment for many years. I wanted to have flexibility." It is important to note, however, that one governor married at twenty-nine and did not start having children until after she was a lieutenant governor. Her experiences are somewhat unique to this group.

Being a mother has been one of the most important roles the governors have had in their lives. In fact, motherhood taught these women powerful lessons and helped them develop unique competencies that have been important to their leadership throughout all aspects of their lives. Many of the women mentioned that motherhood came very naturally to them and felt that their families were essential to their happiness and success. I have compiled all of the statements made by the governors during my interviews regarding what they learned from motherhood that has been helpful to them in their leadership. The list is interesting because they have credited motherhood with helping them develop and strengthen many competencies:

Motherhood taught me to . . .
    Accept that everything can't be perfect
    Balance multiple responsibilities and demands
    Balance priorities
    Balance work and life
    Be able to just survive and endure at times
    Be challenged and survive
    Be creative and look for creative ideas
    Be empathetic
    Be fair
    Be flexible
    Be nonjudgmental
    Be patient
    Be productive
    Be strong and tough
    Become an advocate
    Become more responsible and dependable
    Challenge authority figures appropriately

College Years and Life Roles

Communicate effectively
Comprehend the connection between responsibility and relationships
Confront situations and issues when appropriate
Continuously learn
Deal with being blamed unjustly
Delay judgment
Delegate
Develop new skills
Develop others
Dig deep to understand myself
Effectively network
Expect frustrations
Express my nurturing side
Get the best out of people
Go with the flow
Have confidence in new and undefined situations
Have humility
Have internal strength and resolve
Have self-discipline and self-control
Help others
Hold firm to a decision that has been made
Learn more about myself
Let my faith positively influence all dimensions of my life
Listen and observe others
Look ahead and have a vision
Manage conflicts
Manage my time
Manage schedules
Mediate arguments and situations
Motivate others effectively
Move from issue to issue very rapidly
Multitask
Negotiate and mediate
Organize and plan effectively
Pick battles wisely
Prioritize
Reason
Recognize and nurture an individual's unique gifts and capabilities
Respect others' choices
Sacrifice
Seek for self-knowledge
Set broad parameters in life so that I can empower others
Stand back and watch
Teach others
Trust my instincts and judgment

Trust myself
Understand the importance of learning from challenges
Understand that things won't always be black and white
Use time wisely
Work out and deal with differences

The governors shared many insights regarding what specific things motherhood helped them develop. For example, Governor Roberts was able to move forward productively and did not allow her circumstances to become a roadblock because of her experiences in being an advocate for her disabled son. She rose to the challenge when others would have given up. She learned that she could survive in the face of being challenged to her very core. Another governor raised children and worked part time for years. She spoke of crying herself to sleep many nights because she thought she wasn't the best mother or the best employee as she struggled to balance both of these domains in her life. Yet, dealing with these dilemmas helped her strengthen her skills in dealing with various conflicting demands as a governor. She learned to move forward without expecting perfection and peace. For many, motherhood has influenced legislation they have written and/or supported as legislators or in other elected positions. It has also provided a focus for many of their political efforts and agendas. Although trying to be both good mothers and good politicians has been challenging, these women have learned to use their time wisely and make good choices between important commitments. Finally, motherhood has taught them the importance of letting others make their own choices and providing support as needed.

Work-life Strategies
I asked the governors what strategies they used in balancing their work, family, and other life responsibilities. Most said that they chose to have flexibility in their employment and other responsibilities outside the home for many years. The governor who was a single mother for many years chose jobs that did not require extra time outside of the regular workday. She did not take work home in the evenings so she could focus solely on her boys. This helped her separate work and family by compartmentalizing each role. Another governor also used the compartmentalization strategy as her mother moved close by when she gave birth to her first child. Her mother then took care of her children full time for many years. This provided an amazing benefit for the governor, but it was also fulfilling for her mother. It seems the other governors compartmentalized at times but then closely integrated their work and family domains at others. Two governors made specific comments regarding their use of both types of work-life strategies, choosing to use the strategy that worked best for the situation that presented itself. It seems that balancing work and family through situational strategies may have been a precursor to their development of a situational leadership style that emerged as they became leaders in their communities, professions, and government.

Most of the governors struggled with work-life issues for many years. Most chose to work part time for years so they had flexibility to be home with their children, as needed. Yet, it seems they reinvented their lives as they moved through various stages. They tried to make choices based on their families' needs and their own desire for meaningful contributions outside the home. Many spoke of their love for community involvement and professional work, paid or unpaid. A number of governors said they have been asked to speak on how to balance work and family, and they told me that they didn't have any good answers. For example, Governor Shaheen explained, "After working on a speech about balancing work and family, I finally realized that I couldn't write it because I didn't have a real strategy. My idea of work-life balance has been learning to live with the guilt!" Governor Kunin stated, "Some sense of conflict remains for every woman who has obligations outside of the home."

Support System
As already mentioned, the governors' husbands were the most important source of support these women had throughout their married lives. Some of these men had fairly flexible employment and were able to spend time with the children while their wives were working and/or volunteering. The governors also spoke of the support provided by other family members (particularly parents, in-laws, and siblings). For example, while one woman was at work, her mother cared for both of her children for many years. Other family members also provided either temporary and regular childcare or other kinds of assistance, when needed. The governors' children, particularly as they got older, became important sources of support for their mothers inside and outside the home. For example, Governor Walker spoke of her children having an extended network of friends, which helped immensely during her first election. Governor Kunin said, "My children's networks became my networks as they got older and I became politically active." Many governors said their children became very encouraging when they were teenagers and young adults as well. Older children, in particular, were active and involved in campaigns and other efforts.

The governors also spoke of a number of non-family sources of support. Finding good childcare was the most important priority for all of these mothers as they chose to do work and volunteerism that took them out of their homes. Some had good friends, neighbors, or others who came into their homes to provide childcare and housekeeping. One spoke about hiring someone she had not previously known and said, "She was a gift to me and my family." The governors said it was critical for them to know that their children were happy and safe. Friends were also a critical source of support for the governors throughout their adult lives especially during the years when their children were small and they struggled with the challenges of being a full-time homemaker or juggled both work and family responsibilities. For example, when Governor Hull lived on an Indian reservation with small children, her primary support group was the other doctors' families. The governors mentioned neighbors, co-workers, and staff also being important sources of support even outside of the work environment. One governor found a parent group to be one of the most important sources of support she had for many years. Governor Roberts spent many years being an advocate for her disabled son, thriving on opportunities in which she was able to talk to and work with other parents on these issues.

Challenges

Again, the greatest challenge mentioned by the governors was their work-life struggles. Clearly, balancing work and family continues to be challenging for most women today. One governor used the term "pure exhaustion" when describing the challenge of "being a good mother and having a career." The complexity inherent in marriage and parenthood was clearly one of the greatest challenges these governors spoke about. For example, the challenges Governor Roberts faced with her son's disability provided her years of challenges, which she used to learn and grow. She believes that this personal challenge helped shape her character and provided insights, which eventually led to her strong leadership as a governor. She remarked, "There is not much question that my son's disability gave me the ability to do many meaningful things in my life." Challenging toddlers and teenagers were also mentioned by some governors as difficult times from which they learned. For some, not working full time outside the home was a challenge as they were driven and enjoyed working.

Relocation with children seemed to be at the top of the governors' lists for challenging times as well. Governor Walker spoke of the struggles she went through as her family moved time and time again during a thirteen-year period when she was bearing and rearing many young children. Some governors spoke of moving to slum-like areas during their early lives, particularly as their husbands were finishing their schooling. Although frightening at times, they spoke of learning very important lessons about society including the real struggles that low-income families face, diversity issues, the challenges faced by poor single mothers, and more. Governor Hull spoke about the adjustments she and her husband had to make when living and working on an Indian reservation in Arizona for a few years. She loved this unique experience and the challenges taught her some great lessons about life and priorities despite the difficulties. Moving and its associated changes taught these women about adapting, changing, and flexibility, all of which became useful skills in their later leadership roles.

The governors also spoke of some unpleasant challenges they faced—sometimes just endured—during their political years. Most spoke of difficulties with the press. In fact, some of these governors were attacked outright many times in harsh ways while serving in public office. Although some spoke of learning from these challenges, it seemed that "the pain that comes with these kinds of challenges never quite goes away." The women said they developed "thicker skin" throughout their political careers but most never fully got used to unjust media coverage. For example, Governor Swift had some very unique challenges as she went through a pregnancy while running for lieutenant governor and then another (twins) while serving as governor. The press was relentless at times. As expected, being in high-level posts with very young children was very challenging on many fronts.

LESSONS LEARNED

The themes I have shared in this chapter are only broad highlights of the findings discovered in this study of women governors and their lifetimes of developing leadership related to 1) college years and 2) non-work-related roles during adulthood. Based on the results of my research, I have been asked to speak to many audiences (e.g., faculty, advisors, counselors, student leaders, college administrators) on how female college students can develop leadership. They often ask the following questions:

- What types of college experiences are the most beneficial for developing strong leadership skills?
- What are the leadership competencies most important for female students to develop while in college?
- Who are the individuals that seem to have the most important influence on college students and why?

The governors' stories provide many good examples of the types of influences that can be most effective in facilitating the development of leadership.

Non-work-related roles are also critical sources of leadership development during adulthood. I've discovered that many women do not realize the important developmental experiences that marriage and motherhood can have on their lives. Some of the related questions that I've been asked are as follows:

- What are the attributes of a man who can successfully be married to a strong woman leader?
- How can motherhood help me develop leadership competencies?
- How can I better juggle the demands of my family, work, and community involvement?

This chapter, and book as a whole, has addressed each of these questions and, although there are no magic answers for any of them, the governors' insights and experiences may provide some understanding and clarity as you consider your own situations. I have summarized and categorized the following lessons learned and suggestions in three sections: college experiences, influential individuals, and family life.

A. College Experiences

1. *Full educational experience:* Young women who have the opportunity

to become fully engaged in their college experiences, during at least part of their higher education, may have an advantage in developing leadership competencies during these years. Students who are committed to well-rounded intellectual, emotional, and social development can increase their confidence and desire by being actively involved in many facets of the college experience. Emerging leaders are passionate about their college educations and find joy in the journey. Although many individuals can help facilitate an enriching environment for the development of women students, it is the student herself that determines the actual learning and growth she acquires. Communication-related degrees and coursework (e.g., English, speech communication, and journalism) may be helpful in preparing for effective leadership.

2. *General leadership competencies:* College students who take advantage of the full opportunities available through involvement in their courses and other campus activities, can develop and strengthen the following leadership competencies mentioned by the governors:

   Accountability
   Analysis of motivations
   Articulating positions
   Being candid without offending
   Building a program
   Building relationships
   Communication skills
   Creating and moving forth a vision
   Creating goals and objectives
   Critical thinking
   Dealing with difficult situations
   Delegating and organizing people
   Dependability
   Flexibility
   Focus and concentration
   Focusing on results
   Handling complexity
   Integrating knowledge
   Listening
   Logic
   Management
   Managing budgets
   Negotiation
   Networking
   Organization
   Organizational skills
   Overseeing and supervising people

Planning skills
Political skills
Preparation and studying skills
Presentation skills
Reflection
Representational skills
Representing the institution to stakeholders
Responsibility
Seeing strengths in self and others
Seeing weaknesses in self and others
Spirituality
Teamwork
Time management
Voicing views
Work ethic
Writing

For example, the competency of flexibility can be particularly beneficial for considering future career options. Career flexibility can provide women, who want to be heavily involved in rearing their children, a wide range of opportunities and choices throughout their lives.

3. *Activities:* A wide variety of extracurricular activities can provide developmental opportunities for college students. Particular opportunities to practice leading in venues, such as student government, political volunteerism, and academic/social entities (to mention only a few), can be particularly useful in the development of leadership-specific skills. These experiences teach the student new concepts and skills and provide challenging opportunities that allow students to stretch.

4. *Internships, student teaching, and employment:* Meaningful internships and student teaching experiences in college can be powerful hands-on learning opportunities for young women as long as the experiences provide new, challenging environments and circumstances in which they can develop fresh insights and perspectives. The most beneficial situations seem to be those in which students are required to perform in new roles that open their minds to the impact their future work can have on others. Basic employment opportunities can also be helpful if they provide means for women to work hard, keep busy, be challenged, and strengthen and develop competencies.

5. *Challenges:* Young women can learn dramatic life lessons from being immersed in challenging events and experiences in which a variety of emotions are felt (e.g., conflict, fear, chaos, anger, injustice, confusion, and loss). However, it is critical that they are surrounded by strong

support systems and have already developed reflective skills or are guided through sense-making processes by experienced individuals (peers, friends, advisors, professors). They need to be able to talk and reflect about what they are experiencing.

B. Influential Individuals

1. *Families:* Parents, siblings, and other close relatives can remain an important source of influence for college students even when they are living away from home. A positive relationship with parents and other family members serves as a foundation for feelings of security, support, hope, and optimism during these college years. In fact, family members who listen and encourage seem to be important developmental influences throughout one's life.

2. *College professors*: College professors from a variety of disciplines can be a very important source of influence during college. Young women who have a desire to receive an education (not just a degree) can be positively influenced by classroom experiences as well as one-on-one interactions with college instructors. Professors who respectfully challenge college students (emerging leaders) to enhance their critical thinking skills, deepen their real and perceived intellectual capacity, strengthen their interpersonal confidence, and share their thoughts and opinions in a non-threatening environment can facilitate important developmental experiences for their students.

3. *College staff, administration, advisors:* Any number of authority figures within college settings can also positively influence the development of leadership amongst female students. Emerging leaders seem to be impacted most often by those that they perceive respect and value their ideas, opinions, and contributions. Young women look for those who see potential in them. These individuals can provide the motivation for students to seek excellence in whatever endeavors they choose. In addition, college staff, administrators, advisors, and others can serve as important role models for young women to see critical leadership characteristics, such as strength, integrity, independence, competence, ethics, and perseverance.

4. *Friends/peers:* Emerging leaders can be profoundly influenced by friends who give them accurate and honest feedback and are open and candid (same findings as youth years). Those peers with whom young women have strong, healthy, trusting relationships are those who provide an important source of encouragement, a sense of reality, and optimism for the future. Close friends can be particularly helpful for women during college as they can assist others in understanding them-

selves. College-aged women can also be profoundly influenced by their peers' family members who reach out and provide stability, and who serve as positive role models for them.

5. *Political figures:* Male and female political figures can serve as important role models for young women. They can inspire interest in and commitment for community involvement, political activism, and public service—all of which provide important forums for the development of leadership within young women. For young women to have positive political role models, they need to be exposed to the individual on a personal level (lives, passions, efforts, and work) through any number of mediums (e.g., media, face-to-face).

6. *Influential moments:* The leadership development of young women can be influenced substantially by small, short, and seemingly insignificant moments in one's life. It is in these moments that an individual (even a passing acquaintance) shares an observation with them that can provide insight into themselves, confidence in their talents and abilities, encouragement or ideas to move forward in specific directions, and new perspectives about their potential. These moments can truly make a difference.

C. Family and Life

1. *Marriage and spouse:* To be most successful in the workplace, home, and life, married women need spouses who provide encouragement and support (emotional, physical, family, and financial), and who are not threatened by them. This kind of partner takes genuine pride in his wife's successes. Remarkable spouses are those who have strong listening skills and are willing to share their opinions and advice, while at that same time respecting their wives' personal and professional decisions. A spouse of a strong woman leader must be willing to sacrifice at times and also provide a stable, valued source of support throughout her career. It is clear that spouses of powerful women can also lead influential and successful lives.

2. *Motherhood:* Women with children can attain some of the highest leadership positions in government and beyond. In fact, being a mother can provide valuable experiences critical for the development of leadership skills. Motherhood can teach women powerful lessons—if they are willing to learn—that are directly applicable to leadership in government, business, higher education, and other industries. Women can remain engaged in the community and politics while raising children. Although challenging, it is clear that women can not only reach high leadership positions while choosing to keep their families as their high-

est priority, but that they can become better leaders because of the role that motherhood plays in their lives.

3. *Work-life strategies:* A career in public service can provide the flexibility needed to balance work and life responsibilities. Each woman must choose a work-life strategy that fits best in her life, taking into account her sources of support. A compartmentalization strategy works well for a woman with a strong support system in the home so that she can focus solely on her work when she is at work. This strategy only works successfully if she can then focus primarily on the family when she is at home as well. Other women balance home and family more successfully by using a more integrated approach. They transfer their focus between work and family based on the needs at the time. These women typically have more flexible work schedules and have the option of doing work at home, as needed. Women need to realize, however, that neither strategy makes life easy. Yet, true emerging leaders are not looking for "easy"; although stressful at times, their focus is on making a difference and enjoying the complexity of being active in multiple life domains.

4. *Support system:* A broad base of individuals can be part of an important support system for emerging women leaders. Supportive spouses, parents, in-laws, siblings, extended family members, neighbors, friends, childcare providers, housekeepers, colleagues, and support groups can be elements of a complete package that will provide emerging and current leaders the foundation needed to lead successfully. Providing the same support to others builds these types of relationships throughout one's life. Women who try to move forward without appropriate support from those around them will have a challenging time being successful in any role. The best support systems are the ones you build through years of healthy relationships. Giving support and accepting support are the hallmarks of a successful woman.

5. *Challenges and struggles:* Women who desire to have partners, children, and professional careers must expect that they will face continuous challenges and struggles in life. In fact, women should expect this complexity throughout their lives. However, a true sign of an emerging leader is the way in which she responds to these challenges. She does not quit when things get tough. She may get discouraged for a short time, but she quickly gets back on track and has the confidence that she can move forward in whatever her goals and desires may be. She is optimistic and determined amidst life's storms. Most importantly, she has the ability to learn important life lessons from these experiences.

FINAL THOUGHTS

The discovery of what lies within us, as Ralph Waldo Emerson inferred, is a critical element in our search to understand ourselves (QuoteDB, 2005b). Remarkable leaders are those who learn to see and believe in their own potential. Leadership development is a lifelong journey that is made up of every aspect of our lives. Each experience can help us grow and develop into a more competent, capable, and contributing human being. Therefore, this study confirms Peter F. Drucker's statement, "Leaders grow, they are not made" (HeartQuotes Center, 2007). These women somehow discovered that there are lessons in everything, and they had the desire and developed the ability to learn from them.

I have come to believe that a portion of leadership development is incidental. It just happens because of life experiences. However, the women who become successful leaders are those who thrive on learning and personal development. They want to learn and find opportunities all around them. They love challenges, although often unconsciously, because of the growth opportunities they provide. Learning *is* the foundation for successful leadership. Each of these women governors described unique journeys of developing and "growing" leadership throughout their college years and in their various life roles. And, as I stated at the beginning of this chapter, from every life role these women acquired critical perspectives and skills that helped them become who they became—strong, successful leaders. I believe that we can do the same, and we can influence many others to do so as well.

Chapter 13

Career Paths and Political Years

Leadership is not really about the leader. It is about accomplishing a goal, moving an effort forward, influencing others toward action, and assisting people in making some type of difference. It is about what the followers can accomplish as individuals, teams, organizations, and communities. As a leader, it is not about you—it is about them. Robert Townsend said, "True leadership must be for the benefit of the followers, not the enrichment of the leaders" (Thinkexist.com, 2006). On the other hand, leadership *development* is focused on the leader. It is about helping individuals become competent and influential. As Napoleon Bonaparte noted, it is about assisting people learn to be "dealers in hope" (LeaderValues, 2008). As Sheila Murray Bethel explained, "Leadership is not something that you learn once and for all. It is an ever-evolving pattern of skills, talents, and ideas that grow and change as you go" (Motivation Point, 2008). Leadership development is about human development. This book has demonstrated these sentiments as I have shared the stories and experiences of ten remarkable women who have served as governors within the United States.

In the last two chapters (Eleven and Twelve), I have shared the themes and general findings about the governors' development of leadership during their childhood, youth, college years, and throughout adulthood, particularly as it relates to the non-career elements of their lives. This final chapter now finishes this book by sharing themes regarding the governors' careers, barriers, influential individuals, training and development opportunities, and leadership motivations and styles. It will conclude by sharing advice from the governors to future potential leaders. I believe that reflecting on these results can assist you in crafting your own formal and informal developmental plan.

CAREER PATHS

There is great variety in the governors' career paths. In fact, each woman had a different and unique background, which ultimately led her toward becoming a state governor. I have struggled with determining how to best present the career path information so that you can best see (at a glance) the similarities and differences among these women. I finally decided that the best strategy would be to briefly list each governor's positions, in chronological order, for a quick review. Afterwards, I will highlight some general observations and themes that I discovered about the governors' career paths. One thing is very clear; there are many different pathways for women toward political leadership.

1. **Governor Barbara Roberts**
   - Office Manager
   - Advocate (focused on son's disability)
   - Citizen Lobbyist
   - Political Volunteer/Campaign Worker
   - School Board Member
   - Community College Board Member
   - Legislator's Chief of Staff
   - County Commissioner
   - State Representative
   - Represented the freshman class in the House
   - House Revenue Committee
   - Majority Leader
   - Rules Committee Chair
   - Secretary of State/Lieutenant Governor
   - Governor

2. **Governor Chris Gregoire**
   - Clerk Typist in Adult Probation and Parole
   - Caseworker
   - Criminal Investigative Assistant
   - Attorney General's Officer
   - Assistant Attorney General
   - Director of Social Health Services Section in the Attorney General's office
   - Head of Attorney General's office in Spokane
   - Deputy Attorney General
   - Director of Department of Ecology
   - State Attorney General
   - Governor

3. **Governor Christine Todd Whitman**
   - College Intern for a state senator
   - Campaign Worker (political researcher for presidential campaign)
   - Office of Economic Opportunity Special Assistant (federal government)
   - Director of the Listening Program (National RNC program)
   - Campaign Manager (Congressional campaign)
   - Teacher (ESL)
   - County Board of Chosen Freeholder's Member

- Deputy Director and Director of Freeholder Board
- President of Board of Public Utilities
- Ran for U.S. Senate
- Governor

4. **Governor Jane Hull**
   - Elementary School Teacher
   - Teacher on a reservation (husband in public health)
   - Community and Political Volunteer (education activist)
   - Girl Scout Leader; PTA; Republican Women's Club member
   - Various positions in the state Republican party
   - Chair of governor's campaign
   - Campaign Leader/Worker (e.g., county attorney, state positions)
   - Legislator in the State House Representative
   - Committee Chair (various)
   - Majority Whip
   - Speaker of the House
   - Secretary of State
   - Governor

5. **Governor Jane Swift**
   - College Intern in a senator's office
   - Retail Manager
   - Legislative Aid
   - Legislative Liaison
   - State Senator
   - Committee Service (Ways and Means and others)
   - Candidate for U.S. Senate
   - Director of Regional Airport Authority
   - Director for State Consumer Affairs and Business Regulation Agency
   - Cabinet Member in governor's office
   - Lieutenant Governor
   - Governor

6. **Governor Jean Shaheen**
   - College Intern in the Missouri Welfare Department
   - High School Teacher
   - Retail Business Owner
   - University Senate Secretary
   - Political Campaign Worker
   - Governor's Campaign Manager
   - Ran Jimmy Carters' presidential campaign in NH, Gary Hart's NH presidential campaign

- Vice-Chair for State Women's Commission
- Chair of the Employment Taskforce
- Co-director of Children's Festival
- Director of UNH Parent's Association
- State Senator
- Governor

7. **Governor Madeleine Kunin**
   - Journalist for local newspaper (community and political events/issues)
   - Guide at the American Pavilion at the World's Fair
   - League of Women Voters member
   - Led study group for Medical Care for the Aged
   - Community Activist (e.g., historical house, sidewalk, crossing at railroad track, children's theatre)
   - Women's Political Caucus
   - College Instructor
   - Leadership in League of Women's Voters
   - Legislator in State House of Representatives
   - Democratic Whip
   - Appropriations Committee Chair
   - Lieutenant Governor
   - Governor

8. **Governor Martha Layne Collins**
   - High School Teacher
   - Church/Community Volunteer
   - Campaign Volunteer
   - Congressional District Chairwoman
   - Ran statewide campaigns
   - State Democratic National Committee Woman
   - Presided over 1984 State Democratic Convention
   - State Court of Appeals Clerk
   - Lieutenant Governor
   - Governor

9. **Governor Nancy Putnam Hollister**
   - Activist at college
   - Worked on levy for a new school for disabled
   - Ran City Council Campaign for friend
   - City Council Member
   - Chair of Police and Fire Committee
   - Chair of Planning and Zoning Committee
   - Mayor

- Governor's Director of Operations for a region
- Lieutenant Governor
- Governor

10. Governor Olene Walker
- Account Manager
- Community Leader (PTA President, United Way board member, Ballet board member, Red Cross board member, church leadership)
- Member of local boards and of state and local taskforces (including a school district)
- Educational Consultant
- Federal Education Program Director
- Director of an educational foundation
- Legislator
- Appropriations Committee Chair
- Majority Whip
- State Community Development Director
- Chair of Health Policy Commission; Chair of Workforce Taskforce
- Lieutenant Governor
- Governor

There are some interesting statistics that emerge from looking closely at the governors' career paths:

1. Six of the ten worked on others' campaigns during their careers.
2. Nine worked in the private sector at least some time during their careers.
3. Eight worked as political volunteers before becoming paid political or government employees.
4. Two worked exclusively in paid political positions during their careers.
5. Seven had political interests that came through advocacy efforts focused on children, family, community, or personal concerns.
6. Nine worked in appointed political positions during their careers.
7. Eight spoke specifically of being encouraged to and asked to run for elected positions by others before they decided to do so.
8. Seven were legislators at one point and all chaired or served on key committees.
9. Six were lieutenant governors.
10. Two specifically mentioned being secretaries of state.
11. Four served in formal legislator leadership positions (e.g., Speaker, majority leader, or whip).
12. Seven were elected outright as governor.
13. Three became governors while serving as lieutenant governor when the office was vacated.

14. Six were educators (five were teachers and one an educational consultant).
15. Ten of ten served in at least one elected position before running for or assuming the state's top posts.

Many governors mentioned being the first women in positions within their cities or states. For example, many said that they were the first female governor within their particular states. Some also noted that they were the first female secretary of state or lieutenant governor in their states as well. A number of women who served in leadership positions in their legislators also said they were the first females in those posts. In addition, this group contains a woman who was the first female deputy attorney general in her state, and another who was the first female mayor in her town. Among all of the members of this group of ten women leaders, they were the first females in many of the positions they held and thus in the tasks or assignments they successfully completed.

After each governor spoke about all of the jobs and positions she had occupied throughout her career, paid and unpaid, I asked her about whether she planned her path early in her career or whether it was informal. It was absolutely clear that not one of the women set out early in their careers to become governors. They took opportunities that either they created or that presented themselves. They worked hard in each position and performed to the best of their abilities. They seemed to be constantly preparing themselves for the next position, even though most did not know what that "next position" would be throughout much of their careers. Each opportunity prepared them for the next. One governor stated, "If you are really paying attention, everything you do will build you." People around them saw their competence and encouraged them to take on new opportunities or positions. Because they had a desire to learn and do more, they began thinking about and considering these suggestions from others. A few governors specifically mentioned that they had a low threshold for boredom and thrived on the steep learning curve and challenges that each new positions or assignment created. These women were driven and had the desire to continue learning by having new experiences. As one woman noted, "I needed to learn everything I could possibly learn. I loved it."

It seems the governors made their career choices based on their interests, passion, excitement, and the challenges the positions would provide. The women wanted to be where they could be influential and make a difference. Because they enjoyed challenging themselves, they were open to and, in some cases, sought out different assignments, positions, or opportunities. They paid attention along the way and learned from everything. Many of the governors also mentioned that they had a deep desire to make a difference at a broader level. One woman noted, "It became clear early on that it wasn't as satisfying to make a difference for one person. I wanted to make a difference for a much broader spectrum of society." The women agreed that a political life provides many opportunities to experience different jobs and assignments in a career. One governor stated, "It is hard to get bored if you are doing your best."

Although some had other career goals in mind, they now believe their lives and careers moved in the direction they did so they could be in the "right place at the right time" to make the true difference they desired. In considering the governors' career paths in conjunction with the life roles already discussed in Chapter Twelve, there are three primary situational influences I would like to highlight that appear to have led many of these women toward political careers. The first is motherhood. Many of these women knew that they wanted to stay home with young children, at least for a time, and they made their career choices based on that decision. They wanted flexible schedules with their positions, duties, responsibilities, and even priorities so they could remain integral in the day-to-day lives of their children. For many women, being stay-at-home mothers provided time to be involved in ongoing volunteerism and service in the community. Also, being a mother provided an opportunity for them to put their heart and soul into the welfare of others. These nurturing qualities then produced a strong advocacy perspective within these women that then extended from the home into the schools and communities. For these governors, advocacy efforts expanded from their children and families into other community needs. Motherhood also helped them look at the differences in the personalities, interests, and experiences of others. This helped these governors broaden their perspectives and interests. It is important to note that, although family priorities came before their careers, these women were still able to become prominent political figures within their states and the nation, thereby showing it can be done.

The second situational influence for many of the women in this book revolved around their husbands and their careers. In their supportive roles as wives, these women often followed their husbands in moving to new locations and environments. These relocations seemed to open their eyes to new issues and challenges that individuals and families can face. It seems these moves often provided the governors with opportunities for involvement in different advocacy efforts they might not have chosen in their prior situations. In many cases, because of their husbands' education or employment, the women learned a great deal from relocating to new areas and situations. Marriages also gave these women the opportunity to be in a supportive role in their personal life and to learn the lessons one only learns from serving and supporting others. It is important to note that their husbands' support for them was also essential in their political career paths. Many governors noted it was because their husbands provided the financial support for the family that they had the flexibility to pursue the volunteer and paid paths they took. The husbands' emotional support was also critical in the women's career choices. In some cases, husbands also had flexibility in their jobs to be supportive of their wives in their endeavors, which was particularly critical in the career choices of the governors. Finally, some of the women noted that their spouses' occupations provided exposure to many individuals and groups (e.g., social clubs, professional organizations) that became very helpful, at least during a portion of their careers.

The third and final situational influence I want to mention is the governors' volunteerism and advocacy work. These efforts naturally lead them toward eventually running for office and future political leadership roles. Success in this work seemed to feed their innate desire to make a difference for their families, friends, and communities. This work provided them a reason and forum to expand their personal interests into the common good of others around them. Volunteerism and advocacy roles also provided a way for them to diversify their interests and experiences, giving them opportunities to learn more about the needs of individuals, families, groups, and communities around them. As I will discuss in the next section, each experience provided new perspectives, insights, and personal developmental opportunities for learning and growth.

COMMUNITY INVOLVEMENT

As outlined earlier in this chapter, many of the governors' career paths toward political leadership started with volunteer positions and assignments. The governors included this work as an important component of where their career paths led and their overall development of leadership occurred. In some cases, unpaid and paid work was heavily intertwined, making it crucial for me to consider all of these opportunities and experiences when exploring their adult development. Two general findings emerge from the ten interviews. First, community involvement provided powerful opportunities for these women to learn, strengthen, and enhance many skills and competencies that clearly benefited them as they became politicians and ultimately governors. Second, for many of these women, community service provided them with more helpful experiences in developing leadership than paid employment. For example, one governor spoke of the benefit of volunteerism in her own development:

> *Non-paid work was very helpful for my development. All of that was critical. All of these volunteer activities and community activities were important. Each gave me a new perspective and new experiences. As I look back on it, I realize that all the work and experience I had helped to prepare me for a life in politics. During that period of community and family involvement, I was unknowingly preparing. . . . Volunteer activities can foster enormous leadership skills.*

All governors addressed the issue of volunteerism in their interviews, and that has been discussed in individual profile chapters; however, I have provided a few quotations here so their beliefs regarding the value of volunteer work can be clear to the reader. One governor stated:

> *My volunteer positions were very valuable. They have helped me learn to take risks. I found that I gained from every one of these experiences. I took advantage of every experience. Each opportunity added depth and breadth to the next. I had a wonderful opportunity to make a difference, to make positive changes, to serve the community, and to be creative in terms of looking for solutions. These positions also helped me develop my selling skills, confidence, and assertiveness.*

Another noted some important lessons she learned from community involvement:

> *I learned important lessons from all of my community roles including each experience I had. I even learned from what I considered my least effective contributions. In this work, I needed to create a vision, delegate, organize, motivate, and so forth. I learned all of these skills and more. I learned time management, priorities, meeting top people, and educational processes. I learned about federal programs, at-risk schools, and skills in terms of the responsibility we have for all of the socioeconomic groups within our state.*

A final governor summarizes her feelings about the helpfulness of all types of work and service:

> *All of my paid and non-paid experiences were beneficial. Each helped me develop competencies and also helped me meet people and network. I learned more with each position about politics, governments, and issues. I was able to analyze and figure things out in every position. If you are prepared and willing, you can make more of a difference when opportunities come. I had to take risks; sometimes I won, sometimes I lost, sometimes I was right, and sometimes I was wrong. This is true for anyone. Every experience and every opportunity helped me learn.*

After analyzing the experiences and insights of the ten governors regarding the core competencies they gained through their community involvement, I have compiled the following list:

- Communication (speaking, writing, interpersonal, listening)
- Coping under pressure
- Courage
- Critical thinking
- Decision making
- Delegation
- Ethics, integrity, and character
- Evaluation
- Focusing on results
- Inspiring and motivating others
- Leading change
- Learning from mistakes
- Lifelong learning skills and motivation
- Listening to feedback; providing helpful feedback
- Networking
- Organization
- Proactivity
- Problem solving

- Reflection
- Self-esteem/confidence
- Thick skin/toughness
- Viewing barriers/failures as learning experiences and opportunities

A number of governors also said that their interest in government and politics emerged out of volunteerism efforts and that, through these efforts, they felt empowered. This interest directly and indirectly related to increased confidence, determination, and purpose. They developed and strengthened the ability to be proactive by seeking out people who could help them make the difference they desired. Because of their successful service in the various positions they accepted, many new opportunities challenged them to continue their developmental path toward leadership competence. Interestingly, it seems that this competence provided a type of incentive or ambition for them to continue seeking out new and different experiences and opportunities.

Even with the preparation community involvement provided, many of the governors spoke about how unfortunate it is that women typically don't get credit for life experience in most employment settings, including politics. As one noted, "Life experience is an incredible preparation for political office and leadership."

GENDER BARRIERS AND CHALLENGES

The governors did describe and discuss some of the barriers they faced throughout the years in their political careers. It is important to note that many of the women I interviewed were some of the first prominent women in politics in the United States. They definitely had to "break new ground" in many respects. Even with gender issues, many would not call them "barriers" and instead referred to them as "challenges." Some did not believe things would have been easier had they been male, but they agreed that it was "different." Some said there were definitely more obstacles "here and there throughout their careers" because of their gender. As noted earlier, many agreed that it was because of their gender and their life choices to have flexible schedules and careers, that they pursued the "paths and opportunities" that eventually led them toward political leadership. Again, for a number of the governors being stay-at-home mothers was the basis for their decisions to become involved in government and politics. In fact, some admitted that because of the women's movement, doors were opened for them to run for office and serve in different roles. These women did not display a victim mentality toward gender. In fact, one governor stated, "It is important that women don't think and complain about gender because you can't get anything done that way!" They are willing to acknowledge the gender inconsistencies, but have used rational, productive approaches through the years as gender barriers and challenges have arisen. As one of the first female governors stated, "Gender made me different from start to finish."

All of the women admitted that gender does play a role in the political environment, and the public and media continue to notice and make judgments based on gender. A governor, who was in office in the 1980s, said that there were "assumptions from the community that men could lead better than women." She and others spoke of a continuous feeling that they had to "prove themselves." However, at least for some, once they were able to show the public what they could do, these feelings subsided—although they never totally disappeared. After the women demonstrated their competence and strength and then "harnessed the respect needed to move forward," they were able to make the difference they desired. Most stated that the general public and media are "tougher on women in many respects." Yet, as one governor said, "I have tried to avoid letting it define who I am as a political figure, but the difference is obvious." Yet, a few noted that it is "a little easier for women today because there have been so many women office holders in many states now."

A number of governors shared examples of little "subtleties" that seem to be present because they were female. The different kinds of questions that come from the media were mentioned by more than a few governors. Reporters asked her questions that men aren't typically asked; including questions about such things as dating, marriage plans, hair and wardrobe, perceived strength and toughness, preparedness for positions, work-life challenges, and gender role expectations. One mentioned that there are sometimes assumptions made for groups of political leaders at conferences or other gatherings that planned activities should be geared toward male interests. For example, even though one governor enjoyed playing basketball, having a woman play with a group of men made some males uncomfortable. The males also didn't pass the ball to this governor so she could play and feel included. A few governors mentioned that they have had to work with conference organizers on such issues in the past. As a whole, the women in this book also believe that women leaders typically work harder than male leaders, as most feel that they need to continuously prove themselves to their superiors, colleagues, community members, and themselves. As one governor noted, "The man thing is always going to be there." A final subtlety I will mention here is that of the challenges around the lack of role models for women in politics, as well as in other settings. Some governors mentioned that for some women this can make their career paths more difficult.

LEADERSHIP TRAINING

I asked the governors to tell me about the leadership training and development programs they attended throughout the years. The Kennedy School of Government at Harvard University was mentioned more than any other program as a profound formal learning experience for the women. As one governor noted, "It changed my life. It was a pivotal experience for me and a springboard for what would come next." Somehow the Harvard experience enhanced these women's confidence in their political leadership abilities.

The women mentioned a variety of leadership programs and seminars within women's political organizations, conferences, and groups. For some, it was the opportunities for networking and open discussions that provided them with new insights and motivation. Others mentioned that the women's conferences, retreats, and group meetings were "refreshing and invigorating." A number of the governors talked of memorable speakers they had heard years prior who spoke of concepts like "balancing work and family in the political environment, decision making, ethics, and other lessons learned." As one women explained, "Women-only retreats were unusual and unique, and I enjoyed them." Two governors mentioned women-only dinner groups held at mixed-gender conferences. One noted, "It was a unique experience and very enlightening." For her, it was interesting to interact with and listen to women in a variety of stages within the political arena. These groups often discussed family and career issues, which provided the governors with new ideas, insights, advice, and support. Another said, "I found it particularly helpful to listen and interact with other women in politics." Although one governor didn't remember any specific women-only conferences or training, she did explain that while she was a state senator she used to meet daily with other women senators to talk about issues and insights. She said, "These informal meetings provided a great deal of training and development for me." Many noted that these women-only environments often result in "powerful bonds being created that last for many years." For some, these environments also provided a sense of encouragement. One governor noted that she believed that women need more encouragement than do men.

A number of governors also spoke of mixed-gender training programs and conference experiences. A few mentioned the value and helpfulness of a three-day new governors' conference. Others mentioned additional position-specific training (e.g., secretary of state, lieutenant governor, agency director) and found them very useful as well. Again, some mentioned the actual helpfulness being more because of the available networking and the collaborative and open environments, while others said the content of the sessions and speeches were most helpful. One woman spoke of a fellowship she had through Western Governors. It was an in-depth leadership development program that broadened her perspectives because she interacted with people from all over the United States. She found it helpful as she listened, and it provided insight. Most women believe that conferences, groups, and sessions that provide a venue for listening to and interacting with those in other states who are serving in their same positions (e.g., secretary of state, Speaker) were very beneficial. One governor mentioned attending a five-day ethics training that she absolutely loved. Overall, it seems conferences and training experiences were "energizing, motivating, and exciting."

Finally, a few governors spoke of the developmental benefits they received from working with formal and informal consultants or coaches. These individuals worked with the women on a range of issues including personal appearance (e.g., hairstyles, clothes, accessories, mannerisms), communication skills (e.g., vocal quality, public speaking, interpersonal), and political knowledge (e.g., policy, legal issues, budgeting, processes).

INFLUENTIAL INDIVIDUALS

In Chapter Twelve, I discussed the influential individuals in the governors' nonprofessional life (spouses, children, parents, extended families, friends, neighbors, and so forth). This section will focus on influential people primarily in workplace environments.

The most prominent finding in this research regarding influential individuals is that the governors learned from a wide variety of individuals. They observed, watched, and listened to people in all types of situations and environments. This helped them figure out what worked well for others, what did not, and why. For example, one woman mentioned being particularly interested in watching people under pressure and seeing how they responded. She was able to use many of the elements she learned through these observations when she confronted the same type of pressure as a political leader. One governor said, "Different people influenced my thinking and helped answer questions and clarified ideas." Some of these influential individuals were solely role models with which the women did not have close contact. The governors observed them from afar and learned from watching and reflecting. A few women spoke of the importance of having a well-development network as a wide variety of interactions were a powerful basis of developmental experiences. Listening to the advice of many seemed to help several of the governors determine the best career decisions to make throughout their journeys.

Colleagues made up a large portion of the influential people in these women's lives, particularly as it relates to workplace influences. They listened and learned from more-experienced colleagues either through direct interactions with them or by watching them interact with and respond to others. From these individuals, the governors learned policy, ethics, listening, decision making, and lobbyist relationships. Some women colleagues were influential as important role models and sources of encouragement and support for these governors. These more-experienced colleagues, particularly in the case of legislators, were not necessarily "superiors" but were clearly more senior and experienced. A few women had strong, experienced, and respected female legislators that they were able to watch and who provided important insight and encouragement. These women were respectful to each other and encouraged one another in their careers. One governor explained, "She taught me to love politics and the system. As I watched women with more experience than me, I saw their courage, skills, and influence." Another woman said, "The encouragement that came from other women who had more experience in politics was particularly meaningful for me. I took this encouragement very seriously."

When in top political positions, the women in this book learned from colleagues in other states who had the same position as they did in their own states.

Interactions with these individuals were particularly important in lieutenant governor and governor positions. A governor explained, "Lots of people influenced me in small ways including my peers and compatriots. We learned from each other." The women who were legislators mentioned that other "freshmen legislators," who were elected at the same time, became important sources of friendship, support, encouragement, and even information. Open, honest friendships helped these women learn more about themselves and others. Lastly, it was also clear that the women learned from negative examples of their peers as well.

Superiors were absolutely critical for the development of most of the governors and, in many cases, these were men. According to one woman, these individuals "provided vital support in my competency development." Superiors saw the women's talent and skills and encouraged them forward. The women often knew they were trusted by their superiors, which gave them added confidence. One governor said, "My boss mentored me through many situations and choices. He liked my ideas, was open, and provided me with valuable opportunities." This superior taught her that she could speak her mind and that he would listen and accept her reasonable decisions. Others spoke of superiors that were wonderful listeners and open to new ideas and suggestions. They learned to speak openly and knew their opinions and ideas were valued.

In a few cases, the women had access to interacting with past governors, even before winning statewide elections, and felt encouragement from them. One worked on a campaign for a popular and charismatic governor, and he ended up becoming an important role model as she watched and learned about the importance of being straightforward from him. Other women enjoyed watching state and legislative leaders to see their leadership styles and assess how they were successful.

Meaningful encouragement from superiors was particularly important for some of the governors in this study. One women spoke of the chair of a powerful committee (who was a member of a different political party) who she knew respected her, and he became very influential. He appointed her to his committee and then gave her important responsibility. Even when they disagreed, they respected each other. She learned that this can be done in politics. Another spoke of a female majority leader and woman state party chairman who both became influential in her life through trusted friendships. The feedback from these women was important as she respected and trusted them. The governors provided many examples of influential superiors who made a crucial difference in their opportunities and experiences in becoming high-profile leaders.

LEADERSHIP MOTIVATIONS AND STYLES

Throughout the interviews, I asked each governor what her motivation was for seeking leadership responsibilities throughout her life. The top twelve motivations for leadership during their adulthoods include the following:

1. To make a difference
2. To positively influence
3. To serve the community and help others
4. To make things happen
5. To fulfill accomplishment and achievement needs
6. To fulfill drives and ambition
7. To do what they are meant to do in life
8. To have power
9. To do interesting, exciting, and meaningful work
10. To learn, develop, and grow (liked change)
11. To get great satisfaction from hard work
12. To have challenges and important responsibilities

These women knew they had good ideas and wanted to be heard. They were goal and task-oriented and enjoyed accomplishing meaningful work. They came to love politics and community involvement in all of its unique facets.

All ten governors described their own leadership styles as "collaborative." They worked with strong teams and asked for ideas and feedback from them as well as from many other constituents around them. Many described themselves as team players because they believe that being a strong leader means that you also need to work well within a team. They enjoy bringing people together to find consensus on topics of concern and, if needed, negotiating so that good things can happen. The governors also said that being collaborative means that they also needed to be strong listeners to a wide variety of individuals and viewpoints. Many described situations that helped them learn how to more productively and effectively listen and learn from others around them. One said that the public knows when you truly listen. She felt it was important to include listening to the public as part of her decision-making process. Reaching out to the public and being willing to listen was a critical strategy of some of the governors. Being a good listener also means that you must be a good "questioner," as one woman noted. Learning to ask the right questions to get solid feedback is an art that most of these governors seemed to have developed. Being truly collaborative also means that an individual needs good observation and analysis skills, which these women developed throughout their lives. Some admit they are still working on these skills, as they believe they can and need to improve.

I asked each of the women to describe their own leadership styles through the eyes of their staff. I combined all of these characteristics into the following list:

The governors are . . .
- Able to change their own behavior when needed
- Able to find employees who are dependable and loyal
- Able to find options and solutions for difficult issues
- Able to find satisfaction from seeing others succeed and from enabling others to develop

- Able to give and take feedback
- Able to give credit and take credit appropriately
- Able to incorporate valuable ideas, behaviors, actions, understanding from others
- Able to laugh and find humor, even it is about themselves
- Able to learn from mistakes
- Able to work with people they don't always agree with
- Aware of details
- Candid
- Caring and committed
- Clear and open about expectations
- Competent
- Competitive
- Compromising when appropriate
- Consistent about having high expectations for themselves and others around them
- Decisive and assertive
- Demanding
- Detail oriented
- Driven and ambitious
- Effective in firing and hiring
- Empowering
- Energetic
- Flexible
- Focused on changing the status quo
- Focused on empowering others they trust to take responsibly
- Focused on goals and results
- Hard workers
- Honest and ethical
- Inspiring and motivating
- Interested in developing others
- Interested in making a difference
- Intuitive
- Joyful in other's successes
- Passionate
- Politically astute
- Prepared
- Ready to act
- Reflective and have strong self-monitoring skills
- Respectful
- Risk takers
- Strong decision makers

- Task oriented and like to "get things done"
- Tough
- Transparent in their decisions
- Understanding of success and failure
- Willing to admit they don't have all the answers
- Willing to hire people who aren't afraid to speak their minds and challenge
- Willing to hire very bright people—often smarter than themselves
- Willing to provide opportunities for others
- Willing to reach out to other women and minorities
- Willing to take the heat when needed
- Willing to take things as they come

Overall, it seems the governors demonstrate a number of leadership styles or types that the literature has discussed, including emergent leadership, situational leadership, transformational leadership, and androgynous leadership. Although each style or theory has some unique characteristics, the previous list and the data I gathered throughout the interviews demonstrate that these women have many characteristics of these styles (see previous list).

ADVICE FROM THE GOVERNORS

The governors said that they are often asked to give advice to girls, young women, and women about how they can develop themselves to become future leaders, particularly within politics. So, instead of a "Lessons Learned" section, such as the ones I have included in Chapters Eleven and Twelve, in this final chapter I am concluding with the governors' advice to others who are interested in becoming influential leaders. All of the advice they shared with me fit well into the following five broad categories: 1) start early; 2) get involved; 3) develop critical competencies; 4) understand yourself, and 5) look beyond yourself.

1. Start Early

Most of the governors provided some advice about preparing early in life to develop leadership skills, primarily during high school and college. According to the governors, obtaining a good education is critical to develop leadership. One governor said that youth should not "short change themselves" by getting on a "fast track" to complete high school sooner than needed. She stated, "No book can teach you some of the things you need to know." It takes time and experience to develop the competencies needed to be successful in college and beyond. Many governors noted that powerful learning experiences can occur during high school and college if individuals seek to become open to learning, personal development, and change. The women believe that having positive educational and developmental experiences in high school and college can provide a firm foundation for continued development later in life. The governors suggested that young women can find leadership opportunities in many different places, including Girls Scouts, sports, clubs, activities, and so forth. They also suggest that female students should become involved in politics at the local, state, and even national levels.

A few governors suggested specific college courses they believe would be helpful in developing political leadership competencies. First, some mentioned that political science, nonprofit management, or operations courses can be helpful, but "even more important are courses that let you strengthen the competencies you will need." These may include accounting, management, finance, public speaking, and debate. One explained, "You must become comfortable being in front of an audience and articulating your ideas. Take courses that require you to do this." Many governors said that women should get as much education as possible while they are young and then continue learning throughout their lives.

Overall, the governors encourage young women to become as competent as possible through various kinds of experiences and opportunities, particularly during their formative years. They will need this foundation to be prepared for future development and opportunities they may confront. They urged students to study and learn everything they can early in life because "they don't know what they will be doing in the future." As one noted, "They may think they know, but they really have no clue!" Another stated, "When opportunities arise you need to be prepared to take them." A third woman noted, "Each opportunity and experience can help. In fact, everything can help if you know how to learn!" A critical point that needs to be made is that women of all ages need to believe they *can* make a positive impact and have an influence in their communities. This understanding needs to be engrained within women as early as possible so it becomes an assumption rather than an ongoing internal question.

2. Get Involved

All of the governors suggested that jumping in and getting involved is one of the best strategies to prepare for future political leadership positions. They advise women to study the issues by reading the papers, listening to the local and national news, and becoming informed and aware of what is happening around them. Women should consciously try to understand various perspectives and arguments. They should stretch themselves to learn how to "effectively argue a side." As one governor noted, "Women need to become as competent as possible throughout their lives to be prepared for what is ahead. Everything can help." Another said, "Prepare now to live an engaged life. There is a great deal of hope because you have more leadership abilities than you think!"

Another important component of "getting involved" is to understand that unpaid opportunities and part-time work can provide very valuable developmental experiences. In fact, one governor stated, "All paid and unpaid experiences are important, as you can develop from so many things." All of the governors advised that women get involved in their communities in any number of ways including advocacy efforts, political volunteerism, schools boards, committee work, and such. For example, women should look around and see what needs to be done in their communities and "step forward to make things happen." One governor suggested that women "watch a political campaign as close up as you can by working and volunteering so that you can learn political strategy and other campaign details." A few governors said that working on local campaigns (such as city council, school board, community legislative races) can really help, as they give you the opportunity to see the decision-making process at the ground level. One said that starting slow and small gives you time to develop a deeper understanding of the challenges and issues at the local level. Knowing regional politics can help women "build a base of knowledge" that can be quickly strengthened and developed.

Getting involved in a wide variety of government, political, and social efforts can help women spend quality time with the issues and "earn her dues." Experience is critical, both life experience and professional experience. These experiences can help you learn to energize others to get involved. One governor said, "These opportunities can help you see if you even like the types of tasks that are needed to go to the next level." Finally, one woman just simply said, "Go for it!" It is clear that community involvement can be a powerful tool for the development of leadership.

3. Develop Critical Competencies

Although I have already addressed a few leadership competencies in the two previous categories as well as outlining many leadership competencies earlier in this chapter, the governors mentioned two specific competencies in their advice to young women wanting to become future leaders. First, one that came up over and over again throughout the interviews was that women need to learn to be willing to take risks if they are going to become successful leaders. A few noted that women in general sometimes struggle with taking risks but that leadership is all about "putting yourself out there and taking chances." The governors also advised women to learn to win and learn to lose. As one governor noted, "If you can't lose gracefully, you'll have a tough time making the difference you desire." The second competency is focused on becoming honest and ethical individuals. This was also mentioned time and time again as a critical competency for effective leadership. The practice of understanding yourself (see next category) will help you clarify and strengthen your commitment to be the most ethical individual you can become. Two governors also stressed the importance of learning to "walk away from things if there is a problem with ethics." Being able to do this takes confidence, risk-taking skills, a strong ethical commitment, and internal strength.

A number of other competencies were also mentioned as the governors provided advice for future leaders, such as:

- be observant and reflective
- build a reliable network

- develop good, healthy interpersonal relationships
- keep things in perspective by stepping back and looking around you
- learn collaboration and collegiality skills by establishing a comradeship with others
- learn from following, not just leading
- learn to problem solve
- listen and absorb what is going on around you
- map out your goals
- network early
- practice working with others in various settings and in different roles
- remember humor
- stretch yourself
- take on new experiences

Developing these competencies can help individuals prepare to make the difference they desire. Along with these competencies, one governor concluded, "Dream big, envision yourself doing something you want, think about the changes you can make, and then start moving forward."

4. Understand Yourself

The majority of governors also spoke about the importance of understanding one's own desires, needs, ambitions, and goals. One explained, "Women need to figure out who they are and what they want in life. They need to find out what their passions are and what they really love and care about." Emerging leaders should also figure out fairly quickly, if they don't know already, what their personal values and principles are. By doing this, they can, as one governor mentioned, "discover what their personal core is made of." They become comfortable with themselves and find peace in personal and professional decisions and ambitions. A number of governors argued that coming to know yourself also includes understanding your reasons for wanting to pursue political leadership. As one noted, "Politics is not for the faint of heart. It is a pretty brutal job. Politics can only truly be satisfying if there is a reason bigger than yourself to do it."

Learning to know and understand yourself takes time. Some of the governors noted that you don't have to make a decision tomorrow about whether you want to become a high-profile political leader or not. They suggested that women enjoy what they are doing when they are doing it and not always worrying about a position or assignment being a stepping stone for the next position. One stated, "If you want to make an impact or difference in the world, then do the best in what you are doing right now and enjoy the experience. This will naturally lead to more opportunities."

The final piece of advice under this category is that women should learn to give, receive, and understand helpful feedback. Although it is sometimes difficult, women who can give and receive accurate and open feedback in a logical and rational way seem to be those most intimately interested in learning and developing. The most effective developmental relationships are those with whom you can develop a deep trust and respect. It is important to note that most of the governors spoke about the need to develop "thicker skin" so that the ongoing criticism that is inherent in political leadership does not derail you from the tasks and vision at hand.

5. Look Beyond Yourself

The governors stated many times that emerging female leaders need models of success; hence, each women leader should plan to become an example for others around her. Emerging female leaders should develop coaching and mentoring skills so they are able to mentor others. One governor noted that emerging leaders should also concern themselves with family-friendly policies within their areas of influence. These in turn can assist other women in reaching their goals to make a difference. Women should also support and strengthen each other. They need to help others understand that they can learn from everything around them. Finally, women who are becoming influential leaders should always look for people inside their organizations to develop and promote. They should be willing to nurture them, provide them with opportunities, let them stretch, and also empower them so that they can feel and become success.

FINAL THOUGHTS

By the time this book is published, it will have been a few years since I have interviewed the governors. Some may have moved on to new projects, challenges, or positions; but whatever they go on to do, they will always be leaders. As I concluded in my previous leadership book (Madsen, 2008), "It is in their blood, it is in their hearts, and it is in their souls. They yearn to make a difference. They already have, and they will continue to do so throughout their lives" (288). After spending time with each of the governors, I know that they are continuously learning new concepts, challenging themselves to develop new abilities, and seeking to lead change in a variety of ways. Through studying the lifetime developmental journeys of these ten women, I have had the opportunity to think about my own goals, ambitions, and life. I have also been inspired to continue to discover how to reflect at a much deeper level and reflect on what has happened in my life that has influenced my own development toward competence and leadership. I would challenge you to allow this book to do the same for you; internalize its content, stories, insights, and advice.

Developing strong, sound leaders is a crucial issue in politics and government throughout the world today. In fact, I believe it is imperative that we develop a greater number of strong, prepared, and ethical individuals who can lead effectively and successfully in our homes, schools, businesses, nonprofits, communities, states, nations, and world. All women can and should become leaders in some domain. It is our responsibility as humans who care about the people and world around us. Women *can* and *must* make a difference. Let's start by seeking to learn from everything around us and by taking the opportunities that present themselves. In fact, let's create opportunities to lead within our realms of influence. Let's find new and different experiences and opportunities to strengthen ourselves and others so we can become the leaders the world needs whether in our homes, in the world at large, or anywhere in between. And most importantly, let's appreciate the journey toward becoming the best we can become.

References

Bennis, Warren. *On Becoming a Leader*. Boston: Addison-Wesley, 1989.

Hartman, Mary S., ed. *Talking Leadership: Conversations with Powerful Women*. New Brunswick, NJ: Rutgers University Press, 1999.

HeartQuotes Center. "Leadership Quotes and Proverbs." *HeartQuotes: Quotes of the Heart*. 2007. http://www.heartquotes.net/Leadership.html (26 March 2008).

Hennig, Margaret, and Anne Jardim. *The Managerial Woman*. Garden City, NY: Anchor Press/Doubleday, 1977.

Kunin, Madeleine. *Living a Political Life: One of America's First Woman Governors Tells Her Story*. New York: Alfred A. Knopf, 1994.

LeaderValues. "Quotes." *Quotes "N."* 2008. http://www.leader-values.com/Content/quotes.asp?Letter=N (26 March 2008).

Madsen, Susan R. *On Becoming a Woman Leader: Learning From the Experiences of University Presidents*. San Francisco: Jossey-Bass, 2008.

Mezirow, Jack. *Transformative Dimensions of Adult Learning*. San Francisco: Jossey-Bass, 1991.

Motivation Point. "The Motivational Speakers Hall of Fame: Sheila Murray Bethel." *Motivation for Your Achievement and Success*. 2008. http://www.getmotivation.com/sheilambethel.html (26 March 2008).

QuoteDB. "John F. Kennedy." *QuoteDB*. 2005a. http://www.quotedb.com/quotes/1412 (26 March 2008).

QuoteDB. "Ralph Waldo Emerson." *QuoteDB*. 2005b. http://www.quotedb.com/quotes/1670 (26 March 2008).

Smith, Frances. *The Little Girl Who Grew Up To Be Governor: Stories from the Life of Martha Layne Collins*. Lexington, KY: Denham Publishing, 1991.

Thinkexist.com. "Robert Townsend quotes." *Thinkexist.com Quotations*. 2006. http://thinkexist.com/quotes/robert_townsend/ (26 March 2008).

Whitman, Christine T. *It's My Party Too: The Battle for the Heart of the GOP and the Future of America*. New York: Penguin Press, 2005.

Index

accomplishments, 3, 7, 19, 27, 31, 71, 112, 143, 163, 170, 248, 251, 256, 271, 299
achievements, 5, 23, 31, 64, 71, 78, 98, 112, 143, 160, 164, 167, 170, 256, 271, 299
administration, 24, 34, 41, 107, 108, 117, 165, 186, 214, 217, 227, 228, 270, 280
adolescent, 7, 9, 29, 31, 33, 170, 173, 193, 197, 219, 239, 244, 246-247, 249, 257, 258, 261
advice, 25, 45-47, 72, 73, 93, 94, 112, 117, 119, 135, 139, 140, 157, 159, 165, 173, 187, 210, 230, 235, 251, 267, 271, 281, 285, 296, 297, 301, 303-305
advisors, 12, 79, 107, 126, 130, 139, 185, 246, 250, 251, 253, 258, 267, 277, 280
advocacy work, 17, 291
advocate, 3, 18, 27, 156, 189, 202, 265, 272, 274, 276
alcoholism, 29, 190, 196, 240, 243, 254
ambition, 18, 110, 149, 163, 164, 256, 294, 299, 300, 304, 305
analysis, 105, 228, 299
ancestors, 3, 189
anger, 110, 196, 197, 199, 263, 279
animals, 124, 125, 172, 174, 240
appearance, 117, 296
athletics, 6, 17, 32, 242, 245, 247, 263
attorney general, 27, 39, 40, 41, 42, 44, 45, 46, 116, 270, 286, 290
aunts, 5, 30, 33, 53, 58, 77, 98, 110, 124, 146, 147, 154, 168, 169, 191, 216, 217, 251, 252, 258
awards, 31, 32, 53, 76, 173, 176, 218, 222, 233

babysitting, 43, 102. 249

balancing, 17, 21, 46, 81, 91, 109, 159, 208, 274-276, 296
balancing work and family, 21, 81, 91, 109, 159, 274-276, 296
band, 99, 125, 127, 247
barriers, 20, 87, 116, 117, 118, 163, 182, 209, 233, 285, 294
becoming, 14, 36, 40, 49, 67, 87, 88, 112, 115, 116, 132, 137, 141, 156, 158, 160, 163, 165, 172, 176, 181, 188, 194, 198, 207, 213, 224, 232, 233, 239, 246, 248, 255, 256, 270, 285, 289, 298, 301-306
behaviors, 8, 9, 13, 31, 59, 81, 93, 118, 125, 138, 168, 183, 187, 198, 240, 243, 245, 255, 256, 258, 268, 299, 300
Bennis, Warren, 14, 239, 259
Bethel, Sheila Murray, 285
birth order, 241
boards, 22, 52, 188, 215, 227, 230, 235, 236, 289, 303
Bonaparte, Napoleon, 285
bossy, 54, 192, 244
boyfriends, 6, 7, 107, 117, 129, 197
brothers, 4, 8, 30, 37, 50, 55, 95, 97, 98, 100, 106, 108, 131, 143, 145, 147, 149, 151, 152, 153, 162, 169, 190, 192, 213, 218, 221, 222, 241
Bush, George W., 49, 89, 115, 232

camp, 54, 101, 107, 177, 193, 196, 266
campaigns, 19, 21, 24-26, 26, 37, 44, 46, 56, 61-64, 84-85, 87, 91, 97, 106, 107, 109-114, 132-136, 138, 159, 167, 178-183, 187, 197, 201, 204, 230, 231, 264, 275, 286-288, 289, 298, 303
candid, 25, 58, 91, 149, 184, 192, 210, 245, 252, 258, 268, 278, 280, 300
career goals, 291

Index

career paths, 16, 40, 65, 75, 87, 116, 137, 178, 181, 233, 285, 289, 291, 292, 295
career plan, 65, 134, 209, 233, 270
Carter, Jimmy, 132, 133, 135, 138
challenges, 13-15, 22, 32, 40, 46, 55, 57, 59, 62, 63, 66, 68, 79, 83, 86, 87, 90-93, 96, 102, 108, 110, 114-117, 119, 131, 133, 134, 146, 159, 161, 163, 170-171, 174, 177, 179, 181-183, 186, 190-194, 196-199, 206, 209-211, 221, 228, 232, 234, 239, 240, 243, 245-247, 253, 254, 256, 258, 261, 266-267, 270, 274-276, 280, 282, 283, 290, 291, 294, 295, 299, 301, 303, 305
cheerleader, 6, 7, 22, 49, 66, 125, 148, 171, 173, 177, 248, 271
cheerleading, 245, 246, 248
childcare, 42, 136, 208, 270, 275, 282
childhood, 4, 6, 8, 29, 31, 33, 55, 76, 78, 96, 118, 121, 122, 125, 126, 146, 148-150, 171, 172, 192, 194, 216, 217, 239, 244, 246, 247, 252, 253, 258, 261, 268, 285
children, 4, 9, 10, 13-17, 27, 30, 35, 38, 43, 44, 49, 50, 51, 53, 54, 57, 58, 61, 66-68, 77, 80-88, 90-92, 96, 97, 114, 117-118, 120, 123, 131, 133, 134, 136, 143, 144, 146-148, 151, 154-157, 159-164, 168-172, 178, 181-183, 187-193, 195, 196, 200-203, 205-209, 211, 213-215, 217, 220, 224-230, 232, 234, 235, 241-245, 247, 251, 252, 255, 257, 265, 270, 271, 274-277, 279, 281, 282, 288-291, 297
choirs, 194, 247
chores, 28, 31, 172, 247, 255
chorus, 7, 24, 99
church, 8, 78, 98, 101, 123, 167, 168, 171, 173, 178, 192, 194, 214-216, 218, 225-227, 233, 234, 236, 240, 242, 247, 257-259, 289
city council, 26, 153, 191, 201, 202, 203, 208, 243, 303
cleaning, 44, 163, 174, 234
clothes, 3, 5, 145, 215, 234, 296

clubs, 7, 31, 32, 56, 60, 79, 84, 125, 154, 173, 177, 178, 218, 219, 222, 247-249, 257, 263, 287, 291, 302
coach, 6, 9, 10, 90, 126, 127, 128, 130, 137, 168, 171, 177, 220, 222, 250, 251, 253, 267
coaches, 33, 243, 267, 296
coaching, 120, 127, 130, 200, 305
collaboration, 91, 304
colleagues, 11, 19, 20, 22, 41, 46, 67, 69, 111, 117, 135, 209, 210, 282, 295, 297
college boards, 17, 18, 286
college degree, 20, 28, 68, 79, 81, 122, 200
college years, 33, 34, 36, 37, 59, 60, 122, 128, 129, 175, 176, 199, 222, 223, 224, 244, 266, 277, 280, 283, 285
Collins, Martha Layne, 167-188, 288
committees, 18, 86, 92, 101, 179, 203, 227, 236, 247, 289
communication, 11, 20, 32, 79, 90, 91, 94, 97, 110, 134, 152, 208, 227, 247, 250, 257, 264, 267, 269, 278, 293, 296
community involvement, 5, 76, 84, 166, 225, 275, 277, 281, 292, 293, 294, 299, 303
compartmentalization, 88, 274, 282
competencies, 13, 19, 20, 22, 26, 27, 40, 43, 49, 63, 67, 70, 75, 83, 86, 95, 99, 101, 104, 110, 121, 132, 136, 137, 139, 143, 150, 174, 183, 208, 231, 233, 243, 247, 249, 255-258, 264, 268, 272, 277-279, 292, 293, 301-304
competent, 20, 25, 38, 58, 71, 92, 94, 103, 137, 165, 203, 207, 210, 235, 241, 243, 258, 259, 262, 267, 280, 283, 285, 290, 294, 295, 300, 302, 305
competition, 6, 11, 46, 93, 99, 170, 181, 219
competitive, 5, 6, 7, 10, 11, 21, 31, 32, 46, 54, 78, 98, 99, 100, 101, 104, 112, 120, 125, 126, 147, 165, 170, 193, 217, 245, 247, 256, 257, 300

Index   311

complexity, 39, 177, 192, 197, 198, 202, 209, 232, 245, 253, 254, 256, 266, 270, 276, 278, 282
conferences, 21, 22, 161, 183, 207, 208, 213, 219, 232, 295, 296
confidence, 4, 5, 11, 16, 17, 19, 21, 28, 30, 31, 32, 40, 45, 62, 70, 78, 79, 84, 96, 99, 100, 104, 105, 110, 112, 119, 126, 134, 135, 138, 147, 148, 162, 174, 192, 216, 219, 222, 223, 224, 244, 247, 249, 253-256, 262, 264, 266, 267, 269, 273, 278, 280-282, 292, 294, 295, 298, 303
conflict, 67, 84, 107, 109, 130, 160, 181, 219, 234, 247, 263, 275, 279
conflict resolution, 107, 109
Congress, 112, 113, 129, 138, 191, 231
consensus, 112, 139, 164, 184, 299
continuous learning, 55, 261
control, 8, 54, 58, 83, 163, 247, 273
conversations, 9, 50, 70, 72, 75, 97, 113, 116, 129, 153, 181, 191, 209, 210, 241, 247, 255
counselors, 12, 14, 54, 103, 107, 177, 193, 194, 196, 242, 250, 258, 265, 266, 277
county commissioner, 17, 18, 21, 286
courage, 21, 24, 27, 42, 67, 119, 147, 151, 160-163, 170, 172, 197, 244, 271, 293, 297
critical thinking, 94, 105, 110, 139, 173, 178, 195, 267, 268, 269, 278, 280, 293
criticism, 70, 105, 114, 164, 165, 180, 231, 305
current events, 56, 106, 121-123, 178, 241, 243, 263
current issues, 50, 97, 241, 255, 268

dating, 6, 29, 40, 42, 65, 66, 79, 111, 115, 171, 197, 200, 217, 219, 223, 241, 243, 247, 264, 295
death, 16, 100, 126, 143, 145, 154, 213, 254, 263
debate, 25, 42, 60, 64, 79, 97, 107, 110, 124, 132, 153, 155, 173, 180, 193, 194, 195, 197, 216, 219, 220, 221-223, 241, 245, 247, 248, 253, 257, 263, 267, 302

debates, 64, 86, 97, 110, 178, 194, 214, 219
decision making, 21, 22, 23, 26, 139, 246, 250, 296, 293, 297
delegating, 226, 249
Democrat, 9, 19, 135, 139
Democratic, 16, 19, 22, 110, 117, 135, 157, 158, 159, 167, 179, 183, 230, 231, 288
dependability, 248, 250, 257, 266
dependable, 4, 25, 31, 242, 247, 272, 299
depression, 214
determination, 16, 197, 202, 294
determined, 39, 51, 52, 138, 164, 191, 192, 204, 220, 231, 241, 282
development, 3, 7, 10, 11, 17-22, 24-27, 33, 37, 40, 45, 52, 55, 71, 79, 86, 89-92, 96, 97, 102, 105, 108, 109, 113, 117-119, 125, 129-133, 137, 138, 141, 145, 156, 159, 162, 166-169, 174, 175, 179, 182, 184, 185, 188, 189, 193, 207, 210, 213, 219, 221, 226, 229, 231, 232, 239, 240-243, 246, 249, 250-252, 253-258, 261, 262, 265-267, 269, 271, 274, 277-283, 285, 292, 295-298, 301-305
died, 30, 34, 42, 60, 76, 77, 106, 108, 123, 143, 144, 146, 148, 168, 169, 191, 193, 195
dinner table, 9, 50, 75, 97, 121, 123, 162, 191, 214, 241, 243, 245, 247
disability, 14, 16, 17, 23, 126, 276, 286
discrimination, 39, 41, 131, 161, 198, 263
diversity, 75, 82, 83, 166, 178, 192, 195, 229, 249, 276
divorce, 4, 10, 15, 20, 27, 270
doctoral degree, 227, 270
dorms, 36, 58, 77, 80, 103, 128, 137, 150, 198, 199, 262, 264, 268
drama, 57, 58, 125, 127, 166, 247
dramatic productions, 57, 148, 173, 248, 263
Drucker, Peter F., 261, 283

economic, 26, 51, 95, 98, 167, 169, 185, 189, 243

education, 3, 12-17, 20, 23, 27-29, 34, 35, 38, 47, 49, 52-54, 59, 75, 77, 79, 80, 81, 85, 87, 91-96, 103, 108, 121-124, 131, 132, 143-145, 149-153, 167-169, 175, 181, 189, 190, 192, 200, 203, 205, 210, 213-215, 220-224, 227-229, 231, 233-235, 239, 240, 242, 243, 246, 253, 255, 257, 262, 265, 268, 269, 278-281, 287, 291, 301, 302
elementary school, 30, 81, 126, 144, 214, 215
emerging leaders, 254, 258, 263, 280, 282, 305
Emerson, Ralph Waldo, 261, 283
emotional support, 119, 271, 291
empathy, 83, 106, 140, 208
employment, 11, 33, 40, 57, 61, 77, 80, 86, 101, 107, 128, 129, 133, 151, 174, 197, 207, 218, 221, 224, 228, 230, 232, 234, 243, 249, 250, 258, 261, 265, 266, 272, 274, 275, 279, 288, 291-294
empower, 16, 107, 118, 239, 249, 273, 305
encouragement, 5, 12, 28, 45, 88, 89, 108, 119, 136, 138, 146, 151, 159, 161, 162, 182, 188, 216, 220, 222, 228, 253, 258, 267, 269, 280, 281, 296-298
encouraging, 9, 22, 45, 58, 59, 136, 149, 150, 158, 165, 208, 230, 242, 249, 266, 267, 275
EPA, 49, 64, 232
ethics, 21, 22, 25, 26, 27, 63, 81, 86, 90, 92, 93, 96, 139, 140, 178, 235, 280, 293, 296, 297, 300, 303, 305
expectations, 8, 12, 25, 29, 35, 46, 52, 58, 68, 96, 103, 108, 119, 129, 149, 214, 226, 240, 242, 243, 251, 255, 262, 263, 267, 295, 300
extended family, 5, 12, 77, 97, 98, 102, 145, 149, 171, 191, 216, 225, 250, 251, 255, 270, 282
extracurricular activities, 37, 125, 128, 130, 176, 223, 246, 253, 257, 264, 279

failure, 120, 155, 301

family background, 3, 27, 49, 75, 95, 121, 167, 189, 213
farm, 28, 33, 38, 49, 51, 55, 56, 73, 77, 95, 124, 169, 172, 213, 214, 215, 218, 220, 240, 247, 250
father, 4-6, 8, 11, 14, 27, 30, 37, 44, 45, 50, 51, 52, 53, 54, 55, 57, 58, 61, 75, 76, 77, 78, 80, 97, 98, 102, 106, 107-110, 116, 121-123, 127, 143-148, 160, 168, 169, 172, 175, 177, 180, 190, 191, 194, 196, 197, 201, 213-214, 216, 218, 221, 241-243, 250, 254, 255, 267, 268, 271
fear, 143, 150, 151, 155, 163, 164, 166, 252, 263, 279
feedback, 59, 108, 149, 163, 164, 252, 253, 256, 258, 268, 280, 293, 298, 299, 300, 304
firing, 92, 300
first child, 13, 43, 154, 170, 177, 200, 224, 274
flexibility, 71, 73, 80, 83, 85, 87, 91, 134, 135, 141, 148, 234, 271, 272, 274-276, 279, 282, 186, 200, 208, 270, 272, 275, 282, 291, 294, 300
friends, 4, 6, 16, 18, 22, 29, 31, 37, 45, 52, 54-56, 58-60, 70, 78-82, 84, 85, 88-90, 94, 96, 99, 104, 106-108, 113, 117, 119, 122, 127, 128, 133, 137, 148-150, 153-155, 168, 171-174, 193, 194, 197, 199-201, 211, 215-218, 220-225, 230, 244, 245, 250-254, 258, 262, 263, 268, 271, 275, 280, 282, 288, 292, 297, 298
fun, 7, 32, 37, 46, 47, 56, 57, 64, 71, 81, 82, 84, 124, 134, 186, 193, 194, 209, 228, 248
fundraising, 104, 112, 133, 159, 229, 230, 264, 266

gender, 20, 41, 68, 69, 87, 116, 159, 161, 182, 209, 233, 234, 241, 262, 270, 294-296
Girl Scouts, 6, 100, 104, 120, 193-194, 247-248
glass ceiling, 182, 209
government, 13, 16-19, 21, 23-25, 50, 57, 59, 65, 72, 82, 86, 88, 93, 94, 113, 120, 128-130, 134, 158, 180, 181, 189, 203, 206, 210, 211, 221-

Index 313

224, 230-232, 248, 257, 262, 264, 265, 267, 274, 279, 281, 286, 289, 294, 303, 305
graduate school, 130, 132, 151, 201, 222, 242
graduation, 12, 52, 61, 65, 108, 127, 132, 175, 223, 262, 269
grandfathers, 30, 52, 77, 98, 124, 146, 189, 191, 252
grandmothers, 5, 30, 53, 58, 77, 81, 94, 97, 98, 124, 146, 160, 169, 188, 191, 151, 158, 196
Gregoire, Christine, 27-48, 286
groups, 8, 15-17, 21, 31-33, 36, 39, 40, 46, 52, 56, 61, 62, 69, 76, 78, 84, 89, 90, 100, 104, 125, 133, 135, 136, 138, 148, 155, 161, 166, 168, 172-174, 178, 180, 183, 184, 186, 189, 193, 194, 196, 198, 199, 205, 217-219, 223-225, 229, 233, 235, 244, 246-251, 254, 257, 272, 275, 282, 288, 290, 291-293, 295, 296

hair, 89, 200, 204, 295
hard work, 11, 56, 77, 174, 215, 240, 299
Hart, Gary, 133, 134, 138, 287
Hartman, Mary S., 49
helping others, 19, 26, 34, 43, 111, 170, 181
Hennig, Margaret, 241
high school, 4, 6-8, 10-12, 23, 28, 31, 32, 34-36, 47, 52, 56-58, 65, 77-80, 100-107, 112, 117, 120, 122, 125-129, 131, 144-146, 148-150, 160, 167, 171-175, 190, 193, 194, 197, 201, 214, 217-219, 220, 226, 227, 242-244, 248, 254, 262, 266, 301
hiring, 25, 38, 41, 92, 133, 139, 165, 186, 208, 210, 275, 300
Hollister, Nancy Putnam, 189-212, 288
home environment, 50, 76, 192, 255
homemaker, 4, 154, 242, 275
honest, 52, 70, 93, 96, 122, 139, 140, 149, 184, 235, 242, 252, 256, 258, 268, 280, 298, 303
hope, 30, 43, 72, 145, 196, 242, 255, 261, 280, 285, 302
House of Representatives, 75, 85, 86, 157, 158, 213, 230, 231, 288

housekeeping, 160, 275
Hull, Jane, 75-94, 275-276, 287
humor, 44, 77, 211, 300, 304
husband, 12-16, 20, 22, 29, 30, 42-45, 49, 62, 65, 66, 79-84, 86-88, 94, 107, 111-114, 119, 124, 132, 134-136, 144, 146, 154, 156, 157, 160, 171, 178, 182, 193, 196, 197, 200-202, 208, 227, 236, 271, 276, 287

identity, 104
illnesses, 253, 254
immigrant, 145, 146, 147
income, 27, 51, 76, 87, 101, 135, 144, 167, 213, 215, 240, 276
independence, 14, 27, 43, 58, 77, 79, 81, 100, 102, 130, 145, 149, 155, 225, 240, 241, 245, 249, 251, 258, 268, 280
influence, 16, 23, 28, 35, 37, 39, 45, 50, 53-54, 59, 69, 73, 75-77, 79, 94, 97, 102, 107-108, 118, 126, 129-130, 135, 145, 158-159, 171, 189-192, 195, 207, 208, 216, 220, 221, 233, 243, 246, 247, 251, 252, 253, 254, 258, 264, 266-268, 273, 277, 280, 283, 291, 297, 299, 302, 305-306
influential, 8, 9, 22, 30, 33, 34, 37, 45, 52, 53, 57, 59, 62, 70, 77, 79, 87, 89, 92, 97, 98, 102, 108, 117, 118, 124, 126, 127, 129, 137, 138, 143, 146, 149, 152, 159, 162, 169, 171, 175, 182, 184, 195, 210, 217, 220, 221, 228, 249, 251-253, 255, 258, 261, 266-270, 277, 280, 281, 285, 290, 297, 298, 301, 305
integration, 118, 125, 131
integrity, 70, 280, 293
intelligent, 25, 145, 196, 210, 243
internships, 60, 61, 82, 106-109, 129, 265-267, 269, 279
involvement, 5, 6, 37, 62, 77, 79, 84, 85, 86, 95, 97, 101, 131, 132, 155, 156, 157, 168, 173, 179, 191, 194, 216, 223, 224, 227, 228, 230, 246, 247, 264, 268, 278, 291, 292
isolation, 263

Jardim, Anne, 241

jobs, 6, 17, 33, 68, 93, 102, 109, 122, 129, 134, 172, 173, 174, 175, 184, 185, 189, 197, 211, 242, 249, 250, 266, 274, 290, 291

journalism, 76, 78, 80, 151-153, 157, 247, 262, 269, 270, 278

journey, 27, 140, 141, 213, 214, 239, 278, 283, 306

junior high, 31, 32, 167, 172, 173, 175, 190, 214, 218, 227

Kennedy, John F., 27, 32, 34, 36, 100, 121, 251, 261, 263, 268

Kennedy School of Government, 21, 45, 46, 121, 295

Kunin, Madeleine May, 143-166, 271, 275, 288

law school, 37-42, 45, 46, 58, 73, 108, 131, 200, 201, 210, 223, 270

leadership motivations, 70, 152, 164, 285, 298

leadership philosophy, 24, 92, 139, 165

leadership programs, 21, 90, 296

leadership roles, 21, 23, 48, 62, 79, 86, 104, 158, 181, 193, 218-219, 223, 226, 234, 243, 248, 257, 265, 276, 292

leadership style, 23, 46, 71, 91, 119, 138, 139, 164, 184, 185, 209, 210, 235, 274, 298, 299, 301

leadership training, 45, 69, 104, 138, 161, 182, 183, 264, 295

leading change, 156, 293

learning, 10, 11, 14, 15, 21-26, 31, 33, 36, 45, 47, 48, 61-65, 67, 71, 77, 79, 83, 86, 90, 96, 99, 105, 113, 126, 127, 131, 133-136, 138, 148, 158, 159, 163, 168, 170-173, 176, 177, 181, 182, 189, 200, 204, 205, 208, 211, 220, 223, 239, 242, 246, 247, 249, 250-253, 255, 257, 258, 261-265, 274, 275, 276-279, 283, 290, 292-294, 295, 301-305

legacy, 26, 94, 145, 188, 189, 215

legislative, 16, 17, 20, 23, 24, 26, 89, 90, 92, 109, 113, 117, 155, 158, 222, 230, 233, 264, 298, 303

legislative bill, 12, 13, 15, 17, 91, 155, 159, 230

legislators, 17, 19, 21, 22, 81, 87, 89, 112, 160, 162, 209, 228, 230, 231, 233, 235, 269, 270, 274, 286-290, 297, 298

legislature, 7, 15-18, 22, 85, 88, 104, 153, 156, 158, 159, 162, 207, 219, 230, 231

lessons, 15, 21, 37, 43, 57, 58, 62, 72, 78, 85, 95, 101, 125, 139, 145, 148, 158, 172, 174, 177, 194, 196, 204, 215, 219, 225, 226, 239, 247, 253, 254, 261, 272, 276-279, 281-283, 291, 293, 296

lessons learned, 21, 43, 72, 239, 254, 277, 296

lieutenant governor, 21, 95, 110, 113-117, 159, 161, 167, 179, 180, 189, 206, 207, 213, 231-233, 235, 272, 276, 286-289, 290, 296, 298

life experience, 68, 140, 199, 283, 294, 303

life roles, 261, 283, 291

listening, 22, 23, 31, 34, 36, 46, 61-63, 70, 71, 77, 90, 102, 107, 131, 136, 137, 139, 168, 172, 178, 180, 186, 191, 208, 227, 247, 249, 251, 252, 256, 264, 266, 268, 271, 278, 281, 286, 293, 296, 297, 299, 302

lobbyists, 91, 286

Madsen, Susan R. 305, 319

majority leader, 19, 86, 89, 286, 289, 298

majority whip, 86, 213, 230, 287

make a difference, 23, 26, 34, 35, 39, 53, 58, 59, 61, 64, 68, 71, 73, 85, 87, 120, 129, 146, 147, 163, 164, 166, 170, 185, 188, 207, 210, 211, 213, 226, 248, 252, 254, 265, 281, 282, 290, 292, 299, 300, 305

marriage, 14-16, 29, 37, 51, 62, 66, 80, 81, 82, 117, 143, 154, 155, 159, 182, 190, 199, 200, 242, 270, 276, 277, 281, 295

math, 30, 34, 158, 171, 175, 178, 229, 253

mayor, 4, 64, 89, 134, 153, 203, 204, 205, 206, 208, 288, 290

mentors, 16, 22, 33, 72, 117, 118, 126, 137, 162, 165, 183, 221, 222, 250, 257, 267, 268, 305
Mezirow, Jack, 263
middle school, 32, 77, 97, 99, 122, 127, 177, 178
mistakes, 8, 113, 138, 149, 164, 189, 190, 211, 293, 300
mothers, 4-6, 8, 9, 13, 14, 27-37, 42-45, 50-58, 66, 67, 72, 76-81, 83, 84, 87, 96-100, 107, 114, 118, 123-125, 127, 136, 143-151, 154-157, 160, 162, 167-174, 183, 190-197, 199, 200, 206, 208, 209, 215-218, 221, 224, 225, 234, 235, 240-243, 248, 267, 268, 272, 274-276, 281, 291, 294
motherhood, 13, 15, 43, 62, 67, 83, 94, 117, 118, 136, 154, 159, 162, 182, 183, 208, 234, 235, 261, 271, 272, 274, 277, 281, 282, 291
motivation, 23, 32, 38, 70, 71, 85, 86, 103, 110, 120, 136, 161, 164, 227, 249, 266, 278, 280, 293, 296, 298
moved, 4-7, 12, 13, 34, 38, 42, 54, 61, 66, 80-84, 99, 109, 110, 111, 121, 127, 131, 132, 136, 143, 144, 150, 154, 156, 159, 167, 172, 177, 189, 190, 198, 200, 201, 214, 220-227, 232-233, 247, 274-276, 291, 305
moving, 6, 45, 65, 71, 78, 84, 85, 98, 122, 131, 144, 147, 148, 152, 164, 178, 196, 201, 225, 228, 231, 245, 253, 268, 276, 278, 285, 291, 304
multitasking, 67, 83, 118, 136, 151, 163, 178, 183, 197, 208, 234, 250, 258, 266
music, 58, 81, 148, 155, 186, 217, 230
musical, 80, 122, 192, 219, 221, 225, 263

network, 18, 19, 21, 57, 93, 94, 111, 118, 133, 140, 160, 178, 264, 268, 273, 275, 278, 293, 296, 297, 303, 304
newspaper, 4, 7, 9, 24, 31, 53, 75, 76, 78, 79, 101, 125, 151, 152, 154, 157, 191, 204, 243, 247, 251, 253, 257, 263, 288

non-paid work, 17, 131, 133, 178, 207, 214, 232, 255, 272, 293
non-work-related, 68, 131, 261, 277

obedient, 31, 78, 124, 170, 245
obligation, 72, 105, 145, 146, 216, 242
observant, 78, 138, 170, 245, 303
observation, 117, 125, 256, 281, 299
obstacles, 137, 156, 159, 294
only child, 27, 28, 30, 31, 42, 50, 56, 75, 78, 81, 83, 98, 167, 191
optimism, 30, 145, 146, 242, 255, 280, 282
orchestra, 218, 219, 220, 247
organization, 15, 33, 41, 45, 46, 81, 83, 100, 104, 122, 134, 136, 143, 155, 157, 161, 174, 178, 215, 226, 227, 233, 258
outdoors, 51, 55, 73, 125, 172, 193, 240
outgoing, 31, 47, 124, 216, 244

parents, 3, 4, 8, 9, 12-15, 27, 30, 43, 50-52, 54-57, 75-81, 95-103, 106, 119, 123, 125, 127, 143, 156, 167-168, 171-172, 177, 189-197, 201, 214-215, 218-220, 226-227, 229, 240-243, 251-255, 258, 262, 266, 268, 275-276, 280, 282, 297
passion, 16, 24, 26, 34, 59, 73, 92, 94, 126, 150, 190, 191, 193, 252, 253, 257, 258, 267, 269, 290
patience, 13, 15, 43, 44, 52, 66, 67, 84, 118, 136, 160, 162, 163, 272
peers, 12, 32, 54, 65, 70, 80, 98, 99, 124, 170, 174, 192, 193, 213, 217, 220, 232, 246, 258, 263, 268, 280, 298
personality, 5, 30, 31, 39, 52, 53, 54, 77, 78, 98, 104, 124, 147, 169-171, 192, 216, 217, 245-256
perspectives, 17, 18, 24, 57, 60, 67, 86, 88, 89, 103, 106, 113, 118, 121-123, 130-133, 139, 158, 163, 164, 166, 168, 173, 194, 199, 201, 211, 223, 225, 229, 249, 252, 261, 263, 279, 281, 283, 291, 292, 296, 302, 204
philosophy, 25, 47, 93, 101, 102, 116, 119, 132, 139, 164-168, 185, 211, 265
Plato, 239

plays, 6, 7, 94, 192, 194, 208, 225, 282
policies, 72, 106, 130, 166, 206, 207, 224, 230, 264, 305
political figures, 60, 251, 268, 281, 291
political process, 16, 85, 106, 157, 265
political science, 25, 59, 73, 128-130, 137, 150, 165, 221, 223, 227, 230, 267, 270, 302
popular, 7, 63, 64, 110, 116, 148, 174, 180, 182, 217, 244, 298
power, 54, 143, 153, 159, 164, 166, 255, 299
powerful, 3, 14, 15, 18, 40, 44, 48, 61, 84, 92, 97, 137, 161, 187, 195, 196, 204, 210, 241, 242, 245, 246, 254, 255, 258, 263, 265, 272, 279, 281, 292, 296-298, 301, 303
pregnancy, 8, 82, 83, 114, 115, 132, 170, 177, 200-202, 224, 263, 276
principal, 10-12, 98, 168, 169, 214, 218, 243, 251
prioritize, 13, 15, 88, 222, 234
problem solving, 33, 36, 40, 72, 170, 187, 231, 250, 264, 293, 304
professors, 16, 21, 45, 59, 60, 105, 107, 108, 129, 130, 137, 143, 150-152, 157, 197, 221-224, 227, 228, 233, 262, 266-267, 270, 280
PTA, 77, 84, 85, 96, 123, 213, 225, 226-227, 287, 289
public service, 34, 50, 53, 106, 112, 156, 213, 268, 281, 282

rational, 137, 219, 223, 235, 245, 269, 294, 304
reading, 24, 31, 34, 83, 93, 96-100, 123, 125, 137, 148, 171, 193, 218, 228, 232, 242, 247, 252, 257, 302
recognition, 13, 53, 63, 64, 99, 159, 176
reflection, 29, 59, 72, 105, 119, 129, 139, 146, 239, 245, 246, 256, 261, 268, 269, 279, 285, 294, 297, 300
rejection, 247
relationships, 3-5, 15-16, 29-30, 44-45, 66, 77, 97, 106, 107, 109, 111, 124, 130, 135, 140, 162, 181, 196, 224, 242, 251, 253, 262, 267, 268, 271, 273, 278, 280, 282, 297, 304, 305
religion, 76, 192, 240

reporters, 76, 117, 153, 243
Republican, 9, 50, 52, 53, 60-62, 64, 70, 76, 84, 86, 89, 97, 110-112, 135, 138, 159, 162, 191, 198, 230, 287
research, 57, 61, 130, 133, 185, 241, 243, 244, 245, 261, 262, 277, 297
resiliency, 257
respect, 20, 29, 30, 50, 59, 63, 190, 197, 201, 202, 220, 232, 241, 243, 258, 280, 295, 305
responsibility, 4, 7, 15, 19, 28, 31, 33, 57, 63, 67, 70, 78, 85, 88, 92, 105, 108, 114, 115, 119, 121, 125, 128, 129, 139, 140, 158, 159, 162, 174, 178, 183, 184, 189, 196, 216, 229, 235, 235, 242, 245-247, 249, 250-253, 257, 264, 266, 272-273, 293, 298, 305
retail, 108, 129, 131-132, 174, 250, 266, 287
reward, 24, 75, 94, 99, 107, 153, 170, 173
risk taking, 24, 164, 172, 247
Roberts, Barbara, 3-26, 274, 276, 286
role models, 12, 33, 58, 60, 72, 77, 89, 117, 118, 149, 150, 162, 182, 221, 233, 250, 251, 258, 268, 280, 281, 295, 297, 298
roles, 6, 42, 48, 52, 86, 88-91, 135-136, 160, 163, 168, 187, 208, 210, 213, 222, 226, 246, 257, 261, 264, 271, 272, 277, 279, 291-293, 294, 304
Roosevelt, Eleanor, 150, 268

sacrifice, 234, 271, 281
scholarship, 106, 149, 151, 152, 197, 201, 221-224, 266
school board, 12, 17-19, 21, 22, 26, 71, 93, 153, 202, 303
secretary of state, 17, 19, 20, 21, 24, 26, 75, 81, 85, 86, 87, 90, 286, 287, 289, 290, 296
self-discovery, 8, 176, 269
self-doubt, 163
self-esteem, 4, 104, 192, 249, 252, 255, 256
self-knowledge, 239, 273
self-monitoring, 138, 164, 256, 300
self-sufficiency, 77, 147
sense making, 269

servant, 94, 239, 258
service, 3, 7, 19, 32-34, 60, 65, 83, 86, 87, 94, 95, 109, 113, 122, 139, 166, 169, 170, 175, 178, 189, 192, 200, 211, 215, 218, 219, 222, 225-227, 231, 233-235, 240, 241, 243, 245-249, 255, 258, 264, 268, 291-294
Shaheen, Jeanne 121-142, 272, 275, 287
shyness, 30, 147, 151
siblings, 30, 37, 43, 50, 57, 58, 80, 95, 98, 99, 119, 126, 143, 167, 168, 169, 171, 190-192, 196, 214, 218, 241, 251, 254, 266, 275, 280, 282
sisters, 3-5, 8, 9, 28, 30, 50, 56, 72, 95, 121, 123-125, 131, 136, 144, 146, 168, 169, 190, 192, 193, 214, 215
situational, 274, 291, 301
small town, 3, 6-8, 11, 27, 30, 122, 148, 152, 167-168, 189, 195, 208, 240, 262
social activities, 79, 104, 174, 264
society, 7, 23, 35, 39, 57, 60, 82, 94, 103, 125, 150, 155, 164, 216, 233, 240, 242, 247, 255, 263, 267, 276, 290
sorority, 36, 104, 108, 120, 128, 150, 176, 221, 262, 264, 268
Speaker of the House, 19, 75, 81, 86, 92, 230, 287
speakers, 22, 37, 60, 264, 296
speaking, 7, 10, 16, 19, 25, 32, 62, 79, 84, 90, 100, 110, 131, 143, 147, 150, 151, 157, 173, 175, 176, 178, 194, 204, 207, 216, 219, 221, 231, 236, 244, 245, 247, 253, 254, 257, 264, 266, 269, 293, 297, 302
sports, 6, 7, 32, 47, 57, 78, 95, 99, 101, 112, 120, 125, 148, 218, 219, 243, 246, 247, 249, 254, 257, 302
spouse, 22, 29, 43, 44, 49, 66, 88, 135, 160, 211, 243, 261, 270, 271, 281, 282, 291, 297
stability, 4, 5, 37, 80, 126, 146, 163, 191, 197, 216, 233, 252, 281
staff, 18, 24, 25, 46, 47, 61, 71, 90, 91, 93, 100, 101, 109, 115, 119, 125, 132, 133, 138, 139, 164, 165, 170, 181, 184, 186, 207, 209, 210, 228, 232, 235, 247, 266, 275, 280, 299

stay-at-home mother, 52, 76, 77, 87, 96, 123, 145, 168, 224, 225, 272, 291, 294
strategy, 16, 36, 40, 44, 62, 88, 112, 117, 118, 136, 274, 275, 282, 285, 299, 303
struggles, 15, 56, 57, 67, 81, 118, 163, 173, 180, 190, 196, 217, 234, 243, 244, 253, 256, 261, 276, 282, 303
student body, 7, 12, 37, 101, 218, 222, 223, 247, 264
student government, 128, 264
student teaching, 265, 267, 279
styles, 23, 149, 251, 253, 258, 285, 298, 301
success, 11, 15, 18, 27, 28, 34, 40, 64, 66, 72, 77, 78, 108, 111, 112, 120, 156, 157, 166, 182, 186, 226, 235, 271, 272, 301, 305
suicide, 60, 144, 145, 263
supervisors, 45, 70, 258, 267
support, 13-18, 22, 24, 32, 35, 37, 40, 44-46, 49, 61, 66, 72, 81, 85, 87-90, 93, 99, 107, 108, 110, 113, 115, 117-119, 127, 133, 135, 136, 138, 145, 146, 158-160, 162, 165, 178, 180, 182, 187, 188, 191, 197, 201-203, 206, 208, 216, 220, 226, 228, 231, 235, 244, 246, 251-253, 258, 261-262, 267, 270-271, 274, 275, 280-282, 291, 296-298, 305
supportive, 18, 66, 81, 84, 88, 111, 112, 113, 114, 117, 119, 127, 135, 136, 138, 160, 162, 202, 240, 291
Swift, Jane, 95-120, 271, 276, 287

task force, 227-228
teachers, 6, 9-11, 19, 33, 34, 38, 58, 79, 81-83, 90, 94, 98, 102-103, 105, 108, 126, 127, 145, 147, 149, 150, 162, 167, 169, 171, 172, 175, 176-178, 181, 190-193, 195, 196, 202, 208, 215, 217, 218, 220, 221, 242, 243, 247, 250, 251-254, 258, 262, 267, 290
team, 5, 6, 8, 47, 50, 70, 71, 99, 101, 104, 120, 126, 128, 139, 148, 168, 172, 173, 174, 177, 184, 185, 186, 194, 195, 200, 204, 210, 219, 222,

226, 232, 243, 246, 247, 248, 249, 257, 263, 285, 299
themes, 190, 239, 241, 245, 246, 253, 254, 261, 269, 270, 277, 285
thick skin, 70, 91, 164, 294
time management, 13, 15, 229, 293
toughness, 17, 165, 181, 219, 248, 257, 294, 295, 301
Townsend, Robert, 285
transformational, 263, 301
trust, 15, 71, 84, 93, 104, 139, 151, 183, 256, 300, 305

U.S. Senate, 26, 63, 135, 178, 182, 287
uncles, 5, 30, 33, 98, 110, 124, 169, 191, 192, 251, 252
United Way, 227, 289
unpaid work, 18, 19, 87, 94, 166, 220, 275, 290, 292, 302

values, 47, 96, 98, 101, 140, 215, 257, 304
victim mentality, 41, 294
victimization, 161
Vietnam, 37, 42, 58, 60, 114, 123, 129, 130, 198, 200, 263
vision, 47, 85, 143, 145, 165, 166, 216, 268, 273, 278, 293, 305
voice, 8, 58, 90, 91, 107, 110, 123, 157, 204, 241, 255
volunteer activities, 157, 292
volunteerism, 57, 60, 88, 155, 210, 242, 263, 268, 272, 275, 279, 291, 292, 294, 303

vote, 9, 20, 57, 68, 89, 93, 110, 123, 135, 154, 155, 180, 227, 288

waitress, 129, 150, 151, 197, 250
Walker, Olene, 213-236, 265, 275, 276, 289
Whitman, Christine Todd, 49-74, 270, 286
women's movement, 21, 68, 157, 294
women-only training, 21, 46, 161, 262, 296
work ethic, 4, 27, 33, 47, 77, 93, 101, 139, 167, 184, 213, 235, 250, 255, 258, 268
work-life, 16, 261, 274, 275, 276, 282, 295
writing, 48, 58-62, 103, 105, 108, 139, 149, 151, 153, 154, 157, 179, 229, 230, 231, 236, 247, 253, 264, 265, 267, 269, 293

yearbook, 7, 78, 101, 125, 247, 253, 257
youth, 3, 4, 8, 11-14, 23, 28, 32-35, 40, 47, 53, 57, 59, 61, 76-78, 84, 90, 95, 96, 100, 101, 104, 106, 110, 120, 122, 123, 146, 149, 150, 170-174, 187, 192, 194, 216, 218, 220, 233, 239, 243-249, 251-253, 255, 256, 257, 258, 262, 268, 280, 285, 301
youth activities, 56, 239, 249

About the Author

Susan R. Madsen is a leadership and change researcher, scholar, educator, and practitioner. She is an associate professor of management and has been an independent leadership and change consultant for over fifteen years. She has done research and consulting in a variety of settings (higher education, government, non-profit, and corporate). For the past four years, she has been heavily involved in researching the lifetime development of prominent women leaders. She has personally interviewed a host of women university presidents, governors, and international leaders. Her first book titled *On Becoming a Woman Leader: Learning from the Experiences of University Presidents* was recently released by Jossey-Bass. Susan has also published over forty-five articles in peer-reviewed scholarly journals and speaks and presents often in local, national, and international academic and non-academic settings. Susan's research and consulting work have focused on leadership development, change, ethics in higher education, strategic faculty development, academic service-learning, and work-life integration. She serves as a reviewer and/or editorial board member for many academic journals. She was a guest editor for the 2007 work-life integration issue of *Advances in Developing Human* Resources—a Sage journal. In 2007, she received a prestigious research award from the Academy of Human Resource Development and has also received numerous awards and honors for her teaching and scholarship at her institution and beyond. Susan holds a doctorate degree from the University of Minnesota in *Work, Community, and Family Education* with a specialization in human resource development. She has other degrees in exercise science/wellness and speech communication education and started her career many years ago as a junior high speech and debate teacher. She currently lives in Highland, Utah with her husband and teenage children and enjoys racquetball, soccer, golf, hiking, and community involvement.